MW00675532

Successful Teaching in the Elementary Classroom

PHILLIP S. RINER
Western Washington University

Merrill
an imprint of Prentice Hall
Upper Saddle River, New Jersey   *Columbus, Ohio*

Library of Congress Cataloging-in-Publication Data

Riner, Phillip S.
      Successful teaching in the elementary classroom / Phillip S. Riner.
         p.   cm.
      Includes bibliographical references and index.
      ISBN 0-02-401613-6
      1. Elementary school teaching—United States. 2. Elementary school teachers—
United States.   I. Title.
   LB1555.R53   2000
   372.1102—dc21

                                                 99-26331
                                                  CIP

Editor: Debra A. Stollenwerk
Editorial Assistant: Penny S. Burleson
Production Editor: Mary Harlan
Copy Editor: Colleen Brosnan
Design Coordinator: Diane C. Lorenzo
Text Designer: Mia Saunders
Cover Designer: Jason Moore
Cover art: © Stephan Schildbach
Production Manager: Pamela D. Bennett
Electronic Text Management: Marilyn Wilson Phelps, Karen L. Bretz, Melanie N. King
Photo Coordinator: Sandy Lenahan
Illustrations: Tom Kennedy
Director of Marketing: Kevin Flanagan
Marketing Manager: Meghan McCauley
Marketing Coordinator: Krista Groshong

This book was set in ITC Garamond and Lydian by Prentice Hall and was printed and bound by R. R. Donnelley & Sons Company. The cover was printed by Phoenix Color Corp.

©2000 by Prentice-Hall, Inc.
Pearson Education
Upper Saddle River, New Jersey 07458

All rights reserved. No part of this book may be reproduced, in any form or by any means, without permission in writing from the publisher.

Photo credits: Scott Cunningham/Merrill: pp. 175, 232, 256, 334; Kevin Fitzsimmons/Merrill: p. 219; Dan Floss/Merrill: p. 69; Anthony Magnacca/Merrill: pp. 1, 58, 85, 121, 155, 190, 207, 308, 371; Barbara Schwartz/Merrill: pp. 32, 100, 139; Anne Vega/Merrill: pp. 266, 289, 346, 409; Robert Vega/Merrill: p. 387.

Printed in the United States of America

10 9 8 7 6 5 4 3 2 1

ISBN: 0-02-401613-6

Prentice-Hall International (UK) Limited, *London*
Prentice-Hall of Australia Pty. Limited, *Sydney*
Prentice-Hall of Canada, Inc., *Toronto*
Prentice-Hall Hispanoamericana, S. A., *Mexico*
Prentice-Hall of India Private Limited, *New Delhi*
Prentice-Hall of Japan, Inc., *Tokyo*
Prentice-Hall (Singapore) Pte. Ltd., *Singapore*
Editora Prentice-Hall do Brasil, Ltda., *Rio de Janeiro*

Preface

This text asks 12 questions from the perspective of a reader inquiring about teaching elementary age children. The questions pose a broad conceptualization of what is needed to become a successful teacher in today's elementary classroom. The answers to these questions are always complex and always answer only part of the question. Although every attempt has been made to expose the problems and potential solutions systematically, any answers provided are always subject to controversy and reconsideration.

Because the reader must develop adequate understanding of the issues before implementing any reasonable solutions, I kept two special considerations in mind while developing this text. First, all knowledge about teaching is founded in some type of value structure that may not be wholly accepted by all parties. All learning has some purpose, even if that purpose is an unwarranted compliance to an irrational and covert set of assumptions. Successful teaching is deeply rooted in a broad understanding and careful articulation of the many purposes for the instruction provided in the elementary classroom. Further, students themselves establish additional purposes for learning (or not learning). If the teacher is to be successful consistently, those purposes must be understood and incorporated into daily instruction.

Second, knowledge is neither constant nor absolute. What is generalized from research and theory may persist as viable for many centuries. However, no knowledge base is comprehensive enough to serve as an adequate basis to complete the decision-making cycle involved in daily instruction. Teachers must construct an active understanding of many different areas of knowledge. They must then apply that knowledge to ever-changing school contexts by constructing and testing many hypotheses about what the effects of a specific sequence of teacher activity will be. In short, while teachers must construct an understanding of what is known about teaching, they must also construct an understanding of the applications for each strategy, taking into account the specific instructional context and students.

Organization of the Text

This text is deliberately designed to assist the student in assembling philosophical perspectives, value structures, meta-cognitive strategies, instructional techniques, learning assessment, management, and motivational techniques. Although these topics are often studied separately, this book operates from the assumption that an introductory unified study of a broad conceptualization of successful teaching assists the student in developing the complex interaction and interdependence of research, knowledge, experience, and values necessary before detailed study of any individual component.

Chapter 1, "What Is Successful Teaching?," introduces the reader to historical exemplars. Three important points are made that frame the substance of the entire text. First, many compelling and opposing views have been advocated for the education of children throughout the millennia. Second, successful teaching means successfully mitigating the inherent conflict that arises from those opposing viewpoints. Finally, the diversity represented by our students, their parents, our communities, and the teaching profession provides a forum for a rich, compelling, and continuing examination of the purposes, methods, and outcomes of our schools. Chapter 1 also introduces the reader to linear and concurrent models, why they are constructed, and how the reader is expected to construct personal models to explore teaching issues.

Chapter 2, "How Do I Learn about Successful Teaching?," examines in detail the lessons of Chapter 1 with an emphasis on personal development of explicit and articulated theories about what and how to teach to obtain specific goals. Models that demonstrate how teachers attempt to resolve instructional issues are presented, and the major variables in the decision-making process are examined. The different types of knowledge about pedagogy and specific suggestions on how to develop each area are presented. Chapter 2 closes with an examination of how teachers can train themselves to be more systematic in making decisions and the areas of information necessary to make successful decisions.

Chapter 3, "Can I Really Succeed with All the Children?," discusses the many ways in which students vary. Students can vary as members of groups or as individuals within and among groups. Attention is given to bias and overgeneralization and how these characteristics are developed and controlled by the successful teacher. Building on the prior chapters, methods of exploring personal beliefs and the construction of understanding and knowledge that enable teachers to deal effectively with student differences in the classroom are described. Finally, questions are presented to help teachers ascertain what part of their personal repertoire needs attention so that they can teach diverse children successfully.

Chapter 4, "How Do I Get the Children to Work with Me?," focuses on the proactive teacher activity needed to create an environment that promotes the type of behavior best suited for classroom learning. Reactive strategies are examined, and an array of teacher behaviors to deal with emerging misbehavior are presented, with an emphasis on strategies for teaching a child how to self-monitor and make personal judgments about the appropriateness of his or her behavior. The role of teacher beliefs, personal and community values, and proactive planning is examined in detail. The development of a personal set of strategies for assisting children in establishing and maintaining an appropriate learning behavior is emphasized. The role of students' needs in determining behavior is used as a connecting theme among the various strategies examined.

Chapter 5, "How Do I Get Started in the Right Direction?," examines the issues of what to teach and why it should be taught. This chapter serves as an arch between diversity issues, conflict in beliefs about the purpose of education, and the needs of students for determining what is to be taught. Emphasis is placed on making learning meaningful to the child and communicating that learning is a purposeful behavior.

Chapter 6, "How Do I Get There?," explores the many variables involved in lesson planning. In addition to determining what is to be taught and how to teach it, the model of planning also includes promoting student motivation, managing the physical space and instructional materials, using routines to facilitate transitions between lesson components, developing strategies for effective time use, and minimizing the opportunity for disruption. As each lesson is introduced, criteria are provided for judging the effectiveness of the planning involved in that component.

Chapter 7, "What Do Successful Teachers Do?," presents four models of the teacher knowledge base. Although the summaries of research on successful teaching sometimes overlap, each lends a special perspective to the analysis. Emphasis is placed on assembling research findings into rubrics or models that assist the teacher in systematic growth.

Chapter 8, "How Do I Teach Factual Knowledge?," examines teaching from the perspective of making the learning of specific information or skill as easy as possible for the learner. Emphasis is placed on the teacher's skill in identifying highly structured knowledge and developing specific learning goals. The limitations of instructional approaches such as direct instruction are also examined, and strategies for appropriately implementing various direct instruction strategies are explored. Explicit instructional strategies examined include mnemonics, direct instruction, demonstrations, presentations, and mastery learning.

Chapter 9, "How Do I Teach for Inquiry?," takes the earlier emphasis on the development of knowledge about teaching and applies it to the task of assisting children to develop an understanding of ill-structured and abstract concepts about a variety of topics. Questioning is examined as a tool for both explicit and implicit instruction, and the questioning strategies employed in implicit or indirect instruction are contrasted. Emphasis is placed on collateral or affective learning that results in changes in students' attitudes, which, in turn, affect whether the student actually uses what he or she has learned. A number of implicit instruction strategies are examined, including discussion, inquiry, and investigations.

Chapter 10, "How Do I Engage Children in Learning?," explores the vast array of activities for children. In each area, readers are referred to earlier chapters in which decision making, planning goal-oriented lessons, and appropriate use of instructional strategies were presented as essential skills of successful instruction. Each of the areas and activities examined can be used in a variety of ways. Therefore, it is argued that teacher interaction, modification, and appropriate implementation are far more effectual in obtaining successful lessons than any inherent advantage that the instructional method may contain. Once again, emphasis is placed on the teacher obtaining skill in critically examining a variety of alternatives and matching the instructional method to instructional intent, attributes of the learners, classroom context, and the skills of the teacher.

Chapter 11, "How Do I Know When I'm Successful?," introduces teachers to the inherent difficulty involved in a variety of assessment methods. Although each method has benefits, each also contains limitations. Strategies for communication that are examined include grades, letters to parents, conferences, and portfolios. Methods of acquiring information and establishing the documentation of learning include tests, papers, demonstrations of learning, product portfolios, projects, and recitations. Special care is taken to examine three common scales used in evaluation: norm-referenced, criterion-referenced, and personal best.

Chapter 12, "What Classroom Climate Should I Build?," examines two major classifications of management strategies and how those strategies lead (or fail to lead) to the development of self-responsibility, internal loci of control, and internal motivation factors. Instrumentalists are represented as believing in an inherent connection between specific teacher behavior and resulting predictable effects on student behavior. Developmentalists, on the other hand, are represented as believing that specific teacher behaviors can, over time, assist the child in developing internal skills for personal monitoring of behavior. Although instrumentalists view misbehavior as something to be extinguished by teacher reaction and alteration of the environment, developmentalists view misbehavior as an unsatisfactory but understandable attempt to resolve personal dilemmas and a signal that the student needs assistance in understanding and making better decisions. The chapter ends with a suggestion for combining the many beliefs, understandings, and research knowledge into a coherent program for developing students' basic intellectual skills as well as helping them to understand how they can use the knowledge in their lives.

Web Site

No text can do it all or anticipate the unique interests and sequences of preservice teacher education programs across the nation. To better assist instructors in preservice teacher education programs as well as readers of this text, I am pleased to announce a Web site dedicated to the support of preservice teachers and teachers interested in improving their skills. This is an interactive Web site based on a successful prototype that I developed with the assistance of the National Supercomputing Center for Energy and Environment at the University of Nevada, Las Vegas. The site will continue to develop and will reflect educators' interests and participation. Users of this text are invited to participate. The site will contain asynchronous discussion groups for students, so that students across the nation can interact on specific questions related to teaching. Also provided will be vehicles for linking instructors, communication with the author, additional activities, supplemental appendices, presentation overheads, and other features suggested by readers. The site's primary mission is to prepare teachers for service in our nation's schools. Although designed with this text in mind, the site will have support for all inquiries into teacher growth. The Web address is www.prenhall.com/riner.

Instructors using this text and associated materials will find both factual descriptions of the research knowledge base and invitations for teachers to interact with that material. This interaction is considered necessary to create understanding, construct complex schema for decision making, and develop skills in practical applications. The text should assist the reader in examining many personal beliefs about the relationships among children, schools, and teachers while building a complex array of skills necessary to be a successful teacher.

Acknowledgments

A deep sense of appreciation and gratitude is extended to the following reviewers of this text: Robert Bullough, University of Utah; Zeph Davis, California State University, Sacramento; Linda Distad, College of St. Catherine; Bruce Drewlow, Augsburg College; Elinor V. Ellis, Florida A&M University; Ruth Ferguson, Pace University; Margaret M. Ferrara, Central Connecticut State University; Jerry L. Irons, Stephen F. Austin State University; Jacob M. Kagan, Brooklyn College of CUNY; Honor Keirans, Chestnut Hill College; Frank Miller, Pittsburg (KS) State University; Connie H. Nobles, Southeastern Louisiana University; Lillian Norris-Holmes, Morgan State University; Rosemary F. Schiavi, Brescia College; Betty J. Simmons, Longwood College; Harry M. Teitelbaum, Kutztown University; and Kay W. Terry, Western Kentucky University. Their critical analysis and suggestions not only enhanced the development of this text but also helped make the author a more thoughtful and diligent educator.

A special appreciation is extended to Debbie Stollenwerk, Penny Burleson, Mary Harlan, and Colleen Brosnan for their patience, wisdom, and copious contribution of skill and encouragement. The author has been an elementary teacher for 17 years and, with their assistance, has made the transition from teacher to teacher-educator and from storyteller to author.

I would also like to thank some special people who not only taught me reading and writing but also taught me about the effects of personal goodness. My seven teachers in elementary school practiced many of the lessons captured in this book, and they reinforced my notion that teaching excellence is obtainable with fierce determination tempered by thoughtful practice and a kind heart. So, Mrs. Price, Mrs. Brown, Mrs. Herndon, Mrs. Bingham, Miss Atwell, Mrs. Story, and Mr. Chandler, wherever you are, I want you to know you made a difference.

My wife, Patsy, a teacher for nearly three decades, has taught me that every child can learn. At times, however, successful teaching and learning are obtainable only with persistence that is fueled by an undaunted belief in the worth and ability of every child, even when everyone else has given up hope. Patsy has made a formidable contribution to the evidence that teachers do make a difference.

Ezra and Miriam, my children, have provided me with some of my most humbling lessons and have served as effective teachers, even when the student was unwilling. They constantly remind me that not everyone is the same, not every adult decision is a good one, and that children are often far wiser than their parents...but not always! Through them I have learned that all students deserve the encouragement of an enthusiastic teacher, a kind word, and the satisfaction that only successful teaching can bring to their lives.

Brief Contents

Contents

CHAPTER 2

CHAPTER 3

CHAPTER 4

How Do I Get the Children to Work with Me?   100

MANAGING STUDENT BEHAVIOR

CHAPTER 5

How Do I Get Started in the Right Direction?   139

UNDERSTANDING AND MANAGING THE CURRICULUM

CHAPTER 6

How Do I Get There?   175

SHORT-TERM PLANNING FOR TEACHING AND LEARNING

CHAPTER 7

What Do Successful Teachers Do?   207

THE RESEARCH ON EFFECTIVE INSTRUCTION

CHAPTER 12

What Classroom Climate Should I Build?   387
A REVIEW OF CURRENT THEORY AND RESEARCH ABOUT MANAGEMENT

CHAPTER 1

What Is Successful Teaching?

Making Sense of Many Views

Outline

Teachers clearly need to be made aware that the schools are state-sponsored institutional processes responsive to economic, social, and political demands extending beyond the local arena. . . .

MAXINE GREENE

From the superintendent down, all school managing is difficult, but teaching—the daily face-to-face managing of many resistant students—is not only the hardest job in the school, it is the hardest job there is.

WILLIAM GLASSER

◆

A Slice of Life

Mr. Roberts hunched over his desk in a corner of the busy room. It looked like a collection of leftovers from last year's flea market. The wooden shelves under the windows held the treasures of childhood. There were turtle shells, raccoon skeletons, and hornets' nests found by his students and parents on hikes and hunting trips. Small boxes held seashells, shell casings from a local Civil War battlefield, a collection of bird's nests, and several dolls dressed in historical costumes followed by an endless clutter of objects, paper, paints, and glue. There were also a half-dozen model rockets built during the class's study of aerodynamics as part of the science curriculum.

Six jars lined the windowsill turning a bright spring green. There was only one more week before the algae growing contest would be over. Prize ribbons hung nearby with hand-labeled declarations: "Greenest," "Thickest," and "Most Disgusting." Several aquariums containing crawfish, minnows, catfish, snails, and tadpoles bubbled away. Some were class pets. Some were just visitors. The walls were covered with so many posters, pictures, and stories that it was hard to tell where the bulletin boards ended and the walls began. A few mobiles hung from the ceiling near the walls sporting fish, birds, and airplanes.

About 30 autographed paper airplanes arranged in honored groups were thumbtacked securely to the ceiling. A hand-lettered sign on one group read, "Flight Duration Hall of Fame." Another was labeled, "Distance and Accuracy Champions." Some of the planes had yellowed with age and were in sharp contrast to the fast-changing classroom environment, but some were new. Mr. Roberts had sponsored the paper airplane derby every spring right after his aerodynamics study. Soon it would be time for his sixteenth.

Although Mr. Roberts rarely taught any lesson the same way twice, the continual success of the unit on aerodynamics was the exception. Children always enjoyed building paper airplanes and the end-of-unit contests.

There was quick knock on the door, and Mr. Roberts, without looking up, gave a friendly, "Come on in . . . just a minute. Let me finish this paper." When he glanced up, a handsome young man in his mid-twenties stood looking at him. "Do you remember me, Mr. Roberts?"

Mr. Roberts thought quickly. When all else failed, he usually could remember former students by their eyes. Eyes seemed to be the only thing about children that didn't change as they grew up. "Dan Lane, I think. You certainly grew up well."

Dan was pleased to be remembered. What he couldn't know was that Mr. Roberts was amazed at Dan's appearance. Dressed in jeans and a sweater, he looked relaxed but nevertheless dignified. His childhood speech impediment, and his accent as well, had disappeared. Dan started talking quickly. "Mr. Roberts, I just wanted to tell you that you were right. It is a big world out there, and there was a place for me. You helped me find it. I've been in San Diego for the last four years." Dan spied the airplanes. He laughed. "Mine's still there! You know, I got into trouble when I was a teenager, but I joined the Navy eight years ago and got on a carrier. I'm in avionics now. I track big planes. I guess studying that aerodynamics stuff in fifth grade was the first time I ever enjoyed school."

The Challenge of Being a Successful Teacher

Perhaps you were lucky and had a "special teacher" like Mr. Roberts in elementary school. If you did, you probably remember the excitement of learning and the energy that follows nurtured and directed curiosity stimulated by that special teacher. These special teachers are successful because they have incorporated a complex array of knowledge and skill into a vibrant active classroom. Their classrooms are surrounded by the substance of investigation and activity that form the very basics of learning. Successful teachers described in this text use knowledge about teaching that is not far removed from common sense. However, being a professional teacher requires not only common sense, but also a specialized knowledge that has taken millennia to assemble. The knowledge base of teaching has been greatly enhanced during the past three decades with systematic research on teaching and learning. Combining this specialized knowledge with the more generalized lessons of the past to create successful classrooms requires energy, skill, sensitivity, intuition, rational decision making, and timely assessment that rivals any occupation in the world.

This book is designed to illuminate the complexity of teaching in the modern elementary school. Much of this complexity is a result of emerging knowledge about teaching effectiveness, the challenging societal changes in our nation, and the maturing of our social conscience in that we believe all children should be educated successfully. Further, the concept of public education continues to develop and has extended beyond basic reading and math skills to include an array of social, economic, and academic skills that focus on individual needs, abilities, and backgrounds.

Difficulties of Teaching

A basic starting point for developing teaching skill is to recognize that being a teacher in an American elementary school is a difficult task. One of the first dilemmas that a teacher faces is the public's preoccupation with short-term gains in basic academic skills while expecting schools to work systematically toward long-term outcomes such as citizenship, productivity, responsibility, and lifelong learning. Teachers work in a system where, as Glasser (1990) points out, much of what teachers have to offer is presented to children who often have little interest in school and learning. The percentage of children living in poverty continues to rise, and these children are more concerned with fundamental needs such as safety, shelter, and a sense of belonging than with education. Even in more affluent families, children are surrounded by a world that is bright, loud, fast-moving, and caters to their "me now" perspective.

For many children, learning to multiply negative numbers or writing a persuasive letter are activities far removed from their everyday concerns. To teach these children, the teacher must do some thoughtful planning and skillful instruction. Although the teacher also finds children who learn eagerly and successfully, many of these children's thirst for knowledge goes unquenched because of limited teacher time and other resources. The teacher may also encounter eager children who find learning, despite the best efforts of teacher and child, to be a disconcerting, if not overwhelming, challenge. For these children, constructing a hypothesis for a science demonstration or explaining the motives of a story character is simply too difficult and tedious. Today, far too many children have no common language of success, esteem, and hope with which to accept teachers' invitations to learn.

As insurmountable as these problems may seem, teachers, like our Mr. Roberts, routinely overcome these barriers and provide classrooms where children not only learn but also enjoy themselves, begin to value learning, and discover self-respect and personal hope. The primary topic of this book is to assist the reader in understanding how these successful teachers operate and what strategies they employ. However, to understand how these teachers succeed, we must first explore the many different perspectives of teaching.

Knowledge and Goal Development

Successful teachers initially develop knowledge about successful teaching from two distinct areas. First, each individual in an initial teacher education program brings a set of beliefs about teaching, developed from years as a student and from personal interactions with others, both as a teacher and as a learner. Second, each teacher draws from a knowledge base derived from the findings of educational and psychological research on successful classrooms that has accumulated and is continually being codified.

Teachers vary greatly in their views of what the appropriate goals of education are and how they are to be obtained. There are, by necessity, competing and sometimes conflicting research findings. This lack of a clear, cohesive definition of effective teaching presents a real challenge to the beginning teacher. However, successful teachers realize that knowledge about teaching is not enough. Teaching requires considerable skill, interpretation, and persistence. Learning occurs with the interaction of teacher, student, context, and instructional intent. Successful teachers attempt to apply what they know with a healthy respect for what they do not know. Thus, successful teachers offer tentative solutions, test for results, and alter their behavior accordingly. Additionally, they combine a pervasive caring for children with their teaching so that the child's mind and heart are informed, educated, and transformed (Bettelheim, 1971).

This process of experimentation within a value-laden context is intricate and not totally understood. Educators should expect that their professional knowledge must be reevaluated and reassembled repetitively for each context and interaction. Teaching can be compared to architecture. Architecture has a wide array of knowledge elements that determine load factors for walls, insulation requirements for efficiency, and material schedules for foundation strength. Yet, whether a building is considered beautiful by the clients, whether it projects the owners' values as a company, and whether the workers feel comfortable and productive inside the building is determined by the aesthetics of the design as well as by the architect's engineering competence. Engineering competence is a basic essential but is not sufficient for a successful building. Thus, architects must build from the scientific and be shaped by the artistic. Although teaching is far less precise than architecture, teachers still must build on foundational knowledge, incorporate emerging evidence, and modify teaching plans to meet the needs of students. The remainder of this chapter examines some of the foundations of teaching and the teacher's role. As you will see, some of the knowledge is as old as the human race, whereas some has emerged only from the systematic study of teaching conducted during the past three decades.

Universality of Successful Teaching

Virtually everyone is a teacher in some capacity. Teaching is a fundamental human activity. This simple fact is often overlooked in classrooms where children, who can be wonderful teachers in their own right, work in isolation at tasks developed by the teacher, supervised by the teacher, and evaluated solely by the teacher. The first lesson in successful teaching is to look for the successful teacher in others.

Teaching is the method by which each culture has passed its skills, knowledge, and values from one generation to the next. Even before humans mastered spoken and written language, teaching had to have occurred to transmit necessary skills to others. The most powerful language in the classroom is the language of a teacher's actions. What we *do* in our classrooms as well as what we *say* teaches children what they need to know to live productive lives, as well as passing along our basic values to them.

Modeling

The value and behavior commitments of significant people in a child's life, such as parents and teachers, are observed and emulated by children. While making these incidental observations of adults, children construct powerful interpretations of right and wrong, of their personal role in the world, and how the world works. This process is called *modeling*. Researchers have repeatedly studied the various methods and impact of modeling as a teaching method (Bandura, 1986; Bryan & Walbek, 1970; Good & Brophy, 1991; Marshall, 1988; and Roberts & Becker, 1976). Their consensus is: People naturally learn from watching each other.

Modeling by Teachers   Cook (1988) described this situation: His six-year-old son astounded the entire family by demanding swordfish steak with extra lemon at a restaurant instead of his usual hamburger. Mystified, they watched their son finish his fish with a relish. Finally, the parents inquired why he had chosen swordfish when he had never eaten it, didn't like fish, and had his favorite hamburger readily available. His reply, "Mrs. Lavan said it was great." Mrs. Lavan was their son's first-grade teacher. His teacher's offhand remark encouraged the child to try something new which his parents could not.

Cook, who is a teacher himself, further revealed that, in a moment of extreme irritation and disgust, he chastised one of his students by saying, "Don't act like a retard to me." Within days, he heard his students calling their classmates "retards." When he scolded them for their cruel taunting, one child stated that he was sure that "retard" was an acceptable word in this class. . . . After all, Mr. Cook had used it! Cook then used this opportunity to model to the children how to express an apology and admission of guilt as well as how to correct his behavior. The children were, as they typically are, quite forgiving.

Modeling can, of course, be a positive experience. Cook describes a number of students who, after having grown up and with children of their own, still read for 30 minutes every day because of sustained silent reading in his class. What impressed these students, they recalled, was the enjoyment that Cook derived from the activity and his little phrase, "A day without reading a good book is a very sad day."

Modeling by Others   Adults, however, are not the only models in the classroom. Important insights can be learned about how to teach children by watching how they teach one another. Good and Brophy (1991) describe the fundamental aspects of modeling in the following story about Rayvon, a precocious eight-year-old. Rayvon decided that Cleat, his younger brother, needed some encouragement in growing up and set about teaching him to shoot spitballs. Rayvon, in the process of teaching Cleat, illustrated an effective use of modeling to teach a specific skill. Rayvon's first strategy was to focus Cleat's attention by talking about the "merits" of such endeavors. This piqued the admiration and interest of his little brother. Next, Rayvon demonstrated the whole process of chewing the paper to the right degree of malleability, wadding the mass into the empty carcass of a disposable ballpoint pen, aiming, and finally firing the projectile at the ceiling of their bedroom where it magically adhered with aplomb. Finally, Rayvon inquired if Cleat could perform the task.

When Cleat claimed he could also shoot a spitball, Rayvon encouraged him to try. Cleat first bit off too big a piece of paper, chewed too little, had trouble getting it into the pen, and finally couldn't blow it out. Rather than poke fun at his younger brother, Rayvon laughed, claimed a good try, declared his brother was a "natural," and offered another demonstration. This time, Rayvon was slow and deliberate, telling Cleat at each step what problems to expect and how to avoid his previous mistakes. After the successful demonstration, Rayvon encouraged Cleat to try again. This time, however, Rayvon watched Cleat more closely. When Cleat erred, Rayvon corrected him immediately. Rayvon, however, didn't actually say, "Cleat, that's wrong." Instead, he encouraged Cleat by giving suggestions such as "Too big, try half that size" and "Not wet enough, chew some more." This time, Cleat's attempt was more successful, and the shot almost reached the ceiling. Rayvon squealed with delight, clapped encouragement, and prompted Cleat to try again. Soon, with continued coaching from Rayvon, Cleat was accomplishing the ceiling goal about half of the time. Rayvon kept up the encouragement, and Cleat was truly enthralled by his efforts—until their mother appeared in the doorway.

Modeling and a Teaching Process

Rayvon intuitively followed what Good and Brophy (1991) classify as basic principles of a good demonstration (see Figure 1.1). Rayvon first captured Cleat's attention, allowed Cleat to demonstrate prior learning, helped Cleat understand the new concepts, demonstrated slowly and step by step, and finally gave gentle corrective feedback designed to create a more refined and effective performance. We, as teachers, can learn a new skill just as rapidly as Cleat did. Like Cleat, however, our new lessons may require knowledge and considerations that are not readily evident, such as when to use a skill. Because teaching has so many contexts and interrelated events that affect the success of particular strategies, it is very difficult to talk about successful teaching in terms that are meaningful in *all* teaching situations.

Difficulty of Defining Successful Teaching

Teachers throughout history have tried to determine what constitutes successful teaching. Although today we know more about teaching than ever before, the limitations of our knowledge are even more evident and frustrating. Excellence in teaching has been identified since the dawn of modern civilization (Broudy & Palmer, 1965).

1. Focus attention.	5. Repeat the process if necessary.
2. Give an overview.	6. Have learner repeat the process.
3. Label objects and concepts.	7. Observe and give corrective feedback.
4. Go slowly through the process in small stages.	8. Encourage and redemonstrate; don't dwell on errors.

FIGURE 1.1 Basic principles of a demonstration.

From *Looking into Classrooms,* 5th ed., by Tom Good and Jere Brophy. 1991. New York: Harper Collins.

However, no culture has been able to capture that excellence and make it widely available to the youth of the next generation. Throughout history, several problems have faced those who strived to be successful teachers:

◆   No singular concept of "good" teaching is acceptable to all. Even existing conceptualizations keep changing.

◆   The results of good teaching are diverse and difficult to measure. Short-term and long-term goals must be considered.

◆   Concepts of "good" teaching and the value that society places on the results of teaching are often conflicting.

◆   Concepts of "good" teaching tend to be situational ("context riddled").

◆   The targets of instruction (students) vary greatly in experiences, readiness, willingness, ambition, and ability. Therefore, the "best" methods of teaching to accommodate these difference vary, just as students vary.

◆   Changes in any of the preceding issues change the other four factors; thus, teaching knowledge is always in a state of flux.

Successful Teaching Exemplars and Their Lessons

In trying to define what successful teaching is, we can point to certain teachers who are recognized as teaching exemplars. Each of these teaching exemplars contributed to our rich conceptualization of teaching and learning, although they varied widely in their aims and methods. Examining their contributions and the difficulties that they encountered in accomplishing their goals can illuminate the dilemma of competing conceptualizations of education.

Among the many successful teachers, some, like Rayvon, simply transmit to each ensuing generation the skills and secrets of many trades, arts, and manufacturing techniques. Others have achieved historical importance because their abilities to teach are among the richest demonstrations of teaching skill and expressions of cultural values. These exemplars were able to convey those skills across generations and among many different cultures. We will study four individuals who were selected because of their diverse contributions: K'ung Fu-tse (Confucius), Socrates, Pestalozzi, and Dewey.

K'ung Fu-tse: Educating the Spirit

The aim of Chinese education at the time of K'ung Fu-tse (Confucius: 551?–479? B.C.) was to preserve the given order of Chinese life. Chinese education was designed to educate the young well enough so that the Chinese way of life would remain essentially as it was. Chinese intellectuals had convinced themselves that they had reached the summit of civilization (Wilds & Lottich, 1970), and the focus of education was to maintain that status. Within that frame of reference, however, the pursuit of noble living (the pursuit of human relationships, order, duty, and morality) was a particular challenge. For K'ung Fu-tse, the pursuit of noble living and the instruction of the ruling classes for whom that pursuit was reserved became his life's mission. His teaching style, similar to that of Socrates, was based on questions that led to reflection. He used contrasts and contradiction to urge the pupil toward more difficult and more accurate analyses.

Five Fundamental Relationships   The focus of Chinese education during the time of K'ung Fu-tse was to study and understand five fundamental relationships (Brubacher, 1947). The curriculum was focused on these virtues: benevolence, justice, order (conformity of established ways), prudence, and fidelity (sincerity). These, of course, are still considered to be virtues. Marx (1993) redefined the five virtues basic to Chinese culture as follows:

Jen:	A love of one's fellow human being (benevolence).
Yi:	Respect for individual personality (justice).
Li:	Traditions, law, customs, and conventions that serve as a standard for measurement and the balance between liberty and responsibility (order).
Sin:	Confidence in institutions and in each other (prudence).
Cheng:	Truthfulness, honesty, moral integrity, and being true to oneself. Finding what is good and holding fast to it (fidelity).

Notice how different these intents are compared to the traditional basic "3 R's" curriculum (reading, writing, and arithmetic) advocated throughout the history of American education. Yet, the appeal of K'ung Fu-tse's basic curriculum is nearly universal.

Methodology   In Chinese life during this period, the family was the center of education, and the family initiated the study of the five virtues. Schools only supported and extended the basic education provided by the home. K'ung Fu-tse described a teaching methodology in which the teacher functioned more as a guide and facilitator than as a knowledge expert or source of answers. He wrote in Book XVI in the Hsio Ki (Record on the Subject of Education):

> When a superior man knows the causes which make instruction successful, and those which make it of no effect, he can become a teacher of others. Thus in his teaching, he leads and does not drag; he strengthens and does not discourage; he opens the way but does not conduct to the end without the learner's own efforts. Leading and not dragging produces harmony. Strengthening and not discouraging makes attainment easy. Opening the way and not conducting to the end makes the learner thoughtful. He who produces such harmony, easy attainment, and thoughtfulness may be pronounced a skillful teacher. (U.S. Department of Education, 1986, p. 6)

Fundamental to K'ung Fu-tse's pedagogy was a desire for students to reason and struggle with views and presentations: "Learning without thought is labor lost . . . thought without learning is perilous" (Brubacher, 1947). K'ung Fu-tse, by expressing *Yi*, practiced pedagogy that highlighted an adjustment to individual differences. When two pupils asked K'ung Fu-tse when they should put into practice something they had learned, he gave contradictory advice. This concerned one of his followers who asked for an explanation. One student acted impulsively on ideas; therefore, he was told to consult family and friends. The other student delayed action and was timid in his activity. This student was told to act immediately. K'ung Fu-tse provided the advice best suited to the pupil (Brubacher, 1947).

K'ung Fu-tse advocated students to be involved with life. He believed that education should not be confined to classrooms. He sought to excite, perplex, encourage, and mystify his pupils. Yet, he condemned pressure, exhortation, and force in bringing about learning. He felt that the supreme art of teaching was in getting pupils to ask themselves questions.

K'ung Fu-tse also viewed with skepticism the educational structure of his time. He was particularly critical of teachers. Consider how modern his observations seem when compared to American perceptions of teachers, yet this passage from the Hsio Ki was written 2500 years ago:

> In what they (teachers) lay on their learners they are not sincere, nor do they put forth all their ability in teaching them. What they inculcate is contrary to what is right, and the learners are disappointed in what they seek for. In such a case, the latter are distressed by their studies and hate their masters; they are embittered by the difficulties, and do not find any advantage from their labour. They may seem to finish their work, but they quickly give up its lessons. That no results are seen from their instructions—is it not owing to these defects? (Ulich, 1965, p. 21)

Socrates: Educating the Mind

Socrates (470?-399 B.C.) is well known throughout the world as a teacher and philosopher. He was a free and influential thinker in a Greek society that hotly debated the nature of learning, its purposes, and teaching methodology. Socrates found himself contemplating one of the dilemmas that still face educators today: What is the fundamental purpose of education? Two views of educational purposes existed in the Western world at that time. The first view considered education as a means for immediate economic success (Good, 1960). The competing view argued that the primary purpose of education was the pursuit of virtue. For Socrates, the pursuit of virtue was the pursuit of wisdom and that required constant questioning. Notice the contemporary parallels to twin views of American education as education for citizenship and education for the workplace.

Questioning Current Beliefs   In his personal pursuit of virtue, Socrates found himself embarrassing leading citizens as he questioned them publicly about their beliefs, teachings, and orations. This led, eventually, to his alienating very influential citizens of Athens. It also made him very attractive to his students, the young intelligentsia of his time.

Socrates was eventually ensnared by the logic of his own wisdom. Virtue, according to Socrates, was the pursuit of wisdom through the employment of didactic reasoning unfettered by the desire for gain or the fear of loss. Virtue was self-discipline and the control of emotions, keeping the baser physical needs for shelter and safety subdued by reason while searching for truth and understanding. Eventually, the continued conflict resulted in Socrates being convicted of the crime of attempting to corrupt the youth of Athens; Socrates was sentenced to death. While he could have easily escaped, he was forced to choose between his pursuit of virtue (the search for wisdom with little regard for the baser physical body), or abandon the pursuit and escape from Athens. Socrates chose to pay the price of virtue and accepted his death penalty by drinking hemlock, thereby locking in for centuries his teachings of the nobility of man through the pursuit of understanding and wisdom.

Methodology   Socrates' practice of teaching was characterized by the creation of plausible hypotheses—that is, obtaining tentative explanations to structure rigorous inquiry (Seeskin, 1987). He believed that education had three products: *episteme* (knowledge), *phronesis* (wisdom), and *nous* (good sense or intelligence). The process of obtaining knowledge, wisdom, and good sense through rational inquiry that he taught is known as the *Socratic method.* The method is described here as a four-stage process (Figure 1.2) and as an accumulation of rational tools (Figure 1.3).

---

1. **Disillusionment**   Recognition of a lack of knowledge. Inability to predict, explain, or understand.

2. **Unenlightened truth**   Accurate prediction without understanding or explanation. Inability to use knowledge fully.

3. **Explanation**   Provision of a testable hypothesis that remains tenable. The construction of a logical syllogism that cannot be refuted.

4. **Integration**   Combination of a new explanation with existing knowledge so that a greater understanding results. Typically leads to disillusionment because of the increase in complexity of the conceptualization of the world.

FIGURE 1.2   Socratic model for the creation of knowledge.

FIGURE 1.3   Elements of the
Socratic method in teaching.

From "Socrates in the classroom" by
James C. Overholser, 1992. *The
Social Studies* (March/April), p. 79.

S:	Systematic questioning
O:	Objective and critical thinking
C:	Collaborative investigation
R:	Rational problem solving
A:	Active participation
T:	Tested hypotheses
I:	Inductive reasoning
C:	Comprehensive generalities

Stage one of the Socratic method is a negative stage that is characterized as disillusionment (Gulley, 1962). This stage is a recognition that knowledge has not been obtained and that propositions once thought to be true (or false) are not supported by reason and evidence. Simply put, the first step of inquiry is to recognize one's ignorance and lack of knowledge in a given area.

Stage two is to recognize that certain propositions are true (that is, the proposition provides a rationally sound and accurate explanation), but the learner does not yet know why it is true. This is not considered to be knowledge because the learner does not understand why a proposition is true (or inversely, why it is false).

Stage three is to determine the conditions that are necessary for proving (testing) the solution to a problem. Stated another way, this is the process of providing an explanation for a phenomenon in a way that can be tested and evaluated. These conditions allow the learner to convert a "true belief" (we do not know why something is true) to knowledge (we know why something is true).

The final stage in the Socratic method is integrating this knowledge into a coherent system that provides an explanation for more complex phenomena.

Summarized, the process of the Socratic method is (1) recognizing ignorance, (2) developing an hypothesis, (3) testing the belief, and (4) generalizing the knowledge into the learner's understanding. This is the basic structure of what has been referred to as the "scientific method" and is widely taught in elementary schools throughout America.

The Socratic method has long been recognized for the rigorous and insightful questioning that forces a pupil toward critical reasoning. These questions offer a challenge to existing interpretations or beliefs. Generally, the questions lead to contradictions or refutations. At this stage, although true knowledge is not yet obtained, an unconscious ignorance has been revealed and converted to conscious ignorance. This is a fundamental step that is not designed to discourage the learner, but rather to get the student to recognize the inadequacy of his or her current understanding and to initiate a need for further study, thought, and analysis. With this resynthesis, a new understanding emerges.

The elements of teaching and learning in Figures 1.2 and 1.3, like the descriptors of a good demonstration (Figure 1.1), are called *models of instruction.* A model is simply a representation or approximation of something. Models are used extensively in this book to help you clarify basic elements of a concept or method. The model of a good demonstration (Figure 1.1) and the model representing the four stages of the

Socratic method (Figure 1.2) are linear models—that is, the order of the items in the model represent the order of human activity in enacting the model. Figure 1.3, which outlines the basic elements of the Socratic method, is a nonlinear model in that the activities can occur in any order or even concurrently with one another. In this case, combining a linear model of the stages of Socratic inquiry with a nonlinear model describing the tools used to travel from stage to stage, allows the learner to grasp a complex array of interactive variables in its most simplistic or ideal form. This type of reorganization of knowledge is called *structuring*. Structuring is a prerequisite to understanding.

Socrates' model emphasized the role of questioning to get students to structure concepts for themselves. To do this, the Socratic method requires a teacher who thinks rationally and logically and sees the relationships among many diverse entities. The method used by K'ung Fu-tse, on the other hand, relies heavily on the use of paradox, apparent contradiction, metaphor, and intuitive relationships. Both Socrates and K'ung Fu-tse, however, used carefully posed questions, linked in a skillful sequence to make "telling" an unnecessary instructional tool. Socrates' model of instruction forms the inquiry-based instructional family, examined in detail later in the text. Without doubt, the questioning skill is of critical importance in a teacher. However, is questioning the only tool necessary for successful teaching? Our experience with Rayvon and the criteria for a demonstration seem to define another set of strategies for teaching.

Johann Heinrich Pestalozzi: Educating for Survival

K'ung Fu-tse and Socrates supported a world view in which families were the central units and the providers of education. This view persisted until the major social reorganization brought about by the emergence of the Industrial Revolution. Historically, the world had been organized by a set of stratified societies in which some were born to rule and others were born to servitude. Basic education for life and work had been considered to be domestic education—a duty of the home. By the nineteenth century, the concept was beginning to break down under the encroaching complexity and specialization of work instituted by the Industrial Revolution. Our current notion of free public schools and the universal expectation of successful learning for all are quite recent. Pestalozzi's work can be considered as an important transitional link between ancient and modern views of the family and educational success.

Experience and Social Conscience   Pestalozzi (1746–1827) carefully defended the virtues of domestic education (the education provided by the family at home) yet recognized the limitations of that method. While working to create homes for Swiss orphans, he quickly formulated general ideas and broad concepts regarding successful schooling.

Pestalozzi was inspired by a consistent social conscience and his belief in others.

From childhood, it lay in the peculiarity of my character and of my home training to be benevolent and kindly and to have unlimited confidence in those about me. I came early into association with the suffering and the poor and, in a thousand experiences with them, came to feel the deepest sympathy with them and their many sorrows; and I likewise came to feel the urgent call to attempt to remove the multifarious causes of the evils which they endured. (Pestalozzi's *Views and Experiences* as reported by Good, 1960, p. 231)

Pestalozzi was considered to be a hopelessly impractical idealist. Although his orphanages were financial failures, his ideas were triumphant over the current educational thinking of his day. He enjoyed sharing his ideas and soon became a writing success, but he was frustrated. His writing seemed to him to change nothing. He began in earnest to convince others of the effectiveness of an instructional method based on "realistic" endeavors. He believed that learning should be based on experience and provide children with powers of intellect that would allow them to succeed in more practical endeavors than the mental gymnastics of classical studies.

Methodology   Pestalozzi's view of contemporary educational activity was that it was abstract and not realistic. His solution was to emphasize the role of *Anschaung* (observation) in developing children's skills at exploring and understanding the world around them. Observation begins when the child enters a situation by being barraged with an array of sensations, resulting in a confused sense of order. As the child attends and explores the surroundings, his or her sense impressions grow vivid and definite. Objects and their qualities separate themselves into logical entities with common functions or attributes. These perceptual units can then be recognized, described, named, and classified. To complete the learning cycle, these sensations are combined into logical structures that allow the child to employ intuition and to extend understanding to what cannot be experienced. In short, learning is observation and results in confused sensations. The understanding process is cultivated by continued contact and observation that results in increased detail in clarity, definition, and classification. Because of his orientation to learning as a perceptual activity, Pestalozzi emphasized guided individual and social experience in directing the learning process.

Good (1960), in order to illustrate the process, quotes one of Pestalozzi's students:

The first elements of geography were taught us from the land itself. We were first taken to a narrow valley. After taking a general view of the valley, we were made to examine the details, until we had obtained an exact and complete idea of it. We were then told to take some of the clay which lay in beds on one side of the valley, and fill our baskets which we had brought for the purpose. On our return to the Castle, we took our places at the long tables, and reproduced the valley we had just studied, each one doing the part which had been allotted to him. In the course of the next few days [we took] more walks and more explorations, each day on higher ground, and each time with a further extension of our work. Only when our relief was finished were we shown the map, which by this means we did not see until we were in a position to understand it. (p. 240)

Pestalozzi's educational methods were guided by pupil intuition, interest, and purpose. This was followed later by guided analysis and the employment of scientific technique to obtain enhanced comprehension and skill refinement. Pestalozzi's method was embedded in the following global beliefs about learning and teaching (Bowen, 1981; Good, 1960):

◆ A good home is the ideal educational institution because it is the center of love and active cooperation.
◆ Schools are necessary to give a broader educational base than the home can offer.
◆ The aim of education is the harmonious development of all human powers.
◆ The regenerative needs of the poor and neglected must receive first attention prior to education in order to vitalize the child so that learning is possible.
◆ Education in the school is to be social and universal.
◆ Instruction is to be based on knowledge of individual development, and education is based on the stages of growth of the child.
◆ Meaningful education is initiated by observation starting with the basic elements first.
◆ Curriculum is expanded by practical and scientific lines of inquiry.
◆ Teaching is a skilled occupation and a moral vocation.

Pestalozzi was determined to derive the knowledge of teaching from his experiences with children, rather than through the ontological discourse favored by K'ung Fu-tse and Socrates. Pestalozzi opened the discussion of modern topics in education that are still unresolved. These topics include educational opportunity, developmentally appropriate instruction, concrete–experiential learning, and social improvement through education.

John Dewey: Educating for Change

Among the most influential of modern educators is John Dewey (1859–1952). Dewey made many varied contributions to education. He wholeheartedly embraced the belief that education should not just preserve and sustain a society, it should be the primary route for the improvement and development of a society.

The Central Role of Change   Dewey (1897/1959) argued that curriculum should primarily exist to reconstruct thinking and free individual capacity:

> Any significant problem involves conditions that for the moment contradict each other. Solution comes only by getting away from the meaning of terms that is already fixed upon and coming to see the conditions from another point of view, and hence in a fresh light. But this reconstruction means travail of thought. Easier than thinking with surrender of already formed ideas and detachment from facts already learned, is just to stick by what is already said, looking about for something with which to buttress it against attack. (p. 91)

Dewey believed that the only way to solve societal ills and to expand the individual's mind was to free an individual's capacity through a unique process revealed for each individual. This freeing of capacity, however, must not be turned inward (personal gain); it must be directed toward social relationships. A democratic society provides for equal participation in its good for all its members. Thus, a democratic society develops and secures flexible institutions that are readjusted through critical inquiry, experimentation, and reconstruction. A democratic society must have an educational system that gives individuals a personal interest and control in social relationships and develops the "habits of mind" that secure social changes without introducing disorder (Dewey, 1916/1980).

Foundational Beliefs   Dewey's life spanned an age of almost incomprehensible change. He was born before the Civil War and died on the threshold of the Space Age. As American social conscience continued to emerge in the first half of the twentieth century, rapid change in technology and industrialization radically transformed the basic societal elements. American education was about to come of age. With it, certain fundamental beliefs emerged:

- ◆ *Social amelioration comes through education.* Students must be empowered with the intellectual and social tools to obtain the desired outcomes of both the individual and society. Schools cannot eliminate discrimination and antisocial activity. However, schools can empower students with rational modes of thinking, reflecting, judging, and acting. Education allows each ensuing generation to work closer toward that ideal.
- ◆ *Subject matter comes from the interest of the child.* In determining the best method of education, the nature of interest and its role in guiding the learner is vital. A single list of what constitutes culture is not possible. American culture is a living heritage of action and pluralism. Culture is the social group's hopes and dreams cast against the realities of its time. To transmit the culture and knowledge of our society, the subject matter of schooling must attach itself to living in the present while building the future.
- ◆ *Learning is the reconstruction of experience and knowledge.* The learner must engage the world if learning is to occur. The school must be a stylized version of the world in which people learn primarily and most effectively by direct experience (learning by doing). Children must learn about their world and gain knowledge of the past by contrast to the present. Schooling must be more than preparation for some later day; it must be a part of living.
- ◆ *Education requires reflection.* The reconstruction of experience requires an attitude of thinking. Effective thinking requires a complete act of thought. Thinking rationally about the past and future gives rise to the process of reflection. Reflection always contains some type of challenge to our current ideas and interpretations. This doubt causes further assessment and a critical examination of relevant data. Data examination leads to the formation of hypotheses. The new tentative beliefs are then tested through experimental interactions leading to new knowledge (Axtelle & Burnette, 1970).
- ◆ *Education is experimental.* To be useful to the individual, education must be flexible and prepare the learner to deal with a rapidly changing environment. Democratic education will always be experimental. Education cannot be dictated externally. Excellence in education originates within the teacher-student interaction with the teacher functioning as guide while the student explores ever-increasing bits of reality.

Dewey's work is often a point of division rather than unification in American education. One can, however, safely conclude that Dewey has led us toward a renunciation of any expectation of an easy or permanent solution to educational dilemmas.

The unerring thread weaving Dewey's ideas about a philosophy of experience, the scientific method, the guidance of learning, the nature of democracy, and the social role of the school is that the only true answers in education must come through the process itself. This process requires continuous experimental participation.

Teaching Exemplars and Successful Teaching

Importance of Conflict

K'ung Fu-tse, Socrates, Pestalozzi, and Dewey illustrate that, at its core, education is a search for truth that requires questions to be asked, new concepts to be entertained, and conflicting ideas to be confronted. Successful teaching in elementary schools requires a commitment to all children and exploration of many ideas and values. Conflict—confronting the daily dilemmas of the classroom—is inherent to success.

Necessity of Student Cooperation and Engagement

The exemplars discussed here tell us that although conflict is almost inevitable, the final determiner of truth must be the student's successes, not the ideologies of others. Support, respect, and helping students to think and decide for themselves are persistent arguments from our four exemplars. Successful teaching must respect the unique qualities, beliefs, and heritage of each child. It is not enough for the teacher to use effective methods of instruction; the successful teacher must match the method to the needs of the child. It is this guiding and catalytic function of instruction aimed at unique qualities that Glasser (1990) found so challenging when declaring that teaching is the hardest job there is.

Purposes of Schooling and Forms of Knowledge

Our exemplars demonstrate that there are many conceptualizations of the purpose of school and how those purposes are to be realized. The modern teacher faces an increasingly diverse world and must develop comprehensive understanding of many outlooks. Unfortunately, elementary schools have often been targeted at "mainstream Middle America," offering an homogenous education that requires children to adapt to the needs of school. The intermingling of competing sets of expectations and needs of children with many diverse backgrounds presents a major challenge to the modern teacher.

Unity in Diversity

Figure 1.4 provides a comparison of the four exemplars. They are first compared according to the vehicle on which education is to be based. K'ung Fu-tse examined the spiritual aspect of people and humanity and elevated the role of mysticism. Socrates, his near contemporary in the West, argued strict structural guidelines for the creation of knowledge that adhered to the fundamentals of logic. K'ung Fu-tse's form of knowledge resided in the paradox of conflicting everyday events in which reason was to be tested and was not to be trusted without the involvement of the soul.

Socrates' form of knowledge was the syllogism resulting in a logical truth, carefully built by stringent rules of logic in which emotions were not allowed or desired. Pestalozzi felt all this was too distant from the "real" world of sensation and activity. He argued that the only way to knowledge was through the senses. The senses best operated in a world filled with rich experiences and yielded countless perceptions that could then be assembled and reassembled in order to make sense of the world.

Dewey extended Pestalozzi's view. However, rather than passively collecting sense data, Dewey argued that it was necessary to manipulate and act on the world in various ways. The world was not composed of just material things; it was composed of relationships. The result of experiments allows new assemblages or reconstructions of understandings and relationships. These reconstructions are the products of education.

Varied Uses of Knowledge

Our exemplars varied in their opinions of the intended use of knowledge. For K'ung Fu-tse, the aim of education was to preserve the given order of civilization and life, whereas Socrates was more concerned about what the perfect order really was. Pestalozzi was less concerned about the perfect order than he was about assisting

	K'ung Fu-tse	Socrates	Pestalozzi	Dewey
Vehicle for learning	Spiritual	Reason	Observation	Experimentation
Form of knowledge	Paradox	Syllogism	Experience through perception	Reconstruction of experience
Aim	Spiritual virtue (Harmony)	Virtue of logic (Understanding)	Life skills	Societal improvement
Purpose	Maintain current society	Discover truth that is permanent	Provide skills to live successfully	Change society to preserve and improve it

FIGURE 1.4   A comparison of four exemplars.

children to simply survive successfully (and happily) in whatever order surrounded them and, if possible, to improve their lot in the process. Dewey viewed education as the primary method of improving the lot of everyone even if the ideal human condition was not defined or realized. Whereas K'ung Fu-tse wanted to preserve society, Dewey wanted to change it. Whereas Socrates wanted to discover truth, Pestalozzi wanted to help individuals learn to feed, clothe, and enjoy themselves.

Teachers and Conflicting Concepts of Education

Although our four exemplars' concepts of education differed, it is apparent that all of their beliefs concurrently exist in public schools, in the minds of teachers, and in the views of the public. The goal is for schools to make life better for everyone while retaining the traditions and values that define the oldest continuous democracy. This goal demands experimentation for discovering new truth and understanding while preserving, or reclaiming, the values of the past. Whether teachers and students work together in mutual trust or spiteful fear, in excitement or boredom, or in faith or despair, they do so in an emotional climate established by their hearts as well as their heads. Teachers want students to watch as well as do, to think as well as listen, to accept some ideas and challenge others. Teachers want students to develop work skills and knowledge that allow them to find a good job, but they also want much more for their students than a good paycheck. Teachers want students to help themselves and to help others. It is this combination of demands that adds to the difficulty of teaching, as well as to an understanding of what and why teachers do as they do.

Personal Beliefs about Successful Teaching

Although it is important to examine historical teaching exemplars and teaching excellence in those you meet (including your own students), the most important set of teacher beliefs to study is your own. Teaching is a basic fabric of life and is present everywhere. Teaching and learning surround virtually every human activity. It is accepted as an ordinary, very routine, and often unexamined aspect of life. When you help a friend program a VCR, or help a stranger navigate buying a subway ticket, or even give directions on how to make your favorite cake, you are being a teacher. You may not realize that your teaching is guided by a set of beliefs. You have already formed many beliefs, developed extensive skill, and have many experiences that relate to the issues of teaching in schools (Anderson, 1984; Book, Byers, & Freeman, 1983; Hollingsworth, 1989; Lanier & Little, 1986; Lortie, 1975). You will not abandon those beliefs as you begin your training as a professional teacher. These skills, beliefs, and experiences will have an immense influence (potentially both positive and negative) on your development as a teacher and your future success as a teacher.

Many students enter preservice teacher education programs so confident in their teaching ability that they feel they have little to learn from a teacher education program. Some students realize the immense difficulties of successful teaching and have little confidence at all. It is important to recognize that everyone has established beliefs and unexamined views about teaching. Beginning teachers need to analyze carefully their views about teaching because their beliefs will greatly affect the kind of teachers they become.

Examining Teacher Views: An Activity

Read the following vignette and answer the questions that follow. When you finish, find someone else to do the same thing. Then compare answers.

◆

Juanita Muddles Through Another Day

Juanita was upset. She didn't have any paper to do her math homework. Just that morning, her teacher had told the class that for now on all homework was to be done. She had looked straight at Juanita with a rather grim face that foretold evil tidings for missing homework. Juanita had a problem of forgetting and doing things at the last moment. It was 10 P.M. that night when Juanita remembered her teacher's admonition and began her work. Her mom was already asleep, and her dad wouldn't be home for another hour. Juanita woke her mother. "I need some notebook paper!" she said urgently.

Her mother was not pleased. "Why aren't you in bed?"

Juanita began to cry. "I have a lot of math homework to do, and if I don't do it, the teacher is going to kill me."

Her mom pulled the pillow over her head. Then, in total frustration, she shouted, "Juanita, you've had all afternoon to do that homework. If you needed paper, you should have told me. You have six brothers, and they never got me out of bed for notebook paper. You'll just have to let the teacher kill you tomorrow. I'll sit beside her at the funeral." Her mother looked up and said, "Forgive me. Now get out, I've got to get up at five in the morning. You know that. Juanita, why do you do this all the time?"

Juanita left angry. She sulked until her father came home. He was tired. He was a self-employed mechanic by day and a textile worker in the afternoon. Juanita's dad had been working since before she went to school that day. All he said was, "I'm tired. I'm going to bed. You're a smart girl. Figure out something. Do it on a paper bag or something."

Juanita did just that. She got two grocery bags and cut out four sheets of paper about the size of notebook paper. She made up her "kitchen math" problems and illustrated how to solve them. Then she wrote the beginning of her story that was due the day before. She fell asleep at the table.

At 5 A.M., her mother woke her and made her go to bed. At 8:30, Juanita woke up and realized she was late. Her dad was working on a car in the backyard and had forgotten to call her. She rushed and arrived at school 15 minutes tardy. Her teacher was not happy. "And I suppose, Juanita, that you don't have your home-work either?"

Juanita held out the finished math and the half-done, two-day-late story, all written on grocery bag paper. The children laughed.

Ask yourself the following questions:

◆ If you were this teacher, what you would do?
◆ Whose behavior has to change first if Juanita is to learn to get her work completed on time?
◆ Does Juanita's effort in doing her work on a grocery bag represent progress toward accepting responsibility?

There are, of course, many diverse answers to these questions. Your answers and how you go about arriving at those answers are based on many past experiences and beliefs. Those experiences and beliefs vary with each individual. For example, if you determined that you would accept the work from Juanita (incomplete and on a grocery bag), you probably believe that any effort that Juanita gives is improvement toward the established goal. No matter how slight this effort is, it needs to be recognized and appreciated as progress. You would probably argue that Juanita has, at least, recognized that she must begin to correct her bad work habits.

If you chose to praise her for her ingenuity in using grocery bags, you are probably assuming that Juanita was earnest in her efforts at completing the assignments.

If you chose to talk to Juanita in private about both the appearance of the work and the incompleteness of the already late story, you are probably assuming that you have established reasonable work standards and that those standards must be maintained. Although it is important to acknowledge progress and the unique difficulties that individuals must overcome in order to achieve, it is equally important to remember the value of attaining reasonable goals in a reasonable manner. In this view, although it is important to communicate to Juanita that her efforts are appreciated, you must recognize that Juanita could still have achieved the goal of completed quality work. Juanita has to learn to make a different series of decisions.

Consider, for a minute, your own experiences. What type of family schedule, family support, and teachers did you have? How do you feel about large families? Should mothers work? Should parents have children they cannot afford? What is the appropriate level of assistance a parent should give their child? The circumstances of your early school years have an important impact on your behavior as a teacher.

One teacher, when given this scenario, was adamant that the work not be accepted and Juanita be held totally accountable for her actions. Others in her group were somewhat startled by the strength of her conviction. They thought that this teacher was being insensitive and pressed her for a defense or retraction of the view. The teacher staunchly maintained that giving in to Juanita was telling Juanita that she couldn't be any more than a rattled student halfway struggling through what everyone else found simple. The teacher furthered her position by revealing that, at one time, she, too, was a "Muddled Juanita." She knew that her teachers felt sorry for her, and she used it to minimize her effort. However, when she was in the fifth grade, her teacher matter-of-factly told her that she was grown up now and that her excuses would no longer be accepted. By being held to the same standards as the other students and with the confidence projected on her by her teacher, she began to reassess her status. "I was told that I could succeed. However, success didn't accept excuses."

Some teachers openly admitted that they felt sorry for Juanita, others thought she needed more encouragement and guidance, and still others began to insist that Juanita do her work according to the established standards. Those in the group who had overcome substantial hardship appeared to be the least sympathetic. As one teacher tersely declared, "Juanita's parents aren't so bad. It just means Juanita has to take more responsibility to work harder." The correct solution, of course, cannot be determined without actual contact with Juanita, her parents, and the teacher. There are many possible answers with varying degrees of probable success. What is important to understand is that we all have "hidden" assumptions that result from our past experiences and personal beliefs. Recognizing your own beliefs and values is important because these form the foundation of your understanding of teaching and teaching skill.

Successful Teachers Are Professionals

Teaching is a ubiquitous fundamental human activity. Each of us is a teacher in some capacity a great deal of the time. However, being a teaching professional distinguishes you from your previous teaching experiences. When you accept the responsibility to teach in the elementary classroom, your role, the expectations others have of you, and the methods you employ will radically change. There are many different dimensions on which professional teaching differs from the informal teaching that everyone does. Exactly what we mean by "professional" as it relates to teaching is often debated and has multiple interpretations (Sikes, 1987). For the purposes of this book, the fundamental definition of professional teaching is a vocation in which teaching for pay is distinguished from the essential everyday teaching activity in which we all engage. Essentially, professional teachers are specially trained, licensed by government bodies, regulated for the public good, and paid for their services. Professional teachers in public schools establish an expectation that they are knowledgeable experts, skilled practitioners, and ethically driven. Unlike informal teaching, professional teaching implies an accountable, proficient expert.

Successful Teachers Are Knowledgeable Experts

As professionals, teachers are expected to be knowledgeable experts not only in the subject matter that they are expected to teach, but also in matters related to children. As professionals, they are expected to have an extensive understanding of the methods and strategies used to teach children. These strategies should reflect a more sophisticated and successful approach to learning than that supplied by typical parents. As experts, teachers represent a higher level of skill in dealing with and understanding children than is ordinarily expected of parents. There is no widely shared term for what a "teacher expert" is, just as there is no widely accepted understanding of what a "professional" is. Several distinguishing areas have been identified by the research in this area. According to an analysis by Borko, Bellamy, and Sanders (1992), expert teachers differed from novices by the following:

- The way in which problems are structured
- The facets of situations that receive attention and treatment
- The differential treatment of those facets
- The strategies selected to achieve outcomes
- The selection of information used in solving problems
- The development and use of routines to govern daily events

Going back to the original premise that everyone is a teacher, those who wish to be professionals must be experts compared to their lay colleagues. In this way, teachers must think, behave, and achieve instructional results in a different way from the rest of society. Borko et al. describe three key concepts that identify teaching as a complex cognitive skill: schema, pedagogical reasoning, and content knowledge.

Professional Schema

A *schema* is a mental construct that identifies the variables involved in a complex system. A schema (plural *schemata*) attempts to explain how those variables interact and describes the processes by which a system works. The models presented thus far are simplified schemata; they are mental constructs put to paper and are designed to illuminate very complex mental processes. Expert teachers become adept at developing schemata that identify and explain phenomena from their accumulation of knowledge about teaching, at seeing the relationships among various components of teaching, and at creating hypotheses to guide behavior directed at unique events in their students' learning. Such detail and rationalization are rarely found in lay and novice teachers. Developing a rational and detailed understanding of the instructional environment, the learner, the content, and the method of instruction is a central key role of the professional teacher and an obligation that should not be taken lightly. Novice teachers should practice developing visual models of teaching activities and concepts to direct concentrated study of instructional improvement. Many examples of these models are provided in this text.

Pedagogical Reasoning

Pedagogical reasoning is, in its simplest interpretation, the conversion of facts, events, skills, action sequences, concepts, constructs, attitudes, and values into teaching strategies that can be discovered by the learner from reflective experience.

Pedagogical reasoning assists in developing or identifying instructional strategies for attaining carefully considered goals and aims. Pedagogical reasoning is like a tailor who designs and fits a suit to a man so that it not only meets his present needs, but anticipates his future requirements as well. The tailor obtains an excellent fit but also leaves sufficient cloth in the seams in case the man puts on weight. The tailor selects the cloth for durable wear as well as for appearance, and provides sufficient design consultation so that the suit empowers, rather than overpowers, the man. The professional teacher is an expert in adapting curriculum to the individual needs of learners so that they do not become entrapped, overcome, or resigned to the present by their experiences in learning. Instead, successful teachers help individuals develop so that they are successful, feel successful, and subsequently act as successful citizens.

Content Knowledge

Being an expert in content knowledge is problematic for the elementary teacher but is, nonetheless, a constant expectation. Since elementary classroom teachers typically teach all subjects, they are expected to know all of these subjects. Although the curriculum for elementary students is considered to be general knowledge that all citizens should know and understand, this assumption either overestimates the knowledge of citizens or underestimates the sophistication of the current curriculum. In short, few citizens have mastered the basic elementary school curriculum as it is typically defined. Consider these three questions aimed at children regarding rudimentary knowledge about the physical world:

- What is required for a seed to germinate?
- What is peristalsis?
- If you put three 1.5-volt batteries in a circuit to light a bulb and one of them is "backwards," what happens to the light?

First, write your answer to each of the questions. Then consider in which lessons you might discuss these issues: How old are the children? What questions might be asked? What situations illustrate the concepts? How is this knowledge used in life? Finally, decide if you currently have enough information to answer these questions so that children understand. These illustrations are not trick questions but standard material from elementary classrooms.

- Children might ask, "How does the plant know to start growing?" Your response might be, "Germination is the 'waking up' of the little plant that is already in every seed. Break a seed open, and you can see the 'baby plant' inside with a hand lens. A typical seed needs only warmth and moisture to germinate. It does not need soil or light of any kind." This information is typically taught in kindergarten and first grade when the children get to grow a plant for the Easter holidays and the celebration of the returning spring.
- Children are marvelous creatures who, even when left to their own devices, often find unique outlooks on simple questions. When a child asks, "When I eat

bread hanging upside down on the monkey bars, why doesn't the bread come out my nose?" the child is asking about peristalsis. Obviously, this student has attributed the flow of food from the mouth to the stomach to be a function of gravity. You might answer, "In actuality, the flow of food and liquid to the stomach is governed by a wavelike muscular action in the esophagus that forces food into the stomach when it is swallowed. This is called peristalsis." This subject is studied along with digestion and nutrition in the third or fourth grades.

◆ A child might ask, "Why do I have to put the batteries pointing in the same direction?" Electricity, the flow of electrons, defies a simple concrete explanation. To really answer this question, you may need to perform many experiments with electricity to give children even a grasp of what a "flow of electrons" means. However, you might reply, "If one battery in a three-cell flashlight is put in 'backwards,' the light will still shine but only with the strength of one battery. The two batteries that are opposed to each other cancel each other out. Turn the backwards battery back to its proper position, and the light will shine about three times brighter. Think of the equations $1 + 1 - 1 = 1$ and $1 + 1 + 1 = 3$. The '−1' is the reversed battery." This concept is typically studied in fifth or sixth grade when electricity and DC current are introduced.

How did you do? As a successful elementary teacher, your subject matter knowledge must be quite vast. Because of the young child's intriguing curiosity, teachers must often deal with areas of knowledge that ordinary humans may not have mastered (or even thought about since they were children). While an honest "I don't know, let's find out together!" is one of the best responses to a child's special question, it does not sufficiently counter the need for extensive subject matter knowledge. It is difficult, if not impossible, for a teacher without adequate subject matter knowledge to perform the necessary pedagogical reasoning to construct an appropriate curriculum. Borko et al. claim that schemata for pedagogical content knowledge are almost nonexistent in novices. Developing these knowledge structures and learning pedagogical reasoning skills that can be employed successfully with students are major components of learning to teach as an expert.

Successful Teachers Are Skilled Practitioners

The image of the teacher as a skilled practitioner interacting with students in crowded classrooms is such a powerful icon of teacher work that it almost completely overpowers other facets of the job. Even among teachers, this vision is so strong that other facets of the teaching task (such as student records, planning, and noninstructional duties) is often considered wasted time or "not work." It always fascinates the author when working with teachers in instructional strategies meetings, to hear teachers say, "That was fun, but it's time to get *back* to work."

The view of the active teacher is, of course, an important one. What a teacher does, however, is of minor consequence if those actions are not illuminated by rational direction, purpose, and understanding. The adage, "Success is not just doing things right; it's doing the right things," is an appropriate guidance for teachers. Researchers have accumulated a powerful array of findings that indicate certain teacher behaviors are more indicative of teaching effectiveness than others are. Collectively, this has been labeled "process–product" research, and its finding has been codified into effective teaching profiles. The North Carolina Teacher Performance Appraisal Instrument (TPAI) is an excellent example of a collection of extensively researched teacher behaviors (Figure 1.5). Although there is controversy surrounding the use of research codification to evaluate teacher effectiveness, there is consensus that these descriptions of effective teaching form a partial but important

1. **Major Function: Management of Instructional Time**
1.1 Teacher has materials, supplies, and equipment ready at the start of the lesson or instructional activity.
1.2 Teacher gets the class started quickly.
1.3 Teacher gets students on task quickly at the beginning of each lesson or instructional activity.
1.4 Teacher maintains a high level of student time-on-task.

2. **Major Function: Management of Student Behavior**
2.1 Teacher has established a set of rules and procedures that govern the handling of routine administrative matters.
2.2 Teacher has established a set of rules and procedures that govern student verbal participation and talk during different types of activities—whole-class instruction, small-group instruction, and so on.
2.3 Teacher has established a set of rules and procedures that govern student movement in the classroom during different types of instructional activities.
2.4 Teacher frequently monitors the behavior of all students during whole-class, small-group, and seatwork activities and during transitions between instructional activities.
2.5 Teacher stops inappropriate behavior promptly and consistently, yet maintains the dignity of the student.

3. **Major Function: Instructional Presentation**
3.1 Teacher begins lesson or instructional activity with a review of previous material.
3.2 Teacher introduces the lesson or instructional activity and specifies learning objectives when appropriate.
3.3 Teacher speaks fluently and precisely.
3.4 Teacher presents the lesson or instructional activity using concepts and language understandable to the students.
3.5 Teacher provides relevant examples and demonstrations to illustrate concepts and skills.
3.6 Teacher assigns tasks that students handle with a high rate of success.
3.7 Teacher asks appropriate levels of questions that students handle with a high rate of success.
3.8 Teacher conducts lesson or instructional activity at a brisk pace, slowing presentations when necessary for student understanding but avoiding unnecessary slowdowns.
3.9 Teacher makes transitions between lessons and between instructional activities within lessons efficiently and smoothly.
3.10 Teacher makes sure that the assignment is clear.
3.11 Teacher summarizes the main point(s) of the lesson at the end of the lesson or instructional activity.

FIGURE 1.5   North Carolina Teacher Performance Appraisal Instrument: Functions and indicators.

description of the behaviors of a minimally competent teacher. However, it is becoming increasingly apparent that assembling these listed teacher behaviors into a coherent and unified teaching approach is more important than just being able to demonstrate skill on demand. Thus, for example, "starting on time with materials ready" may be indicative of effective teaching; it is effective only to the degree in which the instruction is worthwhile, the materials used are applicable to the intended instruction, and the lesson is matched to the abilities and interests of the children. Chapter 7 deals with these research findings in detail. For now, the reader is encouraged to actively consider the advantages and limitations of the types of behaviors listed in Figure 1.5.

4. Major Function: Instructional Monitoring of Student Performance

4.1 Teacher maintains clear, firm, and reasonable work standards and due dates.

4.2 Teacher circulates during classwork to check all students' performance.

4.3 Teacher routinely uses oral, written, and other work products to check student progress.

4.4 Teacher poses questions clearly and one at a time.

5. Major Function: Instructional Feedback

5.1 Teacher provides feedback on the correctness or incorrectness of in-class work to encourage student growth.

5.2 Teacher regularly provides prompt feedback on assigned out-of-class work.

5.3 Teacher affirms a correct oral response appropriately, and moves on.

5.4 Teacher provides sustaining feedback after an incorrect response or no response by probing, repeating the question, giving a clue, or allowing more time.

6. Major Function: Facilitating Instruction

6.1 Teacher has an instructional plan that is compatible with the school and system-wide curricular goals.

6.2 Teacher uses diagnostic information obtained from tests and other assessment procedures to develop and revise objectives and/or tasks.

6.3 Teacher maintains accurate records to document student performance.

6.4 Teacher has instructional plan that matches/aligns objectives, learning strategies, assessment, and student needs at the appropriate level of difficulty.

6.5 Teacher uses available human and material resources to support the instructional program.

7. Major Function: Communicating within the Educational Environment

7.1 Teacher treats all students in a fair and equitable manner.

7.2 Teacher interacts effectively with students, co-workers, parents, and community.

8. Major Function: Performing Noninstructional Duties

8.1 Teacher carries out noninstructional duties as assigned and/or as need is perceived.

8.2 Teacher adheres to established laws, policies, rules, and regulations.

8.3 Teacher follows a plan for professional development and demonstrates evidence of growth.

From *Teacher Performance Appraisal System: The Standards and Processes for Use* by North Carolina State Department of Public Instruction, 1986, Raleigh, NC: Author.

Visualization of the practice of teaching is a powerful tool in assisting all teachers to understand the meaning of teacher behavior and to get beyond simple imitation. As you visualize the beginning of a class period, starting on time is an obvious goal. But what do you do to prepare for that eventuality? Do you stand at the door, welcoming the students, distributing an outline of the introductory activity in science? Are you sitting behind your desk, collecting absence notes and lunch money while the children are settling in? Are the children "checking in" at the bulletin board, taking their name tags off the wall and placing them in the pocket that indicates which lunch they are choosing? How do you handle the obviously unhappy child? Do you take the time to inquire about difficulties or rush into the lesson? If you spend individual time with that student, what are the other children doing? Teaching is an incredible array of complex and staccato events that taxes even the most aware and energetic people. Preparing for the role of expert teacher requires active inquiry, constant analysis of routine events, and robust energy and movement.

◆ ◆ ◆

Summary

1. Teaching is a complex activity that has been illuminated by empirical research but still remains incomplete and open to interpretation and new lines of inquiry.

2. The foundation of knowledge about teaching comes from an unstable mixture of empirical inquiry, societal values, and theory.

3. Teachers must interpret events before knowledge can be applied effectively through a decision-making process not totally understood.

4. Successful teaching is present everywhere and constantly changing. Teaching is a basic human activity and varies with the people involved and their needs.

5. Teaching may be performed deliberately when the learning is intended by the teacher or covertly when the learner models the behavior of the teacher even when that behavior is not the focus of the lesson.

6. Successful teaching is difficult to define, and no single concept of "good teaching" is acceptable to all.

7. Teaching exemplars vary in their approach to purpose, method, and result.

8. Examining and comparing these exemplars tell us that conflict is almost inevitable, a supportive respect for students is desirable, and a universal purpose of teaching is to help learners solve problems.

9. Each individual carries many beliefs about teaching, and this affects the way in which decisions about teaching are made. These beliefs vary radically among teachers.

10. Teaching as a profession differs from teaching within a general social context in that the professional is considered to be an expert in the subject matter of instruction, in the methods and strategies used to foster learning, and in the consistent attainment of positive results.

11. Expert teachers differ from novice teachers in the way they structure teaching problems, the strategies they use to obtain outcomes, and the routines they develop to handle daily events.

12. Expert teachers develop sophisticated schemata through intense pedagogical reasoning that increases the probability of obtaining predetermined learning goals.

13. Developing teaching skill at the professional expert level requires active inquiry, constant analysis of routine events, robust energy, and activity.

◆ ◆ ◆

Activities and Questions for Further Understanding

1. Think about the most effective teachers you had in elementary school. Make a list of the things they had in common. Of the items on the list, which do you think are components of successful teaching? Why?

2. Compare your list of traits of successful teachers with another student (or with the list provided in Figure 1.5). How are they alike and different?

3. From "A Slice of Life," it is obvious that Mr. Roberts has repeated some activities every year. Doing the same things over and over is a prime indication of a lack of growth. Do you think that applies to Mr. Roberts and his paper airplanes? Why?

4. Interview two people: one several years older than you and one several years younger than you. Ask them to answer the first question in the activities list. Do the three perspectives produce similar views?

5. When have you taught someone outside of a school-related context? How did you go about doing it? Compare responses with others. Which of the traits you developed in question 1 did you demonstrate? How many of the traits in the TPAI (Figure 1.5) did you use?

6. Select a historical figure that you consider a teaching exemplar. Determine the individual's vehicle for learning, form of knowledge, aim, and purpose. Compare the results with the four exemplars in Figure 1.4.

7. John Dewey is one of the most influential American educators. Examine each of the progressive beliefs outlined in the section on Dewey and determine if those perspectives are still evident in American schools. Should they be?

8. Reread "Juanita Muddles Through Another Day" with a group of friends. As a group, discuss whether the teacher accepts Juanita's homework. What should the teacher do to teach Juanita responsibility? If the primary goal was to assist Juanita in developing a more positive self-concept, would the teacher's behavior toward Juanita be different?

9. Compare the description of Rayvon's lesson to Figure 1.1. Identify which parts of Rayvon's lesson represent each activity of an effective demonstration.

◆ ◆ ◆

References

Anderson, R. C. (1984). Some reflections on the acquisition of knowledge. *Educational Researcher, 13*(9), 5–10.

Axtelle, G. E., & Burnett, J. R. (1970). Dewey on education and schooling. In J. A. Boydston (Ed.), *Guide to the works of John Dewey*. Carbondale: Southern Illinois University Press.

Bandura, A. (1986). *Social foundations of thought and action: A social cognitive theory*. Upper Saddle River, NJ: Prentice Hall.

Bettelheim, Bruno. (1971). *The informed heart*. New York: Macmillan.

Book, C., Byers, J., & Freeman, D. (1983). Student expectations and teacher education traditions with which we can and cannot live. *Journal of Teacher Education, 34*(1), 9–13.

Borko, H., Bellamy, M. L., & Sanders, L. (1992). A cognitive analysis of patterns in science instruction by expert and novice teachers. In T. Russell & H. Munby (Eds.), *Teachers and teaching: From classroom to reflection*.

Bowen, James. (1981). *A history of Western education* (Vol. 3). New York: St. Martins Press.

Broudy, H. S., & Palmer, J. R. (1965). *Exemplars of teaching method*. Chicago: Rand McNally.

Brubacher, John S. (1947). *A history of the problems of education*. New York: McGraw-Hill.

Bryan, J., & Walbek, N. (1970). Preaching and practicing generosity: Children's actions and reactions. *Child Development, 41*, 329–353.

Butts, R. F. (1973). *The education of the West*. New York: McGraw-Hill.

Clark, C. M., & Peterson, P. L. (1986). Teachers' thought processes. In M. C. Wittrock (Ed.), *Handbook of research on teaching* (3rd ed., pp. 255–296). New York: Macmillan.

Combs, Arthur W. (1972). Some basic concepts for teacher education. *The Journal of Teacher Education , 23*(3), 286–290.

Cook, J. E. (1988, April). Growing pains: Speaking of broccoli. *Teaching K–8*, pp. 33–34.

Dewey, John. (1959) . My pedagogic creed. In M. S. Dworkin (Ed.), *Dewey on education: Selections* (p. 91). New York: Columbia University Press. (Original work published 1897)

Dewey, John. (1980). Democracy and education. In D. Tanner & L. Tanner (Eds.), *Curriculum development: Theory into practice* (4th ed., p. 266). New York: Macmillan. (Original work published 1916)

Glasser, William. (1990). *The quality school: Managing students without coercion*. Upper Saddle River, NJ: Prentice Hall.

Good, H. G. (1960). *A history of Western education* (2nd ed.). New York: Macmillan.

Good, Tom & Brophy, Jere. (1991). *Looking into classrooms (*5th ed.). New York: Harper Collins.

Goodlad, J., & Klein, M. F. (1970). *Behind the classroom door*. Worthington, OH: Charles A. Jones.

Greene, Maxine. (1989). Social and political contexts. In M. Reynolds (Ed.), *Knowledge base for the beginning teacher* (pp. 142–154). New York: Pergammon Press.

Gulley, Norman. (1962). *Plato's theory of knowledge*. London: Methuen & Co. Ltd.

Hollingsworth, S. (1989). Prior beliefs and cognitive change in learning to teach. *American Educational Research Journal, 26*(2), 160–189.

Kilpatrick, William (1959). Reminiscences of Dewey and his influence. In W. W. Brickman & S. Lehrer (Eds.), *John Dewey: Master educator* (p. 59). New York: Society for the Advancement of Education.

Lanier, J. E., & Little, J. W. (1986). Research on teacher education. In M. C. Wittrock (Ed.), *Handbook of research on teaching* (3rd ed., pp. 527–569). New York: Macmillan.

Lortie, D. C. (1975). *Schoolteacher: A sociological study*. Chicago: The University of Chicago Press.

Marshall, H. (1988). In pursuit of learning-oriented classrooms. *Teaching and Teacher Education, 4*, 85–98.

Marx, G. (1993, October). Confucius and Sun Yat Sen. *USA–Sino Teacher Education Consortium Newsletter*.

Marx, R. W., & Peterson, P. L. (1981). The nature of teacher decision making. In B. R. Joyce, C. C. Brown, & L. Peck (Eds.), *Flexibility in teaching:*

An excursion into the nature of teaching and training. New York: Longman.

North Carolina State Department of Public Instruction. (1986). *Teacher performance appraisal system: The standards and processes for use.* Raleigh, NC: Author. (ERIC Document Reproduction Service No. ED 271 453)

North Carolina State Department of Public Instruction. (1986). *Teacher performance appraisal system training: A report of outcomes.* Raleigh, NC: Author. (ERIC Document Reproduction Service No. ED 271 452)

Northwest Regional Educational Laboratory. (1990). *Onward to excellence: Making schools more effective*. Portland, OR: Author.

Overholser, J. C. (1992, March/April). Socrates in the classroom. *The Social Studies*, pp. 77–82.

Peterson, P. L., Marx, R. W., & Clark, C. M. (1978). Teacher planning, teacher behavior, and student achievement. *American Educational Research Journal, 15*, 417–432.

Purkey, W. W. (1989). *The heart of teaching is teaching from the heart.* Address to the Association of Teacher Educators Annual Conference, Las Vegas.

Riner, Phillip S. (1989). Dewey's legacy to education. *Educational Forum, 53*(2), 183–190.

Roberts, C., & Becker, S. (1976). Communication and teaching effectiveness in industrial education. *American Educational Research Journal, 13,* 181–197.

Seeskin, Kenneth. (1987). Meno 86C–89A: A mathematical image of philosophic inquiry. In B. P.

Hendley (Ed.), *Plato, time and education*. Albany: State University of New York Press.

Shavelson, R. J. (1973). *The basic teaching skill: Decision-making* (R & D Memorandum No. 104). Stanford, CA: Stanford University, School of Education, Center for R & D in Teaching.

Sykes, G. (1987). Reckoning with the spectre. *Educational Researcher, 16*(6), 19–21.

Taylor, P. H. (1970). How teachers plan their courses. Cited in C. M. Clark & P. L. Peterson (Eds.), *Teachers' thought processes*. Slough, Berkshire, England: National Foundation for Educational Research. In M. C. Wittrock (Ed.), *Handbook of research on teaching* (3rd ed., pp. 255–296). New York: Macmillan.

Ulich, Robert. (1965). *Three thousand years of educational wisdom*. Cambridge, MA: Harvard University Press.

U.S. Department of Education. (1986). *What works: Research about teaching and learning.* Washington, DC: Author.

Wilds, E. H. & Lottich, K. V. (1970). *The foundations of modern education* (4th ed.). New York: Holt, Rinehart, and Winston.

Yinger, R. J. (1977). *A study of teacher planning: Description and theory development using ethnographic and information processing methods.* Unpublished doctoral dissertation, Michigan State University, East Lansing.

Zahorik, J. A. (1975). The effects of planning on teaching. *Elementary School Journal, 71,* 143–151.

CHAPTER 2

How Do I Learn About Successful Teaching?

Constructing Understanding About Knowledge, Knowing, and Belief

Outline

Thus the wit was not wrong who defined education in this way: "Education is that which remains, if one has forgotten everything that he learned in school."

ALBERT EINSTEIN

No longer can we be satisfied with a life where the heart has its reasons, which reason cannot know. Our heart must know the world of reason, and reason must be guided by an informed heart.

BRUNO BETTELHEIM

A Slice of Life

Mrs. Sanchez raised herself on tiptoe as she trained her eyes on Marcus and Ronnie. They seemed to be involved in a conversation that was supposed to be about Dorothy's confrontation with the wizard, but Mrs. Sanchez wasn't sure. Marcus looked up and found Mrs. Sanchez's eyes staring straight at him. His body jerked in embarrassment while his head and eyes attempted to let Ronnie know that Mrs. Sanchez was observing their every act. Both boys' attention turned to the task at hand but seemed a little lost. "Now," thought Mrs. Sanchez, "they'll be talking about the wizard."

She leisurely started walking toward Marcus and Ronnie, but then stopped by Maria's desk and quickly checked her story introduction. Mrs. Sanchez smiled approvingly at Maria, "You've made the lion seem so real. How did you do that?" While most of the class were working on trying to understand why the wizard was so fussy and harsh, Maria and a few others wanted to explore the characters after Dorothy's encounter with the wizard. Although this wasn't the assignment that she had in mind, Mrs. Sanchez felt that initiative should be nurtured and was glad that these children were taking responsibility for their education. She believed in giving students choices and generally allowed students to modify assignments if they could give her a good reason for doing so. She concluded that they could do character sketches and possibly write a play about the adventures of the lion, the scarecrow, and the tin man after Dorothy left the Land of Oz. She wanted the children to understand that authors often developed characters in literature to explore problems or issues they were thinking about. To help children develop this understanding, Mrs. Sanchez generally had the children talk about a character and explore why the character acted in a certain way. Maria and several others, however, wanted to develop this understanding in another way.

Mrs. Sanchez smiled as Mary and her partner Ginnie pointed out the "special" words they had been getting from the thesaurus. Mrs. Sanchez turned and pulled a tissue from her apron. "Need this?" she asked Tom as she laid it gently on his desk. Tom smiled and immediately blew his nose. By that time, Mrs. Sanchez had read his first paragraph and had circled three separate phrases topped with smiley faces. "I'm going to send you some visitors. Show them your explanations for the wizard's fussy behavior."

In three more steps, Mrs. Sanchez stood beside Marcus and his partner. Very aware of her presence, the two boys were trying hard to cover their tracks. They had quickly brainstormed three reasons why the wizard was so grumpy.

Mrs. Sanchez was proud of Marcus. He came into her class with a chip on his shoulder, but there was something about him that she liked. She invested a little extra time, used a little extra patience, and tried not to correct everything he did wrong. She had concluded that Marcus needed to be trusted by others before he could trust himself. With a few setbacks, the plan seemed to be working. "Good start," Mrs. Sanchez said mildly. "But you've got some distance to go. What are some other reasons, other than the wizard being sad, that could explain the wizard's attitude?"

"Embarrassment?" Marcus grinned aloud.

"What could a wizard be embarrassed about?"

Marcus looked down. "Getting caught doing something that . . . "

Mrs. Sanchez raised her hand. "No, don't tell me. Write it down, and we'll share in a few minutes. Now hurry. You two are behind."

Teacher Belief and Teacher Action

A look at Mrs. Sanchez's behavior helps to demonstrate two important aspects of the classroom. First, Mrs. Sanchez was very busy observing, interpreting, and reacting to her children. Second, she made meaning of what she saw and heard based on what she knew and believed about the children. With Marcus, a kid who came to her class angry and hostile, Mrs. Sanchez developed an implicit belief that Marcus's behavior could change but that, as a teacher, her behavior toward him must change first. Because of this belief, she altered her behavior and maintained those changes even when the desired results remained elusive. When Marcus's behavior failed to meet both her expectations and her standards, Mrs. Sanchez maintained her supportive attitude because she believed that Marcus needed support and trust from others before he could support and trust himself.

Teacher beliefs have a covert, and often dominant, influence on teacher actions. Had Mrs. Sanchez believed that Marcus needed more structure and a firmer hand in monitoring his minute-by-minute behaviors, she would have acted much differently than in our scenario. Because she believed that Marcus could— and would—self-correct, she decided to wait for him to notice her. She believed that she could send, and he would receive, a work reminder delivered through eye contact. She believed it was the best way to get Marcus back on task. This strategy allowed Marcus to control his actions rather than to respond to some overt external source of authority. In this case, Mrs. Sanchez concluded correctly. Marcus self-corrected, and Mrs. Sanchez successfully created a situation in which she could return to Marcus later in the period and give him positive, reinforcing feedback on his work. Mrs. Sanchez successfully engineered a scenario in which Marcus could exercise personal responsibility.

Mrs. Sanchez could have been wrong in her assessment of Marcus' needs. In fact, Mrs. Sanchez, like all successful teachers in elementary classrooms, creates hundreds of hypotheses each day. Many are correct, but many are wrong. Even more remain indefinite. Mrs. Sanchez tests her hypotheses repeatedly, refining, modifying, or reinforcing them to help her interpret and react to her students. Many of her actions will change as a result of her experiments. However, some hypotheses will be tested repeatedly and, regardless of results, Mrs. Sanchez's actions will persist because she values certain solutions to problems even if they don't appear to work successfully. In this scenario, Mrs. Sanchez's actions were refined and directed by empirical experiments and observations and are considered *knowledge*. The process of testing, refining, and reformulating knowledge is called *knowing*. The actions based on value judgments, hypotheses without empirical verification or support, and intuition are considered *beliefs*. Knowledge, knowing, and beliefs are employed by teachers in every classroom. They are very personal, often unarticulated, but very powerful determinants of a teacher's action. Obviously, the accuracy and efficiency of this knowledge, knowing, and belief process as it is employed in the classroom have a direct effect on the outcomes of the teacher's efforts. The more accurate and efficient the process is, the more successful the teacher is.

Belief and Action: A Complex Interaction

As Glasser (1990) noted, teaching may well be the hardest job there is. Researchers in both psychology and pedagogy are beginning to unravel some of the mysteries involved in determining teacher effectiveness. One of the earliest findings (quite tangential to the major thrust of the research on teacher effectiveness) was that far more variables are involved in successful teaching than the current research paradigms could handle.

Louden (1991) summarized the emerging view of teaching as more than teacher behavior:

> It is what teachers think, what teachers believe and what teachers do at the level of the classroom that ultimately shapes the kind of learning that young people get. . . . Teachers teach in the way they do not just because of the skills they have or have not learned. The ways they teach are also grounded in their backgrounds, their biographies, in the kinds of teachers they have become. Their careers—their hopes and dreams, their opportunities and aspirations, or the frustration of these things—are also important for teachers' commitment, enthusiasm and morale. (p. vi)

It may seem odd that Louden felt the need to state the obvious: Teachers simply do not react to situations based solely on prior training, predefined curricula, or packaged methodologies. Training, curriculum, and instructional methodologies are transformed from abstract concepts into classroom activities through the perceptions and cognitive structures of teachers. Each teacher's unique perceptions of the problem and personal teaching skill result in many potential solutions to teaching problems. However important this process and each teacher's cognitive structures are, information and verified knowledge about teaching exist that transcend a teacher's individualistic beliefs. That is, knowledge about teaching is available to assist teachers in consistently obtaining certain objectives with a wide range of students.

The knowledge about teaching that is empirically verified and applies to diverse situations is collectively referred to as *research-based knowledge*. However, just what constitutes this research knowledge base is widely debated and open to many interpretations. Two things are quite certain: (1) Research-based knowledge is still inadequate to provide *exclusive* guidance to teachers, and (2) teachers still need to interpret and customize this knowledge for a particular educational setting. The North Carolina TPAI (Figure 1.5) is an example of this controversial dilemma. At first glance, this listing of basic knowledge about teaching seems self-evident. The first five sets of items are thoroughly grounded in empirical research that has been verified in a wide range of settings. What, if anything, could cause controversy and embittered debate?

Benefits and Limitations of Pedagogical Research

The collective research on time management, instructional presentation, monitoring student performance, and instructional feedback forms a curricular approach often referred to as *direct instruction*. Direct instruction has many applications in the successful elementary classroom and is best applied when the objective is to reproduce a certain activity, recall information, or develop a specific predetermined skill. However, direct instruction has some very definite limitations. For example, what if the goal is less structured or requires continual adaptation to circumstances? If the goal of instruction is to teach observation and hypothesis generation, students are required to generalize and apply covert skills based on their own abilities. There is no single way of developing a hypothesis from observations. Since this objective requires students to structure the unknown to make it familiar, it requires the student to act initially by structuring personal observation to develop a comprehensible structure. However, in direct instruction, the specific outcome is generally predetermined; the teacher directly structures the lesson so that students are provided a logical sequential route toward understanding. In teaching hypothesis generation, direct instruction is simply inadequate because of the many appropriate approaches that can be employed and because individual skills vary that can radically alter what may be considered an acceptable solution.

To apply knowledge to new, unique, or continually changing contexts requires skills that can be taught only indirectly through experiences, questioning, and encouragement. These instructional strategies are known collectively as *implicit, inquiry-based,* or *indirect instruction.* Inquiry-based instruction requires that the teacher *not* perform many of the functions of direct instruction but rather allows the child to perform those tasks experimentally.

The teacher, by projecting likely outcomes for different choices, must choose when and how to employ knowledge about teaching to obtain the desired results. Teachers must consider the needs and abilities of students, the context of the environment, and their personal skill level as teachers. This process of making decisions requires sophisticated skills in thinking as well as in fitting many methods to student abilities. These skills are not included in the TPAI model, and those who believe strongly in the purposes of inquiry instruction may find this model of successful teaching to be very limited.

Models that assemble research-based knowledge also identify important teacher behaviors and illustrate how they are interrelated. However, few indicate the conditions under which those behaviors can be used effectively. The listed behaviors alone are also not sufficient to reliably predict effective teaching. The circumstances and style of implementing the listed teacher behaviors appear to be as important as the acts themselves. Determining what, when, and how to react to classroom events is a teaching skill that cannot be directly observed. To understand this process, researchers have had to engage in theoretical inquiry on teacher thinking.

Research on Teacher Thinking

What teachers think before, during, and after instruction is somewhat of a mystery. With the publication of Philip Jackson's 1968 book *Life in Classrooms,* educators began to be less obsessed with determining what teachers *ought* to think and more concerned with examining what they actually *do* think. The results have been paradoxical. For example, although rational planning for instruction plays a major role in virtually all teacher preparation programs, teachers rarely acknowledge planning as an integral, important part of their job (Clark & Peterson, 1986). The importance of thinking about instructional objectives offers a similar incongruity. Although rational approaches to instructional design, starting with a selection of purpose, are almost universally taught in preservice teacher programs, teachers consistently report spending the least amount of time reflecting on the objective of their lessons (Goodlad & Klein, 1970; Peterson, Marx, & Clark, 1978; Zahorik, 1975).

Unobservable Teacher Skill

Many different views exist on which fundamental attributes should be used to determine teaching success. Most perspectives consist of lists of observable teacher behaviors that have repeatedly been shown to be correlates of desirable student outcomes. However, the most critical teacher activity may not be observable at all. Shavelson (1973) speculated that any teaching act must be the result of a conscious or unconscious decision. The process of arriving at a decision must be the result of a complex cognitive processing of available information. This reasoning led Shavelson to conclude that the basic teaching skill is decision making. Although this conclusion may seem to be straightforward, the implications are not. First, this conclusion implies that teaching is more than simply enacting predetermined behaviors. Instead, successful teaching is an interactive process involving the teaching contexts, environment, and students. Second, it implies that teacher decisions are made rationally using perceptions to define the event and to predict the outcome of various teacher behaviors that are possible under the circumstances. Third, it implies that the outcomes in classrooms are determined, at least in part, by the perceptual acuity and reasoning power of the teacher. The "Slice of Life" discussion of Mrs. Sanchez in this chapter illustrates each of these three implications.

Decision Making as a Skill

If decision making is fundamental to effective teaching, how often do teachers make decisions in their classrooms? Research done after Shavelson's inquiry consistently found that teachers make an average of one interactive instructional decision every two minutes (Clark & Peterson, 1986). It is simple to conclude that an active teacher working to provide the best instruction for a class of students is involved in a rather intense process of observing, interpreting, and responding. The process may be so intense that what is intended (determined by the objective and planned prior to the beginning of the lesson) may be secondary to the behavior and cognitive understandings that students bring to the immediate situation. Oversimplified, the proposition is, "Teachers teach children, not lesson plans."

The continual changing of the classroom environment, reflecting variations in student moods, attitudes, and reactions to the day's events, leads to the conclusion that classrooms are unpredictable (Doyle, 1986). Further, since teaching occurs in an unpredictable environment, planning (at first glance) appears to be impractical. However, unpredictability is only half of the picture. The other half reveals a preponderance of research that clearly shows that teachers who establish learning goals correlated to a preplanned curriculum, develop sequenced materials, and use instructional strategies to facilitate student understandings are more successful in improving student learning and performance (Northwest Regional Educational Laboratory, 1984). Clearly, at work here is an immensely complex web of interrelated activity where the teacher's deliberate activity and thinking must occur on all temporal planes: proactive, active, and reactive. Making sense of our incomplete picture of teacher thinking demonstrates the complexity involved in establishing successful teaching in the elementary classroom.

Weaving long-term thinking into short-term situations is a dilemma that taxes the decision-making skills of even the most successful teachers. It is certainly one of the most difficult skills to learn as a new teacher. The first steps toward understanding and developing teacher decision-making skill are to take a covert process and create cognitive models that identify the major components of the decision-making process. Models may not accurately depict reality, but they can stimulate thoughts and, more importantly, hypotheses about how to conduct the decision-making process more effectively. To do that, the major variables involved in teacher decision making must be isolated and then studied to determine how these variables interact and influence teacher behavior.

Major Variables in Teacher Decision Making

Teaching is a thinking, reasoning, and experimental occupation. Therefore, to facilitate their growth as teaching professionals, teachers need to increase their capacity to understand and deal with the complexity of the classroom. This requires the development of constructs that support and structure teacher thinking. Several models exist that attempt to describe how teachers arrive at decisions.

Yinger's Model

Most cognitive models are similar to Yinger's seminal model (1977) in that they are linear, rational, and progressive. Yinger advanced a model of three stages (Figure 2.1). In the first stage, the teacher, through a process of awareness, discovers a problem or dilemma that requires further exploration. In the second stage, the problem is formulated and structured. The teacher generates possible solutions and mentally tests the various possibilities and either modifies the solution or seeks additional ones. In the third and final stage, the solution is implemented, evaluated, refined, and later becomes a part of the teacher's routine or, if the solution was an inappropriate one, discarded and the process reinitiated.

Yinger's model attempts to describe how teachers go about their business of implementing instruction and improving their effectiveness. Yinger, however, built the model from a study involving a single teacher. A number of questions remain: Do all teachers employ the same strategies? Is this strategy the most effective one? Do teachers employ a single strategy, or do they employ many strategies simultaneously? Other theorists have provided additional explanations when examining teachers' planning and decision making.

FIGURE 2.1 Yinger's theoretical model of teacher planning.

1. **Awareness:** The problem is discovered and judged worthy of consideration and effort.

2. **Solution finding:** The problem is redefined and refined; solutions are generated and tested mentally.

3. **Implementation:** The solution is put into action, evaluated, refined, and reimplemented until the desired outcome is obtained.

Taylor's Model

Taylor (1970) found that when teachers plan, the needs of pupils are central to their deliberations about method and content (Figure 2.2). Taylor concluded that the major concerns of teachers during planning were, in order of importance,

1. The needs and abilities of students as perceived by the teacher
2. The subject matter to be taught
3. The identified goals of instruction
4. The method to be used with the students (Clark & Peterson, 1986)

Taylor's model differs from Yinger's in several ways. First, it identifies the entities that teachers tend to think *about*. It describes the "what" of teacher thinking as well as the "how." Second, it is nonlinear. It requires the teacher to consider simultaneously several facets (students, subject, method, and purpose). The teacher must recognize that modifications in thinking made in one area require modifications in others.

Yinger's and Taylor's models demonstrate several facets of teacher thinking and the teacher's role in the classroom. Once again, these models point out that what

FIGURE 2.2 A model of Taylor's conceptualization of instructional concerns.

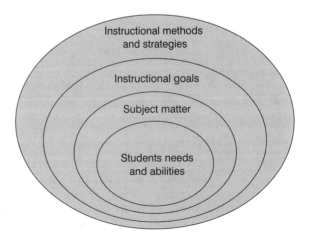

teachers do is quite complex. When Yinger's and Taylor's works are compared, it becomes very evident that teachers probably work in more than one paradigm while teaching. Teachers work both *sequentially* (planning and executing activities that are based on prerequisite events) and *holistically* (where many variables are examined concurrently with the implementation of any learning event). Further, it appears that at least some teachers do both at the same time.

Guiding the Development of Professional Thinking

As demonstrated by K'ung Fu-tse and Socrates, an enduring issue in education is how to promote effective thinking in students. Promoting effective thinking in teachers is similarly problematic. Armed with the knowledge of centuries of thinking and writing about teaching, the novice teacher must still determine what educational aims can be accomplished and what teaching acts will accomplish those aims in the given circumstances. Developing professional thinking in teachers remains the most illusive, yet critical, issue facing teacher education. Good and Brophy (1992) have argued convincingly that the initial step in developing sound thinking and reasoning skills in teachers is to make them more aware of their own thoughts and actions. This text has argued that every preservice teacher has extensive ideas and experiences in teaching others. Being aware of those generalizations can assist teachers in assimilating the ideas of others. Recognizing the foundational strengths and flaws of their personal thinking provides a cognitive structure that can either unify the knowledge that novice teachers acquire about teaching in their preservice programs or isolate the areas of conflict so that these beginning teachers can develop a deeper understanding of both views.

Student Awareness of Success Traits

Figure 2.3 provides a list of attributes that preservice teachers in an effective teaching methods class generated regarding their ideas about successful teachers and teaching. Working in small groups, the students first generated the list that describes what successful teachers think, believe, and do. They were then asked to classify those attributes into four groups. The first group consisted of the attitudes, beliefs, and personality traits of successful teachers. Clearly, this first group dominated the thinking of the preservice teachers. Virtually every positive human trait seems to be valued as an attribute of successful teaching. The next list consisted of the skills necessary for successful teaching. It is difficult to determine how the skills on this list, particularly as they were classified by these students, differ from attitudes and personality traits. Students were, for example, unsure whether "patience" was a personality trait or a learnable skill. In the final two lists, students were asked to include what they believed successful teachers needed to know and needed to do. Notice the sharp decline in the number of items in these lists.

Attitudes, Beliefs, Personality	Skills	Knowledge	Behaviors
patient	understanding	constant learning	prompt
enthusiastic	listener	knowledgeable	patient
dedicated	energetic	objective	role model
realistic	patience	logical	understanding
humorous	assertive	educated	energetic
fallible	organized	good assessment	motivated
creative	flexible	intelligent	accepting
relentless	effective communicator	learner	enthusiastic
open to criticism	class manager	"common sense"	humorous
optimistic	leader	nonjudgmental	approachable
firm beliefs in teaching	follower	creative	takes risks
self-confident	reflective	aware of backgrounds	involved in the school
self-satisfaction	effective	realistic	open minded
cooperative	learner		creative
happy	organized		
compassionate	relevant		
motivated	intuitive		
stable	exciting		
conversive	interesting		
enjoys teaching and	humorous		
children	versatile		
flexible	organized		
spontaneous	controlling		
warm fuzzies	skill in presenting		
young at heart	material		
enjoys challenge	independently wealthy		
caring	sense of awareness		
positive	eyes in the back of the		
desire	head		
goal oriented	able to present simply		
diplomacy	task oriented		
exciting	responsive		
lifetime learner	positive interpersonal		
nonjudgmental	skills		
willing	good observer		
moral	makes learning fun		
encouraging	motivates others		
healthy			
sincere			
loving, brave			
sensitive			

FIGURE 2.3
Attributes of successful teachers and teaching: Views of preservice teachers at the beginning of training.

This exercise made the novice teachers aware that their ideas about teaching were quite global. Preservice teachers were able to identify many characteristics of successful teaching, but most of the characteristics that they identified did not distinguish teaching from the general skills of any occupation requiring contact with others. If asked to list the attributes that describe a good friend, a spouse of many years, or a desirable employer, these preservice teachers would create very similar lists. What makes a successful teacher is difficult to separate from the more general question, "What is a good person?"

Students in this exercise became aware of a subtle difference between basic personality and learned behavior. If teacher skill can be developed, it must be teachable and, therefore, learnable. If successful teaching is primarily dependent on personality, attitudes, and beliefs, teachers must be able to learn these attributes, or only those teachers who already have these attributes in abundance will be successful. In short, teachers must be able to learn patience, flexibility, kindness, understanding, and so on, and learn how and when to use these traits. Students were asked to compare themselves to the list of attributes of a successful teacher that they had created. The students were then asked, "According to your assessment, would you be a good teacher? Are these the only skills needed? Can teaching effectiveness be taught?"

Student Self-Analysis of Beliefs

Awareness, although a good first step, does not make substantial progress toward developing teaching skill unless it is followed by action. The second step toward deliberate development of knowledge about teaching is to compare the knowledge and beliefs about teaching to real-life situations to see how well the knowledge and belief can guide behavior. When comparing their list of attributes to the complexity of successful teaching in a classroom, the novice teachers concluded that their list was a good start but inadequate to guide their development. They were then asked to examine several of the items more carefully. Specifically, they were asked if an item was singular or was composed of several elements. If the item was a composition, what were its subcomponents?

These preservice teachers' examination of patience is instructive. They began by identifying the many basic components that collectively allow a teacher to be patient:

- Knowing how to delay judgment and give encouragement
- Providing corrective feedback that supports (rather than replaces) the child's thinking
- Being able to use more than one way to explain a concept
- Understanding the concept thoroughly
- Identifying the child's actions with what is known about child development
- Having confidence of being able to help struggling children based on past experiences of success

After developing awareness and examining a critical comparison, the preservice teachers began the third step in developing teacher knowledge: building conceptual models to visualize the relationships among attributes. Figure 2.4 shows a conceptual web of the novice teachers' thinking about patience. Their views of patience are somewhat demystified by their examination. According to their analysis, patience is developed by four contributing factors:

- The support given the teacher by parents, peers, and society
- The extent of understanding of the material being taught
- The past success of the teacher with students in similar circumstances
- A knowledge of child development that leads to an understanding of children's reasoning methodology and capability.

The lists compiled by these preservice teachers illustrate their beliefs that patience can be taught via knowledge about child development and enhanced understanding of the material being taught. However, these teachers also isolated environmental factors and past experiences as being strong contributors. Notice how they structured knowledge so that it can be applied or "tested" to real-life situations in attempting to obtain predetermined educational goals. This is often referred to as a *constructivist approach* to knowledge and understanding.

By conceptualizing and building models to explain abstractions, these teachers gained insight into complex phenomena that enabled them to make plans for improving their skills in that area. This constructivist component is critical to developing teacher skill in rigorous inquiry and decision making. Figure 2.5 depicts the process of deliberately creating teacher knowledge about successful instruction. Awareness, both of experience and academic information, leads to a mental process of comparing, contrasting, and incorporating new information with previous knowledge.

To understand how various pieces of knowledge are interrelated, we use a process called *structuring* in which we assimilate this knowledge into a comprehensive whole. We go through an additional step of testing the new structures in real-life applications that, in effect, provides meaning and direction for the process. Since the purpose of acquiring knowledge about teaching is to improve teaching practice and student learning, the rewards of accurate understanding should result in increased student success in the classroom. Thus, the new structures are tested by the teacher both *cognitively* against current knowledge and belief and *empirically* against the actual conditions of the classroom. This testing process leads to new levels of awareness that, in turn, propels the process forward cyclically and continuously. This process is not to be taken for granted. With the speed and complexity of most classrooms, we can become overwhelmed with the immediate and simultaneous demands of student needs, activity, and questions. Much of the actual development of teacher skill comes at the end of the day after the students leave. It is essential for the successful teacher to reflect on the day's events and restructure activity and results into plausible hypotheses.

Two models, one depicting the types of professional knowledge and the other showing the major variables in applying that knowledge, can assist preservice teachers in developing this process for understanding successful teaching.

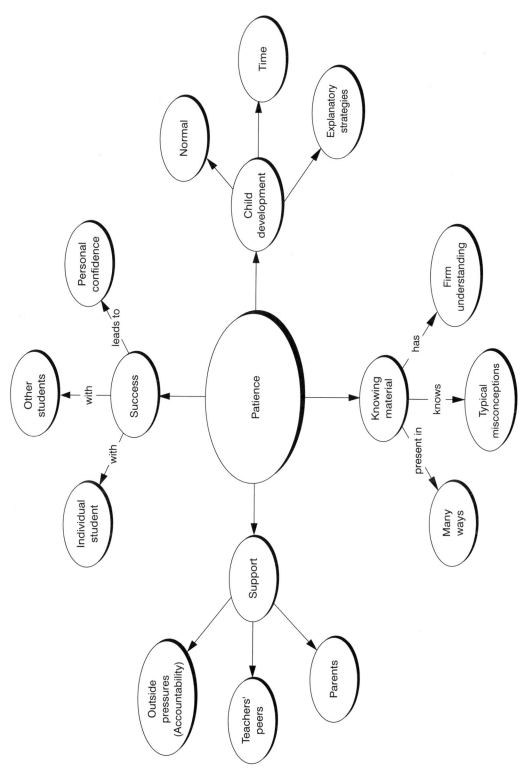

FIGURE 2.4
Teacher analysis of patience.

FIGURE 2.5
Deliberate building of teacher
knowledge.

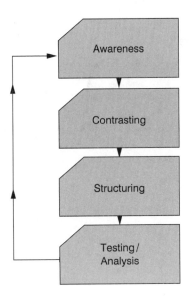

Types of Professional Knowledge

Teaching is often compared to other professions such as law, accounting, and medicine partially because of the status of those professions and partly because of the relative success those professions have in preparing novices to become practitioners. Central to each of those professions is a body of knowledge that must be mastered and from which all decisions are grounded. Teaching, however, is unlike those other professions. Although much knowledge exists about teaching, most teaching success is defined in relationship to cultural and philosophical values, not to empirically verifiable phenomena. For instance, the practice of law has built into it a codified context of opinions in addition to legal statutes from which to develop decisions and courses of action. Teaching, however, has many goals and many different avenues from which to obtain those goals. Teaching goals are not systematically codified, and legislative attempts to define what teaching should be have never matched the reality of the classroom.

Teaching differs from law, medicine, and accounting in that teaching is a cooperative activity that depends as much on the willingness of the student (client) as it does on the abilities of the teachers. Medicine has a similar situation when preventive medicine is the focus of attention. A heart surgeon can perform bypass surgery or even a heart transplant to remedy his patient's distress. However, if his patient refuses to comply with the requirements of diet, exercise, medicinal therapy, and surgery, the surgeon has few options left for helping his patient.

Teaching, however, works with a different set of assumptions. Unlike the surgeon with the reluctant patient, teachers are not excused from serving their defiant client. Instead, the teacher is expected to create a desire in students to alter their habits and become productive, contributing members of society. Many types of heart disease can be prevented with relatively simple diet, exercise, and lifestyle changes.

If the doctors' only role was to prevent heart disease, they would face the same types of problems as teachers in the classroom. Simply knowing about heart disease, conveying that information to others, and having diagnostic skill fail to have an adequate impact on the public. Changing the outlook and habits of people is far more complex and difficult. Far greater knowledge is available for preventing and curing heart disease than for convincing massive numbers of people to alter their lifestyles. Teachers face a similar problem. We have a vast amount of knowledge about the methods that work in teaching compliant eager children, but very little knowledge about educating children when lifestyle changes are required for success.

Three Components of Teacher Knowledge and Use

Because the knowledge base for teachers is ill-defined and based on values as much as empirical evidence, learning about that knowledge and how to use it is an intricate, if not enigmatic, lifelong journey. The knowledge base for teaching can be broken down into three rudimentary components: "knowing what," "knowing how," and "choosing to" (see Figure 2.6).

"Knowing what" is the raw material for developing decisions in the classroom. It is the subject matter knowledge of math, science, and social studies. It is also the pedagogical knowledge gleaned from the literature on education. Applied to an earlier example, "knowing what" is the cognizance that the teacher must apply patience in the classroom to give students adequate time to develop a certain skill.

"Knowing how" is basically the mechanics of taking information and turning it into effective action. In our example with patience, "knowing how" involves being able to encourage the child, giving corrective feedback based on accurate diagnosis of the child's conceptual misunderstandings, and explaining the concept with multiple strategies. This is often referred to as *action-system knowledge* because it indicates those special understandings and insights that allow an individual to materialize productive activity from cognitive knowledge.

"Choosing to" refers to the self-understanding of meta-cognitional apparatus that permits individuals to guide and direct their own behavior. Peterson (1988) identifies meta-cognition as the learners' self-awareness of the processes in which they acquire information, gain understanding, and learn in specific settings. For purposes of promoting successful teaching, this core definition is extended to include the desire and ability to direct and control these processes in any given situation.

An Example of Knowledge Types

Consider the number of times that someone has yelled at you, been insulting, or rude toward you because they were angry at something that you did. What was your reaction? Were you greatly improved by the experience? Most individuals respond to such treatment with a combination of hurt and anger. Often, the resentment alone causes you to do the *opposite* of what was requested. Only rarely does anyone claim to have been improved by a humiliating experience. The "knowing what" component of the knowledge base is the information that sarcasm directed at an individual results in hurt feelings, anger, or a combination of both. If you were trying to coax a

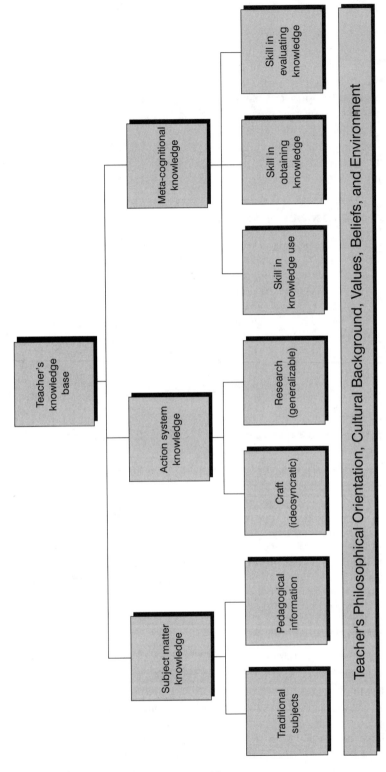

FIGURE 2.6
Teacher's knowledge base.

48

reluctant student into completing an overdue class assignment and the student was uncooperative, you know that yelling and sarcasm most likely will produce hurt feelings and anger from the student. Encouragement and patience is clearly indicated here. This is an example of "knowing what."

How do you display actions that are kind and patient yet progress toward your goal of complete work assignments? In "knowing how," the teacher first isolates the reason why the student did not complete the work. Is the work too difficult? Is the child tired of doing the same things? Is there a misunderstanding about how the work is to be completed? Is there some event outside of school that is interfering with the student's ability to concentrate?

The "knowing how" function directs action toward establishing the reason for the child's resistance. The "knowing how" function also creates more of the "knowing what." Depending on circumstances identified, additional actions may be required. "Knowing how" may require providing encouragement and setting up a time and place for individual help, or it may require empathizing with the student's boredom or discontent. In "knowing how," the teacher collects the necessary information, diagnoses the situation, and responds with appropriate skill.

In this example, perhaps the teacher determines that the student does not understand the assignment and cannot picture the end result. The teacher then concludes that some private time is needed to consult with the student, to get the student started, and to extend the deadline. The teacher's actions may be a soft pat on the back with a reassuring voice, "This is a tough assignment to get started. Let's meet during lunch so I can help you."

There are many different interpretations for a child's reluctance to do a particular assignment. How a teacher directs and controls the process, uses knowledge about patience, encouragement, and incomplete assignments, and turns it into a course of action is the meta-cognitive or "choosing to" function. Even if an individual teacher knows that being patient and encouraging is the best course of action and the teacher is quite capable of demonstrating those feelings, the ability to follow through with this "best solution" remains problematic. Regardless of the reasonableness of any solution and its probability of success, emotions also play a part. A teacher may just as easily conclude the event with the declaration, "You won't leave here until you do it!" The teacher can also simply dissolve the issue by not caring, issuing the student a zero score, and informing the reluctant student, "I'll care when you do!" In classrooms, the latter two strategies sometimes dominate even though they carry a much lower probability of success and certainly violate the general concept of teaching as a helping profession. Simply knowing what and how to do something does not ensure that good practice will appear in the classroom. Why?

Constructing a Teacher's Knowledge Base

The worth of all teacher outcomes is grounded in the values and needs of a society. Society shapes all its participants in some way, but rarely in the same way. Although dominant beliefs, values, cultures, and philosophies exist, none dominate so completely that there is no room for uniqueness and diversity. Teachers, being products of society, have their values shaped by that society. Likewise, as employees of one of society's enterprises, teachers are obligated to perpetuate those beliefs that society believes to be essential for the common good. What subjects are important, what methods are used in teaching, even how we experiment and go about implementing solutions to ambiguous problems are all imbedded in the philosophical values and beliefs of society. However, teachers are also individuals: unique, varying, and variable. They also have values and needs and reflect society's diversity and competitiveness of philosophical outlooks.

When teacher's build knowledge about teaching, they follow many paths because teachers, like society at large, are quite diverse and have many ways of thinking and knowing. Teacher's build knowledge about teaching based on their philosophical orientation, cultural background, values, beliefs, and their unique experiences. The philosophical orientation, cultural background, values, beliefs, and cumulative experiences are referred to collectively as *teacher beliefs*. These beliefs

---

001   The elementary teacher understands, applies, and encourages higher-order thinking skills in various language arts contexts across the curriculum.

002   The elementary teacher recognizes the interrelationships of reading, writing, listening, and speaking and knows how to plan instruction that reflects the interrelated nature of these processes.

003   The elementary teacher understands and applies a variety of methods, materials, approaches, and classroom organization strategies used for language arts instruction.

004   The elementary teacher understands reading as a process in which reader, text, and context interact; recognizes how reading competence emerges; and applies this knowledge in instructional contexts.

005   The elementary teacher understands and applies comprehension strategies used to construct meaning for various purposes from printed language.

006   The elementary teacher recognizes difficulties in the development of reading competence and knows how to use appropriate instructional methods and resources to help students compensate for such difficulties.

007   The elementary teacher understands indicators of student reading competence and knows how to apply appropriate instructional approaches in relation to these indicators.

008   The elementary teacher is familiar with a wide variety of children's literature, understands its uses in the classroom, and applies such knowledge to the selection, appreciation, and critical evaluation of literary works.

009   The elementary teacher understands the role of written language in thinking and communicating, recognizes factors that a writer considers when selecting topics and composing, and knows how to use the composing process for effective communication.

FIGURE 2.7
ExCET test framework for the English Language Arts Elementary Comprehensive examination.

vary widely among teachers. Because these differing beliefs cause wide meta-cognitional differences among teachers and teacher educators as well, building a common knowledge base has been a difficult task for the teaching profession.

Examples of the Knowledge Base

The North Carolina Teacher Performance Appraisal Instrument (TPAI) (Figure 1.5) is typical of many attempts to outline a knowledge base for teaching. Since most of the efforts to codify a common knowledge base for teachers have had teacher evaluation as their impetus, they are generally limited to teacher behavior. However, if a pencil-and-paper test is the format for evaluation, as it tends to be for preservice teachers, the teacher knowledge base is organized as a cognitive rather than a behavioral entity. The test framework for the ExCET test, the Texas certification test for preservice teachers, exemplifies this orientation(Texas Education Agency, 1992). Figure 2.7 shows the 19 elements of the English Language Arts Elementary Comprehensive examination.

---

010   The elementary teacher recognizes effective written communication, can analyze areas in need of improvement in written work, and understands strategies for working with students to improve their writing.

011   The elementary teacher recognizes the role of effective listening in communication, understands listening strategies appropriate for a variety of purposes, and analyzes factors that affect listening and instructional approaches that enhance listening.

012   The elementary teacher relates the development of oral language to thought and communication and understands appropriate and effective strategies for promoting oral language development.

013   The elementary teacher recognizes the role of vocabulary development in all aspects of language and applies strategies for vocabulary development in meaningful contexts.

014   The elementary teacher understands self-monitoring strategies used to improve reading, writing, listening, and speaking.

015   The elementary teacher understands individual language development and factors influencing language development and is able to apply this knowledge in instructional contexts across the curriculum.

016   The elementary teacher recognizes the importance of language competence for learning across the content areas and knows how to apply language arts strategies and concepts in relation to content in a variety of subjects.

017   The elementary teacher understands study skills and strategies and knows how to apply these skills and strategies across the curriculum.

018   The elementary teacher understands the role of multicultural perspectives in language arts education and plans activities to promote understanding and appreciation of cultural diversity.

019   The elementary teacher is familiar with recent developments and issues in language arts education.

From *ExCET Preparation Manual: 04 Elementary Comprehensive* by the Texas Education Agency, 1992. Austin: Author. Permission granted by the Texas State Board for Education Certification.

Other attempts to create a common knowledge base for teachers have included the development of teachers, particularly preservice teachers, as the primary focus. Washington, as part of its statewide school reform, redefined essential teaching, knowledge, and skill into 22 broad areas (Figure 2.8). This model borrows heavily from the national standards published by the National Council for Accreditation of Teacher Education (NCATE, 1995). Individual theorists have also developed models. Ayers (1990) provides a description of an abbreviated sample of the knowledge base for effective teachers (Figure 2.9).

Limitations of the Models

The four depictions of essential knowledge for teachers (TPAI, ExCET, Washington, and Ayers) are singularly inadequate to illustrate the breadth of the knowledge base about teaching. They do, however, illustrate the competing conceptualizations of the knowledge base about teaching. Figure 2.6 depicts the three major components of

---

WAC 180 78A-16S Approval standard: Knowledge and skills. Building on the mission to prepare educators who demonstrate a positive impact on student learning based on the Improvement of the Student Achievement Act of 1993 (1209), the following evidence shall be evaluated to determine whether each preparation program is in compliance with the program approval standards of WAC 180-78A140(S):

(1) Teacher candidates will complete a well-planned sequence of courses and/or experiences in which they acquire and apply knowledge about:
    (a) The state goals and essential academic learning requirements.
    (b) The subject matter content for the area(s) they teach, including the essential areas of study for each endorsement area for which the candidate is applying (chapter 180-79A WAC).
    (c) The social, historical, and philosophical foundations of education, including an understanding of the moral, social, and political dimensions of classrooms, teaching, and schools.
    (d) The impact of technological and societal changes on schools.
    (e) Theories of human development and learning.
    (f) Inquiry and research.
    (g) School law and educational policy.
    (h) Professional ethics.
    (i) The responsibilities, structure, and activities of the profession.
    (j) Research and experience-based principles of effective practice for encouraging the intellectual, social, and personal development of students.
    (k) Different student approaches to learning for creative, instructional opportunities adapted to learners from diverse cultural backgrounds and with exceptionalities.
    (l) Instructional strategies for developing critical thinking, problem solving, and performance skills.

FIGURE 2.8
Washington administrative code defining teacher knowledge.

the knowledge base as subject matter knowledge, action system knowledge, and meta-cognitional knowledge. Each major component has certain subdivisions that further delineate the sources of teacher knowledge. When compared to Figure 2.6, the ExCET formulation fits the subject matter conceptualization of the knowledge base. The TPAI represents the action system knowledge. The Washington model and Ayers's framework, while covering both subject matter knowledge and action system knowledge, primarily reflect the meta-cognitional knowledge aspects of the knowledge base. Teacher growth in instructional effectiveness depends on harmonious development of all three types of knowledge. A teacher who has skill in teaching but lacks an understanding of subject matter and its underlying concepts is incompetent. Likewise, a teacher who is knowledgeable of the subject but is unable to convey that knowledge meaningfully is ineffectual in developing student academic competence and only creates frustration in students. A teacher who is self-aware but does not exercise individual talent in obtaining and using subject matter knowledge and action system knowledge is unprofessional and makes no impact on the learning of the students.

(m) Classroom management and discipline, including:
 (i) Individual and group motivation for encouraging positive social interaction, active engagement in learning and self-motivation.
 (ii) Effective verbal, nonverbal, and media communication for fostering active inquiry, collaboration, and supportive interactions in the classroom.
(n) Planning and management of instruction base on knowledge of the content area, the community, and curriculum goals.
(o) Formal and informal assessment strategies evaluating and ensuring the continuous intellectual and physical development of the learner.
(p) Collaboration with school colleagues, parents, agencies in the larger community for supporting student learning and well-being.
(q) Effective interactions with parents to support students' learning and well-being.
(r) The opportunity for candidates to reflect on teaching and its effects on student growth and learning
(s) Educational technology including the use of computer and other technologies in instruction, assessment, and professional productivity.
(t) Issues related to abuse including identifying physical, emotional, sexual, and substance abuse, information on the impact of abuse on the behavior and learning abilities of students, discussion of the responsibilities of a teacher to report abuse or provide assistance to students who are victims of abuse, and methods for teaching students about abuse of all types and their prevention.
(u) Strategies for effective participation in group decision making.
(v) The standards, criteria, and other requirements for obtaining professional certification.

1. Knowledge of self
2. Knowledge of human development
3. Knowledge of the learning process
4. Knowledge of historical, social, political, economic, and cultural contexts
5. Knowledge of the disciplines
6. Knowledge of explicit and hidden curricula
7. Knowledge of learning environments
8. Knowledge of group process as well as individual behavior
9. Knowledge of the interaction between affective and cognitive domains
10. Knowledge of individual differences
11. Knowledge of parents and communities
12. Knowledge of children's meanings
13. Knowledge of the complex interplay of forces that motivate learning

FIGURE 2.9
Sample of an abbreviated knowledge base for teachers.

From "Rethinking the Profession of Teaching: A Progressive Option," by William Ayers, 1990. *Action in Teacher Education,* 12(1), 1–5. Reprinted by permission.

Constructing Individual Understanding

Only teachers who systematically develop their knowledge base in all three areas grow as teachers and achieve teaching success. Unfortunately, although experience should be a primary indicator of this growth, research has failed to show a significant relationship in student learning success and years of experience possessed by the teacher. Likewise, advanced degrees are no predictor of teacher success (Riner, 1992). A speculative hypothesis may be instructive. The evidence tends to indicate that the first few years of teaching are filled with questioning, experimentation, and evaluation. Many teachers leave during this novice period. Those who stay tend to develop a "comfort zone," and their torrid pace of experimentation, primarily driven by survival needs, diminishes. When teachers stop experimenting and expanding their knowledge base, their growth and effectiveness as educators diminish until the major predictive variable of teaching success that remains is the entering behavior of students. If this hypothesis is true, it can be avoided by establishing lifelong habits of teacher reflection and growth.

Developing Subject Matter Knowledge

In all 50 states, a college degree is now required for certification for teaching in public schools. The emphasis of the college degree program for teachers is based on a belief that teachers must possess substantial subject matter knowledge. However, a teacher discovers, before long, that children want to learn about many things that the teacher does not know. Pedagogical reasoning (the process of locating and converting facts, concepts, and constructs into instructional strategies) is fundamental to teaching success. However, simply taking the view that "everything can be looked up" and failing to develop comprehensive knowledge actually limits the development of pedagogical reasoning. Although some consider subject matter knowledge to be the *only* requirement for teacher success, others argue that the role of subject matter knowledge is an important, but woefully insufficient, characteristic of the successful teacher.

What Is Meaningful Information?

Although subject matter knowledge is important, inappropriate emphasis on factual information can have devastating effects on both teacher and student growth. Whitehead (1929) argued that inert knowledge is not only useless but also harmful. For Whitehead, inert knowledge was isolated factual information that was not integral to the individual's perspective of the world and the manner in which that world was engaged. He argued that emphasis on gaining this type of knowledge was harmful when the demands for its acquisition mask the true utility of knowledge. For example, which of the following pursuits may be considered meaningful and which may be inert for students in a fourth-grade class?

The names of all the state capitals
How animation is made from clay figures
The names of the U.S. president's cabinet members
The first 10 prime numbers
The calculation of pi
The origin of "ninja"
Where math is used in a video game
How ancients fired clay pots without natural gas or electricity

Of course, with no imagination, all instruction regarding these items will be inert. Similarly, a very skilled teacher can capture children with all of the items. In general, state capitals, pi, prime numbers, and the U.S. president's cabinet contribute less to a child's concept of the world than animation, ninja, math in video games, and ancient societies. Children are surrounded with animation, ninja, and video games. Children are usually fascinated about what people did in the past before electricity and television in much the same way that they are attracted to dinosaurs. By selecting topics that enlarge the child's world, inert teaching can be avoided and student motivation enhanced.

Increasing the Pool of Information

The need to develop subject matter knowledge in elementary teachers is directly related to Whitehead's argument. If an assembled hodgepodge of isolated facts is considered to be subject matter knowledge, that knowledge has little relevance to teaching success in the elementary classroom. However, if the way in which a teacher perceives and understands the world is considered to be subject matter knowledge, that contributory knowledge is central to the pedagogical reasoning that helps the teacher translate the child's curiosity into a learning experience. With that in mind, here are some suggestions for building subject matter knowledge for success in the elementary classroom:

◆ Constantly attempt to understand conceptually isolated facts by asking yourself questions: "Why this way and not some other way? How can I visualize that concept? How would this information be used?"

◆ Empathize with the child. "What would a child think about this? How would a child react to this event?"

◆ Learn to ask questions. Ask questions of others who may have a more developed understanding. Think about their answers.

◆ Learn to observe. When you look closely at things or events, the "why" and "how" questions are naturally triggered.

◆ Read a wide range of nonfiction materials. "How and Why" books that are so popular with children can often illustrate some of life's real mysteries, such as how a vacuum cleaner works or how the refrigerator light turns itself on and off.

◆ Cultivate curiosity. Make an "I wonder . . ." time a daily fixture. "I wonder how grocers can get a head of lettuce from California to North Carolina faster than I can send a letter through the mail?"

◆ Participate in summer programs in the arts and sciences that allow participants to work in the field. Work alongside a biologist for the local power company or help produce the local newspaper.

◆ Take courses through continuing education or the community college that are designed to help you develop skills in everything from auto mechanics to tole painting.

◆ Take advantage of your school district's inservice education opportunities.

◆ Invite speakers to your classroom.

◆ Travel not only outside your region but also inside your customary environment. Children are fascinated with the mechanical room in their school, particularly when the gas-fired boiler turns on with a whoosh.

◆ Be a lifelong learner. Model curiosity and a love of learning to your students.

Developing Action System Knowledge

Experience can be a very punishing teacher, yet experience is one of the fundamental building blocks of action system knowledge. Taking conceptual knowledge about subject matter and the characteristics of children and then matching it to an appropriate teaching strategy is a difficult task. Putting that strategy into action is also a complex and arduous process. Fortunately, researchers and other educators can guide at least part of that process. Action system knowledge is composed of two different, yet related, aspects of a teacher's personal knowledge about teaching: research-based knowledge and craft knowledge.

Research-Based Knowledge

Research-based knowledge results from systematic empirical investigations into the learning processes of children and the successful instructional strategies of teachers. Some of this empirical research has come from experimental designs in which groups of teachers are trained in differing methodologies. Each methodology is then represented by a group of teachers attempting to employ the method with individual classrooms of children. The effects of the instruction from these groups of teachers are then compared statistically.

Researchers have also studied the effects of characteristics of individual teachers and learning outcomes by examining normal classrooms using sophisticated observational instruments. Common characteristics of teachers are then tested statistically. A relationship between frequency of these behavior characteristics (as measured by classroom observations) and the measured outcomes of student activities is computed and evaluated for significance. The relationship of teacher behavior and student outcomes is then reported as a correlation coefficient demonstrating the covariance of one entity with the other.

Other researchers "shadow" teachers during their workday over a period of time making observations and often interacting with the teacher. Although the methods of empirical investigation vary widely, most methods attempt to study teachers while systematically controlling for the unique differences of teachers, children, and their schools so that the findings are generalizable over a wide range of situations, children, and teachers. This empirically derived research attempts to give teachers information about which particular teaching strategies or teaching acts may result in certain learning outcomes. The research falls short, however, of claiming that certain teaching acts *cause* student learning outcomes. The actual interactions have varying effects on student outcomes, and results are often inconsistent. Nonetheless, this research provides general outcomes that are predictable from observations of teaching acts. This subtle difference between causal effects and associative effects basically tells the teacher that, if they act in accordance with the research, most children will respond with the predicted changes in learning but the effects on learners will vary. Some children will respond appropriately, some will not respond, and some will respond in a contrary manner. Therefore, research should be regarded as a very valuable guide, but not as ultimate fact. Some teachers will not follow the conclusions of this research and still achieve positive results. This aspect of a teacher's personal knowledge base forms the individual's "bag of tricks," or craft.

Craft Knowledge

Craft knowledge is idiosyncratic in that it represents the discoveries of an individual teacher and often depends on the unique skills of the teacher and environmental factors of a single classroom (Figure 2.6). Knowledge of teaching as a craft has numerous dimensions worth considering. First, most research or empirically verified knowledge is a systematic examination of craft knowledge. Second, craft knowledge may be tacit or undisclosed by the teacher. Teachers may be able to explain their effectiveness, can describe the diagnostic processes involved in the solution of a teaching situation, and generally be very aware of their actions that result in their success. More likely, teachers have difficulty separating many conflicting beliefs about teaching and the teaching antecedents that precipitate instructional success. Teachers may mistakenly prescribe instructional results to a constellation of events and behavior when only a few are actually shown to be effectual when studied systematically. Third, the creation and utilization of craft knowledge is required to fit research knowledge into the context of each individual teaching situation. The specialized contextual attention needed to employ research knowledge successfully is best understood as a variant of craft knowledge. Our discussion about the differences between research and craft knowledge is not intended to value one and scorn the other. On the contrary, both types of knowing greatly enhance the systematic success of teachers. The point is that it takes more than simply finding exemplars and imitating them, or acting on unverified beliefs, to become a good teacher.

Teachers create models in order to further understanding.

Increasing Action System Knowledge

Developing action system knowledge requires participation and reflection. Unlike subject matter knowledge that can be learned separate from participation, developing action system knowledge requires that you employ mental conceptions of teaching in actual teaching. These experiences must be analyzed if the construction of action system knowledge is to yield accurate information. Some ways to initiate the process of the construction of systematic action system knowledge are as follows:

◆ *Develop personal statements of goals and strategies for achieving them and schedule times to assess the outcomes.* Schools often support teacher attempts at enhancing practice by encouraging or requiring the setting of professional development plans or high priority objectives.
◆ *Practice peer coaching.* This matches up two teachers who mutually assist in observing and assessing instructional activity in the classroom. Peer coaches analyze teaching on the basis of goals and criteria established by the partners and discuss strategies for improvement or practice.
◆ *Videotape your own teaching and privately view the tape.* This can be enlightening in making you more aware of your teaching performance.
◆ *Participate in action research in which groups of teachers participate in obtaining schoolwide goals by data collection and analysis.* In short, action research is a method by which teachers do research in miniaturizing their own classrooms as research labs.

Developing Meta-Cognitional Knowledge

Meta-cognitional knowledge is best conceived as the mediator between desire and activity, rather than as a separate entity. The term "meta-cognition" is a fuzzy one in the literature and is subject to many interpretations (Pintrich, 1990). In general, meta-cognition refers to the way in which individuals control and regulate their own thinking processes. However, it is important to include that regulation of the thinking processes also entails the control of activity. Brown, Bransford, Ferrara, and Campione (1983) identified three major components of teachers' meta-cognitive knowledge: planning, monitoring, and self-regulation. Essentially, meta-cognition refers to the ability of a teacher to

◆ Deliberately plan experiences that provide opportunity to rationally and critically explore personal beliefs and assumptions,
◆ Monitor their ability so that active thinking is converted into action resulting in teacher-initiated changes in the environment and personal behavior, and
◆ Regulate and adjust teacher behavior to control and react to the results of those actions.

"Choosing to" and Making Meaning

Meta-cognitional knowledge is widely considered by teacher educators to be central to the development of the successful teacher's knowledge base. Compared to the two conceptual components of the teacher's knowledge base (subject matter and action system knowledge), meta-cognitional knowledge can be viewed as the mediator between "knowing what" and "knowing how" and the primary regulator of teaching activity. In building your knowledge base for successful teaching, it is critical that all three aspects of knowing are developed. Mere skill acquisition without a discriminating analysis of the learning contexts for appropriate implementation is insufficient for successful teaching.

Strategies for developing meta-cognitional learning naturally include those for acquiring subject matter and action system knowledge. Any conscious attempt to initiate and regulate learning leads to some manifestation of meta-cognitive knowledge. However, to extend significantly the awareness and regulation of cognitive processes, it is necessary to go beyond simply acquiring and implementing information. These diverse and isolated bits of knowledge must be conceptualized into schemata or relational models that form tacit hypotheses about how certain aspects of the environment interact. In short, meta-cognition is both "meaning making" that leads to some sort of prediction about future events *and* using those predictions to develop and implement strategies that assist in the shaping of successful teaching experiences.

Increasing Meta-Cognitional Knowledge

Following are some suggested activities for leading teachers toward developing meta-cognitional knowledge:

◆ Learn about the construction of models designed to explain important components of teaching. Webbing, concept mapping, organizational charting, and analogous and metaphorical comparisons all assist in unifying experiences and information.

◆ Study your personal motivation in a systematic manner. What are the circumstances that allow you maximum control of your thoughts and actions? Why are some activities easy to undertake while others are difficult? Why do you look forward to some things and dread others? How do you initiate and accomplish unpleasant tasks? How does this differ with pleasant tasks? What makes an activity satisfying or unsatisfying?

◆ Learn to understand yourself and why you feel and act as you do. Describe and analyze your personality with the help of interest, personality, and learning style inventories; journal keeping; introspection; and studying literature.

◆ Ask questions of others who demonstrate behaviors that you want to imitate. If someone is particularly happy most of the time, ask him or her why they are happy so often. Almost universally, the answer will consist of meta-cognitive awareness rather than good fortune.

◆ Work toward remedying problems and difficulties, rather than concentrating on blame. Redirecting the impulse to externalize the causes of daily setbacks into positive self-initiated behavior is a useful meta-cognitive activity that can become habitual.

◆ Understand and nurture your patience with others, particularly in situations where you do not have influence or control.

Major Classroom Variables

Figure 2.10 illustrates a helpful model for developing meta-cognitional knowledge and guiding the daily decision making of the classroom. It identifies three pivotal variables from which teachers must collect information: the needs and abilities of students, the intent of instruction, and the environmental contexts that constantly vary within classrooms. With changes in one of the variables, changes in the teacher's instructional strategies generally occur. The teacher's skill, attitudes, beliefs, and knowledge are central to interpreting and responding to changes in students, instructional intent, or the context. How well a teacher responds to such changes is determined by his or her ability and willingness to employ various instructional strategies. Together, the four variables are basic to understanding how successful teachers determine the instructional strategies in their classrooms.

Instructional Intents

The intent of instruction is often taken for granted, and when it is, the purpose of the lesson is rarely communicated to the students. Without purpose, learning in

FIGURE 2.10
A basic model of dimensions of teacher decision making.

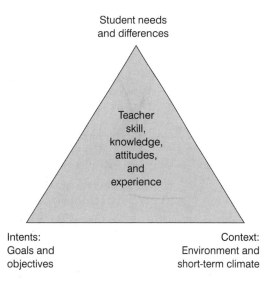

school becomes lifeless and boring. This learning is what Whitehead (1929) refers to as "inert"—that is, incapable of interaction, lifeless, or dead. Learning mandated by some authority is not fair to the child and demeans the learning process. Educators often agree to the "what" of education without understanding the "why." When this happens, the learning process is always artificial and remote to children's lives.

Learning without understood purpose has cumulative effects that diminish the development of positive attitudes about learning. Establishing purposes that are understood and valued by learners avoids undesirable negative reactions to skill acquisition and use. For example, what is the effect of teaching a child to read when the child learns to hate reading and avoids the activity whenever possible? All learning intents are, therefore, dual in nature: There is an intellectual (or rational) component and an affective (or emotional) component. To maximize the effectiveness of any instructional decision, both the intellectual intent and affective intent must be considered as well as the short-term and long-term effects. By considering all dimensions deliberately and rationally, a teacher's decision making can undergo various permutations in which a number of alternatives are considered and the potential results projected and evaluated.

Contexts

Take a few minutes to project yourself well into the future. You are now a successful teacher and can claim, after only 10 years of teaching, that your classroom is exactly as you envisioned it. What are you doing in that classroom? What are the children doing, saying, and feeling? Collectively, the answers to these questions form the classroom context. Classrooms are isolated from other types of social life in this country. Perhaps the most dominant feature of a classroom that separates it from other forms of social life in the United States is the relative lack of freedom. Children, and their parents for that matter, have little or no choice about whether they go to school, which school they will attend, who will be their teacher, what they will learn, where they will sit, when they can move, or even when they can take care of basic personal needs such as going to the restroom. The density (the square footage allowed per child) in which children are housed in their classrooms is among the highest of all social environments, rivaling crowded elevators and theaters. Even when classrooms are designed to accommodate the special attributes of young children such as in seating, tables, and bathroom fixtures, these areas radically differ from the out-of-school social environment where children typically sit with adults in adult-sized chairs in rooms sized to accommodate adult needs.

Ironically, however, each schoolday, hundreds of thousands of teachers adapt these environments so that children not only learn successfully, but also enjoy being in the classrooms with their teachers. Unfortunately for all of us, but particularly for children, the transformation of straw into gold does not occur in every classroom. The context of schooling can be an exhilarating or defeating experience for any child. Although the teacher cannot control each and every aspect of the classroom environment, the teacher is central to creating a context of support, caring, curiosity, experimentation, and learning.

The contexts of the classroom include the following:

- Time available for instruction
- Physical surroundings
- Immediately preceding events as well as historical patterns of events for that classroom
- Attitudes and behaviors of the students
- Attitudes and behaviors of the teacher
- Outside influences

Two examples can quickly illustrate the importance of considering the classroom context and its effects on the success or appropriateness of any lesson. Normally, a unit on death and dying presented to a kindergarten class would raise questions among parents. However, if the class had just lost a class member in a tragic school bus accident, discussing this topic would not only be considered appropriate, but would also be welcomed by most parents. The circumstances and timing are, in this case, important determiners of the classroom curriculum.

Even the sequence of typical daily lessons can be greatly influenced by classroom context. For example, Mrs. Bresinsky has planned the following work on a long-division algorithm, a study of peristalsis in health, and a social studies lesson concerning the use of evidence in judiciary proceedings. She concluded that she would begin by telling the children about the morning's schedule and the health lesson in particular. She promised them that if all the morning's work was completed before lunch, they could hang upside-down and eat bread to see what happened. Although most children already knew the result, it was, nevertheless, something to anticipate. It was also a brilliant conclusion to a presentation on peristalsis. With a sense of excitement, the children and teacher buckled down to the more mundane math at hand. Mrs. Bresinsky reasoned that "grandma's rule" (do what I want before what you want) would make the difficult math more bearable.

Ten minutes into the lesson, the fire alarm went off. When the class returned, the principal announced over the intercom that the fire drill was not planned and that someone had deliberately tripped the alarm. The principal required that each teacher send any child who was out of the room at the time of the fire drill to the principal's office. Tomisha, who always did everything right, was out of the room taking the morning's attendance report to the office. The children began to "oo-oooh" as Tomisha was asked to go to the office. The children were now quite removed from the long division and quite excited about Tomisha's visit to the principal. What does Mrs. Bresinsky do?

Such emergencies and interruptions arise almost daily in classrooms. Mrs. Bresinsky decided to use this one to her advantage. She asked the children to put away their math. She then began asking what the children were thinking when Tomisha had to go to the office. Soon she was well into her social studies lesson on judiciary evidence using the morning's false alarm as the context for the lesson instead of well-publicized trials that were constantly in the news. The math was done after lunch with the promise that, if the children worked hard on their math, the principal would talk to them about how he conducts an investigation when there was major wrong-doing in the school. Mrs. Bresinsky had successfully captured a "teachable moment" by responding to the classroom context.

Student Needs and Abilities

When lessons are planned and teachers teach, the needs and abilities of the children in the classroom are central to teacher thinking. If the instruction planned is too simple for the abilities of the children, children cannot learn what they already know. Likewise, if the lessons are too difficult and require knowledge that the children do not have, they cannot learn successfully without backtracking and mastering the needed material. Matching lesson difficulty with student ability is a critical skill for successful teaching in the elementary school. Unfortunately, the difficulties involved in this process are almost beyond resolution in classrooms where many children of differing abilities, backgrounds, and needs compete for the attention of a single teacher. One of the most startling realities of the elementary classroom is the incredible diversity among children. Although this diversity presents substantial challenges to the teacher, it is also the source of many of teaching's most cherished rewards.

Because of this great diversity among children, singular instructional approaches to instruction are almost always contraindicated. Children radically differ in needs, motivation, past learning, backgrounds, and abilities. Likewise, attempting to meet individual needs of a class of 25 children by planning 25 lessons is an equally untenable solution. A calculated compromise is usually made in which teachers match the needs and abilities of students to the resources available in the classroom to maximize successful instruction. This process almost always results in less than ideal solutions for both teachers and students.

Corno and Snow (1986) classified the following student differences that require adaptive instruction: intellectual abilities, specific prior knowledge, academic motivation, related personality characteristics, and cognitive (or learning) styles.

A teacher can adapt to differences in intellectual abilities, specific prior knowledge, academic motivation, and learning style by varying the following:

◆ Amount and type of attention given to the student by the teacher (including teacher expectations)
◆ Amount of time that the student is given to accomplish the learning
◆ Instructional strategy (direct instruction, lecture, mastery learning, demonstration, inquiry, experimentation, cooperative learning, and so on)
◆ Type of materials used (books, films, TV, audio recordings, computerization, real objects, and so on)
◆ Type of reinforcement or reaction given to both successful and unsuccessful attempts at learning

When teachers make decisions, they must react to the individual differences of students. This requires them to identify those individual needs, assess how those needs affect the current learning goals, and develop accommodation strategies for satisfying those needs within the given context.

Teacher Skill, Beliefs, Attitudes, and Knowledge

When considering the instructional intent, environmental context, and student like-nesses and differences, teachers develop instructional strategies based on various hypotheses constructed from their cumulative knowledge and experience. There are a variety of ways in which teachers can attempt to solve instructional problems. Teachers' views change over time, and those changes can have profound effects on the substance of the classroom. Cohn (1992) compared the results of a 1964 survey of Dade County (Miami) Florida teachers with the results of a follow-up survey in 1984. She identified a massive shift from teachers who desired students who were creative and intellectually demanding to those who wanted "nice" kids from average homes who were respectful and hard working.

What types of societal changes may have occurred to alter teachers' views in this fashion? How would a classroom of a teacher who preferred intellectually demand-ing children be different from that of a teacher who wanted "nice" kids?

Beliefs among teachers not only vary, but an individual teacher may also have widely disparate beliefs about children and education. Following are the results of a single veteran teacher's efforts to identify personal assumptions about children. This teacher believes that children

are a product of their environment	are self-fulfilling
have poor decision-making skills	need guidance
need recognition	are sweet, aware, fun to be with
need structure	are mean and cruel
need affection	are forgiving/hold grudges
have trouble dealing with the abstract	like movement
lack empathy	are mischievous
are materialistic	need praise
like to be listened to	are easy to please (want to please)
don't like to listen	need pay-offs
want to control surroundings and events	like sports and music
vacillate	can achieve if determined
are sensitive/insensitive	are culturally different from adults

Several interesting observations can be made by examining the list. First, even though the teacher identifies children as being substantially different from adults, the list of assumptions is true for adults as much as for children. Also, even within the list, extreme differences in the assumptions are noted. For example, the teacher indicates that she believes children vacillate and, therefore, can be forgiving/unfor-giving and sensitive/insensitive. Finally, the teacher believes children are "fun to be with" even though it is quite evident she feels that children are somewhat egocentric and preoccupied with their own needs.

This belief structure continuously filters events and assists in the construction of the hypotheses that teachers use to make decisions. Examining your belief structure, your assumptions about children, your attitudes toward the purpose and meaning of education, and your attitudes about yourself will always assist you in your journey toward successful teaching in the elementary classroom.

◆ ◆ ◆

Summary

1. Teacher beliefs have subtle, and often dominant, effects on teacher actions.

2. Teacher beliefs can be so powerful that they continuously support teacher actions that do not yield the results expected or sought.

3. The interaction between teacher beliefs and teacher actions is complex, not well understood, and demonstrates major variation among teachers as well as within individuals as they change over time.

4. Research-based knowledge has been emerging in increasing detail and relevance. This knowledge is based on empirically verified conceptualizations of teaching and applies to a wide range of situations.

5. Research-based knowledge is interpreted and transformed by teachers according to differences in teacher skill, student need, instructional intents, and educational context.

6. Determining which techniques to employ and when to employ them is as important as the skill needed to demonstrate them.

7. Teacher thinking has been examined but has not resulted in a comprehensive understanding of the processes that teachers use in making decisions. The processes of assessing the school environment, determining teacher activity that directs successful learning, and the developing strategies to evaluate their success is highly complex.

8. Researchers have developed conflicting and complementary models that outline the processes that teachers use to determine teaching activity. Some are linear (see Yinger in Figure 2.1) while others are non-linear and concurrent (see Taylor in Figure 2.2).

9. Teacher development is guided by development in teacher's professional thinking.

10. Increasing teaching success is thought to be a function of the complexity in which the teaching environment is analyzed and the accuracy of the resulting hypotheses.

11. Building conceptual models about the variables involved in teaching assists the growth in understanding about those variables.

12. Professional knowledge about teaching can be classified into "knowing what" (subject matter knowledge), "knowing how" (action system knowledge), and "choosing to" (meta-cognitional knowledge). These relationships are shown in Figure 2.6.

13. Meta-cognitional knowledge allows teachers to direct and control the processes used to determine, enact, and evaluate instructional activities.

14. Each teacher's knowledge base appears to be unique, although there are many shared conceptualizations.

15. Successful teaching is the result of systematic growth in subject matter knowledge, action system knowledge, and meta-cognitional knowledge.

16. Teachers can grow substantially in each area of knowledge by using personally guided programs of professional improvement.

◆ ◆ ◆

Activities and Questions for Further Understanding

1. There is a guiding phrase for improving teacher practice: "If it doesn't work, quit doing it." In the "Slice of Life," Mrs. Sanchez maintains *faith* that Marcus will change his behavior and continues her course of action of being supportive rather than controlling. How does a teacher reconcile observed outcomes with beliefs when the teacher's current behaviors are not getting the desired result?

2. What are the implications of the following argument: "What a teacher uses most is belief and craft. Knowledge from research is too scarce to build a teaching repertoire."

3. Louden's statement, "It is what teachers think, what teachers believe, and what teachers do . . . that ultimately shapes the kind of learning that young people get" appears to conclude that thinking, believing, and doing are separate entities. What are the relationships among these three teacher activities?

4. Shavelson concluded that the basic teaching act is decision making. Is it reasonable to conclude that decision making is more important to successful teaching than imitation of effective teacher exemplars?

5. Yinger's model of a teacher's decision-making process is shown in Figure 2.1. Does this describe the way that you make deci-sions? How is your decision-making process similar and dissimilar to Yinger's model?

6. How is Taylor's model (Figure 2.2) similar and dissimilar to your decision-making process?

7. Make a model showing how you think you make most decisions. Compare your models to others.

8. Create a model similar to that shown in Figure 2.3. What characteristics would you include in each column heading?

9. Choose one of the characteristics that you think is most important for successful teaching and develop a concept web that examines its basic elements and their relationships.

10. The author makes a distinction among "knowing what," "knowing how," and "choosing to." Create a web map that describes the elements involved in your "choosing to."

11. Make a model of what you think composes a teacher's knowledge base.

12. The model depicting the major variables in teacher decision making (Figure 2.10) included students, intents, contexts, and teacher skill and beliefs. Are there variables left out of the model? If so, what are they? Are the elements in the model of equal importance? How would you defend your answer?

◆ ◆ ◆

References

Ayers, William. (1990). Rethinking the profession of teaching: A progressive option. *Action in Teacher Education, 12*(1), 1–5.

Bettelheim, Bruno. (1971). *The informed heart.* New York: Macmillan.

Brown, A. L., Bransford, J. D., Ferrara, R. A., & Campione, J. C. (1983). Learning, remembering, and understanding. In J. H. Flavell & E. M. Markham (Eds.), *Handbook on child psychology: Cognitive development* (Vol. 3, pp. 77–166). New York: John Wiley & Sons.

Clark, C. M., & Peterson, P. L. (1986). Teachers' thought processes. In M. C. Wittrock (Ed.), *Handbook of research on teaching* (3rd ed., pp. 255–296). New York: Macmillan.

Cohn, Marilyn M. (1992). How teachers perceive teaching: Change over two decades, 1964–1984. In A. Lieberman (Ed.), *The changing contexts of teaching: Ninety-first Yearbook of the National Society for the Study of Education*. Chicago: University of Chicago Press.

Corno, Lyn, & Snow, Richard E. (1986). Adapting teaching to individual differences among learners. In M. C. Wittrock (Ed.), *Handbook of research on teaching* (3rd ed., pp. 605–629). New York: Macmillan.

Doyle, W. (1986). Classroom organization and management. In M. Wittrock (Ed.), *Handbook of research on teaching* (3rd ed.). New York: Macmillan.

Glasser, William. (1990). *The quality school: Managing students without coercion*. Upper Saddle River, NJ: Prentice Hall.

Good, Tom, & Brophy, Jere. (1992). *Looking into classrooms* (5th ed.). New York: HarperCollins.

Goodlad, J., & Klein, M. F. (1970). *Behind the classroom door*. Worthington, OH: Charles A. Jones.

Jackson, Philip. (1968). *Life in classrooms*. New York: Holt, Rinehart and Winston.

Lichtenstein, Gary, McLaughlin, Milbery W., & Knudson, Jennifer. (1992). Teacher empowerment and professional knowledge. In A. Lieberman (Ed.), *The changing contexts of teaching: Ninety-first Yearbook of the National Society for the Study of Education*. Chicago: University of Chicago Press.

Louden, William (1991). *Understanding teaching: Continuity and change in teachers' knowledge*. New York: Teachers College Press.

National Council for Accreditation of Teacher Education. (1995). Standards, procedures, & policies for the accreditation of professional education units. Washington. D.C.: Author.

North Carolina State Department of Public Instruction. (1986). *Teacher performance appraisal system: The standards and processes for use*. Raleigh, NC: Author. (ERIC Document Reproduction Service No. ED 271 453)

North Carolina State Department of Public Instruction. (1986). *Teacher performance appraisal system training: A report of outcomes*. Raleigh, NC: Author. (ERIC Document Reproduction Service No. ED 271 452)

Northwest Regional Educational Laboratory. (1984). *Onward to excellence: Making schools more effective*. Portland, OR: Author.

Peterson, P. L., Marx, R. W., & Clark, C. M. (1978). teacher planning, teacher behavior, and student achievement. *American Educational Research Journal, (15)*, 417–432.

Peterson, Penelope L. (1988, June/July). Teachers' and students' cognitional knowledge for classroom teaching and learning. *Educational Researcher*, pp. 5–14.

Pintrich, Paul R. (1990). Implications of psychological research on student learning and college teaching for teacher education. In W. R. Houston (Ed.), *Handbook of research on teacher education*. New York: Macmillan.

Riner, Phillip S. (1992). A comparison of the criterion validity of principal's judgment and teacher self-rating using a high inference rating scale. *Journal of Curriculum and Supervision, 7(2)*.

Shavelson, R. J. (1973). *The basic teaching skill: Decision-making* (R & D Memorandum No. 104). Stanford, CA: Stanford University, School of Education, Center for R & D in Teaching.

Taylor, P. H. (1970). How teachers plan their courses. Slough, Berkshire, England: National Foundation for Educational Research. As cited in C. M. Clark & P. L. Peterson (1986), "Teachers' thought processes" in M. C. Wittrock (Ed.), *Handbook of research on teaching* (3rd ed., pp. 255–296). New York: Macmillan.

Texas Education Agency. (1992). *ExCET preparation manual: 04 Elementary comprehensive*. Austin, TX: Author.

Whitehead, A. N. (1929). The aims of education. New York: Macmillan.

Yinger, R. J. (1977). A study of teacher planning: Description and theory development using ethnographic and information processing methods. Unpublished doctoral dissertation, Michigan State University, East Lansing. As cited in C. M. Clark & P. L. Peterson (1986), "Teachers' thought processes" in M. C. Wittrock (Ed.), *Handbook of research on teaching* (3rd ed., pp. 255–296). New York: Macmillan.

Zahorik, J. A. (1975). The effects of planning on teaching. *Elementary School Journal, 71*, 143–151.

CHAPTER 3

Can I Really Succeed with All the Children?

Student Diversity and Student Differences

Outline

We hold these truths to be self-evident, that all men are created equal, that they are endowed by their Creator with certain unalienable rights, that among these are Life, Liberty, and the pursuit of Happiness.

DECLARATION OF INDEPENDENCE

There exists in the human heart a depraved taste for equality, which impels the weak to attempt to lower the powerful to their own level, and reduces men to prefer equality in slavery to inequality with freedom.

ALEXIS DE TOCQUEVILLE

A Slice of Life

Mr. O'Connell enjoyed the team reports that his fifth graders had given on the Bill of Rights. He was especially pleased that the children had recognized that the real meanings of the amendments were constantly being interpreted. Mr. O'Connell had taken the opportunity to tell the children that the U.S. Constitution was called a "living document" because it allowed interpretation. The children appreciated the idea but weren't quite sure what interpreting laws meant, especially when laws mean so many things to different people. Mr. O'Connell was pleased. "Tomorrow, we will talk about the judicial system and how it interprets what laws mean and how they are to be fairly administered," he said with a smile. Privately, he thought how lucky he was this year to have such an inquisitive and challenging group. A swell of optimism overcame him, and he began to whistle cheerfully as the bell rang for dismissal.

Tuesday, Wednesday, and Thursday were pure bliss. Mr. O'Connell explained about the court structure set up by the Constitution, and the children kept interrupting with "What if's?" and "How can that be?" Mr. O'Connell told his students that, in the beginning, America was a great experiment and people, even today, wanted to leave their home countries to live here because of the freedom and opportunity. The children quickly shared how their families had moved to the city from other states to find work. Several children told how their parents had lived in another country and why they had moved. Liu, one of the most hard-working, kind children in the class, told the class how he had loved his home in Vietnam but admitted that he had more fun here. Liu volunteered that his father was trying to bring Liu's two uncles to the United States but was unable to do so because of the Immigration Service. Liu lamented that the people at INS were unfair. His remark was like a gauntlet had been thrown down in front of Tomeka, one of the most polite children that Mr. O'Connell had ever taught. "They shouldn't be coming here taking all the jobs anyway!" she shouted. He was stunned by her challenge.

Liu, however, had an immediate retort, "Who are you calling they?" There was something in the "they" that was ugly and mean . . . or was it hurt? Mr. O'Connell intervened.

"Well, it seems we have a disagreement about whether people from other countries should be allowed to come to the United States and live. That's a good topic for tomorrow. Talk to your parents about their feelings about immigration, which is when others move from another country into your country." Mr. O'Connell wrote the definition on the board along with some questions to ask and suggested that the children look in the newspapers and magazines for more information.

While Mr. O'Connell was completing the writing with his back to the class, there was a sudden yell, "Am not!", followed by the loud thump of a thick book bouncing squarely off the top of a youngster's head. Mr. O'Connell turned to see Liu, bent over with his hands over his head, rearing up to thrust kick at Tomeka. His foot landed right on her diaphragm, and Tomeka doubled over trying to catch her breath. Mr. Tuner had no time to react. Tomeka gurgled, while the rest of the class stared in shock. Not knowing exactly what had happened, Mr. O'Connell was struggling for some idea of what to do. He hustled over to Tomeka who, by now, was beginning to gasp small breaths. In just a minute or two, Tomeka was breathing normally, more or less. Mr. O'Connell held both children by the shoulders, and the class started buzzing wildly with both taunts and inquiries.

Independence and Social Norms

The right to be different, the right to self-determination, the right to freely express oneself—these are cherished privileges that have made the United States one of the most desirable nations in the world for oppressed people. The tenacious resistance of Americans to violations of these rights has resulted in a nation of diverse and competing views. Although these rights are zealously protected, the democratic values of Americans also make a tyranny of the majority a constant threat to individual self-determination and to ethnic and ideological minorities. This threat is very real and presents a constant impediment to free expression and access to economic security.

In America, diversity and respect for individual differences are concurrently lauded and ignored, usually without consistency or reason.

Cultural diversity is not a unique characteristic of the world's oldest democracy; it is endemic to social life in all societies (Conner, 1978). However, the diversity that is special to American democracy results from widespread access, equity, tolerance and mutual coexistence, not a struggle for survival. Historically, diversity has provided a way of sorting and classifying people. Such classifying provides a sense of order and group affiliation that is considered necessary for social living. Many Americans prize their cultural heritage and attempt to keep alive many of the most sacred traditions that connect them to their ancestral legacy. However, diversity is also used in harmful ways to identify groups that are targeted for servitude and discrimination, resulting in restricted freedom and lowered economic opportunity. Clearly, the latter use is not acceptable under the democratic ideals of our current society, but it does exist, although its manifestation is increasingly more implicit and covert. Discrimination always has the same result: intentional harm directed toward groups and individuals that puts the basic ideals of our society at risk.

Differences among individuals have followed a similar pattern. Distinction and honor are granted to those possessing differences that are valued by society. Thus, American society affords special status to notable professional athletes, captains of industry, political leaders, heroes demonstrating great bravery at personal risk, and the like. However, that same society has often selected some individual differences to be shunned. This has resulted in "closed doors" for individuals who can and do make substantial contributions, but their contributions are minimized because of a lack of tolerance or understanding. Children with bright, inquisitive minds, children with weight problems, children from fundamental or orthodox religious groups, children with learning disorders, and children with crippling diseases are frequently targeted for inappropriate differential treatment that limits their access and their development.

The solutions to inappropriate treatment of both individual differences and diversity within the school environment are very similar and focus on tolerance, encouragement, and thoughtful adaptation of the learning environment. However, as with most instructional and curricular problems, solutions require significant teacher effort in dealing with the context, students, and intents. This chapter explores the two related areas of individual differences and diversity education.

Diversity Education and Multicultural Perspectives

Diversity has varying meanings and implications. Whether diversity is a topic of academic study or casual interest, there are numerous points of dissension and few points of agreement. However, there are several key points that teachers can consider as core components of appropriate ethical and pedagogical standards.

First, no child should be at an educational disadvantage because of his or her cultural or ethnic affiliation. Although there are culturally related events that assist or hinder student achievement, the school should not act to perpetuate those inequalities. Second, a child should never feel that success or failure in school is related to his or her acceptance or abandonment of his or her cultural heritage. Finally, there are common core values that support and maintain a democratic society. One such value is equality under the law. Therefore, while the school should not seek to elevate or demote one cultural perspective over another, it cannot abandon the basic beliefs imbedded in democratic ideals and protections afforded by the Constitution. There will always be inherent contradictions in values held by individuals in a democratic society. There will be conflict as diverse groups and individuals engage and express the rights afforded in the American democracy. Creed, gender, and racial equality are firmly established under American law and is a fundamental premise of a free society. Although there are ethnic groups that claim cultural superiority or attempt to demean the status of women, the school must firmly assert the rights of all races and both genders to equal education and equality in access and participation. Thus, while tolerance education is a laudable goal, tolerance is not an absolute concept, and not all ethnic practice can or should be tolerated or embraced.

When narrowly defined cultural, ethnic, or religious views conflict with the predominant values of a democratic society, the teacher faces this challenge: how to protect students' rights to an educational experience free of prejudice and at the same time provide them the freedom of self-determination. The principles of providing diversity education and promoting tolerance are admirable; however, attempts to implement these can introduce problems for which simple resolutions and platitudes are inadequate.

What Is Meant by Diversity?

Diversity is a result of self-identification of a group of people with similar characteristics that differentiates them from the masses. These common bonds provide identity and belonging. Diversity is typically confined to group differences and has a social connotation. Differences that are unique to a single person or are not contained within the individual's group identification are considered individual differences. This distinction is arguable. One view is that individuals with similar characteristics, such as those with physical handicaps, form a social group with a distinct community possessing their own unique values. Another view is that such generalization is simplistic and yields inappropriate stereotypes. One of the difficulties involved in diversity education is that there are wide-ranging opinions on what constitutes diversity and what should be the appropriate goals of a diversity curriculum.

Regardless of your concept of diversity, issues involved in gender identification, regional identification, ethnic, political, religious, social, and occupational affiliation play major roles in defining who we are, how we are special, and how we belong.

A common tendency of mankind appears to be denying others opportunities based solely on group identification. Yet, the group identity that is often used to exclude and punish others is also necessary to meet the basic need of belonging. Belonging has been eloquently argued by humanistic psychologists (Dreikurs & Cassel, 1972; Ginott, 1972; Glasser, 1986) as being an essential fundamental need that drives and directs our behavior. This ancient need to seek and find others who give us physical protection and increase our chances of survival has evolved today into a social need for personal meaning and psychological safety in our increasingly complex social life. Although a few individuals choose isolation over social living, the universal tendency of humankind is to form groups, establish group norms, and secure essential needs of protection, shelter, safety, and meaning through group ties and associations.

Dimensions of Diversity

The debate, controversy, and emergence of a diversity curriculum each incorporate elements of the following:

Empirical verification	External measures of "what is" based on the broadest shared measures
Theory	How and why "what is" operates
Ideology	What "ought" to be

When we talk about diversity, the logic behind our positions is always a mixture of empirical verification, theory, and ideology. For each of us, what is "known" about these three elements is greatly affected by the differences in our experiences. Unfortunately, the distinctions among "is," "how," and "ought" is often blurred in dealing with diversity, resulting in much confusion. In discussions and policy debates about diversity issues, these elements are almost always tinged with an emotionalism that cannot be readily contained. Tolerance or acceptance is not easily practiced. When the values and social policies to be pursued in public schools are being considered, the results, not surprisingly, are quite unsettling and indefinite.

Multicultural Education

The foremost effort to educate American youth about diversity is contained in a curriculum orientation known as *multicultural education.* Banks (1995) identifies five different dimensions or conceptual orientations toward multicultural education: content integration, knowledge construction, prejudice reduction, equity pedagogy, and empowering school culture.

Creating a curriculum that emphasizes multiple cultural perspectives is referred to as *content integration.* Content integration is an important avenue for learning about others. Studies of societies, ethnic groups, or communities different from our own are important components of any effort to expand students' views of the world. However, when content integration is the only avenue of educating students about diversity, the study of academic content of diversity does not reflect the dynamics of living in a multicultural world. In extreme cases, diversity then becomes solely academic content. However, content integration should be considered one of several avenues that are required to educate students about living in a diverse world.

Another approach involves *knowledge construction*. According to Banks, knowledge construction describes the procedures by which a cultural group builds knowledge in social, behavior, and natural science areas. This study includes the frames of reference or perceptual orientation of various cultural groups. Individuals who have not been exposed to diverse cultures may find this very difficult to comprehend. These individuals often consider their personal or cultural outlooks and approaches to understanding as the only logical approach possible. In short, some individuals are said to be culturally myopic. Americans, for example, have historically viewed individual achievement and free expression as a fundamental process. However, many cultures view collaborative effort within a group far more valuable. These cultures view free expression by individuals as a weakness since they value the collective view over any individual assertion of personal prerogative or right. For many Americans, these propositions simply do not make sense. Nevertheless, combining knowledge construction with content integration is a powerful strategy.

Banks identifies the third area of conceptual orientations toward multicultural education as *prejudice reduction*. This dimension focuses on students' racial and cultural attitudes and emphasizes tolerance and cooperative coexistence. A number of studies indicate that educational intervention can assist children in being more understanding, inclusive, and tolerant. Unlike content integration and knowledge construction, which are primarily modes of knowledge acquisition, prejudice reduction dynamically deals with values, value assertions, and behavior. It is one thing to know about the literary and cultural history of a group and how they interpret themselves and the world. It is an entirely different instructional goal to promote positive attitudes toward differences with tolerance and understanding committed to action. By combining knowledge of cultural history, norms, and perceptual outlooks with the teaching of tolerance, understanding, and negotiation, a realistic image of a multicultural program begins to emerge. However, there are two additional considerations that must be included.

It seems a reasonable proposition that if cultural groups create, view, and use knowledge in differing ways, differing instructional strategies should optimize the learning for different groups. Banks refers to this perspective as *equity pedagogy*. Attempts have been made to create special instructional programs for minority groups or economically impacted populations. The results have been mixed. A real danger is that members of these groups receive instructional programs based on overgeneralized cultural traits that result in stereotypes and limited instructional opportunities. On the other hand, some programs that directly address dominant group problems have found success and acceptance without the stigma and harm of stereotyping and without the institutionalization of low expectations. The work of Levin (1988) and Comer (1988) has demonstrated that by accepting the needs of student groups and intentionally developing programs to meet those needs, schools can make a substantial contribution not only to the students' academic achievement, but also to the vitality of the community and home.

The final dimension of multicultural education is an *empowering school culture*. This concept interprets the school as a social organization with a dynamic that is larger than its individual parts (Banks, 1995). Thus, the goal of a multicultural curriculum is the development of a school culture that is empowering to students from all social and cultural groups. Its purpose is to deal with diversity in contexts that allow students to develop their potential with the least restrictions and with the most support. The systems of Comer (1988) and Levin (1988) contain numerous structures that permit parents, community, teachers, and children to take charge of the available educational resources and structure them into something much more than a program of services. This perspective fosters the development of a sense of community in which education is appropriate to the students as well as effective in meeting specified learning goals.

The critical impact of any multicultural curriculum or attempts at expanding the opportunities of underrepresented populations depends on a careful conceptualization of both the intent and the strategies employed. Research in this area seems to point toward broad conceptualizations encompassing many different perspectives and strategies for improvement. Thus, successful teachers must view diversity education in conjunction with the total school and community context and deliberately strive toward specified goals with targeted strategies.

Diversity and Individual Differences Inside the Classroom

Teachers must be aware that their daily treatment of children in the classroom can be enhanced greatly by a careful consideration and understanding of how teacher actions affect children differently. The differences among children in cultural, physical, and social dimensions are a major contributing factor to the teacher's determination of both curriculum and its implementation. The critical importance of the teacher decision-making skill discussed in the previous chapter emerges as a central element in helping each child, regardless of group or individual differences, to realize the goals of the classroom.

The emotionalism involved in discussions of diversity and individual differences should never be underestimated. Much of what underlies culture and ethnicity are unquestioned perceptions of how and why the world and its societies operate as they do. This emotionalism easily challenges rational approaches to discussions of cultural issues. At a special 1992 American Educational Research Association "Fireside Chat," a packed room of professors and graduate students discussed multicultural and feminist perspectives. Magliaro (1994) described the intense emotionalism and anger vented during the session. Central to the discussion was discrimination— overt, covert, intentional, perceived, and inadvertent. The group universally condemned discrimination. But how it occurs, why it occurs, and what can be done to prevent it were areas of hot debate, and a common ground from which to build a consensus did not emerge. Even among those trained to set aside emotion for reason, diversity issues evoke strong emotional responses.

The inverse of this troublesome issue of discrimination is the concept of fairness. What comprises fair treatment of diverse individuals is tightly linked to what is believed to be fair treatment of any individual and how individual and group differences can be accommodated. When those differences come in direct conflict, effective accommodation requires more than just policies and curricula. Fairness is almost universally endorsed, vaguely understood, and problematic in its implementation. Children need to feel that their diverse needs are being addressed fairly. For that to happen, teachers must first understand the many ways in which children differ and the causes or antecedents of those differences.

Individual Differences Within a Diversity Construct

At the most basic level, students differ in ways that can be readily observed by a teacher who is in daily contact with them. Easily observable differences among children include racial characteristics, gender, and certain physical traits such as height, weight, or pronounced differences in body development. Other differences are not as easily observed. Language potential may or may not result in observable differences. Bilingual children often converse with friends outside of school in their native language while communicating in school with the teacher and other children in English. The teacher may have no idea that English is their second language. Age is another "hit-or-miss" observable difference. Some ten-year-olds easily fit into a group of children three years older, while others resemble students two years younger. Children often dress to illustrate their differences as well as to hide them. Careful observation by the teacher, however, can look past physical characteristics and establish an estimate of the maturation and behavior of the child.

Some significant differences among children are inferred from behavior but cannot be observed directly. Intelligence (broadly defined) can result in behaviors that show uniqueness among children. Some children continually struggle over the most basic activities, while others absorb the information, analyze it internally, ask questions regarding the utility and validity of the information within specific contexts, and make projections about the implications of the information. The ability, or lack of it, to play with other children cooperatively, to make and sustain friendships, and to obey social norms can be proxies for characteristics of intelligence, personality, and social maturity.

Differences among children, whether a result of individual differences or cultural/social diversity, do not yield consistent differences in behaviors. Some traits yield observable differences in some children; yet, equally profound differences cannot be observed at all in other children within the school setting. Children may be labeled "at risk" because of a collection of statistical traits related to low achievement. Within this group of children, researchers have identified a trait they refer to as "resiliency." Resiliency refers to the student's ability either not to succumb to or to overcome educational hardships. Resiliency is not a trait easily identified, but it may have a major impact on academic success. Therefore, when making instructional decisions based on observable and inferred characteristics of children, the teacher must proceed with considerable skepticism accompanied by a readiness to rethink educational decisions.

Ethnicity, while providing observable clues in some situations, can be quite invisible in others. Religion can be a central feature in the ethnic composition of a group and can have profound effects on the perspectives of the individuals within the group. Religious differences are usually unseen in the classroom unless the religion prescribes certain dress or behavior that separates the children from others. Some Islamic sects require their male children to carry curved knives as a display of religious symbolism, whereas other groups within the same religion require no pronounced display of differences. Some religious differences may occasionally be observed by type of dress or the prohibition of certain classroom activities such as participating in the Pledge of Allegiance. Religious and ethnic diversity are protected forms of free speech in America and a teacher's intrusive inquiry (for example, "How can you believe *that?*") is certainly not warranted nor are evaluative judgments (for example, "The family has some weird beliefs."). Some families may find teacher inquiry into personal aspects of the family to be meddlesome and undesirable. Other families welcome the interest, readily share their beliefs and habits, and look favorably toward the teacher's interest and respect. For example, Jehovah's Witnesses provide extensive materials specifically designed to assist the teacher in respecting, with virtually no disruption to the class, the religious practices of their children.

Differences in ethnicity can often frame a child's outlook on what is important and how others should be treated, as well as define the role that the child should play in society. These differences can result in profoundly different responses among children in similar circumstances. Understanding the outlooks of children is an important aspect of constructing effective instructional strategies.

Some sources of student differences can only be inferred and yield no obvious evidence of differences among children. Learning style preferences, cognitive differences as measured by intelligence tests, self-concept and self-esteem, and "within family" differences such as support, a sense of belonging and other values, can and often do have influential effects on the learning success in school settings. These differences are often hard to perceive in most cases and even harder to accommodate successfully because of the indefinite nature of their occurrence.

There are no clear or definite ways to classify and analyze student differences. Multicultural education is a commonly utilized scheme for studying and understanding differences in social groups united by ethnic, racial, or religious similarities. Differences in learning styles, intellect, physical ability, and behavior are usually not addressed in schools unless the differences are pronounced. These differences are then classified by identifying children with "special needs," giving rise to an area of schooling referred to as *special education.* However, not all student differences that affect learning success are covered under this rubric. Some of these differences include research on multiple types of intelligence and motivational characteristics and are considered later in the text.

Separating the academic study of student differences into diversity and individual differences makes sense from an academic perspective. However, the teacher may find that a clear separation of social and individual differences and their effects on classroom learning success is not that easily obtained. The teacher must develop an integrated understanding of how student differences affect learning, how these differences interact, and how these differences have many different outcomes.

Many traits of children that are described as socially determined and traits that are described as individual trait differences are usually not independent of each other and have mutual effects. Some identified "differences" that are thought to unite individuals actually provide only a gross generalization of common ethnic ties and may not be a unifying factor. For example, language is often regarded as a cultural difference; however, many people may speak the same language without sharing the same culture. This is particularly true of children who speak English or Spanish—the most common languages found in American schools.

Some characteristics are so broad as to be meaningless in many instances. For example, ethnicity is often used to classify individuals for affirmative action purposes. The typical categories usually identify only superficial physical differences and use a mixture of ethnic and racial groups such as African-American, Caucasian, Asian, Pacific Islander, Hispanic, Mexican-American, and Native American. Note however, that the differences *within* groups—for example, between African-American immigrants and tenth-generation African-Americans—may be just as substantial as differences *between* groups—for example, between Caucasians and African-Americans. The same applies within Caucasian ranks by including within that classification tenth-generation immigrants of long-forgotten Scottish heritage and first-generation immigrants fleeing political oppression from an eastern European country. Any type of decision made on ethnicity alone increases the danger of unfairly assessing the skill and needs of individual students through stereotyping and overgeneralization. This can be just as harmful, often more so, than ignoring all the differences among groups. Danger lies in both paths; therefore, careful consideration from the teacher is essential for classroom success. An important point to remember is that the perceptions of teachers and students regarding diversity can have profound effects on the effort that students expend, the treatment they receive from others, and the outcomes obtained. It is critical for each teacher to explore the beliefs of others and to read deeply and widely about diversity and individual differences. However, it is even more important for teachers to consider seriously their own cultural outlook and how that affects their views of others.

An additional issue that must be considered is how a student's differences affect his or her learning success in school. When teachers consider the observability (whether teachers can observe a particular trait difference), control (whether the child can influence the emergence of the trait), and effect (what influence the trait has on the behavior of the child), three very important generalizations for the teacher can be made:

◆ The child has a great deal of control over some differences that affect learning and no control over others. The child's learning success comes from concentrating on areas that the student can influence. Teacher-directed adaptations are made for areas that the student cannot hope to influence but that may have an impact on learning. Students and teachers must share the responsibility for constructing the best possible learning opportunities.

◆ The teacher has a great deal of control over some differences that affect learning but no control over others. Teaching success comes from concentrating on areas in which the teacher can exercise control to effect a positive impact on learning. Teachers and students must develop skills in adapting to influences that they cannot change.

◆ Areas that teachers and students cannot influence must not be allowed to diminish educational opportunity, if at all possible. Again, cooperation among students, parents, and the school is essential for educational success.

There is no knowledge that can guide teachers unerringly toward appropriate treatment of children. All teacher decisions must be recognized as tentative and subject to reconsideration based on the results obtained. However, there are beneficial ways and there are hurtful ways to attempt to accommodate the vast differences among children. A reasonable sequence for teacher growth and understanding is to

◆ Attempt to understand what the differences are.
◆ Determine how those differences manifest themselves.
◆ Speculate on what effects these differences have on learning and social growth.
◆ Propose hypotheses regarding the appropriate accommodations that provide positive benefits for the child within the classroom setting.

Teacher/Student Differences

Heath and McLaughlin (1993) examined the building of ethnic and gender identity in urban youth and found that identities are better represented as layered self-conceptualizations. They also concluded that simple labels of ethnicity, race, or gender relationship do not accurately reveal the breadth and the complex interaction among personal and societal variables. An amusing but illustrative way to begin to understand student differences is to compare how students view school to how teachers view school. Spencer and Barth (1991), with tongue in cheek, analyzed the view of students on several issues in the social studies curriculum (Figure 3.1). While humorous, the intent is to show how much more immediate and egocentric student views are when compared to more mature adults.

Most teachers accept that student views differ from their own. However, the successful teacher must attempt to understand those differences and use this knowledge to assist children in developing concepts and attitudes that benefit their educational development. For example, suppose that John is a fifth-grade student and Figure 3.1 accurately portrays his views about social studies and your class. How could you use this knowledge to communicate effectively with John? If John were to do an unusually good job on a particular essay and earned an "A," what might John's reaction be? Would he attribute the "A" to hard work or to having pleased the teacher? What would be the likely response of John to the following comments: "John, you have been so good this week. You're paying attention, and your hard work is paying off. . . . You made an 'A'!" or "You made me think. I'm not sure I agree with you, but you expressed yourself forcefully and with thoughtfulness."

Since the teacher emphasized John's conformity in the first comment, John's perception that grades are rewards or punishments is confirmed. However, the second comment expresses John's work in opposition to the teacher's view but acknowledges his strength of persuasion in the essay. John cannot easily conclude that he is receiving the "A" because he said what the teacher wanted to hear. He could conclude that he pleased his teacher by arguing forcefully for his point of view

Issue	Teacher View	Student View
Important	Epochal moments in world history	Music, Friday night's party
History	The sum total of what has happened that provides us with understanding	Stuff that happened a long time ago and has nothing to do with now
Social Studies	The one subject that allows students to use school to make sense of their lives	The one subject that has no practical purpose whatsoever
Read Pages 80–84	An assignment that will inform students and start them thinking	No homework tonight
Class Attendance	One thing students have to do	Something you have to do if you aren't sick, sleepy, watching cartoons, going to the doctor, sitting with a sick baby sister
Grades	A measure of the quality of student work	A way for teachers to punish students

FIGURE 3.1   Diversity in teacher/student views.

Adapted by permission from "Standing on Uncommon Ground" by J. M. Spencer and J. L. Barth, 1991. *Social Education,* April/May, 212–215.

(which, to his satisfaction, she did not readily share) but that certainly is not capitulation. John might easily conclude that he pleased his teacher, not by conforming to something with which he disagrees, but by expressing himself appropriately. John, however, can easily conclude that he is not being manipulated by grades; he simply is receiving acknowledgment for hard work. And then again, John may not even care on this occasion! However, by understanding and acknowledging John's differences and viewpoints, the teacher enhances the likelihood that John will perform in a way that is ultimately more beneficial to him.

Ethnic/Cultural Differences

Not all diversity issues are as readily accommodated as student attitudes toward grades. Ethnic differences are increasingly a topic of debate regarding their contributions toward learning and school success. A tenuous balance exists between genuine understanding of a child's cultural context and overgeneralization and bias. Campbell-Whatley (1993) accumulated a list of cultural differences established by a host of other writers. The list contrasts the differences between the four dominant minority definitions and mainstream American culture. Her groups were labeled Anglo-American (a misnomer since most Caucasians in the U.S. are not of English descent), Native American, Asian-American, African-American, and Hispanic-American. By combining the views of numerous authors, she developed a series of comparisons, shown in abbreviated form in Figure 3.2.

Minority	Majority
Native American	**Anglo-American**
• Elders to be honored	• The future lies with youth
• Learning through legends	• Learning from books and schools
• Sharing, group ownership	• Individual ownership
• Humble, cooperative	• Competitive
• Not bound by time	• Structured awareness of time
• Expect few rules	• Expect rules for most situations
Asian American	**Anglo-American**
• Quiet, reticent, aloof	• Talkative and outgoing
• Dependent, conforming	• Independent, "do my own thing"
• Respect for elders	• Youth is most valuable
• Sons more valuable than daughters	• Sons and daughters of equal value
• Strong family exerts control over behavior	• Child free to exert independence
• Child misconduct is source of great shame	• Child misconduct is an expression of independence
African American	**Anglo-American**
• Not necessary to look listener in the eye	• Look speaker in the eye
• Seek support from larger families (kin)	• Seek support from smaller immediate family
• Child-rearing a result of extended family	• Child-rearing a result of immediate family
• Cultural pride	• Individual pride
• Usually lower educational expectations	• Usually higher educational expectations
• May interrupt speaker with encouraging remarks	• Use nods and few words to encourage speakers
Hispanic American	**Anglo-American**
• Do not want to be separated from group as being different or excelling	• Competitive, wants recognition
• Stand closer, touch, avoid eye contact	• Respect distance, avoid touch, make eye contact
• Respect extended family	• Loyalty to immediate family
• *Personalismo,* preference for individual contact	• Favor a more organized and more impersonal approach
• Tendency toward lower academic achievement	• Tendency toward higher academic achievement
• Strong commitment to *dignidad, machismo,* and *respecto*	• Do not share this commitment

FIGURE 3.2 Cultural characteristic comparisons.

Adapted from *Multicultural Education Module* by G. D. Campbell-Whatley, 1993. (ERIC ED 364 497)

When members of each of the five cultural groups review these comparisons, they often feel that certain statements overgeneralize their group and cast it in an unnecessarily negative light. Inversely, some of the generalizations are readily accepted as "accurate" without significant disagreement. Although some individuals instantly agree with the comparisons, some generalizations may not correspond to a particular person's contact with that cultural group. For example, a person who grew up in San Francisco, after years of negotiating for vegetables with the spirited street grocers in Chinatown, may have difficulty viewing Chinese-Americans as "quiet, reticent, and aloof." Or, a Southern white male may find it difficult to agree with the assessment that he views his elders as not being from the "real world" when he recounts weekly hunting and fishing with his father and uncles, as well as working together in the family's construction business. Yet, there is little doubt that there are general differences in cultural outlooks of Americans that have relationship to ethnicity. Many believe that the comparisons in Figure 3.2 are accurate, although the reader is strongly cautioned to be acutely aware of the dangers of stereotyping and the dangers involved in assessing a student's needs and habits by group membership. Hopefully, the readers will share the author's skepticism at the value and utility of some ethnic generalizations and remember that the successful teacher always takes the time to value all students as unique individuals.

The essential question when dealing with diversity information is, "What does a teacher do with this knowledge?" Can a teacher use the knowledge constructively to the benefit of children, or do the overgeneralizations help form stereotypes that do more harm than good? Again, the teacher's judgment and deliberate decision-making skills play a direct role in developing appropriate answers. If teachers unquestionably accept the generalizations as being applicable to a certain child based solely on the child's ethnic membership, a disaster of misunderstanding is almost certain to occur. If, however, the teacher uses the information, along with other information about the child, to develop a more complete awareness of the child's social life, then the results can have beneficial results.

For example, one teacher recounts that she often asks children, "At home, who do you ask when you want to get permission to do something special?" That person is always included in the invitation for a conference. This teacher long ago learned that the "parent" in many families was not necessarily the child-rearer. Likewise, when trying to explain to a misbehaving child why certain behaviors cannot be tolerated, a teacher may understand one child's refusal to look directly at the teacher as an appropriate measure of respect while recognizing that another child is demonstrating an unwillingness to accept accountability for his or her actions. Again, the use or abuse of cultural generalizations hinges on the ability of the teacher to use the information to understand better the causes and interpretations of classroom events.

Gender Differences

Faculty at Oregon State University (1987) recognized that racial and sexual prejudices are sometimes deliberate, but sometimes they are just a result of reflecting and transmitting unexamined cultural assumptions. These unintentional messages may single out individuals and diminish student confidence, lower academic self-expectations, and eventually limit career choices. The faculty published a booklet to help raise awareness of how unexamined cultural assumptions affect students. A primary object of their attention was differential treatment of gender. Although acknowledging that males and females differ in very significant ways, they also recognized the difficulty in determining when differential treatments are appropriate.

Areas of differential treatment by gender that have been identified included items related to language, behavior, and expectations. Figure 3.3 illustrates some of the common findings that relate to differential treatment by gender. Most of these treatments are unintentional; probably few elementary teachers are deliberately biased or intentionally show favoritism for one gender or the other. However, differential treatments do occur. Everyone has generalized beliefs about the differences between boys and girls, and this does have an impact on how children perceive and act.

Language
- Boys receive more frequent praise than girls (Sadker & Sadker, 1994).
- Boys receive feedback that is more specific (Sadker & Sadker, 1994).
- Boys receive feedback that redirects them toward correct solutions more often than girls (Sadker & Sadker, 1994).

Behavior
- Classroom teachers pay less attention to girls than boys (AAUW, 1992).
- African American girls have fewer interactions with teachers, although they attempt to initiate the interactions more frequently (AAUW, 1992).
- More girls are sexually harassed than boys (AAUW, 1992).
- Teachers were less tolerant of boys with effeminate behaviors than those with aggressive behaviors (Clarricoats, 1980).
- Teachers tend to spend more time with boys because they think that they have more problems with reading, writing, math, and behavior (Kidder, 1989; Sadker & Sadker, 1994).
- Boys ask questions and get answers (Sadker & Sadker, 1994).
- Boy receive more praise, critique, and help (Sadker & Sadker, 1994).

Expectations
- Girls are expected to be quieter and neater (Byrne, 1975).
- Girls are expected to be better behaved (Byrne, 1975; Delmont, 1980; Stanworth, 1983).
- Girls are expected to be more cooperative and easier to control (Byrne, 1975).
- Girls are expected to answer more quickly (Sadker & Sadker, 1994).
- Boys are expected to succeed outside the classroom more frequently (Sadker & Sadker, 1994).
- Boys are expected to achieve higher status jobs and make greater contributions (Sadker & Sadker, 1994).

FIGURE 3.3   Examples of differential treatment of boys and girls.

The issue of differential treatment becomes more complex when we begin to understand that boys and girls *are* different and that these differences accelerate as children reach puberty. These differences, however, may be only a foreshadowing of physiological and neurological differences that have important effects on how children of different genders learn, how those differences are to be treated, what impact they have on schooling opportunities, and how competing values are to be reconciled. Common cultural values have created gender words that permeate our language. Some, such as "actor" and "actress," have only surface effects. Other gender language, such as how the child refers to a parent, is significantly charged with cultural expectations. Children refer to their parents with gender-specific language, such as "Mommy" and "Daddy" (rarely as "Parents"), and this carries with it many cultural and social messages within the family structure.

There is certainly a wide differential in gender-specific language. For instance, when a child uses "Mommy," the language is not only natural but also carries with it a certain pride and affection. However, the use of other gender-specific language is demeaning, hurtful, or labeling. For instance, calling a person "woman driver," "male hairdresser," "toots," or "jock" carries a message that is usually meant to be demeaning.

In the elementary classroom, the language is much more benign but as potentially influential. Phrases such as "He's all boy!" or "Sit quietly like a proper young lady" may not have harmful intent, but they carry messages that convey unintentional expectations. The phrase "all boy" generally refers to behavior that is active, inquisitive, not easily restrained, and aggressive. Does this mean that a boy who is reticent, quiet, and polite is somehow not "all boy"? Is a young girl who is active, aggressive, and mobile not quite "a proper young lady"?

Open communication improves classroom cooperation.

Although such language certainly has a negative side and it is best to avoid the use of such language, it is equally important not to condemn this type of language. People who use this language rarely have a hostile intent but simply are expressing beliefs that frame who they are and what the proper order of social life should be. Immediate and hostile condemnation of such language would be a de facto violation of cultural tolerance and understanding. This paradox of how to tolerate what one does not value is the central difficulty in dealing with diversity in all its forms.

Exploring Bias and Equity

One of the most stimulating aspects of teaching is the constant requirement to make immediate decisions without adequate information. When John, Ralph, and Tom disrupt the class and force the teacher to spend an inordinate amount of time redirecting their behavior, the teacher rarely has the time to calculate gender equity regarding teacher attention. However, if teachers do not consistently attend to demanding, nonproductive behavior in the class, how can a proactive learning environment be established? The difficulty in eliminating potentially harmful differential treatments and promoting differential treatment that positively recognizes student diversity is generally underestimated. In fact, the concept, at least at first, seems quite contradictory. To clarify the intent of diversity awareness and tolerance, the concepts of bias and equity need to be developed.

Bias results when inappropriate judgments are made about an individual or group that have potentially negative outcomes by creating some type of favoritism. That is, judgments are not made on the basis of facts and evidence but by a predisposition to assist or discourage individuals to possess a certain trait. When these judgments are systematically used to make decisions, they form a core of activity that has become known as *discrimination*. Although discrimination may favor one group over another, it is usually considered to be negative because one of the groups is placed at a deliberate disadvantage. *Equity* results when differences are recognized and differential treatments then devised to accommodate special needs of certain groups so that they can obtain equal access to opportunity and success.

Differential treatment that attempts to maximize the positive opportunity regardless of diversity is considered *accommodation*. This differential treatment is not meant to create a deliberate disadvantage to others. It is designed to minimize the effects of a potential disadvantage that previously existed for an individual or groups of individuals.

This taxonomy makes sense except that, in practice, the terms frequently become entangled. When does accommodation become reverse discrimination? What separates bias from personal preference, individual expression, and self-determination? As you work on the following problems, remember that all of your solutions can be multidimensional.

1. In a group, propose the following scenarios using a note taker to record responses. At the end of the activities, try to determine what you think is the

best policy on differential or equal treatment between boys and girls. Attempt to apply that policy to other identified differences among children.

- Imagine a teacher who consistently demonstrates each of the differential treatments outlined in Figure 3.3. What beliefs does the teacher hold about boys and girls?
- Next, imagine a teacher who consistently provides complete equality in all treatments of boys and girls. What beliefs does the teacher hold about boys and girls?
- Imagine a teacher who genuinely wants to provide complete equality consistently but has several boys who regularly show aggressive behaviors toward the other children. How does the teacher prevent the behaviors outlined in Figure 3.3?
- Imagine a teacher who genuinely wants to provide complete equality consistently but has several girls who regularly show aggressive behaviors toward the other children. How does the teacher prevent the behaviors outlined in Figure 3.3?
- Finally, imagine a teacher who wants all children to be treated fairly. The teacher realizes that the students vary greatly and has noted that there are differences between boys and girls in his fifth-grade class. The teacher consistently argues that puberty does not treat boys and girls alike and bases his opinion on evidence that puberty occurs earlier in girls than boys. The teacher also believes that puberty affects student behavior. What basic tenets should this teacher try to establish to guide teacher decision making?

2. Interview a group of boys and girls and ask them to describe "boy behaviors" and "girl behaviors" that they see in school. Ask them if the teacher treats boys and girls differently and, if so, how they are treated differently. Also ask how they want to be treated. Compare the responses from boys and girls. Share your results with others and attempt to create generalizations about how boys and girls view themselves and the opposite gender.

These two activities demonstrate that simply treating children the same does not hold up under scrutiny as a way of avoiding bias and prejudice. Equally evident is the dilemma that treating children the same is, when effects are considered, treating them inequitably. With so many questions raised about differential treatment on the basis of gender when the children are of like culture, it is easy to appreciate how many more questions must be addressed when race, culture, ethnic affiliation, religion, and regional differences intermingle. When intellect, personal preferences, learning style, and personality are included, the consideration of any systematic appropriate treatment of unlike children becomes intensely complex—if not mind boggling. Are there ways to accommodate student diversity with such a startling array of perceptions, values, and outlooks? Fortunately, there are two situations that salvage the teacher's sanity:

- Children are very resilient and respond positively to many different treatments.
- The values that unite children in a classroom are almost always much stronger than those that divide.

The teacher's job is to recognize teacher and student activity that assists children to achieve academic and social goals. Some of the most critical and difficult tasks for a teacher are learning to identify, recognize, nurture, and constantly model those values that unify children and promote their well-being.

Accommodating the Diverse Needs of Children in School

To accommodate the varying needs of the children in elementary classrooms, begin asking yourself the following questions to develop your self-awareness and introspection.

Do I Give Encouragement to All Students?

It has been repeatedly shown that teachers provide more encouragement to some children than others. Children who are perceived by teachers as "working hard" or "trying" often receive encouragement for their efforts even if they are not successful. Students who fail and who are not perceived as using their talents are often reprimanded for poor performance and encouragement is withheld. Generally, whenever a student is having difficulty, encouraging words and guided suggestions for improvement are needed.

Do I Send Messages of Low Expectations?

It seems unthinkable that a teacher sends messages to children implying that they are incapable of completing an activity successfully. However, acts of kindness often go astray. In working with a child, a teacher may attempt to reduce the performance anxiety by telling the child, "I don't expect you to get all of these right, but try to do what you can." Even subtler is the rationalization for "excuse making" that teachers use when children have certain difficulties. For example, a group of teachers were very defensive about the performance of their children on a standardized test. Their immediate defense was, "These children don't have a chance. They can never be expected to do what others do." Because of the widespread expectation that the children would perform poorly on all academic work, these teachers had built a curriculum that deemphasized critical analysis and higher-order cognitive skills. No wonder the children performed poorly on these skills. They were not given the opportunity to learn what they needed to succeed.

Do I Provide Tutoring and Special Individual Assistance to All Students?

It is a common belief that those in need of tutoring are those who have the most difficulty learning. Some teachers, therefore, spend an inordinate amount of time working with children who consistently have difficulty. As appropriate as this may seem, other children also need the teacher's attention. Many activities, such as creative writing, provide opportunities to tutor the most academically skilled child. This tutoring provides support, displays teacher interest, and offers the opportunity for the teacher to challenge the bright student. This challenge also provides the student with some understanding of the experience and effort that children who are not as academically gifted must expend to learn even the simplest of activities. Likewise, teachers may inadvertently withhold assistance to a child who has difficulty learning because of the implicit belief that the extra assistance will not make a difference. In general, all students need teacher attention regardless of academic performance.

Do All of My Students Participate in All Class Activities?

Just as teachers may concentrate tutoring time on slow learners, they also tend to provide high achievers an inordinate opportunity to participate in class activities such as plays or classroom discussions. The reasons for providing all students appropriate activity time in discussions or class projects are very similar to the reasons for providing quick learners with tutoring activities. The learning needs of all children include the need for challenge and the need for expression and appreciation.

Do I Give Opportunities for Children to Try Many Different Types of Activities?

Variety in instructional activities is necessary for children to grow optimally even if one strategy is most effective for a particular student. For example, children with difficulty in learning are very likely to profit most from activities involving mastery learning. However, every child needs extensive experience and involvement in the use of high-level cognitive activity and creativity. Gender differences may stimulate differential behavior from teachers if boys and girls are limited to specific tasks by gender association. Boys, for example, tend to be asked more questions and receive more feedback than girls do. Girls may be assigned cleaning tasks, whereas boys carry and move furniture as part of classroom maintenance chores. Teachers must always be aware of these possibilities.

Do I Respond to All Students Enthusiastically?

Each child, regardless of differences, wants to belong and to be recognized as valuable and capable. Many teachers (particularly in middle schools where children rotate teachers by subject) greet children as they enter the classroom. This enthusiasm about learning can be contagious. Smiles, encouragement, and expressions of appreciation all add to enthusiasm. Likewise, showing interest in the day's study topic, explaining the relevance of the topic to their lives, and sharing personal experiences about the subject provide an inviting environment for students.

Do I Have a Plan with Resolve?

There is nothing magical or esoteric about treating children who differ in culture, race, and ability in ways that promote learning and self-growth. It does, however, take resolve to maintain a classroom that recognizes and communicates the importance of each child and his or her learning success. Teachers who implement changes in the classroom do so most successfully with simple plans that focus the teacher's thoughts and activities on the transformation of the learning environment. Simple plans start with a statement or goal, followed by a directive statement that provides guidance and suggestions for activity. A teacher received the following plan for teaching in a workshop. It identifies an appropriate goal for all teachers: effective communication about learning. The statements are simple, "do-able," and self-evident. If kept where the teacher can see them every day, these short reminders can make the difference in helping the teacher to remember important strategies for daily use. Over the years, the author has written these on dozens of cards, carried them in his wallet, and read them frequently until the contents have been thoroughly integrated into his daily teaching activity.

*My Plan: Communicate to each child about his
or her learning success and improvement*
1. When the child learns successfully, ask the child, "Why?"
2. When a child has difficulty learning, ask the child, "Why?"
3. Keep notes about the learning successes and difficulties of each individual child
4. Give children choices.
5. Use a variety of approaches for each subject, each day, and each lesson.
6. Help children to recognize how they learn best and what is required in learning successfully.
7. Always keep in mind the purpose of each lesson and what is truly important.
8. When you don't understand why a child does behave in a particular way or has a certain concept, ask the child.
9. Don't overgeneralize based on assumptions and experiences with cultural or racial membership.
10. Acknowledge the child's differences by being as tolerant and accepting as possible

Do I Provide Role Models?

Children learn by watching others. It is a primary way of learning that has endured the total evolutionary history of humans. Children see, analyze, and construct beliefs about what they see. If what they see is different from what they are told, children naturally invoke the old adage, "Seeing is believing." The people to whom children look for guidance on how to act, look, and behave are role models. Role models can provide examples of desirable behavior more readily if there are overt characteristics similar to the child, thus promoting and assisting the child's identification with the model. Teachers should point out the goodness in others. This includes everyone in the school: students, faculty, and staff. Bring visitors into the classroom. Parents, grandparents, friends, businesses, and school neighbors can help in a variety of ways. One message is always special, "I am here; you are important."

Am I Developing My School's Community?

Schools traditionally exist within communities and are usually expressions of community values and norms of behavior. To develop schools, teachers often find that they are expected to assist the community in dealing with persistent social problems. Diaz (1992), writing for the National Education Association, identified the following seven areas of consideration in developing a multicultural school community:

◆ School community dialog
◆ High expectations
◆ Parent/community involvement
◆ Teacher involvement in decision making
◆ Effective leadership of the principal
◆ Focus on developmental and social skills
◆ Regular monitoring of student progress and reinforcement of success

Not surprisingly, the characteristics of schools in multiethnic areas strongly reflect the characteristics of successful schools at large. In developing the school community, parents, teachers, administrators, and children must engage in lengthy discussions about what is important in the school curriculum, how to organize the school structure to serve the children, how to assess learning progress and current needs, and why it is continually necessary to reconsider the educational purposes of the school. Such activity does not happen by accident; all teachers in the school must nurture it. The first hurdle in developing these school building activities is to initiate the dialog for improvement.

This dialog begins by establishing the belief within the school community that each child has both the ability and the opportunity to succeed. Teachers must constantly encourage students and recognize their successes. In turn, the principal and parents must recognize teachers for their contributions. This vision of success and recognition has to permeate all areas of school.

Parents are participating partners in schools and must be given the opportunity to voice their opinions about how the school can assess its achievements. Teachers must be involved in the decision-making process and work with parents to develop solutions to mutually troubling problems within the school environment. The principal is a key leader in guiding and directing the collective effort of the learning community. However, teachers can begin the process in their classrooms by providing students with opportunities to discuss learning, giving them some say in what learning strategies are employed, and recognizing by their words and actions the students' daily contributions and accomplishments.

Do I Look for New Ways to Use Resources?

Many plans for school and classroom improvement are predicated on the assumption that new and additional resources are needed. However, most successful classroom enhancement plans start with existing resources and then use them in new, more effective ways. For example, when a large number of students with minimal

English proficiency are enrolled in the school, it is often considered necessary to allocate additional resources such as special teachers, lower class loads, or additional help from parent volunteers so that more individualized instruction can be provided. All too often these resources are not provided or may take months to obtain. Figure 3.4 is a list that one teacher developed for using existing resources and the natural social tendencies of children to provide supplemental resources for bilingual children who need assistance.

By assigning children as helpmates to other children for various activities, this teacher ingeniously accomplished a multitude of goals. First, by spreading the assistance among many children, the burden on one child is minimized, and another learning hurdle is not created in the attempt to alleviate one. Second, each child is likely to have a skill in at least one of these areas, thus making it possible for all children to make an additional contribution. Third, by having so many different children assist, the socialization and enculturational opportunities for the bilingual student are maximized. Teachers who make plans to use resources in creative ways often find that, besides ameliorating the initial problem, a plethora of additional benefits are derived.

Am I Developing My "People Skills"?

People skills are those traits and behaviors that enable an individual to work and communicate effectively with a large number of people. Some of the most important teaching skills are people skills. However, sometimes too much emphasis in teaching is on being understood and too little, if any, on understanding others. Figure 3.5 lists some strategies for promoting tolerance, which ties in with the plan discussed before for using short statements that guide toward stated goals.

Desk Mate: Sits beside and assists the second-language child with finding materials, books, and page numbers; helps the student during fire drills and to learn how to get around in the building.

Playground Mate: Plays with non–English-speaking child to explain games and rules, sees that the child knows safety rules, facilitates meeting new children.

Bus Mate: Helps the new child navigate the bus ride to and from school, both in behavior and timing.

Cafeteria Mate: Helps the child navigate the school lunch line, introduces new foods and eating procedures, helps avoid isolation.

Academic Mates: Help child during different academic activities; use a different student for each type of activity to increase the child's integration into the class.

FIGURE 3.4   Strategies for working with second-language learners: Providing language mates.

Adapted from "Language Mates" by M. T. Everett, 1991. *Learning 91, 20*(4), 52.

- Examine your own views carefully: What things invoke intolerance from you, why, and how do you express it?
- Show an interest in the uniqueness of your students.
- Share your feelings about your own differences and experiences with gaining acceptance.
- Show videos that illustrate the lifestyles of the world's people; discuss what it must be like to live that way.
- Read many different stories to the class, choosing a variety of characters and regions.
- Model patience, fairness, and compassion when children do things you don't like; deal with the errors but minimize the negative messages sent to the child.
- Ask children to share experiences that made them feel small or unworthy; ask them to share other more positive experiences.
- Ask children to share why they are sometimes hurtful to others; have the class develop strategies that are more productive.

FIGURE 3.5 Strategies for increasing tolerance, understanding, and core values.

People skills are learned primarily by practice and by focusing on the needs, values, and communication strategies of others. Developing people skills requires consistent attention and a reflective disposition, but the results are worth the effort.

Am I Willing to Make Programmatic Change?

American businesses are slowly turning toward customer-driven policies in managing both manufacturing and marketing activities. In considering the needs of customers, companies have found that workers often fail to provide the best possible service simply because company policies prevent it. Careful studies have consistently revealed that a strong majority of workplace errors are a result of the system in which workers function, not in the actual activities of the workers. Schools and classrooms often need to reexamine program policies and implementation strategies with an attitude of change and enhancement.

For example, many believe that the dropout problem in public schools exists because the students and their families fail to take education seriously and do not have a work ethic that provides teachers with prerequisite opportunities for teaching. Unquestionably, this has a ring of truth about it. However, it does not solve the problem. Nevares (1992) examined programmatic changes and isolated the following nine elements of a successful dropout prevention program for working with at-risk youth:

- Maintaining a low student-teacher ratio
- Providing positive physical and mental environments
- Providing well-understood policies and procedures that foster a quiet, no-nonsense atmosphere
- Providing an appropriate curriculum

◆ Establishing attendance incentives
◆ Encouraging student progress by involving all of the child's teachers
◆ Keeping parents well informed
◆ Building bridges with the community
◆ Using ancillary support staff (particularly counselors) effectively

Certainly, schools and their teachers can make a positive influence on all children.

When only seeing the deficiencies of their system, teachers start to develop a sense of helplessness so that improvements are rarely made. By looking at solutions within the programs and policies, however, teachers start to realize that they do have influence in improving the situation. They then find that changes, both in themselves and in their children, can be greatly facilitated.

Am I Being Practical?

Accommodating student differences need not require singling out a student. Careful, thoughtful planning can yield many practical modifications in the classroom to accommodate special needs students while enhancing the classroom for all. For example, Tanner-Halverson (1994) suggests numerous strategies for adapting the classroom environment so that the needs of children suffering from fetal alcohol syndrome or fetal alcohol effects (FAS/FAE) are better met. FAS/FAE children typically have lowered intelligence levels, are prone to hyperactivity and attention deficit disorders, and have marked tendencies toward being impulsive in calculating consequences to their actions. Tanner-Halverson recommends a careful structuring of the classroom so that it provides a consistent environment for these children but does not require rapid adjustment to new demands. Teachers help these students when they provide overt or physical definitions to limits. The teacher can provide physical boundaries for children in interest or activity centers by assigning meaning to the edges of rugs or bookcases. By using instructional devices that permit and encourage concrete experiences using color, shape, and image cues along with words, children can work on the learning task longer with fewer diversions.

The teacher can arrange the classroom physical environment into many different types of areas for study so that the differences in tasks are matched to the work space. For example, study carrels can be constructed from routine desks by using appliance boxes. Students can be supplied individual desks instead of more communal (and distracting) tables and chairs. Conversely, tables can be supplied for children who work least efficiently, thus providing them with increased opportunity to share and interact by having learning neighbors.

In governing participation and group activity, concrete kinesthetic devices can be used to provide clear signals about what is permitted. For example, a toy or puppet can be passed around to indicate whose turn it is to talk or participate. A chart that indicates who gets to be "helper" or "captain" for a particular activity can be posted so that children can clearly see that soon they will also get a turn.

Some activities appropriate for FAS/FAE children, however, can be disastrous if consistently applied to other children, particularly the gifted. Whereas FAS/FAE children need lots of repetition and unchanging environments, gifted children thrive on novelty and change. Whereas clear expectations and clearly defined tasks are usually indicated for most children, gifted children must be supplied with ambiguous, challenging situations on a recurring basis if they are to find school interesting and their intellectual skills appropriately developed. The practical solution is simply to provide many activities and avenues to learning similar content. Such adaptation takes additional teacher time and can be difficult to implement. However, if a learning environment that accommodates a wide variety of student needs and differences is not provided, more problems are invariably caused than if a proactive, diligent attempt is made to provide all children with success opportunities.

Small, practical accommodations to student differences send one message that is at the center of the diversity and tolerance issue: "I care about you, about your success, about your comfort, and about your well-being, and I will make changes to see that you succeed." This message, more than any other, fuels the advancement of learning for children in America and underlies the national debate on diversity, opportunity, and education.

A Slice of Life: Mr. O'Connell's Resolution

"Boy, you're in trouble now! You hit a girl!" shouted Steve and added to Liu admiringly, "She sure deserved it, though!" Most children said that they had seen the "whole" thing.

Mr. O'Connell established order and sent all the children back to their seats. Next, he sat Tomeka and Liu on either side of his desk and said with an unusually stern tone, "Now sit there, and don't move a muscle."

Mr. O'Connell was quite angry at the outburst. He did not condone that type of behavior and had taken great care that the children knew that. He even had a "time-out" corner for students to go when they were mad. There, no one could bother you or even talk to you. It was a haven where students could go when they had had enough; it was actually the most comfortable spot in the whole room.

Liu and Tomeka stared hatefully at one another. It was this glaring anger that bothered Mr. O'Connell most. Obviously, this dislike for one another had not just developed during a social studies discussion. Yet, he had been totally unaware of any tension in this class. "All good things come to an end," he thought privately. "Or had they?"

Mr. O'Connell decided that he would have each child write down what they saw and knew about the conflict between Liu and Tomeka. Liu and Tomeka were asked to write their sides of the story, too. It gave Mr. O'Connell some time to think and, especially, some time to calm down. He was quite angry with them, but he was also very surprised. Liu and Tomeka were among his best students; neither had ever caused any problems. The only thing he could think of was to send them both to the principal to be sent home.

Instead, he opted for a breather and cooling-off period. Lunchtime was next, and he would read the accounts of the fight then. After lunch, he would attempt to sort it out. This was a new experience for him. He had sorted out fights among boys and even among a few girls during his first three years of teaching. This was the first one between a boy and a girl. "Eleven-year-old boys," he thought, "ought to know better." He shrugged at himself. "Now I'm stereotyping. Why does it have to be so difficult?"

When Mr. O'Connell read the papers, he was surprised. Several papers had recorded events of name calling and taunting between the two students as far back as the end of last year when Liu first arrived at the school. About half the papers claimed that Tomeka was justified in hitting Liu first because he had called her a name. About half the class claimed that Tomeka deserved to be hit because she hit Liu with a book on the head "real hard" when Liu wasn't looking. What really bothered Mr. O'Connell was that the boys seemed to side with Liu; the girls, with Tomeka. "Oh, brother," thought Mr. O'Connell, "what do I do now?"

Fortunately for Liu, Tomeka, and the rest of the children in the class, Mr. O'Connell was an exceptional teacher. Instead of viewing the situation as a "class divided," he wisely chose to emphasize those aspects of people with which they identified and how those traits help to form supportive groups. Mr. O'Connell had no problem with the children identifying with others of the same gender backgrounds, but not at the expense of important commonly shared values. What Mr. O'Connell chose to discuss that afternoon was the concept of fairness and what fairness requires of us. What he got was a surprise and a lesson in life.

Mr. O'Connell decided to have a class meeting. He framed the meeting with a short and simple statement that each child in the classroom was different from the others. He noted how some of these differences made children popular and some made children mad. He then asked children about the differences that made students popular. The children readily supplied many examples of differences saying that some were funny, good at sports, and pretty (which made some giggle and others turn red). Differences that made children unpopular had to do with dress, speech, music preferences, grades, and their treatment of others. Mr. O'Connell then simply asked Liu and Tomeka if they would mind if he asked each to share why they were angry and disliked the other. He was ready to talk about gender but was thwarted by what he heard.

Liu volunteered to go first. He pronounced that Tomeka's mom didn't like him and his family and didn't want other people coming to America to live. Mr. O'Connell then remembered that Tomeka's mother was a caseworker at Immigration and Naturalization Service (INS). What he didn't know was that Tomeka's mom just happened to be the caseworker for Liu's father's attempt to bring his aunts and uncles to the U.S. Tomeka was almost in tears. With a loud "Not true!" she explained that there were laws and rules and that her mother couldn't just decide to let people come or keep them out just because she liked or didn't like them. Tomeka was tired of the hassle that she had been getting from Liu.

Mr. O'Connell concluded rather quickly that this was a more personal matter, stopped the testimony, and quickly began to focus the children on ways to look at ourselves as others might see us. After class, he asked Liu and Tomeka if it was all right if he had their parents come in for a conference. He explained that he wasn't angry at them and commented that the students were trying to deal with problems that grownups hadn't yet solved. He even complimented them for regaining their composure so quickly after the little fight.

The conference was tense when Liu's father and Tomeka's mother discovered that not only were they living in the same community, but also that their children were in the same school and the same class. After the children told their sides of the story, Mr. O'Connell smiled and told both parents how difficult the world had become. He then asked them, "What do we do? How can I help?" Liu's father was the first to speak, and he admitted that he had said many derogatory things about the INS and about Tomeka's mom. He had no idea, however, that Liu knew her, much less went to school with her child. He quickly apologized for his comments. Tomeka's mom was gracious and quickly added that her job was often stressful and perhaps she had not been as courteous as she could have been. In a conciliatory offering, she asked Liu's dad to come see her and that they would reexamine the application, but, she added quickly, she didn't want to raise any false hopes. Liu's father was pleased at the offering.

Mr. O'Connell asked both parents to speak to the class about immigration representing the roles of immigration officer and immigrant. They quickly agreed, and the children took careful note of the behavior of their parents. In the following weeks, Liu and Tomeka ended their silent warfare, and both made "A's" on their immigration essays.

◆ ◆ ◆

Summary

1. Diversity issues include a whole gamut of differences among individuals and groups of individuals.
2. Diversity is closely associated with individual determination and basic rights in American culture.
3. Diversity gives us both identity and isolation.
4. Gender, regional identity, ethnicity, religion, political beliefs, preferences, occupations, economic, and physical differences are all dimensions of diversity.
5. A drive for belonging encourages the formation of groups in which individuals share common beliefs or characteristics.
6. The emotionalism involved in diversity issues should never be underestimated.
7. Some diversity characteristics can be reliably identified; others cannot. Some diversity characteristics are changeable; others are not.
8. Differences in diversity do not easily equate into consistent, predictable differences in the behavior of children.
9. There are no clear or definite ways to classify and analyze student diversity.
10. Teachers must recognize diversity among children but must avoid overgeneralization and stereotypes.

11. Many diversity issues must be accommodated. Other diversity issues are individual choices and need no accommodation. Distinguishing between the two can be difficult.
12. Attitudes, beliefs, culture, and values offer some of the most challenging areas of diversity for the teacher to accommodate helpfully.
13. Cultural characteristics can easily become stereotypes. The individual must be central to any attempt to deal successfully with diversity in the classroom.
14. The contribution of diversity issues to learning success or failure is difficult to isolate. However, ample evidence exists to demonstrate that diversity issues can affect a child's education.
15. Accommodation to diversity can have unanticipated results that teachers must recognize so that they can deal with the negative influences effectively.
16. Awareness and introspection are primary entering strategies for successful accommodation of student diversity.
17. Making a plan for communication with students and parents increases the likelihood that effective communication takes place.
18. Providing role models with which children can identify is an important accommodation.
19. Effective schoolwide accommodations for diversity issues involve the community in meaningful ways.
20. Using resources in new ways often precedes, and sometimes supersedes, the acquisition of new resources in accommodation activities of the school.
21. "People skills" are essential in establishing the respect and value of all children in school.
22. Some accommodations require substantive programmatic changes.
23. Being practical and earnest about diversity issues often yield direct and effective solutions.

◆ ◆ ◆

Activities and Questions for Further Understanding

1. Reread "A Slice of Life" and Mr. O'Connell's dilemma. What other courses of action could he have taken? What if the parents were not cooperative but instead were adamant and intolerant? What should Mr. O'Connell do next?
2. Describe the type of home life that you experienced as a child. Compare your description with others in your class. What differences in childhood experiences could result in differences in attitude and perspective?
3. Search the juvenile section of the library to find books from differing cultures on the following themes:
   a. Childhood disobedience
   b. Death
   c. School activities
   d. Friendship
4. Locate several comparisons of ethnic groups such as the one discussed in this chapter. Evaluate your perception of the accuracy of the descriptions. Compare your assessment to others in your class. What differences are found? What is the source of differing interpretations?

◆ ◆ ◆

References

AAUW (American Association of University Women). (1992). *How schools shortchange girls*. Washington, DC: AAUW Educational Foundation.

Banks, J. A. (1995). "Multicultural education: Historical development, dimensions, and practice." In J. A. Banks & C. A. M. Banks (Eds.), *Handbook of research on multicultural education*. New York: Macmillan.

Byrne, E. (1975). *Women and education*. London: Tavistock.

Campbell-Whatley, G. D. (1993). *Multicultural education module*. (ERIC ED 364–497)

Clarricoats, K. (1980). "The importance of being Earnest . . . Emma . . . Tom . . . Jane: The perception and categorization of gender conformity and gender deviation in primary schools." In R. Deem (Ed.), *School for women's work*. London: Routledge Kegan Paul.

Comer, J. P. (1988). "Educating poor minority children." *Scientific American, 259*(5), 42–48.

Conner, W. (1978). "A nation is a nation, is a state, is an ethnic group, is a. . . . " *Ethnic and Racial Studies, 1,* 377–400.

de Tocqueville, Alexis. (1966). "Democracy in America." In J. P. Mayer & Max Lerner (Eds.), *Democracy in America: A new translation by George Lawrence*. New York: Harper and Row.

Delmont, S. (1980). *Sex role and the school*. London: Methuen.

Diaz, Carlos (Ed.). (1992). *Multicultural education for the 21st century*. Washington: National Education Association.

Dreikurs, R., & Cassel, P. (1972). *Discipline without tears: What to do with children who misbehave*. New York: Hawthorn Books.

Everett, M. T. (1991). "Language Mates." *Learning 91, 20*(4), 52.

Garcia, R. L. (1992). "Cultural diversity and minority rights: A consummation devoutly to be demurred." In J. Lynch, C. Modal, & S. Modal, *Cultural diversity and the schools* (Vol. 4, pp. 103–120). London: The Falmer Press.

Ginott, H. (1972). *Teacher and child*. New York: Macmillan.

Glasser, W. (1986). *Control theory in the classroom*. New York: Harper & Row.

Heath, S. B., & McLaughlin, M. W. (1993). *Identity and inner-city youth: Beyond ethnicity and gender*. New York: Teachers College Press.

Kidder, T. (1989). *Among schoolchildren*. Boston: Houghton Mifflin.

Levin, H. M. (1988). "Accelerating elementary education for disadvantaged students." In Council of Chief State School Officers (Eds.), *School success for students at risk* (pp. 209–226). Orlando, FL: Harcourt Brace and Jovanovich.

Magliaro, S. G. (1992). "Multicultural education: An intellectual and emotional debate." *Teaching and Teacher Education: AERA Division K Newsletter,* Spring 1992, Vol. 6.

Nevares, L. (1992). "Credit where credit is due." *The Executive Educator.* December 1992, pp. 50–53.

Oregon State University. (1987). *Eliminating sexism in the classroom*. (ERIC Document ED 286 393)

Pang, Valerie O. (1992). "Institutional climate: Developing an effective multicultural school community." In Carlos Diaz (Ed.), *Multicultural education for the 21st century* (pp. 57–71). Washington, DC: National Education Association.

Sadker, D., & Sadker, M. (1994). *Failing at fairness: How America's schools cheat girls*. New York: Charles Scribner's Sons.

Sewell, Thomas. (1994). "Multicultural charade." *Forbes,* March 28, p. 54.

Spencer, J. M., & Barth, J. L. (1991). "Standing on uncommon ground." *Social Education,* April/May, pp. 212–215.

Stanworth, M. (1983). *Gender and schooling*. London: Hutchinson.

Tanner-Halverson, Patricia. (1994). "Classroom tips: Let's get practical." *NEA Today,* March, p. 17.

CHAPTER 4

How Do I Get the Children to Work with Me?

Managing Student Behavior

Outline

In true listening, we reach behind the words, see through them, to find the person who is being revealed.

J. POWELL

It was worth it!

TIMMY, 10, TOLD HE MUST STAY AFTER SCHOOL FOR A WEEK FOR HITTING ANOTHER STUDENT

◆

A Slice of Life

Mrs. Evans rubbed her temples. She had a headache, a bad one. "Must be allergies," she thought to herself. It was early spring, and the children were restless so she had planned carefully to account for it. She had helped all the children in her fifth-grade class find a book just for them and had developed a series of reading, sharing, and creative activities based on their books. Some children were already writing screenplays for skits and making movie posters. Now, they were listening to nine of the most reluctant readers in the class.

Mrs. Evans heard Stacie falter. Over Stacie's shoulder, Mrs. Evans spotted Stacie's finger on the word. This was part of a routine taught long ago at the beginning of the school year. When students were reading aloud, she told them that if they needed help with a word, they should put a finger on it and try to sound out the first sounds. She then would cue in on the repetition. "Muh, muh. . . . " Mrs. Evans encouraged while looking at Stacie although Stacie didn't look back. She was struggling with a word that refused to give up its secret. The others ignored both Stacie and Mrs. Evans. They were wrapped up in their own reading.

Stacie picked up the clue. "Muh-chet, Muh-chet-tee," she chattered. Stacie looked up confused. "That doesn't make sense!"

"Good go, very close," Mrs. Evans smiled approvingly. "Muh-shet-tee. It's a long knife for cutting brush."

"Oh, OK." Stacie went back to her reading. Mrs. Evans had somewhat of a reputation among the children. She could listen to a third of the class reading aloud at
the same time and just somehow know what was going on. They had gotten used to
it. She seemed to know everything that went on in the class. Even when the children
thought they had gotten away with passing a note or whispering behind her back,
Mrs. Evans always seemed to know anyway. During recess or between lessons, she
would come up to a child's desk with a kind and understanding voice. "I know
that you think it's very important to talk to Jeannie or you wouldn't have bothered
to write the note. But during lessons, we should be doing lessons." She would smile,
and the child would look at her with a mixture of thankfulness, irritation, and
wonder.

"Juan, there are pencils with erasers in the pencil pot. You might find it easier."
Mrs. Evans had watched Juan trying to correct his drawing, but he had less than a
fraction of an eraser. Juan smiled as if to say, "Geez, I knew that." He quickly went
to a shelf that held a vase with over a hundred pencils. He poked around, found
one he liked, grabbed it, and returned to erase furiously. Mrs. Evan wasn't watching Juan, though. Stacie was telling Millie about the machete and cutting through a
jungle full of bugs and spiders. Mrs. Evans listened. She said nothing and looked
around the room one more time. Thump, thump, thump went her throbbing head.
But even with the pain, Mrs. Evans smiled inside. Stacie was really into that book.
Great! She hadn't wanted to do anything at the beginning of the year. "Three minutes to go." Mrs. Evans announced.

Most children ignored the notice. Some, however, wanted to reach a stopping
place in their projects, and a ripple of quiet determination and activity passed
through the class. Mrs. Evans began to circulate through the class handing out a
note-taking guide for the video that the children were going to see in the next lesson. "Time!" Mrs. Evans said aloud. "Who wants to tell about a sad thing in their
book?" Several children volunteered. Mrs. Evans called on Stacie as she looked
about the room at the volunteers.

Stacie immediately launched into how the machete was used to cut the flowers
around the campsite. Mrs. Evans inquired, "Class, what is sad about cutting a
flower?" Mrs. Evans again scanned the room. "Raoul?" Raoul was still reading his
book and looked startled. Mrs. Evans repeated the question, "Stacie thinks it is sad
that the flowers around the campsite were cut. Why would cutting flowers be sad?"
Raoul thought about the question. "I guess because they can't grow anymore?"

Mrs. Evans looked at Stacie. "Is that it?" Stacie said that it was more than that.
The cut flowers couldn't grow seeds so the baby plants never happen. Mrs. Evans
smiled and nodded. "Anyone have something exciting happen in their book?" She
looked at Raoul, and he was paying attention now. Mrs. Evans, however, called on
someone else but seemed to have a smile for everyone. This sharing continued for
five minutes, and Mrs. Evans encouraged the class. "It seems the books are a hit! I
can't wait to see your projects. Tomorrow I'll ask you to write down your ideas
about what you would like to do, so think carefully. Now, it's time to watch the
video that I promised. Juan, do you remember what I said the topic would be?"

Order and Responsibility

Often more worrisome than what to teach and how to teach it, harnessing and controlling the activity of 20 to 30 bright, active, and eager children is viewed as a near-monumental task. One of the greatest concerns among both teachers and parents is managing student behavior in the classroom. Classroom management is too often defined as the manner in which order is established and maintained in the classroom. However, this is only a partial definition. Simply controlling the behavior of children hits the mark far short of the ideal of promoting student responsibility and preparing children for full participation in a democratic society.

Determining the balance between order and responsibility should be a conscious process that is the result of careful and thoughtful analysis of a number of classroom issues. The conclusion reached by the teacher is, in part, a reflection of philosophical underpinnings that define what balance between order and responsibility is appropriate. The beliefs regarding what composes order and responsibility, as well as how to achieve these ideals in the classroom, vary from teacher to teacher. Additionally, the balance of order and responsibility that is established in the classroom can have wide-reaching effects on the success of both the instructional techniques employed and the development of the affective climate surrounding the students (McEwan, 1996). Successful teachers give careful attention to establishing the balance that provides the greatest degree of freedom while still maintaining the order required of an effective learning environment. This balance is not static and requires continual consideration of a number of issues.

What Is Managed?

In general, classroom management focuses on four aspects of classroom life: student behavior, curriculum/instruction, space usage/movement, and the affective climate. Visualize Mr. Hauk, a fifth-grade teacher, sitting at his desk grading math papers. His students have just been given a very competent explanation of multiplication with two digits. Students are now working problems similar to the ones that he had just demonstrated. The verbal disruptions that occur are handled quickly and with stern resolve. The class responds (at least temporarily) by appearing to be more businesslike. An unfortunate but typical paradigm of a well-managed classroom is one in which children are quiet and busily working on today's assignment while the teacher grades yesterday's homework papers. The students are working, the teacher is grading, and disruptions are minimal and handled quickly. However, is learning occurring? Are the children maximizing the benefit of learning time? Are the things that appear to be going on really happening?

Examining this picture a second time reveals some disturbing conclusions about this "ideal" classroom. Is the teacher's activity appropriate? The teacher is working hard to grade yesterday's papers so that students can have them before the end of class. Although this may seem to be a normal and effective practice, a reconsideration demonstrates that Mr. Hauk's efforts are very misplaced. If Mr. Hauk's lesson for today was building on the skills being developed by yesterday's lesson, how does he know those skills were mastered? How does Mr. Hauk know which students had misunderstandings that needed reteaching or additional explanation? Further, does Mr. Hauk have any idea whether the work that the students are doing now is being done properly? It is likely that errors and misunderstandings are being repeated and practiced that will not come to light until the end of the lesson tomorrow. Meanwhile, an opportunity for reteaching today has been lost.

Order in the classroom is only a byproduct of attempts to obtain more meaningful and educationally applicable goals (Schimmel, 1997). Among those basic principles are the following:

- Providing physically and psychologically safe environments for children
- Maximizing their opportunity to learn
- Obtaining cooperation in realizing central classroom goals surrounding learning
- Minimizing the time used in transitions and in completing nonacademic tasks
- Maximizing student responsibility for self-control and for learning
- Minimizing the degree of adult control necessary to maintain order

Mr. Hauk, by focusing on too few of the required management tasks, lost learning opportunity, learning efficiency, and opportunities for developing responsibility.

Dimensions of the Classroom

Doyle (1986) identified five dimensions of a classroom setting that must be managed successfully: multidimensionality, simultaneity, immediacy, history, and an unpredictable/public classroom climate.

Multidimensionality

Many different tasks and events exist in the classroom. Further, any single event may have multiple consequences. This is called *multidimensionality*. In Mr. Hauk's class, for example, it appeared that students were computing math problems. However, closer examination would reveal that many students were also doing other things. Some may have been writing notes, someone else may have been doing homework for another subject, and still another student may have been drawing or reading from a library book. These unsanctioned activities occur regularly in the classroom as a matter of course.

As well as unsanctioned activity, classrooms typically have several sanctioned activities for working toward the same objective. These activities should be the ones occupying student effort. Conversely, students sometimes perform identical tasks but for widely varying reasons. For example, in Mr. Hauk's class, it was possible for two students to be out of the class for special lessons, several students could have finished quickly and were now at the computer center working on a book project, while still another student was quietly doing advanced lessons from a programmed learning kit.

Multidimensionality also suggests that even the same activity can be many different things to different students. For some students, the math activity was routine review and practice. For others, however, the lesson presented great challenges. For example, at least one student may have decided that he or she could not possibly learn this skill and essentially quit trying. Even simple classroom occurrences such as Mr. Hauk's reminder to three students to get back on task can have many different meanings. One student may not even have cared about Mr. Hauk's rebuke, whereas another was crushed because he felt unfairly singled out among many who were being disruptive. The third student was infuriated at Mr. Hauk's unfairness because she was not even involved in the disruption. Mr. Hauk had caught the wrong person. Without an understanding and ability to deal with the complexity in the classroom, teachers cannot manage effectively because they do not have accurate information about what is occurring.

Simultaneity

Many different classroom events happen at the same time. This is called *simultaneity*. In Mr. Hauk's class, some children were angry and preoccupied with feelings of resentment, some were engaged in the lesson, some were working on a lesson at an interest center, and some were worried or confused by the disruptive events. All were experiencing these events simultaneously. Mr. Hauk, to understand the classroom activity, must be able not only to identify many different activities but also to process information about many events at the same time.

Attending to many simultaneous events and tasks always presents a challenge for teachers. Novice teachers may be so focused on presenting the planned lesson that they do not notice student reactions or unsanctioned activities. Attending to the classroom's simultaneity is a critical skill to master. However, making a concerted effort at being aware of classroom events may be one of the best avenues for growth in effectiveness for all teachers. Good and Brophy (1994) argue that being aware of classroom events and reacting to them is essential for teacher growth in decision-making effectiveness. Quality instruction is greatly affected by teacher awareness and comprehension of the complexity involved in the social and intellectual structure of the classroom.

Immediacy

The pace of classroom events can be rapid, and a sharp staccato of major classroom events makes quick teacher action a necessity. Put more simply, when children want something, they typically want it *now*. This is called *immediacy*. Teachers are given little time to respond to most classroom events.

In Mr. Hauk's classroom, students who need help come to him at his desk. While Mr. Hauk is helping a student, other children often request assistance. Although these children may appear to wait patiently, they are really simply doing nothing as they await Mr. Hauk's attention. If they are allowed to line up at Mr. Hauk's desk, others are inspired to seek assistance, line up, and also stop working until Mr. Hauk assists them. Students are exploiting Mr. Hauk's inability to deal with immediacy. They invent a massive time-wasting strategy of standing in line at his desk awaiting their turn to ask an invented question.

If Mr. Hauk hears a disruption in the back, he has little time to investigate if he is helping the waiting students. Worse, by being seated at his desk, he is even more at a disadvantage. The time he spends in moving to the disruption and investigating it results in time that these students are at an impasse in their studies. If he fails to deal with the disruption or does so unsuccessfully, the disruptions can reoccur and worsen, requiring even more time that he must take away from his students. For teachers to be successful managers of student learning and activity, they must develop both strategies and skill in handling many different tasks immediately after their emergence. This requires carefully developed and practiced routines and strategies that minimize the amount of reaction time from the teacher.

Unpredictable and Public Climate

Further eroding the teacher's likelihood of controlling the classroom environment without immediate active involvement is the unpredictability of classroom life. *Unpredictability* describes the classroom as a place where things often happen in ways not expected or intended. Additionally, many other students may see what happens to a student (or to the teacher). Thus, almost all classroom events are public. Some events can be anticipated, but the actual time of the occurrence is unknown. *Foreseeable but unpredictable events* describes situations in which the teacher knows that disruptions are possible, even likely, but does not know when and where the event will occur or who will be involved.

For example, Mr. Hauk can be sure that someone will have difficulty during the seatwork exercise, but he does not know who will be involved or when the help will be needed. Further, when a student needs help, it is almost certain that the other students will know who is having difficulty and who is not. As adults, we take for granted certain degrees of privacy in routine daily living. However, the classroom is decidedly different. Virtually any reprimand, student request, or need is public and likely to be known by everyone in the class. This applies not only to students but also to the teacher. The teacher is always visible, and every action that he or she takes is viewed by most of the children in the class. Teachers who are aware of the unpredictability and public climate of the classroom environment should take care to develop special skills. These include sending subtle signals to individual students, making better use of transitional time, and scheduling private chats during the lunch period to handle personal matters with children.

History

Over time, certain understandings develop as the class meets. After several weeks or months, the classroom develops a history. One important outgrowth of history is the teacher's credibility. *Credibility* is the belief among children that the teacher means what he or she says and says what he or she means. Credibility is simply the believability of the teacher's explanations, promises, requests, or demands.

These understandings influence how classrooms continue to function during the remainder of the year. Evertson, Emmer, Clements, and Worsham (1994) claim that teachers have only a few weeks at the beginning of the school year to establish the rhythm of daily classroom life for the rest of the year. They recommend that students be taught the teacher's expectations and routines during the first weeks of school. Routines are to be practiced and critiqued until they become automatic. Further, rules that are to govern the classroom must be established, taught, and reinforced very early in the school year if major problems are to be minimized or avoided altogether.

How Are Classroom Dimensions Managed Successfully?

A vast variety of effective management strategies and styles exist in public schools today. Kounin (1970) identified a number of teacher traits that appear to be associated with management effectiveness and continue to provide excellent guidance to successful teachers. These behaviors were the result of studying the behavior of teachers and students in hundreds of classrooms. Underlying the effectiveness of teacher behavior was a phenomenon that Kounin called the "ripple effect."

When a teacher responded to a child's misbehavior or activity, Kounin noticed that the teacher's activity affected other children who were not involved in the original incident. For example, if the teacher told Cindi to use better handwriting, other children attended to the message and often improved the handwriting in their work. If the teacher told two children to stop daydreaming and get back to work, other children would start working harder. Recognizing that noninvolved children could be positively (or negatively) affected by teacher actions, Kounin began to focus on teacher behaviors that were common among teachers with classes that were performing well. Kounin examined eight behaviors that seemed to be consistently related to effective classroom management.

"With-itness"

The ability of a teacher to be aware of what is going on in all areas of the classroom and communicate that to the students is called *"with-itness."* Mrs. Evans, in the "Slice of Life" at the beginning of the chapter, provided an excellent example of "with-itness." She was able to listen to reading cues of the children by listening for changes in pace, volume, and rhythm. Further, she was familiar with the children's reading material, both content and vocabulary. This was particularly important to Mrs. Evans when reluctant readers were involved. Mrs. Evans also scanned the room visually, looking for clues about what was happening. She also wandered around the room, listening to her readers and watching the work of the other students. In being "with-it," Mrs. Evans also displayed the next teacher behavior that Kounin felt was essential to effective classroom management.

Overlapping

A teacher's ability to deal with more than one thing at a time is called *overlapping*. Overlapping is simply the ability to manage successfully the simultaneity and immediacy of classroom events. While listening to several readers, Mrs. Evans displayed overlapping behavior. However, Mrs. Evans also attended to the other students in the class. Although she may choose not to deal with the behavior at the moment, Mrs. Evans conveyed to the children that she knew what occurred. Overlapping and "with-itness" are closely associated. Some evidence has demonstrated that both are closely associated with perceptual acuity that is, in part, related to the genetic structure of the teacher (Riner & Jones, 1993). However, for most potential teachers, overlapping and "with-itness" can be developed by employing several strategies. Moving around the classroom, surveying the class using scanning eye movements, and listening attentively are strategies that can lead to high levels of "with-itness." Having routines to take care of mundane tasks, not dwelling on mistakes, and delegating responsibility assist in the development of overlapping behaviors.

Smoothness and Momentum

Smoothness and momentum are characteristics of lessons provided by good managers. *Smoothness* relates to the ability of the teacher to keep the lesson flowing, particularly minimizing the effects of interruptions and the incidence of digressions. *Momentum* is demonstrated by maintaining the lesson pace, constantly building on the major emphasis of the lesson rather than dwelling on a subpoint or student disruption. In switching lessons or tasks within lessons, effective teachers emphasize transitions that minimize disruption as well as the time used to switch activities. Mrs. Evans demonstrated smoothness and momentum when she asked children about the content of their books during the transition between reading and science. By passing out the note-taking guide for the next lesson, she provided time for students to reach convenient stopping places and assistance in switching attention from one lesson to the next.

Group Alerting

The ability of the teacher to maintain the attention and activity of all children is called *group alerting*. Even though a child may not be directly involved in the question or activity that is the current focus of the lesson, successful teachers have devices that signal to the child that attention to the teacher is needed. Getting children to pay attention to the lesson is only part of what is meant by the term. In group alerting, the teacher is able to get the students to anticipate the next step or requirement in an activity. Children not only respond to requests but also look for clues that help them to prepare mentally for the next lesson activity.

Group alerting assists the teacher in building and maintaining smoothness and momentum. Mrs. Evans helped students anticipate the end of the reading lesson by handing out cards. Students, because they were familiar with the strategy, understood the next activity was about to occur and that the activity would require group work. They knew that they would be moving from a solitary to a group activity. Mrs. Evans was reinforcing the requirement that the reading lesson had ended by starting the sharing sessions subsequent to handing out note-taking guides. Likewise, the short question and sharing activity pulled the children together for the introductory part of the next lesson. Group alerting is often a subtle array of teacher/child interactions that are learned and form a part of the classroom's history. Group alerting cues increase with improved teacher consistency as well as the amount of time and experience that children have with recognizing the signals and responding appropriately.

Accountability

The teacher's expectation that all children will engage in activities and assist each other in fulfilling the learning expectations is called *student accountability*. When Mrs. Evans singled out Raoul, she demonstrated that the accountability expectation was not being fulfilled. Note that Mrs. Evans did not attempt to chastise or ridicule Raoul. In fact, by repeating the question, she provided Raoul with the opportunity to fulfill the expectation and regain his attentiveness to the lesson. In this case, Mrs. Evans demonstrated the distinct difference between punitive consequences and holding students accountable. Mrs. Evans was also establishing accountability by assigning each student a specific task in the science lesson, helping to ensure that no one student dominated the lesson activity.

Challenge Arousal

Challenge arousal is the teacher's attempt to establish enthusiasm and involvement in the lesson. Mrs. Evans demonstrated an interest in the selected books and in the children's interpretation of the books even though she did not feel well. According to Kounin, teachers who showed zest and interest in learning had students who also showed zest and interest in learning.

Mrs. Evans carefully cultivated not only the students' behavior but also her own. When Stacie stopped her reading to tell a classmate what was happening in her book, Mrs. Evans deliberately chose not to interrupt and inform Stacie that it was reading time instead of sharing time. Since Stacie was so excited, Mrs. Evans determined that Stacie needed to share and it would promote her future reading as well as the enthusiasm of other students. Previously, Mrs. Evans had discussed appropriate behavior for reading groups and had acknowledged that there were times when you "just had to tell" someone else about the book. Mrs. Evans simply requested that the students keep the discussion short and return to reading appropriately. Mrs. Evans had learned to listen in on the conversations of the children and could almost always tell whether the conversations were on task or not. Maintaining excitement and interest in learning meant providing leeway on the acceptable and unacceptable behaviors of students.

Variety

Variety is the teacher's ability to involve many different learning styles and activities in the daily lesson plan. Variety not only implies the usage of different learning activities among lessons, but also that many different perspectives and learning strategies are used within any lesson period. Mrs. Evans demonstrated a variety of strategies within the short time frame in the "Slice of Life." By allowing students to self-select books and by assisting them in determining various strategies for exploring the book's meaning, Mrs. Evans provided numerous learning paths for each child. Also, in the transition period, she used individual and group learning. Finally, within the next lesson, she planned to employ technology to bring different perspectives and foci for their activity. Variety is important in that it provides several modes of learning so that each child has an opportunity to experience a strategy best suited for them. However, variety is even more important in avoiding satiation. *Satiation* is experienced when repetition of the same stimuli results in decreasing awareness and response from the child. The satiation effect is illustrated by eating a large quantity of ice cream—the first bite generally is better than the last. The use of variety in daily classes is a result of careful and thoughtful planning. With a little reflection and thoughtfulness, variety can be a hallmark of every class.

Purposes of Classroom Management

Classroom management generally refers to development and preservation of order in the classroom. It also includes the notion that the classroom activity should contribute to the well-being of the student in very definite and prescribed ways. However, the appropriate order for the school environment is widely interpreted, and the appropriate goals for learners are frequently debated.

Weber (1990) identified eight different orientations or intents for classroom management. Figure 4.1 shows the label assigned to each orientation, the primary management role of the teacher, and the basic assumption underlying the position.

Few teachers fit neatly in any one category. However, Weber demonstrates that classroom management has many different goals. Each perspective has its advocates, although almost everyone finds at least one approach objectionable in many situations. For example, few parents and fewer children value overt intimidating behavior from teachers and other school employees. However, in dealing with an out-of-control student who consistently and severely deprives other children of peace, property, safety, and security, implementing negative sanctions appears to be a reasonable approach as well as inevitable. However, the number of situations in which the intimidating approach may be appropriate is very small.

Orientation	Role of teacher	Assumption
Authoritarian	Control student behavior	Teacher preserves order through discipline
Intimidation	Compel student behavior	Teacher enforces order by negative sanctions and punishment
Permissive	Maximize student freedom	Teacher frees students to develop and explore with limited restraints
"Cookbook"	Do the "right" things	Teacher follows established patterns of what is considered correct
Instructional	Plan and implement successful lessons	Students who are learning do not misbehave
Behavior modification	Modify student behavior	Teacher fosters positive, eliminates negative behavior
Socioemotional	Maximize learning	Positive environment fosters learning
Social system	Foster effective classroom groups	Learning occurs best within groups

FIGURE 4.1   Weber's eight orientations in classroom management.
Summarized from "Classroom Management" by W. Weber, 1990. In J. M. Cooper (Ed.), *Classroom Teaching Skills* (4th ed., pp. 229–306). Lexington, MA: Heath.

Critics argue that hostile or coercive approaches have virtually no place in schools unless used as a last resort. Some children routinely demonstrate immature behavior because they lack more constructive ways to deal with disappointment. In these cases, harsh punitive measures do little to help with maturation. The potential harm of an intimidating approach is substantial, real, and should never be underestimated. Kounin (1970), for example, found that harsh criticism was negatively related to positive classroom behavior. Positive approaches almost always obtain more effective growth in both attitude and responsibility whereas negative approaches tend to foster more negative behavior (Purkey & Novak, 1984). Yet, the negative side of human nature exists, and even the best teacher sometimes gets angry.

In learning to manage a class, teachers will probably experiment, either deliberately or by accident, with each role identified in Figure 4.1. Each of the orientations has a philosophical background and a set of assumptions about the purpose of classroom management. Each orientation, therefore, expresses a set of values that the teacher holds to be true. For example, the "cookbook" orientation assumes that certain acts are always correct and appropriate, whatever the context of the situation. The social system orientation holds that success lies in being able to communicate and work with others, thus devaluing competition or singular efforts of individual children.

Few teachers, however, consistently maintain such narrow views of the intent of the classroom. For example, there is no doubt that skills in cooperative learning must be developed and that these skills will be needed increasingly in the future. However, society still remains a competitive one in which individuals, as well as groups, vie for recognition and advancement.

The behaviorist view argues that reinforcement is needed if behavior is to be encouraged or discouraged successfully. Thus, the teacher should reward positive behavior tangibly to increase its frequency. Critics, however, believe that some student activity must originate from the character of the child. Kindness and help given to others, for example, are expected to be given without expectation of recognition and reward.

Even the issue of teacher organization and control of the class is continually open to question (Megay-Nespoli, 1993). Many teachers value the ability of their classes to self-regulate, to assist in designing the daily curriculum, and to establish personal goals and behavior independent of the teacher's influence. Other teachers tend to value classes that look to the teacher for direction and readily comply with expressed expectations.

The resolution to competing values is a pragmatic one: Teachers pick and choose among goals and strategies and form eclectic approaches to classroom management. *Eclectic approaches* are a collection of beliefs and behavior—many of which are contradictory—unified into a perceptual filter that determines the outlook of the teacher.

An Eclectic Road Map: Time/Method Matrix to Management

Eclectic behavior from teachers is common because the variety of contexts, student needs, intents, and individual differences demand various approaches if optimal results are to be consistently obtained. As described earlier in the text, the intents of education are varied. Those differences lead to substantive differences in the teaching behaviors and learning activities deemed appropriate for the school curriculum. Those differences are not likely to be resolved and may be fundamental to individual freedom and motivation. Teachers must, therefore, develop strategies that accommodate the vast needs of students, account for the varying behaviors of students in class, and respect the variety of value structures reflected in the homes of students. Obviously, this is not easy.

Time Dimension

Teachers initiate instructional behavior by first thinking of the future. In deciding what and how to teach, teachers consider the needs and abilities of students, the curriculum, and the materials available and then begin to plan for the next learning opportunities in the classroom. This is a *proactive* view of the classroom because the teacher's actions precede the students' actions. The intent of being proactive is to ensure that the students' first actions are the desired ones and unwanted behavior does not occur. Unwanted behavior that is not aggressive or disruptive but that does waste learning time is called "off-task" behavior.

When the teacher enacts a management plan, immediate student reaction can be assessed and subsequent student activity predicted. For example, if the teacher introduces an activity and the students applaud with delight, the teacher is likely to experience active participation from most children. Thus, the teacher's choice of activity diminishes potential misbehavior. If the students' response was a uniform, "Not again!" subsequent responses from children may be suspect. Teacher decisions that deal with early emerging indications of student behavior are considered *active*. A student who complains "Not again!" is not displaying off-task behavior. However, this student is clearly expressing displeasure at the repetition and boredom, which is predictive of off-task behavior. A teacher who makes frequent, minute changes in lessons in response to student reaction is actively monitoring the classroom to prevent a situation from deteriorating.

Many student behaviors are actually a sequence of behaviors. For example, student fights are generally preceded by verbal altercations. These, in turn, are preceded by a precipitating event, such as a perceived violation of individual rights or dignity. If the teacher intervenes in the earliest phases of a sequence of potential events, the teacher is responding to a minor or marginally inappropriate behavior in order to prevent a more serious one. This is the active phase of response.

When the teacher cannot prevent an event by proactive behavior and cannot minimize its escalation by active behavior, student misbehavior occurs, and reactive teacher behavior is required. *Reactive* strategies are generally aimed at eliminating misbehavior, whereas *proactive* strategies are aimed at promoting desirable behaviors. However, the reverse can also be true. A teacher's reactive strategy may also be to respond to appropriate and positive student behaviors, hoping that the attention and appreciation provided will promote similar appropriate behaviors in the future. When reactive strategies have a proactive focus, they extend well beyond the limited effectiveness of "knee jerk" reactions of coercion or reward. All reactive strategies should be designed to either promote or extinguish a current student behavior to improve the chances of successful instruction in the future.

Figure 4.2 illustrates some typical proactive, active, and reactive strategies. Obviously, the goal for every teacher should be to promote student behavior proactively. However, this is not always possible because of the unpredictable nature of the classroom environment. Teachers who have carefully considered strategies for those unexpected times, however, greatly increase the chances of appropriate reaction that promotes further positive behavior.

Method Dimension

Decisions about strategies for managing the classroom involve a fundamental choice regarding who should direct the students' behavior. Gordon (1974) suggests that teachers and parents ask themselves the question, "Whose problem is this?" Although a deceptively simple question with three possible answers (student,

FIGURE 4.2   Examples of behaviors for three time dimensions.

Proactive
- Teacher puts three pencil sharpeners in different parts of the room.
- Teacher practices the routine of gathering completed written work from students.
- Teacher assigns equipment captains for P.E. and trains them carefully.

Active
- Teacher walks around the room during seatwork.
- Teacher makes eye contact with student who is looking around.
- Teacher walks toward two students having a disagreement.

Reactive
- Teacher takes a toy away from a student who is playing with it during math class.
- Teacher sends a child to a corner desk after she was caught talking.
- Teacher requires students to clean the floor under the cafeteria table after a rowdy moment.

teacher, or shared), the reasoning involved in determining whose interests are at stake and who must construct solutions is quite complex. The method dimension determines who takes charge of identifying and correcting misbehavior and who determines and promotes positive ones. When the teacher controls the situation, the teacher's response is *interventionist*. If the teacher determines that the child can identify appropriate and inappropriate behavior for a given situation and employs the behavior successfully, a *noninterventionist* strategy is recommended. If the teacher determines that the student can take a large measure of initiative but may need the teacher's guidance and encouragement, an *interactionist* strategy is used (Glickman, 1981).

Interventionist.   *Interventionist* strategies result when the teacher determines that the child cannot or will not resolve the situation satisfactorily and imposes a solution for the current issue. When an interventionist strategy is used, the teacher takes ownership of both the problem and the solution. The teacher determines who and what the problem is and how it will be resolved. The teacher who says, "Mary, sit in your seat now!" has provided an interventionist strategy. An interventionist strategy requires teacher time and energy. Although in the incident with Mary, the time and energy may seem small, the potential cost of interventionist strategies is always great. For example, if Mary chooses not to comply, the teacher must follow up with additional demands or sanctions and risks being caught in a power struggle. Mary may choose to comply but in a leisurely way that requires additional teacher monitoring. Even if Mary does comply, the teacher would be overwhelmed if 15 students chose to stand up and walk around at the same time. Addressing each errant act of a classroom of children can destroy both the classroom climate and instructional pace. Although teachers always use interventionist strategies, successful teachers must cultivate other strategies for managing classroom activity. The strategies must promote student self-control and responsibility.

Noninterventionist.   *Noninterventionist* strategies result when the teacher determines that the child can and will resolve the situation satisfactorily. The teacher chooses to limit his or her behavior to activity that increases students' awareness of the inappropriate behavior. Noninterventionist strategies are intended to invoke a student's self-judgment about his or her behavior's appropriateness. With a noninterventionist strategy, any problem in student behavior is the problem of the student, and the solution should be developed and implemented by the student. Students at their best expect and deserve noninterventionist strategies. Although teachers are often not aware of it, noninterventionist strategies dominate their classroom management behavior. For example, when a teacher makes eye contact or frowns, he or she is sending a message to the student. Generally the message is, "I see that your actions are inappropriate. I hope that you will agree and find a way of improving immediately." Here the teacher is making a tacit request that the student regain control without assistance from the teacher. Noninterventionist strategies are used countless times each day in classrooms. They often go unnoticed by the teacher because of the subtlety of the acts and because the teacher does not have enough time and energy to monitor each act of every child. The teacher must, therefore, rely on the child for self-control.

Interactionist.   Sometimes, the teacher determines that assistance is needed in both making the student aware of the behavior, judging its appropriateness, and determining a redirection but chooses to involve the student in negotiation. This shared responsibility is considered *interactionist*. In an interactive approach, the teacher assists the student in accepting the responsibility for governing personal behavior by helping the child to become aware of the behavior, to judge the appropriateness of the behavior, and to develop strategies for improving the student's activity.

For example, if Tong has not completed his work during the prescribed time three days in a row, the teacher may ask Tong to develop a plan to complete his work in a timelier manner. She may inquire about the source of the difficulties and point out his talkative behavior during the periods. Additionally, she may evaluate the work completed to ensure that Tong has the skills necessary to complete the work successfully. The teacher may also suggest several strategies to Tong, offering him choices and listening to counterproposals. The object is to provide as much opportunity to the student to self-regulate behavior as the student can successfully use, without leaving any doubt that the behavior must change.

Figure 4.3 provides examples of interventionist, interactionist, and noninterventionist strategies that may be successfully employed in the classroom. Although it is desirable to give students as much responsibility as possible for governing their behavior, remember that some students need extensive assistance in controlling their social behavior and teacher time dedicated to negotiation is somewhat limited. Each orientation has its place in a carefully managed classroom.

Using the Matrix

Time and method dimensions exist for every classroom management situation. Comparing the two dimensions can develop a matrix of activities. An example of current strategies for dealing with a lack of effort is shown in a teacher's time/method matrix in Figure 4.4. By analyzing strategies for dealing with problem behavior in all dimensions, teachers can establish a rich array of strategies for dealing with persistent classroom management problems. For example, rather than relying on rewarding students who perform work successfully (reactive/interventionist), the teacher's attention is directed by the matrix to more proactive solutions. For example, the teacher may carefully consider the reason for learning a particular skill to be taught and emphasize that reason in the beginning of the lesson. The teacher's plan is to make the learning meaningful, hoping that students will put their best efforts forward. This strategy (proactive/noninterventionist) provides additional avenues to solving off-task behavior. By combining attention to the many dimensions of management planning, the teacher has a much larger choice of alternatives readily available for immediate use.

FIGURE 4.3 Examples of behaviors for three method dimensions.

Interventionist
- Teacher requires student to stay after school.
- Teacher designs and creates an interest center determining all procedures herself.
- Teacher provides a pizza party for successful completion of a class project.

Interactionist
- Teacher has a class meeting and negotiates special routines for P.E. equipment.
- Teacher approaches student and asks, "What can I do to help you remember to bring in your homework?"
- Teacher approaches quarreling students and says, "Find a solution you can live with and I can, too."

Noninterventionist
- Teacher walks next to a student who is having an unauthorized conversation with another student.
- Teacher says to a student, "I get angry when I see you throw food."
- Teacher asks daydreaming student, "What are you doing?"

	PROACTIVE	ACTIVE	REACTIVE
I N T E R V E N T I O N I S T	Spend some one-on-one time with Marcus getting to know him better. Write Marcus notes/letters expressing what I like about him. Plan learning activities that engage his interest. "What am I doing? Is it working?" Write positive letters; make phone calls to his mom.	Model self-discipline. Model coping with disappointment, frustration, and anger. Accept and reflect Marcus's feelings without judging. "You seem upset. Can I be of help?" Use active listening to address Marcus's concerns. "It is often disappointing when we don't get our way." Use proximity control, eye contact, overlapping.	Try to enhance Marcus's self-esteem by describing things he does well and wise choices he makes (encouragement, appreciation, praise). I once told Marcus he was a leader—he didn't believe me. Now I describe instances when I see others following his example—both positive and negative!) "Could it be that you want others in the class to pay attention to you?" Ignore minor misbehavior; seek help from school counselor.
I N T E R A C T I O N I S T	Conference with Marcus about what he thinks he does well and what areas he would like to improve. Decide together what the rewards for improvement will be. "I see you are hesitant or unsure about this assignment. Would you like to talk about it?" Establish rules that promote learning with the help of the whole class.	"You need to make a decision, to stay in our class or spend some time in another room." If Marcus chooses by his behavior to go to another room, he fills out a "Time Out to Think" form outlining the problem and what he will do to solve it. This must be done before he returns to our room. Remove materials/papers from him. "I see you are choosing not to do this activity. Let me know when you are ready to work again." "What rules might you need to get your work done?" Ask, "What are you doing? What should you be doing?"	Reward positive behavior with an extra privilege. "I see your behavior interfering with your learning as well as that of other students. What can we do to solve this problem?"
N O N I N T E R V E N T I O N I S T	Have Marcus complete "I" message statements. Ask Marcus to prepare some information, science experiment, etc., to present in an upcoming lesson.	Use cooperative learning groups to hold Marcus accountable in learning situations with peers and to increase sense of belonging. Allow Marcus to peer tutor a younger student in another classroom. Use "I" messages. (for example, "I'm concerned that your talking is interfering with your learning.")	When Marcus apologizes say, "Your determination to do better is all the 'sorry' I need." Have Marcus fill out a daily or weekly self evaluation, assessing his own behavior (make his own value judgment). "I see you're upset. Write down your ideas for making this situation fair for everyone."

FIGURE 4.4 A sample matrix of a teacher's plan for specific misbehavior. A: Marcus engages in attention-getting behavior; he claims things are "not fair" when he doesn't get his way.

	PROACTIVE	ACTIVE	REACTIVE
INTERVENTIONIST	Share with students my feelings about why listening is so important. (Some researchers say 90% of our learning occurs through listening.) Use listening activities that require students to practice good listening to be successful. (Don't repeat directions.) Plan transition routines/activities specifically and in advance.	Review listening skills chart when needed. Use overlapping, movement management, and group focus. Practice using these strategies effectively to hold student attention. Use a soft speaking voice to encourage students to listen. Let students know what signals I will use to get their attention. Use proximity and nonverbal signals to get attention.	Teacher quietly removes materials/papers from students. (Logical consequence of not listening is losing the right to do the activity.) "I feel irritated and angry when I have to wait for your attention (or have to repeat directions.)" "I would like to speak without being interrupted." Point out and describe good listening behaviors: "I saw Marcus move away so he would not be distracted. I saw Megan stop talking as soon as she heard me."
INTERACTIONIST	Hold class meeting to discuss listening skills and strategies. Make a T-chart of what listening looks and sounds like. Discuss listening strategies such as blocking distractions, thinking of question. Generate ideas for signals students can use to remind each other to listen (silent reminders: finger to lips, point to speaker, etc.)	Establish listening/signal routines at the beginning of the year and practice them. Be consistent in stopping and practicing when students start slipping. (I have a tendency to let up too soon!) Ask students to select signals to use. Write on chalkboard/overhead the steps to follow or have students write the steps while listening. Have students verbally repeat directions to a partner or to me (as a whole group).	Class problem solving: "We are having difficulty quieting down. Many students are not listening when directions are given. How can we solve this problem?" (Go through Gordon's no-lose steps.) Ask class to determine consequences for good and poor listening.
NONINTERVENTIONIST	"I'm going to give directions now. What I say will be important." Have students organize themselves into learning teams and brainstorm ideas for helping themselves and others to be better listeners. Student teams tape-record sounds for the class to listen to and identify. Student teams tape-record sounds for the class to listen to and identify. Students record favorite books for others to listen to.	"It's difficult to hear instructions when others are talking." "I am ready to begin." "I would like everyone to be able to hear the directions." Use self-evaluations to increase student awareness of their own listening skills. Use peer tutoring. Allow students to sometimes give the directions in both class and small group settings. Student "team leaders" accept responsibility for learning.	"You didn't hear the directions. What can you do?" Use self-evaluations to increase student awareness of their own listening skills. Allow time at the end of the day for students to list or verbally share things they learned that day by listening.

FIGURE 4.4 *(Continued)* B: Class has difficulty making smooth, efficient transitions.

Getting Started

Developing a comprehensive classroom management program and the teacher skills for implementing it is not easy. Doing so takes substantial effort throughout the teacher's career. Creating time/method matrices for specific management problems is a helpful and thoughtful way to promote personal growth. However, a review of a broader, more basic plan covering all types of desired student behavior is the best starting point for most teachers. The first step in that plan is to establish prerequisite beliefs and attitudes needed by the teacher to guide the development and evaluation of the management plans. Just as a business has a bottom line, the successful classroom must have clearly established goals.

Purpose of a Management Plan

The research in classroom management has focused on orderliness of the classroom with a focus on student compliance to the required behavior necessary for the particular learning task presented by the teacher. Doyle (1986) notes that most of the research tends to focus on individuals rather than the group dimensions of the classroom environment. However, simply maintaining order and developing strategies for dealing with undesired behavior do not promote learning unless accompanied by a set of principles that guide teacher decision making. When order becomes an end in itself, the teacher imposes a regimen that nullifies a positive learning environment.

Each teacher must establish a set of guiding purposes for the classroom management plan and carefully measure day-to-day decisions in light of their contribution or detraction of these goals. The goals of any management plan necessarily reflect the values of the teacher. Earlier in this text, the intent, context, and student characteristics that frame the teacher's decision-making process were discussed. This perceptual picture is created and interpreted by a teacher's values, skills, and knowledge about children and learning. Figure 4.5 provides the author's view of the primary goals of a classroom management plan.

FIGURE 4.5 Classroom management fundamental goals.

- Establish an environment that benefits children
- Ensure the physical safety of students
- Promote basic goodness and caring in all students
- Develop academic skills appropriate for the students' personal advancement
- Improve students' social skills necessary for citizenship
- Exercise each student's self-control and individual responsibility

Beneficial and Safe Environment

At the heart of any classroom is the desire to provide beneficial experiences to children in a safe, healthful atmosphere. The school district's mission as well as the school curriculum should guide the understanding of what constitutes "beneficial experiences." Since children's needs differ, the benefits that children should receive from a carefully managed classroom also differ in focus and emphasis. Some children need to build self-confidence; others need to learn respect for the abilities of others. An appropriate classroom plan, therefore, provides experiences for leadership and followership. More importantly, the plan should provide strategies to match the leadership and followership roles so that followers develop some leadership skills and leaders develop followership skills, thus enabling children to maintain a healthy balance of social growth and role expectations.

Goodness and Caring

Goodness and caring are fundamental to education. Socrates and K'ung Fu-tse advocated that the study and development of virtue were a primary goal of education. This argument has been carried down through the centuries. With the American family under stress, the school must redouble its efforts at providing instruction and experiences for learning basic goodness and mutual respect necessary for responsible citizenship. Externally establishing order in the class without putting a primary emphasis on the development of responsibility and self-control falls short of this goal. The classroom management plan must mirror the mosaic of rights and responsibilities that characterize adult life.

Academic Skills

The classroom management plan should establish an environment in which academic skills assist the child in self-determination and productivity. Although much of the research on classroom management focuses on behavior control (Doyle, 1986), many writers such as Charles (1983) view the management of the curriculum to be central to a total management plan. Ensuring that a variety of instructional approaches are used and studying subjects from varying perspectives avoid satiation and increase both interest and success in learning. Arranging the curriculum so that the student is most productive for the greatest amount of time is a management task that mirrors the roles of other managers in business and industry.

Social Skills

Students' social skills that promote active participation as citizens include more than just self-control and a respect for the rights of others. Social skills that promote citizenship include developing a work ethic, caring about others in a way that promotes positive social action, and making contributions without the expectation of reward or recognition. Classroom management programs that focus on interventionist

Routines simplify the end of the day.

strategies alone cannot provide experiences for the roles that students are to accept in the future. Therefore, the management plan must look toward establishing order in the classroom so that it is valued by the students and is primarily self-regulated. However, student safety and freedom from the hurtful acts of others often make external intervention necessary. This illustrates the typical management dilemma of working toward two goals where the teacher must construct a balanced compromise. It does, however, mirror the dilemma faced in out-of-school life for all of us.

Self-Determination

This compromise is simplified in classrooms where students have developed and use cooperative self-determination. This final suggested goal of a successful management plan can be considered as a general summary of all the other goals. When students understand the purposes of being in school and accept the responsibility for determining personal success, much of the work that results in successful learning has been validated. Instructional methods, no matter how skillfully implemented, cannot educate unwilling and uncooperative students. However, even poorly developed lessons can instruct children who are eager, helpful, and ambitious. Keeping in mind the goals of developing initiative, self-determination, and responsibility assists the teacher in calculating strategies that obtain long-term results and manage the inevitable risks.

Three Prerequisites for Successful Classroom Management

Every building must have a foundation to support the weight and pressures involved in the structure. Likewise, every classroom management plan must have a strong foundation on which to base teacher activity. Without the foundation, teachers are left without sufficient credibility or student goodwill to be successful (Figure 4.6).

Every Student Counts.   A fundamental premise for successful classroom management is that every student counts and is important. There are no "write-offs" in a successful classroom. One of the hidden secrets in public school is the sense of futility that teachers often feel when faced with such overwhelming obstacles. Behind the feeling of futility lies a sense of teacher blame in which earnest and caring teachers feel inadequate to the task.

A teacher's personal remorse revolves around many factors. Students who are neglected often develop coping skills that are hostile, hurtful, and aggressive. Although teachers may acknowledge the source of the student's unacceptable behavior, they feel absolutely powerless to make any alternations in the student's life outside the confines of the school. Teachers may direct kindness, concern, and care toward the disaffected child, but only rarely does their compassion immediately overcome the student's aggressiveness and anger.

Improvements among disaffected children usually take concerted effort by many teachers over years of school. Teachers, missing the sense of progress needed to provide a sense of success and worth, then feel betrayed, hopeless, and frustrated. Ironically, many end up feeling much the same way that the neglected child feels: Nobody cares. The resulting indifferent or unresponsive behavior toward the child is much the same as the child displays toward the adult. There are no simple answers for "keeping the faith" and continually renewing a belief in the value and capability of each child. However, when the teacher mentally loses the battle, the teacher's behavior soon deteriorates. Children then begin to believe that the teacher values student behavior, not the student.

FIGURE 4.6 Prerequisites for successful classroom management.

1. Everyone counts: Everybody is important.
2. Anything can be: Express optimism about students and learning.
3. Academic program is . . .
   • appropriate.
   • valuable to students.
   • conducted efficiently and equitably.

Optimism About Success.   The second prerequisite is a pervasive optimism about children and the teacher's ability to facilitate success. Without feeling empowered and believing that their self-directed activity can bring about the desired result, teachers are less motivated and have a sense of futility that minimizes the effectiveness of planning and implementation. In this way, teachers are very much like students: Motivation is primarily a belief in the value of an activity and the ability of the individual to perform the required tasks successfully.

Much has been written about the decline of education, out-of-control students, and failing schools. With such a dismal picture, it is difficult for teachers to be optimistic. Much of the pessimistic outlook on education is "psychofact," narrowly defined positions that distort the true situation. Today's schools have challenges, but these challenges are probably no greater than during the formative years of the common school movement, during the Great Depression, or during the desegregation movements. Without a belief in the teacher's ability to ameliorate the status of children, there is little impetus to act.

Appropriate Academic Curricula.   The third prerequisite is that the teacher constantly endeavors to provide an academic program that is appropriate to the children's ability, is viewed by students as valuable, and is conducted efficiently and equitably. The teacher must provide learning environments that reflect the changing, varied needs and abilities of children. Without an appropriate curriculum, it is difficult to establish any basis for student effort, self-determination, or responsibility.

Classroom Management Basic Principles

In building a classroom management plan, certain basic principles can assist in guiding the teacher. These principles are derived from the basic goals previously outlined and reflect the ideas of researchers such as Dreikurs, Grunwald, and Pepper (1982), Glasser (1989), Jones (1979), and Kounin (1970). When working with students, a teacher's personal management plan will evolve. However, each of the following sections provides direction considered essential for any management plan (Figure 4.7).

Know Your Students

Sporting events in America are big business. When two opponents meet, they rarely are strangers. Teams and individuals carefully view statistics and film of their opponents to learn all that is possible about them. The belief underlying this careful preparation is that the more you know, the better decisions you can make.

Teaching, while having no opponent except perhaps ignorance, is still enhanced by the idea that the more you know, the better decisions you make. Consider this extreme example of how missing information led to an inaccurate perception.

FIGURE 4.7 Classroom management basic principles.

> 1. Establish clear rules where rules are needed.
> 2. Let students assume independent responsibility.
> 3. Minimize disruptions and delays.
> 4. Plan independent activities as well as organized lessons.
> 5. Stress positive desirable behavior.
> 6. Recognize and reinforce desired behavior.
> 7. Use praise effectively (nonjudgmental; express appreciation).
> 8. Focus attention when beginning a lesson.
> 9. Keep lesson moving at a good pace.
> 10. Monitor attention during lessons.
> 11. Stimulate attention periodically.
> 12. Maintain accountability.
> 13. Terminate lessons that have gone on too long.

Mr. Scott Reflects

While teaching in a gifted child program, one of my new students, Mark, started going to the principal's office regularly for permission to go home because he felt bad. Each time, the principal allowed him to go home. He lived nearby, and although no one was home, the principal knew he was a nice, responsible kid in a very difficult home situation. The principal did not expect or seek much assistance from the boy's mother or the mother's boyfriend.

Mark was ten years old but emotionally mature for his age. He had moved back into the school district a few months ago. Mark had attended the first and second grades here, and his teachers adored him. I was bothered because Mark generally became ill just before he was to go to his special class with me. Although a class for gifted children, this particular group contained many gifted underachievers. Task orientation and work ethic was a constant topic in this class. These children had great potential but failed to do much, if not most, of their classroom work. I took it personally.

After speaking to the principal, we determined that unless there was a fever and/or vomiting (signs of "real" illness), Mark could not go home and would be sent to my class. I was adamant. Mark had to give me a chance if I was to teach him. The next day, Mark didn't show up. Using the intercom, I called the office to see if Mark was there. Indeed, he had been but had been sent home. I was furious! A few minutes later, the intercom rang, and the principal asked me to come to his office at the end of school. I was more than happy to oblige. After all, we had an agreement.

After school, the principal told me that he had sent Mark home. After having denied Mark permission to go home, Mark began to beg, saying that he hurt too much to be at school. In short, Mark finally told the principal that he had an undescended testicle and that it was swollen. Lying down with a heating pad was his only relief. I felt so dumb that I resolved right then and there to see to it he had the proper care. After talking to the department of social services that afternoon, we discovered that they knew about the situation, but Mark's mother would not give permission for the surgery necessary for treatment. They could do nothing except send another worker to the home that afternoon. The next morning, the worker was at the office and sadly told us a long story of neglect and the current troubles of Mark's mother who was under indictment for stabbing Mark's natural father in his sleep. That was why they had moved back to our school. The mother refused to cooperate in any way and "that is that, end of story."

Thankfully for Mark, the principal was a friend of a local judge and immediately placed a call to his friend. Since the early stages of gangrene were evident, the situation was considered life-threatening, and the surgery was done under court order that afternoon. All along, I had made an enemy of Mark because I thought he was just lazy and rebellious. I resolved to judge less quickly and look more carefully for the truth.

Although this is an extreme example, it does illustrate the vast differences that can exist between our perceptions and reality. Successful teachers use on a daily basis their knowledge about children's likes and dislikes, study habits, and the encouragement (or discouragement) that they receive. Each teacher should ask the questions in Figure 4.8 about each child individually. Pondering and developing possible answers to these and other questions are primary keys to becoming what is known as a *reflective practitioner.* Understanding comes only with time, effort, and reflection.

Information can be obtained from many different sources. The child's permanent school record provides information about the student's health status and past school attendance. It usually provides a sketch of the child's home life: with whom the child lives, the family size, the occupations of parents, and where in the commu-

FIGURE 4.8 Questions to guide teacher understanding of students.

- Who are they?
- What do they think? feel? believe?
- How do they view school? you? themselves?
- What motivates them?
- How can you assist their motivation?
- What's normal for them? their age group?
- Why do they behave the way they do?

nity the child lives. Previous work in school can also reveal patterns of growth. Interviewing previous teachers also helps. Finding time to talk to children about their likes and dislikes and listening to their stories during play periods, before and after school, or eating lunch with them can reveal a lot about who the children are. Interest inventories, creative writing, and art can also provide insights that assist the teacher in understanding the child. Even watching some of the Saturday cartoons that they watch can help the teacher establish credibility as a caring, helpful person in their lives.

Establish Rules That Are Necessary

Students must know clearly what is acceptable and what is not if they are to make appropriate decisions to govern their behavior. The successful teacher must establish clear rules and teach them to students. When establishing rules, it is important to understand what the rule is intended to do, whether the rule applies only to school life or also to conduct out of school, and whether the rule can be enforced. In general, rules that apply too narrowly to school conduct should be avoided. Narrowly defined rules, such as "walk in a straight line in single file," should be incorporated into classroom routines so that students can be made aware that these behaviors are either necessary or desirable only because of the special circumstances in the school.

Rules should carry the force of compelling necessity. For example, walking in a straight line and in single file may not be necessary as children move across the playground from building to building on the school site. However, during a fire drill, this behavior takes on a critical importance, and variations should not be tolerated. Classroom rules should govern conduct that applies in almost all school contexts. A rule such as "Do not touch others in hurtful or harmful ways" has few, if any, contexts that permit exceptions. Students should be taught that if another student says that a touch is hurtful or annoying, it must stop. This rule and other rules that are most appropriate for elementary classrooms assist children in understanding citizenship and responsible conduct outside of school. The more relevant and compelling the rule, the easier it is to establish conformity to acceptable norms of behavior.

In establishing rules, the teacher should remember three essential criteria:

- The rule is a "must have." It is necessary.
- The rule is easily understood. The meaning of the rule is taught as well as strategies for obeying the rule.
- The rule can be, and is, enforced.

Rules that are unnecessary detract from those that are. Teachers have limited resources when enforcing rules. Student attention should be focused on the most important aspects of a code of conduct. Requiring students to "raise their hand before speaking" is not in the same category of importance as "students may not harm others." The latter is considered a necessary rule. Raising a hand before speaking, procedures for moving about the room, and methods of getting help should not have the power of rules. In these areas, there are many methods of obtaining appropriate results, and the teacher often has many different structures to govern these needs depending on the situation. For example, students may not speak in a formal discussion without raising their hand but may speak freely during a cooperative work exercise. However, the situations in which students are allowed to harm one another are quite rare. A rule governing student behavior needs to provide consistency across the many school and community contexts.

Children must be able to understand the rules easily. One common set of rules found across the country is, "Be kind, work hard." Although this is a wonderful class motto and should exemplify teacher expectations for children, its utility as a rule is limited. At issue is the rule's effectiveness at regulating student behavior. For example, if Monique is a pencil biter and has no pencil, the kind thing for each student, particularly those near her, would be to loan her a pencil. But the loaned pencil is most likely to be bit, chewed, and in general, decreased in attractiveness. Can you reasonably compel the children to loan a pencil to Monique? If no one chooses to loan Monique a pencil, has a rule been broken? Does "Be kind" mean that students must loan pencils to anyone in need? The rule is too vague.

Another example of a vague and potentially ineffective rule is the common rule, "Respect others." What does this mean? If Stanley is a bully, does it mean that students must respect him while fearing him? Many teachers successfully deal with the vagueness of their rules by extensively teaching the meaning of words such as "respect." One teacher has children practice respect by role playing in a variety of situations at the beginning of the school year. By practicing how to resolve conflicts, disagreements, and uncomfortable situations, children develop immediate skills in resolving a difficult situation. Children also learn explicitly what is meant by "respect," and with the teacher's care and effort, "respect others" can serve as a rule.

There is a management axiom, "What gets done is what gets inspected." Observations of society at large reinforce the belief that "rules without enforcement is wishful thinking." Rule enforcement should not be confused with harsh punishment. Later in this text, various enforcement strategies and methods of reinforcing appropriate behavior are considered. At this point, it is enough to note that rule violation must result in some consequence. If the rule is truly necessary for school functioning, any violation of what is essential must be dealt with explicitly.

For example, if one student strikes another there is a tacit violation of the rule, "Do not harm others." If ignored or slighted, students will infer that hitting is permitted, that it is not so terrible, and that it can go on unnoticed. Rule enforcement need not be harsh. If one student hits another, the offending student may have to sit away from other children for the rest of the day or must remain next to the teacher during the play period. The idea to be conveyed to the student is, "You have violated a rule protecting the safety of others. Right now, you have violated my trust. Therefore, you must stay near me so I can monitor your behavior until you have regained the ability to monitor it yourself."

Rules assist the teacher in obtaining the minimal student conduct requirements. However, rules have little value in influencing the more mature expressions of student responsibility. Rules must apply to all students; therefore, rules must state behaviors that all students are capable of demonstrating continually. However, expressions of maturity, kindness, altruism, and helpfulness require special skills that may not be continually present in each child. Children who have been surrounded with hostility or neglect may not have the necessary beliefs that promote gracious acts of kindness toward others in need. High positive expectations are more appropriate than rules for developing children's moral and work behaviors.

In writing rules, it is important to find the best balance between being too specific and too vague. Also, attempting to put rules into a positive, rather than a negative, statement is also desirable. Often, it is not possible to write a positive rule without increasing wordiness or confusion. Each teacher must determine what is necessary for each class. Following are five rules that governed one teacher's class:

◆ Do not hurt others.
◆ Do not damage property.
◆ Do not take things that belong to others.
◆ Do complete all work.
◆ Do ask for help when you do not understand.

The first two rules are prohibitive statements, but they are direct and to the point. They meet the criteria of being necessary, easily understood, and enforceable. Turning them into an equally simple positive statement would not be an easy task. Some teachers, however, prefer to use vaguer but more positive words, such as "Respect others," but neutralize the loss of specificity by extensive teaching and practice.

The third statement is also concise, direct, and meets the three criteria for rules. This rule, however, can be turned into an easily understood positive statement: "Before using others' things, ask permission." Although not saying exactly the same thing, the functionality of the second rule is at least as satisfactory as the original. The positive version also has the added benefit of directing student behavior as opposed to prohibiting it.

The last two rules are positive statements that compel students to perform certain acts. Although the necessity of the first two rules is self-evident, the last two rules generally create an interesting debate regarding their appropriateness. The teacher-author of these rules simply claimed that doing student work, which included paying attention, was not negotiable. She could not teach without it. She was not going to give students a choice regarding completion of daily assignments. Further, she was adamant that the student was responsible for letting the teacher know when learning was difficult and extra help was needed. This "asking for help" applied to other problems as well. She argued that unless the student let her know about the problem, she couldn't help.

For this teacher, these were necessary rules, and she had carefully considered the impact of these rules on her class. She also claimed the most difficult compliance of all fell on her shoulders. She said that providing activities that each child could complete successfully and the necessary instruction for students to succeed was her responsibility. These two rules "kept her on her toes!" The last rule, however, is still problematic: How is a rule that requires students to seek help enforced? Her logic was quite subtle. The rule for seeking help was necessary if she were to expect children to complete all work. The rule was self-enforcing: Students who did not understand and did not seek help found themselves with the natural consequence of doing poorly on the assignment. Certainly, this teacher was teaching for success. She also illustrated the role of teacher values and expectations in establishing the classroom management plan. This teacher clearly had high expectations for both her children and herself, conveyed those expectations to all, and fulfilled her obligations. Most importantly, this teacher demonstrated that the ultimate purpose of rules is not simply to secure student compliance but to promote learning.

Use Routines to Simplify Decision Making

Routines are potentially one of the most valuable strategies that teachers have for accommodating the complexity and speed of classroom life. Because of the immediacy and simultaneity of the classroom, the demand for the teacher's time and attention exceeds the supply. Teacher time is a limited commodity that must be reserved for important tasks requiring the teacher's skill and knowledge. Predictable or reoccurring tasks are handled with preestablished procedures. Routines are automatic ways of accommodating reoccurring tasks or immediate class needs so that the teacher is free for more important learning endeavors (Hawkins, 1997).

Predictable tasks are events that can be foreseen. Many predictable tasks occur regularly so that both the time as well as the method of completing the tasks can be planned. For example, gathering materials for the recess period outdoors occurs at scheduled intervals during the day as does preparation for lunch and end-of-day dismissal. Many predictable tasks, however, arise when the exact time of the occurrence is not known. Teachers can predict that pencils must be sharpened and noses wiped, but the exact time of such needs is beyond prediction. Routines are the strategies that teachers use to prescribe the methods that children can follow for meeting personal needs with minimal disruption to the class.

The consummate routine is the fire drill. In most states, school evacuation procedures are mandatory by legislative action, and fire drills represent an important routine for the safety of students. Schools typically can evacuate a building of all occupants in just a few minutes. This is taught, rehearsed, and practiced until classes know what to do even if the teacher is out of the room when the necessity arises.

Most classes start the day with prescribed routines. Children enter the building, put away coats and bags, and sit at their desks. Many classes take role, lunch counts, and start the initial learning tasks with little intervention from the teachers. In one class, the children enter the room on arrival at school. They take their name tag off a board that has each student's picture and name. Students then place the tag into one of three small buckets that represent the two lunchroom meal choices and "bag lunch." When the teacher actually takes role, he looks at the board, calls out the name of any student whose name tag is still displayed. The teacher then counts the children to see that the number agrees and records any absences. A student "sergeant-at-arms" then counts the lunch tokens and reports to the cafeteria the lunch requirements. The tags are bound with rubber bands by lunch entree and the teacher takes them to the lunchroom. This helps the children to remember their request and not change their minds so the lunch offerings are skewed for the day.

There are many strategies for taking attendance. Any one strategy may be successful or unsuccessful, depending on the classroom context and teacher preference and skill. The author, for example, took attendance by looking at the desks, noting any empty desks and who sat in them. He called the students' names to double-check their absence and counted the total number of children. Lunch report was a duplicated slip of paper where each child indicated a "1, 2, or 3," which corresponded to the choices on the lunch menu bulletin board for the week. That bulletin board was done every Friday by a student committee who posted pictures of the meal menu for each day of the following week.

Routines have infinite variations, but all are designed to achieve four basic goals. Routines should do the following:

◆ Minimize the time spent on the task.
◆ Minimize the opportunity for disruption.
◆ Maximize student responsibility.
◆ Minimize adult control and teacher involvement.

If possible and desirable, routines should have self-checking capabilities so that children can self-regulate their compliance.

Routines cannot be prescribed but must be developed by the teacher in concert with the school environment, the status of the students, and the teacher's preferences. For example, the location of the restroom in relationship to the classroom and the maturity of the children will greatly influence the development of a routine.

Maintain Positive Reasonable Expectations

The teacher must form reasonable positive expectations and communicate them to students in helpful guiding ways. Teachers must search for the positive contributions of all children and communicate a sincere appreciation of cooperation to all children. Even the most disruptive students are generally in compliance with classroom expectations most of the time. These contributions must constantly be acknowledged. Likewise, when poor or unproductive behavior occurs, it is important for the teacher not to dwell on the negative, but to reassert the positive expectation.

If the teacher has negative expectations for the class or certain students, the teacher must not communicate them. Instead, the successful teacher will develop a strategy to neutralize the negative situation. Teachers sometimes inadvertently ascribe negative expectations to students based on group membership or past experiences. It is natural for a teacher to dread contact with certain students who have repeatedly presented themselves as demanding, uncooperative, and disruptive. However, these feelings should be kept private, and the successful teacher should redouble efforts to promote a positive learning climate for every child. By concentrating on the positive, the teacher is encouraged to consider alternatives that can lead to cooperative and productive behavior for each student. This, of course, is simple to say but very difficult to enact.

Good and Weinstein (1986) offer several suggestions for teachers to assist in creating positive expectations from negative ones:

◆ Vary classroom activities to provide application of learning to novel and relevant situations.
◆ Emphasize the purpose of each lesson and how it benefits the child.
◆ Use student ideas and suggestions in planning lessons and selecting learning activities.
◆ Use active instruction techniques that increase student choices and responsibility.
◆ Ask questions that require more than memory and exercise the student's imaginative and rational skills.
◆ Encourage students who have difficulty by focusing on progress and effort.
◆ Minimize public comparisons with more successful students or classes.
◆ Minimize criticism and maximize encouragement.
◆ Publicly acknowledge accomplishments and progress.

By placing a recurring emphasis on positive expectations for students, teachers can emphasize and focus student attention on what is important in learning. Positive expectations provide teachers with a powerful platform to establish a classroom climate of effort and responsibility.

Positive expectations must be more than teacher rhetoric and must be prefaced by viewing students as capable, able, and valuable (Purkey & Novak, 1984). Building positive expectations for all students is not easy for the teacher. Positive expectations that support the teacher in stressful classroom events are developed by a pervasive belief in both the students' abilities and the teacher's skill in bringing out abilities in useful and productive ways.

Provide Independence as Students Assume Responsibility

Few problems have been more persistent in the historical development of the human race than the development of individual and social responsibility within each individual. To the teacher who feels the need to control children, any principle arguing that students should be given as much independence and self-determination as possible may seem incongruent. From one point of view, however, teacher control can be argued as nonexistent. In reality, students are totally in control of every activity every minute of every classroom day (Glasser, 1985, 1986).

Students seem to be under the control of teachers simply because they have decided to comply with the teacher's expectations. When any student chooses not to comply and instead chooses to disrupt, that child can do so. There is little that the teacher can do to prevent it with one exception: Create a class in which the child receives no benefit from disruption. Providing negative outcomes for disruption does not alter the basic truth that students are in control. Students simply decide whether the outcome is worth the hassle. Timmy, in the opening quotes, demonstrated this reasoning by claiming that a whole week of staying after school was worth the pleasure of pummeling another kid who had vexed him one time too many.

Students need to understand that they are not only in control but that they must also be responsible for what they do. Making students aware of their power and spotlighting the teacher's respect for their autonomy is a primary venue toward developing student maturity and citizenship. Figure 4.9 outlines some of the basic rights and responsibilities of students. Notice that each right is an equal expression of a responsibility. Although a sophisticated understanding of this balance is well beyond primary students, children can, and do, establish a sense of fairness and individuality. Helping students to grapple with responsibility must entail assistance in understanding their autonomy and internal control.

Assisting students to assume responsibility requires daily treatment. Sometimes a simple change in how teachers think about children can convey disarmingly different messages to children. For example, compare the following teacher sequences for beginning a math class:

TEACHER A: "Writing time is over. Don't forget to finish your stories tonight. I don't want anyone coming in tomorrow without their story finished. Okay, take everything off your desk and put it away." (teacher pauses while students clean off desks.) "Cecilia, we are waiting on you." (pause) "OK, students, it is now time for math. Get out your math books." (pause) "Cecilia, we are waiting on you again. OK, now turn to page 34." (pause) "Is everyone on page 34? Show it to me so I can check. OK, now put your finger on the picture of the fraction that shows one half."

TEACHER B: "I certainly enjoyed reading the beginnings of your new stories about how two greedy children try not to share but trick the other into getting less while they get more. I can't wait to read the finished stories tomorrow so please don't forget to finish them tonight. I'm looking at a picture on page 34 of the math book. Who can find the picture of one-half?" (teacher pauses) "Cecilia, the characters in your story don't know what a half is, do they? Can you find the one half on page 34 of your math book? Great! OK, I see that almost everyone has found it. If you have found it, you can help others. Great! I see all the fingers on the one half."

• Right to individual self-determination	• Responsibility to permit others' self-determination
• Right to safety	• Responsibility to others' safety
• Right to free expression	• Responsibility to respect free expression of others
• Right to a positive learning environment	• Responsiblity to protect the learning environment for others

FIGURE 4.9   Student rights and responsibilities governing behavior.

The attitudes expressed by the teachers differ. Teacher A reminds children that the work is not completed and must be done before returning to school on the next day. Teacher B attempts to show appreciation and encouragement as the children move from one lesson to the other and also shows excitement about getting to finish reading the stories tomorrow, but reminds them they must be finished for her to read them.

The conduct of the two lessons demonstrates two different outlooks on student cooperation. Teacher A requires the children to act in unison; Teacher B knows that some students are faster at preparing for the next lesson. Teacher A accepts the role of monitoring students' behavior; Teacher B encourages the students to do so by being helpful to their peers. Teacher A provides meticulous step-by-step orders; Teacher B encourages students to prepare for the next lesson by accomplishing a learning task.

The following strategies assist the teacher in developing a sense of empowerment in children:

- Provide choices.
- Ask for student suggestions and input.
- Allow children to self-correct when caught disrupting.
- Avoid overdirection by telling children to do the obvious.
- Do not tell children what they think or how they feel; ask instead.
- Acknowledge effort.
- Give children opportunities to solve problems before intervening.
- Let children help in planning the curriculum.
- Stress positive desirable behavior.
- Teach for success.
- Accept responsibility and hold students accountable.
- Teach for a reason.
- Communicate purposefulness, intentions.
- Invite participation.

Developing responsibility in children is one of the more important missions of schools and is a formidable challenge to teachers. Working with families and children in developing citizenship is not only as important as the "3R's," but learning is also made much easier and more efficient by responsible caring children.

Give Students Individual Attention

When a student behaves in a manner that the teacher feels is unacceptable, the teacher must direct attention toward the student to correct that behavior. For many students, this is the only individual attention that they receive. One of the most important aspects of behavior management is providing daily acknowledgment and interaction with children that assists them in verifying their value in the classroom. Glasser (1989) called this "giving students the time of day." He argues that the most important step in dealing with any type of misbehavior is to have first developed a relationship with the student based on daily interactions that are not negative.

Teacher interaction with students can become monopolized by the teacher's needs, ignoring the needs of children. The teacher asks a question, requests student work, or directs student movement. In short, it is easy for teacher–student interactions to be completely dominated by directive requests. At its most extreme, the child is "only a student"; the child has no relationship with the teacher other than the teaching/learning interaction. Imagine having a job in which the boss communicated with you only to give directions or make requests. It would be easy to infer that you are "only an employee" and that your only value to your boss or to the company is your ability to perform work. Workers do not perform their best in such an environment but instead rotate around the traditional "grumble/comply" cycle. The same is true in education. Acknowledging the person behind the student role is essential.

Teachers have many opportunities for "giving the time of day" to children. The instructional day is filled with chances that allow teachers to express interest in children:

◆ Greet each child at the door in the morning with eye contact, a smile, and by saying his or her name.
◆ Notice moods; inquire how the child is feeling.
◆ Have a "Hobby Day" where children can bring things to share.
◆ Write biographies illustrated by photos from the child's home and vacations.
◆ Say, "I enjoy having you here" and "We missed you."
◆ Send a thoughtful note complimenting the child on something he or she did.
◆ Ask, "What do you think?"
◆ Remark, "You make me feel good."

Purkey and Novak (1984) labeled the interest and attitude directed toward students as the "teacher's stance." They argue that the teacher's stance needs to be considered at length and that the offhand, noninstructional contact between teacher and student can have a major impact on the learning environment. Being intentional toward students—that is, carefully directing thoughtful activity in all contacts—is a major part of a teacher's stance that promotes responsible behavior. Likewise, interacting with a child in a way that conveys respect and acknowledges that you value the child is extremely important in building a firm foundation to support a cooperative classroom.

Remember Basic Instructional Procedures

The final basic principle for building a successful classroom management plan is to provide solid basic instructional strategies. Students need to know what is expected of them and to have ample avenues for complying successfully with those expectations. Children may misbehave during interesting well-developed lessons, but such behavior is minimized when the fundamentals are successfully in place. The following strategies summarized by Good and Brophy (1994) and others are essential in proactively managing the classroom.

Focus Attention When Beginning a Lesson.   Do not start without the children. As discussed earlier, a focus activity need not be elaborate but must direct the students' attention to the task at hand. During the early parts of the lesson the teacher should explain the learning objective and any special behavioral expectations that are necessary. Students who miss these directions almost always will be confused.

Provide Smooth, Efficient Transitions.   Consider what steps are needed to move from one lesson to the next. Following a painting activity with a math group activity may not work smoothly because children will finish painting and the necessary cleanup at different times. Activities such as painting can be followed by those that have multiple start times built in (such as free reading, editing a story, practice with basic math facts in cooperative groups, or leaving for play period). This method provides children with both a variable time in which to be artistic and an activity that can be begun independently without waiting on the teacher or other students.

Minimize Disruptions and Delays.   Do not stop classes to deal with unimportant things. Have students "write notes" and put them in your mailbox when they want to tell about a special trip when you are trying to have a lesson on a different topic. You can respond with a "note on the note." Have routines for distributing and collecting materials and papers. Do not deal with behavior at the expense of the lesson. Tell the child, "I'm too busy with this lesson to deal with your outburst. I will deal with it after this lesson. Your behavior until then will affect what I do."

Plan Lessons with Variety.   Know your curriculum and utilize your best instructional strategies. Avoid satiation. If a strategy is particularly successful, the successful teacher saves it for the more difficult lessons. Make a basic list of student activities including items such as talk, listen, read, write, act, make-believe, watch, sing, run, and so on. See that each type of activity is accomplished each day.

Stimulate and Monitor Attention During Lessons.   Keep lessons moving at a good pace and promote active participation. Instead of having one child summarize the discussion, have children pair off and summarize to each other. Pick one pair to share. Move about the room. Look at student work as well as check on whether students are working.

Constantly Analyze Your Classroom

Management, whether it is in business, industry, government, or the elementary classroom, requires constant attention. The end result of classroom management is not the result of a few big decisions but the cumulative effect of countless small corrections as the teacher measures the minute-by-minute pulse of classroom activity (Klann, 1996). When novice drivers attempt to steer a car for the first time, they find that driving, even on a straight, flat road, requires constant attention and correction of the steering wheel, brake, and accelerator. At first, the car drifts, and the novice makes major corrections while the car weaves back and forth down the road. As the novice becomes more skillful, the driver anticipates the actions of the vehicle and makes minute corrections that are just barely noticeable by the passengers. As the driver becomes an expert, the road conditions, speed, traffic, and unpredictable actions of other drivers are merged into a smooth, careful ride in which passengers are treated to a dexterous display of skill. Classrooms are equally responsive to minute, immediate corrections based on careful analysis of many observed and anticipated variables

◆ ◆ ◆

Summary

1. Classroom management includes not only the manner in which order is established and maintained in the classroom, but also how curriculum, instructional activities, and student motivation and growth are promoted and governed.
2. Teachers must provide the following, at a minimum:
   a. A physically and psychologically safe learning environment
   b. Maximized opportunity to learn
   c. On-going opportunities for students to develop self-control and increased maturity
3. Multidimensionality, simultaneity, immediacy, history, and public climate are among the five dimensions of the classroom environment that must be managed.
4. Teachers in successful classrooms have strategies for dealing with the five dimensions. These include "with-itness," overlapping, smoothness, momentum, group alerting, accountability, challenge arousal, and variety.
5. Classroom management has many purposes. Many of these are value statements.
6. Negative treatment of children is inversely related to positive student behavior.
7. Teachers may act proactively, actively, or reactively to manage the classroom.

8. Teachers may determine problems and solutions alone (interventionist), with children (interactionist), or by giving children clues (noninterventionist).
9. Teachers must plan in order to have multiple strategies ready for classroom situations that are expected but not predictable.
10. Goodness and caring are fundamental to an appropriate classroom management plan.
11. Three prerequisites for successful classroom management are as follows:
    a. "Every child counts"
    b. Optimism about children
    c. An appropriate curriculum and instructional program.
12. Basic management principles include the following:
    a. Knowing the students
    b. Establishing rules where necessary
    c. Developing and using routines
    d. Maintaining positive high expectations
    e. Providing opportunity for students to assume responsibility
    f. Recognizing students as valued individuals
    g. Practicing effective basic instructional procedures
    h. Constantly analyzing your classroom for improvement strategies

◆ ◆ ◆

Activities and Questions for Further Understanding

1. Analyze the "Slice of Life" sections of other chapters to identify events that illustrate Doyle's dimensions of classroom life. Generalize a list of teacher activity that successfully deals with each dimension.

2. Using the same strategy in question 1, illustrate each of Kounin's eight classroom management behaviors.

3. Provide a critical analysis regarding the suitability of each perspective listed in Figure 4.1.

4. Create an interest inventory and other strategies that assist the teacher in getting to know the student. Share these strategies with others in your class.

5. Develop the rules necessary for your class. Describe the rationale for each one and how you could teach the children to comply with the rule.

6. Develop routines for several typical classroom activities. Test the routine by the five criteria provided in the chapter.

7. Describe the major ideas that create the "teacher's stance" that leads to successful instruction.

8. How does a teacher establish (or lose) credibility?

9. Visit classrooms and interview successful teachers. How do they develop classroom "with-itness"?

◆ ◆ ◆

References

Charles, C. M. (1983). *Elementary classroom management.* New York: Longman.

Doyle, W. (1986). "Classroom organization and management." In M. Wittrock (Ed.), *Handbook of research on teaching* (3rd ed.). New York: Macmillan.

Dreikurs, R., Grunwald, B., & Pepper, F. (1982). *Maintaining sanity in the classroom: Classroom management techniques* (2nd ed.). New York: Harper & Row.

Evertson, C. M., Emmer, E. T., Clements, B. S., & Worsham, M. E. (1994). *Classroom management for elementary teachers* (3rd ed.). Boston: Allyn and Bacon.

Glasser, W. (1985). *Control theory: A new exploration of how we control our lives.* New York: Harper & Row.

Glasser, W. (1986). *Control theory in the classroom.* New York: Perennial Library.

Glasser, W. (1989). *Schools without failure.* New York: Harper & Row.

Glickman, C. (1981). *Developmental supervision: Alternative practices for helping teachers.* Alexandria, VA: Association for Supervision and Curriculum Development.

Good, T., & Brophy, J. (1994). *Looking into classrooms* (6th ed.). New York: Harper Collins.

Good, T., & Weinstein, R. (1986). "Teacher expectations: A framework for exploring classrooms." In K. K. Zumwalt (Ed.), *Improving teaching.* Alexandria, VA: Association for Supervision and Curriculum Development.

Gordon, T. (1974). *Teacher effectiveness training.* New York: Peter H. Wyden.

Hawkins, D. (1997). "It's more than history." *Social Studies, 88*(3), 108–112.

Jones, F. (1979). "The gentle art of classroom discipline." *National Elementary Principal,* June.

Klann, K. (1996). "Observations of a student teacher." *Social Studies Review, 36*(1), 91–92.

Kounin, J. (1970). *Discipline and group management in classrooms.* New York: Holt, Rinehart and Winston.

McEwan, A. E. (1996). "Must teachers bear the moral burden alone?" *Journal for a Just and Caring Education, 2*(4), 449–459.

Megay-Nespoli, K. (1993). *The first year for elementary school teachers: A practical plan for dealing with the short and long term management of teaching duties and responsibilities.* Springfield, IL: Charles C. Thomas.

Powell, J. (1974/1979). "The secret of staying in love." In R. Bolton, *People skills.* Upper Saddle River, NJ: Prentice Hall. (Originally published by Argus Communications)

Purkey, W., & Novak, J. (1984). *Inviting school success: A self-concept approach to teaching and learning* (2nd ed.). Belmont, CA: Wadsworth.

Riner, Phillip S., & Jones, Paul. (1993). "Failure in student teaching: Two case studies." *Journal of Teacher Education and Practice, 9*(1), 39–49.

Schimmel, D. (1997). "Traditional rule-making and the subversion of citizenship." *Social Education, 61*(2), 70–74.

Weber, W. (1990). "Classroom management." In J. M. Cooper (Ed.), *Classroom teaching skills* (4th ed.). Lexington, MA: Heath.

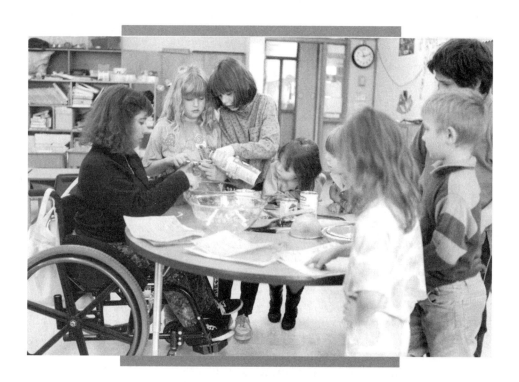

CHAPTER 5

How Do I Get Started in the Right Direction?

Understanding and Managing the Curriculum

Outline

Before there can be a rational curriculum, *we must settle which things it most concerns us to know; . . . we must determine the relative value of knowledge.*

HERBERT SPENCER

We want our children to be able to think for themselves, to be self-directing, considerate, and thoughtful.

L. E. RATHS, S. WASSERMANN, A. JONAS, AND A. M. ROTHSTEIN

A Slice of Life

Mrs. Huskins was beside herself. Her son Duane constantly complained about homework. "What a waste of time this is. This is s-o-o-o stupid!" Duane would drone day after day.

Sometimes Mrs. Huskins actually agreed with her son but always privately to herself. She would always respond, "Duane, the teacher knows why. She is trained as a teacher. She knows what she's doing."

"I wish she would tell somebody! I asked her why we had to do variables in math, and she just got mad." Duane pursed his lips and began to mimic in a singsong voice, "You need it so you can do algebra next year." Duane tossed his pencil. "Who needs algebra? Who needs math? And who in the world needs variables!"

Mrs. Huskins was at her wit's end. "Duane, just do it. Just do it, and forget about it."

Duane was about to object when the phone rang. Mrs. Huskins answered the phone briskly, "Yes, who is it?" Her eyes then brightened. It was Donnie, her oldest son who was a math major at the university. "Donnie, you called at the right time. Talk to your brother. He won't do his math homework."

Duane got out of the chair reluctantly. "Aw, Mom, what does Donnie know?"

As Donnie spoke on the phone, there was a hint of amusement in his voice. "Say, you got old Dawson for math? (chuckling) Have you had to solve those equations that plot her initials on a graph yet?" Donnie inquired.

Duane did not see the humor. "Yeah, that's what I'm doing now. It's so stupid. When I asked why we had to do it, she said we were going to need it for algebra next year. What idiot uses variables?" Duane did not expect an answer.

"You, you idiot!" was Donnie's reply. With a chuckle, he added, "You got your Game Boy handy?"

Duane reached for his game, turned it on, and said, "I've got it on. Ms. Pac Man is running. What does that have to do with math?"

Donnie quickly explained. "When you push the 'up' button, you add one to the Y axis. That would be Y + 1. If you keep it pressed, you keep adding one, and Ms. Pac Man keeps moving up. She stops at the top because the variable is set at a maximum value and can't get any bigger. If you push the 'down' button, it subtracts one from the Y-axis, and she moves down. Keep pushing and Game Boy keeps subtracting one from the Y-axis until she stops at the bottom because she has reached the minimum value for that variable. The same thing happens on the 'left' and 'right' buttons. Right adds one, left subtracts one. Push both left and down, the X- and the Y-axes get one subtracted at the same time. This continues until you quit subtracting, or she runs out of places to go. The game is set up so that the equation variables are no greater than or less than a certain number. That is where the 'walls' are on the game board. The game is nothing more than a whole big set of equations with variables plotted on a graph, Mr. Idiot." Donnie continued explaining how variables were used in video games.

Fortunately for Duane, this made perfectly good sense. He never had trouble doing his homework; he just thought it was a waste of time. He had never really thought about what made video games work. He never expected his homework to be connected to anything fun. It left him a little stunned. "OK, Donnie, you win. I'll go do my homework."

Mrs. Huskins was thankful. After she finished talking to Donnie on the phone, she wrote him a quick letter of thanks and slipped in a ten-dollar bill. She thought, "If only the teacher could talk to Duane that way."

The next day Duane was rather excited about the discovery. Immediately after the tardy bell, Duane caught Mrs. Dawson's attention by waving his hand. "Yes, Duane, what is it?"

"I know what variables are used for!"

"I do, too, Duane. Now would you look on the board and give us the coordinates for the first position?"

What Is Curriculum?

Schools are organized around a series of purposes that emerge from the common welfare of society. When these purposes are made explicit and codified, the curriculum begins to take shape. The most fundamental conceptualization of curriculum is that it is what we teach children in school. But like everything else in education, this simple definition belies the enormous complexity involved in developing a comprehensive guide to the educative mission of the school.

In trying to characterize the state of curriculum scholarship in America, Philip Jackson (1992a, 1992b) summarized the persistent position of curriculum research and theory as "confusion." He offers other commonly cited descriptors: conflict, amorphous, elusive, in disrepair, moribund, and driven into disarray. Jackson speculates that much of the confusion results from an inability, or perhaps an unwillingness, to settle on a common definition for the word "curriculum." Other contributors to curriculum confusion identified by Jackson include perspective issues (how we look at curriculum) and professional issues (how curriculum specialists view curriculum versus how teachers, administrators, parents, and children do.)

The field of curriculum has yet to agree on a common definition of curriculum. However, teachers must have a comprehensive understanding of their curriculum if they are to achieve educational goals with consistent results. To guide the management of curriculum in the daily elementary classroom life, a conceptualization of curriculum with four facets is offered (see Figure 5.1). This broad view not only includes the content of subject, but also the manner in which it is presented and evaluated. Although curriculum debate continues, teachers must still make daily decisions uniting intent, method, rationale, and results.

Curriculum Intent

Curriculum intents are usually described as outcomes that focus on the goals and aims of instruction. Curriculum intent can be stated as a list of *goals* or content areas describing the topics and information that are to be covered. This *content orientation* usually does not examine the relationship between material and learner and, therefore, is not generally favored by educators. A *process orientation* focuses on the

---

Intent (What)
- Goals and aims
- Planned experiences
- Incidental or collateral experiences
- Unplanned experiences

Rationale (Why)
- Value assumptions and assertions
- Desired outcomes
- Understanding the needs of children
- Understanding the contributions of various types of experiences

Method (How)
- Affective environment
- Intellectual environment
- Physical environment
- Material selection and use
- Cognitive structuring

Results (Effects)
- Actual outcomes
- Strategies for assessing what those outcomes are
- Activities leading to validation or redirection

FIGURE 5.1   Four facets of curriculum development and inquiry.

learner's interaction with the experience and emphasizes the role of instructional methods in what the student actually learns. In extreme examples, process orientations may completely omit reference to content. Each of the three variations of stating curriculum intent (goal, content, and process) provides important guidance in describing a curriculum's foundation. Teachers often use the terms interchangeably.

The definition of *content* used in this text refers to a broad, balanced combination of goals, materials, and skills involved when attempting to describe curriculum intent. Selection of content is an essential activity in curriculum design, providing direction and substance to the planning process. *Content selection* is the focal point for determining how the teacher will direct the work of children in school. *Curriculum content* is *everything* that the teacher will have the children do during the schoolday. The teacher may want the children to write descriptively, solve simple arithmetic problems encountered in making change, or envision the size of their country. During this primary activity, the teacher may also want the children to work cooperatively and develop a sense of worth and accomplishment. This secondary intent may be composed of incidental, or *collateral,* experiences. Secondary intents must be carefully considered in developing the curriculum.

In many ways, collateral content may be the most influential part of the curriculum for children. When writing, children need to use materials responsibly, direct their own behavior, employ creativity, and identify their work by signing it appropriately. Although these experiences are not the primary purpose of the activity selected by the teacher, learning these lessons is, nevertheless, an important part of life's successes. Secondary or collateral experiences may hold the keys to successful learning in most activities. These activities teach (or fail to teach) caring, cooperation, responsibility, and pride. None of these can be taught directly with consistent success but rather must permeate successful instruction. Affective goals are taught when they are consistently reflected in the daily work environment of the school. Theorists have referred to the latent affective effects as being the "hidden," or *implicit,* curriculum (Erickson & Shultz, 1996).

Unplanned experiences are part of the curriculum delivered to the students in schools and can play a major role in what students learn. As implied by their name, unplanned experiences happen by chance and, therefore, resist sequenced management approaches. Unplanned activities may range from the trivial to the profound. Dropping a book is a common experience that rarely enters our thinking as a significant event. However, these unplanned and recurring activities can cumulatively have a substantial impact on the characteristics of the classroom and the outcomes of teacher's efforts to instruct. If, for example, the teacher routinely chastises children for carelessness when such events occur, the outcomes of virtually all activities are affected. If the teacher shows children how to care for materials and how to prevent accidents that may damage materials, a cooperative helpful environment is developed. In turn, the cooperative environment encourages children, and the resulting improved effort affects the class's success. These unplanned events, however, should have planned responses. The teacher's consistent reaction to unplanned events can affect the character of each child and that, in itself, is a valid concern of school curriculum.

Curriculum Rationale

Children can learn many things in school. A teacher can design an inexhaustible number of experiences for the students to obtain curriculum intents. The selection or omission of an activity depends on the purpose of the teacher. The process of determining the appropriateness of intents and activities develops the *curriculum rationale.* In selecting and implementing intents and associated activities, the teacher establishes a set of guidelines that include an array of value assertions.

When time is finite and choices are nearly infinite, the teacher must decide what is most critical. Activities and their potential outcomes must be prioritized. In developing and managing the classroom curriculum, the teacher must decide whether an activity is considered a reasonable strategy for bringing about the desired outcome and whether it provides necessary variety. A carefully developed and written curriculum rationale provides a checkpoint to evaluate these differences and provides an opportunity for continual rethinking of the instructional program.

The teacher's understanding of children's needs and abilities and his or her beliefs regarding the value of certain experiences also affect the development of the curriculum rationale. Because a single measure of the relative merit of these considerations is not available, teachers are guided throughout the rationale by a mixture of research, experience, and values.

Curriculum Methods

After the intent of the curriculum has been determined and justified, it must be implemented in the classroom. Curriculum intents are actualized by *curriculum methods.* Some curriculum developers do not consider instructional strategies to be an integral part of the curriculum. Some view the methods of teaching to be instructional decisions and limit curriculum consideration to content issues alone. For this group, curriculum discussion is limited to a scope and sequence of content decisions. Others consider the methods to be the curriculum. For these curriculum thinkers, what students do *is* the curriculum, and the content selected is both arbitrary and incidental. For teachers, a clear demarcation between the relative contribution and importance of content and instruction is probably superficial. *What* students are taught and *how* they are taught greatly affect what they learn. Since teacher activity centers around student learning, both the "what's" and "how's" are integrated into the teacher's daily thinking about curriculum.

From these many views, you, as an individual teacher, will determine what works for you. Although many curriculum developers reject the importance of either content or methods, or the unification of the two, the teacher does not have the luxury of such a theoretical view. The dichotomy between methods and content is often referred to as the *process–product debate.* In most respects, this is a false dichotomy. The interaction between content selection and instruction processes contains the most salient aspects of successful curriculum development. For that reason, method selection is considered integral in determining the process by which students are introduced to the content. The result of curriculum analysis should be instruction that students find both satisfying and effective. Successful lessons are difficult to design, but teachers diligently employ critical analysis of both what they teach and how they teach it.

Curriculum Results

The results obtained from curriculum variations compose the fourth area of curriculum management for the teacher. Why develop a system of schooling if it does not improve children's abilities to demonstrate specific skills and knowledge? The outcomes of instruction are the true measure of the effectiveness of any curriculum. Theory, research, and prior implementation have established support for, and potential of, the curriculum, but if the outcomes are not there, the curriculum is unsuccessful. Unfortunately, determining outcomes is neither simple nor straightforward.

When comparing intended outcomes with actual outcomes, simple, direct comparisons are important but are usually inadequate. For example, if the curriculum design calls for third graders to learn basic multiplication facts by memory with near-instant recall, simply measuring all third graders for this ability would result in a dangerously narrow assessment of the curriculum. In this case, the measure only looks at the proposed desired outcome and ignores any efforts toward assessing the collateral outcomes. Assessment of successful development and implementation of curriculum require measures that are sensitive to outcomes that are unwanted as well as wanted, unintentional as well as intentional.

Another conundrum faces the teacher: The assessment procedures selected may directly influence interpretations regarding the appropriateness and success of the curriculum as much as the actual implementation of instructional strategies. Although the reality of the outcomes does not change, the perceptions among teachers, students, parents, and community radically alter the interpretation. Figure 5.2 illustrates three views of a baseball bat. The first is easily mistaken as being a ball. Actually, the view is looking directly at the large end of the bat. The second looks like a wheel but is actually the view from the other end of the bat. The final view is easily interpreted as a bat. This is the view that is expected and commonly used in interpreting an object as a bat. If parents used one assessment perspective, students a second, and teachers a third, they would rarely agree on what is actually occurring in the school. This echoes the message of previous chapters: The beliefs, values, skills, and experiences of teachers greatly affect every phase of instruction.

When assessments of the curriculum are made and general agreement is reached regarding the interpretation of the assessment, activity must occur that either continues the current curriculum or suggests alterations. These redirection

FIGURE 5.2 View depends on perspectives.

activities are essential for systematic improvement of schooling effectiveness. Tyler (1949) presented this cycle of intent, method, and assessment of results in a four-step system known as the *Tyler rationale:*

1. What is the education goal?
2. What instructional strategies can best meet the goals?
3. Given the context and resource, how can these strategies best be organized and delivered?
4. Once instruction is complete, how will the instructional program and the learner's accomplishments be evaluated?

These four areas—purposes, experiences, organization, and assessment—not only provide a widely accepted approach to enhancing curriculum, but also compose a simple, yet effective, definition of what composes a curriculum. A brief examination of each provides the teacher with a more complete context in which to study these areas in more detail.

Purposes of the Curriculum

Education in this country grew out of a need to preserve the moral propriety of citizens. That need still underlies the preoccupation of education today with job preparation and economic competitiveness. Public education in America soon followed the first permanent settlements. In 1647, Massachusetts enacted a public school law that compelled local communities to establish public schools where children could learn to read the Bible. This landmark event was later called the "Old Deluder Satan" Act because the law referred to the development of adequate literacy in children to read the Bible and keep the devil at bay. Although these first efforts put moral development at the forefront of education, the economic value of citizens who were able to calculate, read, and write was integrally considered. These dual purposes—moral development and economic enhancement—continue to this day as the fundamental underpinnings of public education.

Expanding the Curriculum

As the nation grew more diverse and the importance of public school received greater acceptance, the curriculum offered in public schools was subject to increased scrutiny and more varied interpretation. In the nineteenth century, the curriculum was expanded to include a diversity of subjects, such as algebra, astronomy, chemistry, botany, surveying, and philosophy. The addition of these subjects initiated the public school's retreat from predominantly reading, writing, the classics, and religious instruction (Pratt, 1980).

Just after the turn of the nineteenth century, rapid changes in the industrialization of the world forced another revolution in schooling. Free public education began to be viewed as a right of all citizens in the United States, and the common school movement required increased expenditures to provide that education. During that time, Herbert Spencer began an ambitious attempt to codify the sum of knowledge in a set of encyclopedias. In examining the structure of knowledge, Spencer (1894) concluded that there must be some rational way of determining a priority order of all existing knowledge. Although that view is quite naïve in light of today's knowledge explosion, the question "What learning is of most worth?" continues to pose an unanswerable dilemma for curriculum developers. Spencer, however, went about the task quite systematically and compiled the information he thought most important in a multiple-volume encyclopedia (Spencer, 1894).

Spencer argued that, in building curriculum, human activities must be classified in order of importance. He suggested a five-tiered hierarchy of knowledge. These activities lead to the following:

◆ Self-preservation
◆ Indirect contribution to self-preservation
◆ Rearing and discipline of offspring
◆ Maintenance of proper social and political relations
◆ Gratification of tastes and feelings through leisure

Notice that Spencer clearly establishes self-preservation (productive work) at the top of the pyramid and individual interests and needs at the very bottom. This hierarchy, positing economic success first, morality second, with individuality last, dominated the first half of the twentieth century. However, during the 1960s, societal values began to change, and a series of social and political reforms had turned the pyramid upside down for many teachers and curriculum developers. Thus, we now have a large faction who support individual expression, self-determination, and full assertion of personal rights as the primary focus of school curriculum, with moral development and economic considerations in second and third place. Society is again pressuring schools to provide education for economic success, particularly as it applies to ethnic subgroups and international economic competitiveness. The modifying caveat is that education for success should be provided for all Americans without consideration to race, ethnicity, gender, or disability. The question is whether schools will be able to provide maximized training for vocational access and financial success while simultaneously accommodating individual differences in skill, aptitude, tastes, choice, and values. Schools, however, do try to accommodate diversity and individual determination. Trying to accomplish both goals is not easy, and the results are certainly subject to extensive criticism and debate. Teachers have to deal with these conflicting values when attempting to manage the daily curriculum and often feel that they are placed in "lose-lose" situations when they have to try to please everyone. Pratt (1980) attempts to put some humor into the situation by presenting three approaches to curriculum:

Students should learn what they want to learn:	Romantic
Students should learn what they need to learn:	Programmatic
Students should learn what I want to teach:	Idiotic (p. 51)

Benefits of Articulated Purposes

Although the general goals of curriculum—morality, economic success, and individualism—appear to be fairly uniform, the meaning and prioritization of those goals can leave teachers in a quandary. If curriculum statements are subject to such broad interpretation, are they beneficial to teachers' attempts to effectively manage the curriculum?

Support and Direction.   One of the most important contributions of a clearly defined curriculum is providing support and direction to the teacher. Collectively, teachers can debate, articulate, and compromise on the mission priorities of schooling using the stated curriculum as a focusing point for discussion and action. There have been attempts, however, for the written curriculum to dictate the daily activity of teachers. So-called teacher-proof materials have been introduced as public confidence in teachers has declined, which is usually tied to the economic and social condition of the nation. Curriculum kits, learning activity packages (LAPS), learning machines, individually guided instruction, and teacher's guides to textbooks are examples of the attempt to minimize the teacher's role in determining curriculum. Although these teaching aids have contributed to the teaching arena, their lack of responsiveness to student needs have minimized this impact and influence. A curriculum of carefully articulated activities can complement the teacher's contributions, but the curriculum must guide—not direct—the activities of the teacher. Finding the right combination of the specificity in curriculum development is always a challenge. Fortunately, the "sweet spot" for curriculum specificity appears to be quite broad and varied.

Creating a Learning Environment.   A carefully articulated curriculum can provide guidance for the teacher in creating learning environments. Assuming that the curriculum is dynamic (actively debated and modified), teachers' participation in developing the curriculum provides an exchange of ideas and methods that both instructs the teacher and reviews basic concepts and strategies.

A carefully articulated curriculum can inform students of what is expected and also let parents of very young children know what is expected of the child and what the child can expect from the school. This open expression of intent also provides for appropriate and systematic assessment of school effectiveness and permits wider participation in helpful review of school effectiveness. Finally, a carefully articulated curriculum informs the public of what the school intends to do and provides the first line of accountability.

Attending to Students' Needs

Maslow (1954) established a hierarchy of individual needs that he thought directed individual behavior. Starting with the most fundamental, those needs are as follows:

1. Physiological needs (survival, basic physical needs)
2. Safety (avoidance of harm, absence of threat, sense of protection)

3. Belonging (love, affection, membership, friendship)
4. Esteem (worth, recognition, independence, status)
5. Self-actualization (becoming unique, fulfilling desires compatible with others)

If schools want to educate a child for personal fulfillment, survival needs, safety needs, belonging, and esteem must permeate the curriculum. This is doubly important for those children whose needs are not being met in their homes. Attempts have been made to use Maslow's hierarchy to guide curriculum development. Unfortunately, an explicit statement of student intellectual needs is omitted from the hierarchy. Intellectual needs form a major focus of the elementary school curriculum. Intellectual needs are subsumed indirectly in Maslow's treatment because intellectual development is instrumental to esteem and self-actualization. Because of the hidden emphasis on intellectual development and on individual needs over the economic needs of society, many individuals fail to find an adequate intellectual basis for Maslow's theory in curriculum development. Many compromise efforts have been made, and each provides certain advantages and certain limitations.

Shepherd and Raga (1992) provide such a compromise and suggest that curriculum should clearly outline the school's responsibility to students. They argue that the school must meet student needs or act as a guarantor for those needs in three broad areas: physical needs, social–moral needs, and intellectual needs—basically, a restatement in modern terms of Spencer's systemization. However, the listing does overtly address both society's need for moral behavior and the individual's need for recognition in society. Shepherd and Raga provide several advancements in thinking. First, learner needs are concurrent, not prioritized. If the school is to be successful, all of these needs must be met. By this view, although needs may have a logical prioritization, all are considered essential,. Therefore, resources must be allocated so that these basic needs in all areas are fulfilled concurrently. Second, the structure presented by Shepherd and Raga focuses on the students' current needs as opposed to their future needs as adults. Although Dewey (1916) first posed this proposition decades ago, it is difficult to create a curriculum that is valuable to children now and in the future. Third, this model assumes that by fulfilling individual self-actualization needs, society's needs will be met by the individual's contributions.

Students' Physical Needs. Physical needs of students include appropriate nutrition, rest and activity, opportunity to develop muscular coordination, and safety. Schools also need to demonstrate and teach a tolerance and understanding of the individual variation in height, weight, strength, shape, and functioning of the body. Increasingly, the school is the first point of contact for adequate medical and health services in addition to appropriate first aid and emergency care.

Informally, teachers have long been concerned with students who lack adequate clothing and have unmet nutritional needs. It is not uncommon for teachers to purchase clothing for students and to have it anonymously delivered to the home by friends. Long before federal school meal programs were developed, teachers managed to see that children obtained daily meals, clothing, and care. Teachers have often been involved with local churches and service clubs in obtaining basic fundamental needs for children. As a teacher in a small town, the author was taught the "underground" welfare program of contacts to obtain shoes, eyeglasses, coats, clothing, Christmas toys, and dental and general health care. The system was informal, hidden, shrouded in anonymity, with a careful concern for the dignity of the child and a healthy fear of developing parental dependence. Although loving and well meaning, the system nevertheless was inadequate to ensure the healthful well being of all children. In some schools, these efforts did not even exist. Instead of providing an informal program of goodwill, the school has become the central clearinghouse for a number of formal assistance programs that attempt to provide for the minimal physical needs of children.

Programs that attempt to ensure the physical needs of children vary widely by city and state and are often funded to assist targeted groups or areas. Unfortunately, the responsibility for the healthful welfare of children is widely dispersed among an almost incomprehensible array of agencies and authorities. It is very easy for children to be overlooked in that system. For that reason, it is imperative that the school and teachers act as advocates for all children, particularly those living at or near the poverty level. Systematic programs for assessing student physical needs are conducted routinely in schools for some areas such as vision and specific childhood disorders such as scoliosis. Other childhood disorders, such as diabetes, are not systematically screened; it is up to watchful observant teachers to spot warning signals.

Students also need to be taught about their physical and health needs. Explicit instruction in child health issues, such as nutrition, bodily functions, hygiene, and illnesses, fulfill an important need for information and awareness of healthful living. Additionally, students need guidance on how they can emotionally navigate childhood in a society that has maintained an unprecedented and accelerating focus on change and consumption. Whether using explicit instruction or a watchful eye, all prospective teachers need to be aware of their role in maintaining a healthy environment for children.

Students' Social-Moral Needs.   Students' social and moral needs are defined as needs that can *only* be satisfied through membership in a group. These needs include acceptance, belonging, respect, cooperation, making useful contributions, initiative, individual recognition, conformity, sense of right and wrong, development of moral conscience, and a scale of values. Meeting these needs is important if the child is to mature into a healthy adult, and the responsibility for doing so is shared by the family and the school. Some people, however, feel that this role belongs in the domain of the family, not as part of the school's curriculum. However, as discussed earlier, schools have always engaged in aspects of moral development. The issue facing the school that is particularly problematic to the teacher is, "Whose morals?"

The issue of attending to moral and social needs of students may have no solution that all parents find satisfactory. Should children be taught tolerance of moral judgments that are condemned by personal religious, cultural, and family outlooks but that are valued and held in high esteem by others? Religious tolerance, although a basic foundation of American culture, is nevertheless far from universally accepted by many nations on earth. In many countries, having the wrong religion can subject a family to persecution or even death. Should a "tolerance of those who are intolerant" be taught in hopes of promoting universal understanding of cultural differences? Which social mores are inviolable, and which are mere expressions of culture? A teacher's understanding of the basic moral issues becomes critically important if the right of each student to an appropriate education is to be considered.

For teachers in public schools, some issues supersede individual preferences. Religious tolerance is a fundamental legal entitlement, and the school must make allowances for certain beliefs regardless of the teacher's view. For example, some children are not allowed to participate in a birthday or Christmas party due to religious beliefs. The school must provide alternatives for these prohibited activities. Of course, parents must demonstrate that such practices are an integral part of the exercise of their religion and cannot prohibit activities that they simply do not like or find objectionable. Resolving these differences may seem difficult at first, but most teachers and parents develop amicable solutions. Some religious organizations even prepare comprehensive guides for teachers explaining the nature of these beliefs and suggesting strategies to accommodate individual beliefs that will have minimal or no disruption to the teacher's normal classroom conduct.

Usually, children whose parents take exception to school practices do so out of consideration for their children. More problematic are the children who receive no moral instruction or whose instruction is destructive to the welfare of others. Although a parent's participation in any political activity is a guaranteed right, conveying messages of hate, intolerance, and destruction to their children may cause these students to act in ways that cannot be sanctioned or permitted by the school. Usually, these clashes of values are unpleasant for everyone. Teachers, in close collaboration with their administrators, must work to protect the educational access to a healthy, safe, and appropriate environment for all children. The rise in student violence, drug use, property thefts, vandalism, hate crimes, and pregnancy has demonstrated effectively that moral instruction in public schools is a societal concern where the common good is at risk.

Moral instruction may include discussions and planned experiences regarding conflicts involved in sorting out life's decisions. Being honest with parents while maintaining friendships with peers are common conflicts in a child's moral development when the peer group chooses an activity of questionable value. For example, a student who wants to be accepted by a peer group may lie to his or her parents about alcohol use at a party. By including role playing and discussion activities, teachers combine speaking and reasoning skills from the intellectual arena with an active consideration of moral and social development. Finding the balance between the two is difficult, however, and few areas of the curriculum afford greater opportunities for conflict. Attending to student moral and social needs will continue to present dilemmas for the teacher.

Students' Intellectual Needs. Confronted with the fragmented authority for ensuring that students' physical needs are met and the explosive nature of attending to students' moral and social development, the beleaguered teacher is left hoping for more comfortable territory when the intellectual needs of children are considered. Yet, among the three, understanding and reaching agreement on students' intellectual needs provides the arena where the educational community has the widest disagreements and strongest competing opinions.

There are many areas of contention when debating the intellectual needs of children. Among the foremost is the process–product debate discussed earlier in this chapter. Although this debate may be centered around a false dichotomy, it often dominates the debates regarding the intellectual curriculum. Successful teaching in the elementary classroom requires teaching strategies that both attain specified content knowledge and develop higher-order cognitive skills. Neither of these goals should be left to chance nor neglected in managing the curriculum.

In the following four chapters, specific methodologies for developing lessons for content mastery in low- and high-structured subject matter as well as developing cognitive skills for using that knowledge are addressed. Acquiring and using knowledge requires a multifaceted view of the abilities and characteristics of children. Increasingly, cognitive psychology is revealing a complex pattern of individual learning differences in learning style, preference, and capability. If a student's expected success in learning varies with the type of instruction provided and that variance differs between individuals, no teacher can possibly maximize each child's opportunity to learn. What the teacher can do, though, is to provide many lessons that assist in educating the "whole mind" and to help students develop a broad array of many different learning strategies.

Several theoretical approaches are being developed to assist the teacher in matching instruction to individual differences. Gardner (1983) presents a theory of multiple intelligences that identifies the following seven different learning aptitudes or "intelligences":

- *Linguistic:* Language ability
- *Logical–mathematical:* Number and pattern
- *Spatial:* Perception of the physical
- *Bodily–kinesthetic:* Use of the body in motion
- *Interpersonal:* Relationships with others
- *Intrapersonal:* Inner feelings
- *Musical:* Tone and rhythm

Using Gardner's model, a curriculum must be developed so that children of differing intellectual abilities can have the opportunity to learn intellectual reasoning in all seven areas. The curriculum pattern for any individual child must provide instruction that develops each intelligence. In addition, teaching strategies should be formulated that provide each child with the opportunity to expand his or her individual strengths while helping him or her to increase skills in weaker areas. Currently, no systematic curriculum successfully performs both tasks. Because of the complexity of providing learning opportunities systematically and the infinite variations in students' abilities, such a curriculum is not likely to appear in classrooms in the near future, particularly as they are currently financed. This model does illustrate, however, three fundamental purposes within curriculum management in meeting student intellectual needs. First, there are many abilities that must be accommodated by the curriculum. Therefore, the intellectual curriculum must provide broad cognitive experiences that engage total student abilities. Second, a critical mission of the intellectual curriculum is to teach children to use many different processes and abilities in solving problems. Third, when content is prescribed, the curriculum must make provisions for multiple methods for mastering the material.

Common Purposes of Contemporary Curriculum

Curriculum must reflect the diverse views of teachers, parents, administrators, school boards, businesses, and the public. Therefore, much work goes into synthesizing the views of very different factions so that schools can meet the expectations of a broad range of citizens. As contemporary curriculum is debated, several prominent purposes of curriculum have emerged consistently. When managing the classroom curriculum, teachers may encounter or create goals in a variety of life, economic, and social skills. Figure 5.3 illustrates eight dominant purposes of education contained in contemporary curriculum and provides for each category some examples of curriculum aims.

Basic Skill Development.   To the general public, basic literacy and math skills still rank as the chief purpose of school. The basics of reading, writing, and math certainly have not diminished in importance; any school that does not achieve these goals fails to provide effective education.

Information Acquisition.   The public likewise supports the goal of information acquisition, particularly so-called common knowledge. For example, the public is forever fascinated by American schoolchildren's lack of geographical knowledge. A particular favorite tidbit for the press is the percentage of Americans who think New Mexico is a foreign country.

Specifically what factual information children are supposed to acquire is difficult to ascertain. A number of books have been published about which basic factual knowledge all educated Americans should know. Basic knowledge of our democratic heritage is expected, however; for example, children should learn about due process, the Bill of Rights, and how laws are created and enforced. Although such knowledge seems essential for good citizenship, even these goals have their detractors. Fortunately for teachers, current curriculum guides are typically very broad so that teachers can interpret systemwide goals in a way that best benefits their students.

Processing Information.   Another purpose of curriculum is to teach children how to process information. This skill is fundamental to daily functioning. For example, students need to learn how to understand various forms of savings or investment instruments or to compare the reliability of two competing models of automobiles. Solving problems and condensing information into usable forms are required in almost all occupations. Although the public may not pay attention to this area, processing information remains one of the most critical and elusive goals to actualize.

FIGURE 5.3 Common purposes of contemporary curriculum.

Basic skill development
- Add single-digit numbers.
- Write complete sentences with appropriate grammar and punctuation.
- Form cursive letters appropriately.

Information acquisition
- Identify the major economic activities of the home town and state.
- State the meaning of "due process of law."
- Find nations with a gross national product larger than General Motors Corporation's gross profits.

Information processing
- Develop a recycling collection plan for school (or home or community) refuse and trash.
- Calculate the amount of raw material needed to pour a concrete sidewalk to connect classroom buildings.

Creative production
- Write a dramatic monologue expressing a student's anger regarding mistreatment from a parent.
- Paint a self-portrait.
- Make a short video clip showing children at play.

Development of citizenship and social responsibility
- Attend a District Court and summarize the most important rights of the accused.
- Develop and implement a "Don't Drink" campaign for the junior high student government.
- Identify the basic components of caring.

Vocational advancement
- Develop a personal budget for living alone while earning the minimum wage.
- Write a business letter requesting attention to a complaint.
- Calculate wages and appropriate deductions for a payroll check.

Healthful living and recreation
- Complete a square (or round or line) dance.
- Successfully complete a basketball free throw.
- Describe the appropriate daily dental hygiene.

Affective development
- Orally express polite resentment to someone who is rude.
- Appreciate the skill involved in ballet.
- Be able to judge "correctness" of various approaches to solving a problem involving theft.

Creative Production.   Creative production is just emerging in many curriculum areas. Although music instruction has long been in the curriculum, creative writing, drama, painting, and crafts have become accepted as legitimate studies during the past three decades. Student-run newspapers and literary magazines are common in the elementary school and can be influential components of the elementary curriculum. Additionally, creativity is being recognized as central to achievement in such diverse fields as science, technology, and management.

Citizenship and Social Responsibility.   Citizenship is being redefined in the elementary curriculum. Traditionally, citizenship tacitly meant "doing what the teacher tells you to do." Citizenship in today's curriculum requires teaching responsible behavior, cooperative effort, participation, and caring. Citizenship education is poised for a radical revival as the social fabric of the nation continues to erode and is subject to increasing scrutiny.

Vocational Advancement.   Vocational education has historically been allocated to secondary school. However, many vocational skills are now taught in the elementary school. Promptness, effort, and accountability are considered to be "prevocation"

Solving problems involves multiple goals.

work skills; the elementary school provides early and consistent exposure to these work attributes. Society can no longer rely on the family or happenstance to teach these skills consistently to all children.

Healthful Living.   The United States spends more per person on health care than any other nation on earth and yet is on the verge of a health-care crisis. Substance abuse through alcohol, illegal drugs, and prescription medications is among the worst anywhere in the world. Even more disturbing is that these afflictions are often correlated with ethnicity and economic status. Today, our children are fed diets high in fat and low in nutrition. Healthful exercise is being brushed aside in favor of television, stereo systems, and computer games. Increased attention to healthful living, satisfying use of leisure time, and personal well being will take on broadening importance if current trends continue.

Affective Development.   Affective development remains an elusive area of the curriculum. Teaching children about emotions and helping them to develop positive attitudes is an integral component of effective instruction. However, affective development includes not only basic shared values but also other attitudes and beliefs that appropriately belong in the domain of the family. Conflict in the affective curriculum is common and inevitable. Currently, affective development is best addressed by providing a supportive, safe environment for children, giving encouragement, teaching restraint, correcting behavior, and having faith in a student's self-determination.

The successful teacher addresses each of these areas of affective development daily. Most curricular activities have multiple purposes; almost everything done in the classroom adds to or subtracts from the affective development and maturation of the child. The successful teacher should constantly compare the curriculum being offered with these curriculum purposes to be sure that a broad approach to all student needs is being implemented.

Curriculum Experiences and Organization

Curriculum must be organized and experiences preplanned so that school resources can be allocated. Resources include time, materials, equipment, space, and human support. By organizing the curriculum, key decisions can be made that enhance the likelihood that decisions are made appropriately and school efficiency is enhanced. Three methods of organizing curriculum have emerged: subject matter, needs of students, and problem-solving approach.

Organizing Around Subject Matter

The most common method of organizing curriculum is around subject classifications. The typical curriculum is designed around math, science, social studies, reading, and language arts (Ornstein & Hunkins, 1988). The arts and physical education are added to round out most elementary curriculum organizations. Although considered a tool, technology is being included in many school curricula because of the increasing importance of technological competence in the workplace. There is something both natural and contrived about this organization around subjects. Some subjects, such as math, contain an internal structure that provides a logical sequential course of study. Other subjects, such as literature, do not. These areas are almost always related to other subject areas such as the historical context of a novel. Within low- and high-structured subjects, a sequential, hierarchical presentation can usually be created and defended. This type of order provides assurances that curriculum is not a "hit or miss" affair and covers all of the important aspects of the subject.

On the other hand, knowledge acquired about a specific subject is not always connected to how that knowledge can be used and how it relates to other activities. Accounting, for example, is much more than simply counting and tracking money. Tax law, economic trends, growth projections, and commodity cycles are all involved in tracking and assessing the flow of money and assets through a business. If the effective use of knowledge is considered in curriculum development, aligning the curriculum based solely on subject matter is a process almost condemned to shortcomings from the start.

There are a number of strategies for overcoming the limitations of subject classifications in organizing curriculum. Although single-subject organization is dominant, some curriculum planners attempt to combine topic areas to focus on compatible aspects of study. The resulting curriculum is *multidisciplinary* in that a course of study uses multiple disciplines. An *integrated* approach attempts to merge the subjects further by focusing on broad fields of study. Although the inherent structure of subjects is not totally discounted, an integrated curriculum focuses on the application of subject matter knowledge to a specific problem or line of inquiry. Broudy, Smith, and Burnett (1964) proposed a curriculum composed of symbolics of education (language and math), basic sciences, developmental studies (development of culture and schools of thought), exemplars (aesthetic experience), and molar problems (social problems). Multidisciplinary and integrated approaches are currently fashionable, but generally supplemental, methods of organizing curriculum for delivery.

Organizing Around the Needs of Students

A second method of organizing curriculum eschews the traditional organization by subject matter classifications in favor of an intensive examination of students' needs. Learner-centered designs argue that if a curriculum of value to the learner is to be developed, it must be organized around the characteristics of the learner rather than any inherent or logical structure of the subject matter. This curriculum orientation is propelled by the belief that learning should be directed by the child's natural unfolding of interests and learning. The learner-centered focus has had great impact on curriculum development during this century. The curriculum that has emerged is still centered primarily around subjects but is organized for delivery based on theories developed by cognitive psychologists on the abilities of children. The developmental psychologist Piaget (1973) remains one of the most influential voices in describing the abilities of students.

This approach has a number of advantages. By planning a curriculum around a student's needs and abilities, the probability of the curriculum having and communicating inherent value to a student is maximized. Student motivation should increase, and optimal learning environments should be easier to construct. Even with this critical advantage, though, learner-centered designs have found only intermittent acceptance.

The primary difficulty in learner-centered approaches lies in the assessment of the needs and abilities of students. Although cognitive psychology has enlightened educators on the intellectual abilities, needs, and characteristics of children, consistent successful implementation of this knowledge has been elusive. The interpretations of these works have provided widely varying approaches to teaching.

The most critical limitation of the learner-centered approach is a logistical consideration. Needs and immediate abilities of children vary substantially. With classrooms containing 25 to 30 children or more, the teacher must react to the expressed and emerging needs of students in small instructional groups. Individual treatment of students, except in special circumstances, simply is not possible with the current level of resources. Additionally, wide variations in learner needs and abilities require wide variations in the curriculum to respond to those needs. This reactive approach to curriculum diminishes consistency in the curriculum, increases the burden of the teacher in determining the curriculum, and heightens demands on teacher knowledge and skill.

Organizing Around Problems

A third approach has emerged that attempts to capture the advantages of consistent structure of subject matter and the motivation gained by a curriculum that focuses on fulfilling student needs. Problem-centered designs focus on the problems of living successfully, both from societal and individual self-actualization perspectives (Ornstein & Hunkins, 1988). Problem-centered designs allow developers to develop the curriculum with generalized notions about the learners prior to actual contact with the learners. This provides teachers with substantial support and direction in the planning and execution of the curriculum and minimizes the reliance on immediate interpretations of students' needs. Content is included according to its usefulness in assisting students to resolve common social and personal problems. A great deal of emphasis is placed on understanding living in various societal settings. Of course, what is considered a "problem" can vary widely. Therefore, emphasis is placed on common themes or strands that maintain a certain level of consistency regardless of specific student differences. For example, making purchases and making wise decisions regarding purchases is a problem for all citizens. Assessing costs, adding and subtracting money, comparing weights and other measures of quantity, ascertaining per unit costs, weighing product effectiveness and reliability, and budgeting expenditures with projected income provide a carefully articulated curriculum area.

The advantages of the problem-centered approach make it an attractive alternative to subject matter or learner-centered perspectives. Problems provide a natural vehicle for determining relevance of content and provide a context in which academic skills can be generalized to daily use. However, the problems approach does present some significant challenges. Primarily, problems that integrate the use of skills from varying disciplines or subjects do not necessarily provide appropriate opportunity for the initial development of those skills. In the preceding example, ascertaining per unit costs is a substantially more advanced skill than adding costs of purchases. In fact, finding a sum for a set of numbers is a prerequisite skill for developing per unit costs. Teaching both simultaneously or even in close sequence does not provide an optimal experience. Obviously, this difficulty is a reflection of the problem under study and may be manipulated to minimize the conflict in skill needs.

An additional problem occurs in determining the kinds of problems that children may find relevant. If problems are carefully studied and structured to include only the skills that students can learn, the number of problems to be taught is necessarily limited by the time available for careful planning and development by the teacher.

Perhaps the greatest problem in the problem-centered approach is its hidden assumption that the value and relevance of any knowledge depends on whether it can resolve social or individual problems. For example, literary works, symphonies, and dramatic vehicles may have utilitarian value, but their primary value is the quality that they add to personal development and introspection. Nevertheless, the problems approach certainly provides teachers with a substantial supplement, if not an alternative, to the dominant, subject-centered curriculum.

Selecting Experiences

Erasmus wrote in 1515:

> I have no patience with the stupidity of the average teacher of grammar who wastes precious years in hammering rules into children's heads. For it is not by learning rules that we acquire the power of speaking a language, but by daily intercourse with those accustomed to express themselves with exactness and refinement, and by the copious reading of the best authors. (Binder, 1970, p. 141)

Erasmus's lament is almost identical to contemporary attacks on grammar instruction. Which experiences should accompany curriculum content has been bitterly contested for centuries. Sometimes, the same questions are debated with each ensuing generation. With this lack of consensus, how is a teacher to manage the curriculum? Although contemporary research has attempted an empirical investigation of the effectiveness of curriculum experiences in terms of teacher behavior, student activity, and instructional strategies, the current knowledge only provides a partial picture.

Clandinin and Connelly (1992) describe how teachers' views were not considered during the early literature on curriculum development. Instead, teachers were viewed as mediators between curriculum and its object (students) rather than as creators, evaluators, or specialists of curriculum. The teacher's role in curriculum development was described in terms of a conduit, in which information flowed through teachers from school officials to students. Certainly, teachers are the primary pipeline for the public to realize its educational ambitions for children. However, the progressive flow of curriculum purposes toward a realization of student learning is not as direct as the metaphor implies.

Many aids are available to assist in selecting and using the content and strategies involved in daily instruction. These include curriculum guides, annotated versions of textbooks providing teaching strategies, inservice training programs, curriculum specialists who work with teachers, and commercial instructional packages. Despite these aids, the teacher is still responsible for creating the immediate environment that best meets the needs of the students. These individual alterations were discussed in previous chapters and a model of teacher decision-making was developed (see Figure 2.10). In a similar vein, Hunter (1994) describes three clusters of teacher decisions: content to be learned, learning behaviors to be used by students, and teaching behaviors to be used by the teacher. Notice that these instructional decision groups are nearly the same as those primary decisions made in developing curriculum. Although the curriculum may prescribe certain content, teachers must decide whether the curriculum component is appropriate and timely and which experiences will be effective. This process of teacher decision making can lead to great variations in the actual curriculum. Teachers must pay special attention to ensure that their activities align with the curriculum.

Curriculum Alignment.   The degree in which the teacher's instruction, students' learning, and the stated curriculum correlate or match is called *curriculum alignment*. Alignment depends on the knowledge and skill of the teacher. Hunter (1994) contends that propositional knowledge (what affects learning), procedural knowledge (how to implement instructional propositions), and conditional knowledge (when and why to use propositions) enable teachers to make decisions that result in curriculum alignment and learning effectiveness. To maintain alignment, teachers must continually assess classroom activity using a wide variety of strategies.

Curriculum Heuristics.   Although teacher knowledge contributes to curricular alignment, the *heuristics* (strategies that are used to solve problems) may have an even greater impact. Taba (1970) suggests the following seven steps to curriculum design:

◆ Diagnosing needs
◆ Formulating objectives
◆ Selecting content
◆ Organizing content
◆ Selecting learning experiences
◆ Organizing learning experiences
◆ Determining what to evaluate and which methods to use

According to this sequence, when teachers use their knowledge to select learning experiences, the assumption is that a utilitarian assessment of needs, carefully developed objectives with associated content, and a comprehensive organization scheme is available to them that facilitates their understanding of the curriculum. Unfortunately, these assumptions may be optimistic. When teachers select experiences, the impact of Jackson's (1992) description of curriculum as being "confused" is readily felt. However, across all curriculum documents, several strategies exist to help the teacher select curriculum experiences. Specific strategies for low- and high-structured material have been identified and are commonly referred to as *direct* (expository) and *indirect* (inquiry-based) instruction. Collateral learning has also been studied, and strategies such as cooperative learning, modeling, and counseling approaches appear to be successful.

Variety.   Teachers who employ a *variety* of approaches consistently have a high degree of instructional success according to virtually all comprehensive summaries of teaching effectiveness. The curriculum must provide a variety of experiences that include the full gamut of human skill, cognition, and emotion. Teaching with a variety of approaches, along with communicating clearly, emphasizing success, and maintaining students' and teachers' focus on learning tasks, are essential to teaching effectiveness as identified by empirical research (Borich, 1996; Cruickshank, 1990).

In providing variety, students are given optimal opportunities for success. By avoiding satiation, teachers and students remain fresh to the learning task. To achieve this method of managing the curriculum, many organization paradigms are available to assist teachers in systematically selecting a variety of experiences for their students. In selecting cognitive activities, two models will be examined: Thinking Keywords by Raths et al. (1967) and the Taxonomy of Educational Objectives by Bloom (1956).

Thinking Keywords

Raths et al. (1967) acknowledge that it is common among educational leaders to assume that teachers must take responsibility for changing the behavior of children. However, Raths et al. stress the idea that teachers must only be responsible for providing experiences that will give students the opportunity to change. Thus, giving children the opportunity to assess their learning, its relevance, and their success is an imperative dictate to teachers. Teachers should provide a series of structuring cognitive activities to children daily.

Raths et al. (1967) developed 12 "thinking keywords" (Figure 5.4), which are a series of thinking operations for analyzing student behavior as well as teacher behavior. This list is designed to assist the teacher in explaining to students how to exercise that operation. Raths et al. stress the teacher's role in providing expert personal analysis to develop and provide learning experiences for children:

> Developing curriculum materials is a difficult task, and it is easier to follow the book. Moreover, if thinking is to be stressed, one must pay close attention to what the children say and write; a teacher must also pay attention to what he is saying and writing. (p. 3)

1. **Observing**   Collecting data by the senses (notice, describe, depict, characterize, illustrate, recite, specify)
2. **Classifying**   Grouping concepts or objects using given or created criteria (name, categorize, group, catalog, sort)
3. **Comparing**   Identifying the similarities and differences in two or more concepts or entities (contrast, liken, differ, relate, weigh against, compare, match)
4. **Summarizing**   Isolating the main ideas and characteristics of an event or concept (find the most important part, abstract, sum up, condense, digest, put in a nutshell)
5. **Interpreting**   Finding the meaning of a passage, event, or phenomenon (translate, explain, define, depict, portray, clarify)
6. **Collecting and organizing data**   Assembling information in usable form (gather, accumulate, compile, pull together, assemble, manage, order)
7. **Imagining**   Creating new or novel concepts (invent, devise, suppose, picture, make up)
8. **Looking for assumptions**   Finding unproven conjecture used as fact (reexamine, rethink, reevaluate, review, reconsider, recheck)
9. **Criticizing**   Formulating opinions by reason and attention to data (reflect, consider, analyze, study, scrutinize)
10. **Hypothesizing**   Creating potential explanations or predictions for phenomena (speculate, suppose, guess, conclude, venture)
11. **Applying facts and principles in new situations**   Transferring learning to situations not previously experienced (use, operate, exercise, utilize, explore, apply)
12. **Decision making**   Taking situations, information, and problems and proposing and implementing action (conclude, decide, resolve, settle, finish, carry through, complete)

FIGURE 5.4   Thinking keywords: A guide to thinking operations.

Based on *Teaching for Thinking: Theory and Application* by L. E. Raths, S. Wassermann, A. Jonas, and A. M. Rothstein, 1967, Columbus, OH: Merrill.

Although the rigors of curriculum development require holistic thinking about all aspects of educational endeavors simultaneously, special attention to cognitive processes involved in each experience provides the navigational checks required to steer a straight course. The activities described by Raths et al. provide an active curriculum that treats knowledge as changing and emergent rather than static. Such an array of curriculum experiences provides the opportunity for students to learn how to deal with current problems and also to learn the skills and attitudes that they will need in the future. Providing children with the skills that they will need for an unknown future is what challenges the teacher most rigorously. According to Doxiadis (1967),

Dealing merely with the present is unrealistic because by the time we have analyzed the situation, defined our problems, and planned how to meet them, the present has become the past; by the time we are ready to act and create new conditions, the present is the distant past. (p. 12)

Active use of all thinking operations on a daily basis enables students to deal with the present and to handle possible outcomes and future problems. For example, to provide experiences in classifying in a unit on plants, the teacher may ask students to do the following:

◆ Name what each of the plants in the terrarium (or playground) have in common.
◆ Describe the characteristics that pine trees have that oak trees do not.
◆ Group the flowers on the front lawn and describe the categories.
◆ Sort bark samples into two different categories and describe the differences between the two groups.

By examining each of the thinking operations and its relationship to experiences in a given unit of instruction, the teacher ensures a variety of activities using a wide range of student abilities while still maintaining a coherent academic focus and accountable instruction.

Taxonomy of Educational Objectives

Benjamin Bloom (1956) developed a simpler but equally comprehensive system of examining learning activities. Bloom's taxonomy of educational objectives (see Figure 5.5) is among the most popular and widely used outlines for obtaining variety in the curriculum. The taxonomy includes six classifications of educational objectives: knowledge, comprehension, application, analysis, synthesis, and evaluation.

Unlike the "thinking keywords" of Raths et al., Bloom's taxonomy has an inherent structure that implies a hierarchy of operations. As presented in Figure 5.5, the sequence leads from the item with the least intellectual complexity (recall) to the item with the greatest level of intellectual complexity (evaluation). Do not confuse complexity with difficulty. Many tasks that are classified as recall may be more difficult than tasks in higher levels of the taxonomy. For example, recalling the Preamble to the Constitution may require much more time than providing a critical evaluation of why you enjoyed a particular book. The complexity issue, however, is an important consideration even if it is not predictive of difficulty. When a teacher considers various objectives for use in the classroom, selecting an objective in a complexity hierarchy requires additional care and thought because knowledge and skills contained in lower levels of complexity may be prerequisite. For example, when selecting objectives in the evaluation area, the teacher must expect that the student can use skills developed in virtually all other areas of the hierarchy. For example, in evaluating the contribution of the Bill of Rights to the development of America's sense of freedom, the student must be able to do the following:

◆ Recall basic facts regarding the Bill of Rights
◆ Comprehend what the items mean
◆ Apply that meaning to individual action

Domain	Definition	Verbs
Knowledge	The learner can remember facts, recall terms and procedures, and locate information.	define, describe, identify, list, match, name, recall, recite
Compehension	The learner can demonstrate understanding by translating, paraphrasing and interpreting, changing knowledge from one form to another, and predicting outcomes and effects.	convert, estimate, explain, infer, interpret, rearrange, rewrite, summarize, translate
Application	The learner can use or transfer knowledge or skill to a new situation.	change, compute, demonstrate, operate, show, solve, use
Analysis	The learner can discover and differentiate information and examine the component parts, understand the organization and relationship of its parts, and compare for similarities and differences.	breakdown, categorize, diagram, discriminate, distinguish, order, outline, subdivide
Synthesis	The learner can combine information, ideas, concepts, or skills into new forms.	combine, compile, compose, create, design, generalize, plan, produce, rearrange
Evaluation	The learner can support a judgment with reason and establish the value, quality, or appropriateness of knowledge or activity.	appraise, compare, conclude, contrast, criticize, justify, support

FIGURE 5.5   An explanation of Bloom's taxonomy of educational objectives.
Based on *Taxonomy of Educational Objectives* by Benjamin Bloom, 1956, New York: David McKay.

- Analyze those activities and their relationship to our beliefs
- Reassemble those activities into a comprehensive view of the attitudes that typify American culture

This, of course, is a tidy example; the taxonomy does not present a lockstep hierarchy of complexity or prerequisites. The example does illustrate and reiterate an important point to remember when managing the classroom curriculum: Although information acquisition may be a prerequisite skill, many other learning activities, such as developing cognitive skills that empower students, must be included in the curriculum if knowledge is to be employed successfully.

An Example of Organization

Curriculum is often organized around a singular taxonomy using either single subjects, integrated themes, or problems. Armstrong (1994) provides an excellent example of using more than one organizational structure to prepare a curriculum. Figure 5.6 is a matrix combining Bloom's taxonomy of educational objectives and Gardner's multiple intelligences theory in a unit on ecology.

Bloom's Levels of Educational Objectives

	Knowledge	Comprehension	Application	Analysis	Synthesis	Evaluation
Linguistic intelligence	Memorize names of trees	Explain how trees receive nutrients	Given description of tree diseases, suggest cause of each disease	List parts of a tree	Explain how a tree functions in relation to the ecosystem	Rate different methods of controlling tree growth
Logical— mathematical intelligence	Remember number of points on specific trees' leaves	Convert English to metric in calculating the height of a tree	Given height of the smaller tree, estimate height of the larger tree	Analyze materials as found in sap residue	Given weather, soil, and other information, chart projected growth of a tree	Rate different kinds of tree nutrients based on data
Spatial intelligence	Remember basic configurations of specific trees	Look at diagrams of trees and tell what stage of growth they are in	Use geometric principles to determine the height of the tree	Draw cellular structure of a tree root	Create a landscaping plan using trees as the central feature	Evaluate practicality of different landscaping plans
Bodily— kinesthetic intelligence	Identify tree by the feel of the bark	Given array of tree fruits, identify seeds	Given type of local tree, find an ideal location for planting it	Create different parts of a tree from clay	Gather all materials needed for planting a tree	Evaluate the quality of different kinds of fruit
Musical intelligence	Remember songs that deal with trees	Explain how old tree songs came into being	Change the lyrics of an old tree song to reflect current issues	Classify songs by issue and historical period	Create your own tree song based on information in this unit	Rate the songs from best to worst and give reasons for your choices
Interpersonal intelligence	Record responses to the question, "What is your favorite tree?"	Determine the most popular tree in class by interviewing others	Use survey results to pick a location for a field trip to an orchard	Classify kids into groups according to their favorite tree	Arrange a field trip to an orchard by contacting the necessary people	Rank three methods to ask others about tree preference
Intrapersonal intelligence	Remember a time when you climbed a tree	Share the primary feeling you had while up in the tree	Develop "tree-climbing rules" based on your experience	Divide your experience into "beginning," "middle," and "end."	Plan a tree-climbing expedition based on your past experience	Explain what you liked best and least about your experience

FIGURE 5.6 Matrix of Gardner's multiple intelligences theory and Bloom's taxonomy used in an ecology unit on local trees.

From *Multiple Intelligences in the Classroom* by Thomas Armstrong, 1994, Alexandria, VA.: Association for Supervision and Curriculum Development. Used by permission of ASCD.

Assessing Curriculum Results and Effectiveness

Theoretically, the best way to assess the effectiveness of the curriculum is from the data used to create the curriculum. Unfortunately, few curricula are created from a systematic examination of data about children. Fewer still contain clearly stated goals that lend themselves to accurate measurement and assessment. Making the situation even gloomier is the misconception that assessing the learning of individual children results in adequate assessment of the curriculum. Again, the refrain of Jackson's analysis of "confusion" seems appropriate.

Teachers, however, can help to reverse this neglect of curriculum analysis. By carefully planning the curriculum, teachers can provide simple and effective assessment procedures. It was stated earlier that curriculum views have various sources of origin including the structure of the subject matter, perceived student needs, and perceived societal needs. It was also stressed that the perspective of various individuals, and the way in which individuals approach and judge situations, may have as much influence in determining judgments about curriculum as does any data source. Finally, it was noted that curriculum experiences include collateral effects other than the main intent stated in the curriculum. These collateral effects must also be taken into account when assessing the curriculum. The teacher is faced with an almost overwhelming task when assessing the classroom curriculum's effectiveness. Fortunately, assessing the curriculum is the entire school's responsibility, not just the teacher's. However, teachers can assess several aspects of the assessment on the classroom level. These areas are as follows:

◆ Responsiveness of curriculum to students' needs
◆ Alignment with the stated curriculum
◆ Attainment of teaching goals
◆ Acquisition of desired attitudes toward learning and citizenship by students

Assessing Responses to Student Needs

When curriculum developers conduct student needs assessments, many sources of opinion are solicited. These sources include parents and taxpayers, politically influential individuals and pressure groups, students, teachers, academic specialists, social experts, employers, labor organizations, recent graduates, nongraduates or dropouts, community agencies, and frontier thinkers (Pratt, 1980). When assessing the classroom curriculum, teachers are particularly interested in the opinions of three of these groups.

The opinions of parents, students, and other teachers about the appropriateness and effects of the classroom curriculum are absolutely essential in guiding teachers. Data from these sources are generally collected informally in an ongoing process. For example, parents may say that they appreciate the collaborative homework that children do with parents in a current events unit and the benefits derived from such endeavors. Teachers may comment on the preparedness of students in earlier grades to engage in particular studies. Students are usually quite willing to share opinions about how and what they are learning. The "Slice of Life" earlier in this chapter demonstrates an unfortunate lack of responsiveness by the teacher to an excellent source of student feedback.

More formal methods of obtaining data for needs assessment include packages or evaluation kits, questionnaires, interviews, public hearings, analysis of social indicators, and systematic observation. These methods provide superb opportunities for assessing the classroom contribution to stated goals. A striking example involves a middle school that had experienced a rash of student pregnancies involving about 10 percent of female students. After modifying the curriculum to include a discussion about sexuality in the physical education component on maturation, a follow-up study one year later revealed that the teen pregnancy rate had dropped to less than one percent. The redeveloped curriculum emphasized sexual abstinence during the teen years, but it also included birth control information. A side benefit, revealed from student surveys, was a greater awareness of love and family in sexual relations and a decrease in sexual activity by the teens. The teachers involved in the curriculum response to student needs now had substantial evidence to support continued education involving human sexuality in the physical education curriculum.

Whatever instrument is used to determine student needs, repeating the survey later on is necessary to determine whether the curriculum is continuing to meet that particular need. Annualized standardized testing, grade level unit tests of basic skills, repeated measures of basic skills assessments, evaluation of student attendance, incidence of expulsions, acts of vandalism, or hours of parent volunteerism all afford benchmarks for assessing the classroom curriculum. Even comparing the number of guest speakers from year to year yields illuminating data on whether the curriculum is expanding the learning experiences of children and increasing the involvement of the community. It is important not to overlook such simple data types in assessing the classroom curriculum.

Assessing Alignment with the Stated Curriculum

Consider the plight of a third-grade teacher ready to introduce a unit on multiplication. In the early stages of planning, the teacher gave a short pretest to assess student knowledge of multiplication. The teacher normally expected a range of understanding comparable to the range of student ability. However, several of her brightest students did not know any basic multiplication facts (the teacher had expected student to know 0's, 1's, 2's, 5's, and 10's) or demonstrate any understanding of the basic concept of multiplication as repetitive addition of the same number. On the other hand, some of the students that the teacher expected to have difficulty actually had a firm understanding of both the facts and the concepts.

After discussing this with the second-grade teachers, she was dismayed. One of the second-grade teachers revealed, "Oh, I don't believe in teaching multiplication to second graders. It's too hard. I just skip it. We spend extra time on addition." Accurately enough, the class had shown a similar demarcation when learning to regroup on two-digit numbers. The children had learned what the teachers had taught; they did not know what the teachers had not taught. The problem for this teacher was that, because of such radically different exposures in the math curriculum sequence, the normal differences between students had increased. The problem manifests itself time after time in all areas of the curriculum. In science, a teacher is faced continually with the result of idiosyncratic choices of teachers so that some students have studied magnetism (or adaptation, or mammals, or the hydrologic cycle) while others have not. The same problem source was identified. One second-grade teacher had not taught the curriculum-required second-grade topics whereas another teacher had jumped ahead and taught third-grade topics to the second graders. Even if our third-grade teacher were to go back and teach the second-grade topics, half of the students would already have studied those topics. What had occurred was a lack of curricular alignment.

The competing initiatives among teacher creativity, curriculum responsive to student interests, educational innovation, and sequenced curriculum have provided teachers with mixed messages about the conduct of their classrooms. Obviously, our third-grade teacher has a problem, but the nature of the problem varies with perspective. Some curriculum reformers are quick to point out that the subject matter content of the curriculum is superfluous. What really counts is whether students are able to use such skills as inquiry, critical decision making, and teamwork. From this perspective, the problem lies more with the teacher who teaches prescribed content rather than focusing on an intensive examination of the interests of students. On the other hand, school boards are legally the determiners of school curriculum, and most teacher contracts require that they follow the prescribed curriculum. Although teacher determination of teaching strategies and flexibility on some content selection is essential for effective teaching, complete disregard for the school's curriculum plan can result in chaos.

Teachers can find out whether their classroom curriculum is aligned with the school curriculum by the following:

- Referring to the scope and sequence statement for the curriculum published by the school or district
- Consulting veteran teachers, curriculum supervisors, and the school principal
- Maintaining abbreviated lesson plans and submitting them to supervisors
- Comparing the lessons provided with the scope and sequence of nationally circulated textbooks in skill-based subjects
- Referring to the suggested curriculum content of national organizations designed to promote those subjects
- Consulting with teachers who will teach the students the following year
- Examining the results of standardized tests
- Analyzing the results of systemwide student assessments

None of these methods alone are adequate, but when considered collectively, they will guide the teacher toward appropriate curricular alignment. Developing instructional innovations, meeting individual student needs, and providing for personal professional growth require experimentation, creativity, and departures from traditions. Yet, these activities must be balanced with the students' entire educational needs over the years rather than their needs for day-to-day or situation-specific experiences. Finding that balance is not difficult in most situations when teacher awareness and school cooperation are nurtured.

Assessing Students' Learning

The assessment of students' learning has many purposes and methods. At the forefront are the aims of holding students accountable for their learning and guiding the teacher in assessing the effectiveness of daily instruction. Assessing students' learning to determine the effectiveness and appropriateness of the curriculum, however, differs from typical student assessment in that the focus is not on individual students. Instead, attention is directed at cumulative effects of various patterns of experiences on various groups of students. This perspective also uses assessments, usually standardized tests administered at benchmark grade levels, to determine whether the minimal skills considered essential to public schooling are being taught and learned. Districts that administer annualized testing sometimes also use them informally to assess individual teacher effectiveness. This practice has very serious implications; even the most minimally valid comparisons require extremely sophisticated technical and statistical controls and analyses. Standardized testing, even with its shortcomings, does provide a reasonable starting point for a simple examination of the curriculum's effectiveness in producing student learning, with the following caveats:

◆ *The standardized tests and the school curriculum must be aligned.* Essentially this means that what the test purports to measure and what the school curriculum purports to teach have been examined and are the same.
◆ *The standardized test is viewed as a minimalist expression of student learning.* Standardized tests do not measure the nuances of the curriculum as it must be tailored to the students in a school or classroom. Usually, only the most universally accepted skills and content are assessed; attitudes, values, and collateral learning are not.
◆ *Standardized tests are affected by variables other than the school's instructional program.* The students' economic and regional membership, parent education, and family attitudes are also major influential variables in standardized testing results.
◆ *Standardized tests results cannot be evaluated without additional data.* A high percentile score does not necessarily indicate student success, nor does a low score necessarily indicate failure. Differences in student populations minimize the validity of simple comparisons. A student's progress from the previous assessment provides a more meaningful measure of student growth.

In using standardized tests as part of a program for assessing the curriculum and its effectiveness, the purpose of the assessment must always be remembered. The central purpose of curriculum evaluation must always be to improve the curriculum, thus improve the educational effectiveness of the school and the success opportunities for each student. If, for example, the school composite results show a high level of mastery in reading decoding skills, the school must still work on improving the skill level of the low-achieving students. Likewise, if the composite indicates extreme shortcomings, the school must examine the curriculum to see if the skills were included, if the skills were taught, and if the various methods used by teachers to develop those skills were the correct ones. The school must also examine the relative contribution of other factors, particularly the students' entering behaviors.

An example illustrates the danger of naïve or simplistic use of test scores. A second-grade teacher was completely distraught about the results of a state-mandated standardized test. Her class had managed to score around the fiftieth percentile on virtually every category. She lamented that half her students were below average in every measure. What she found most disappointing was that the class had shown exceptional effort, particularly in reading for pleasure and conducting science projects. She had rated the class one of her best in years, but according to the test, they were actually no better than any of her previous classes. Other teachers in the second grade were also upset.

The principal was upset as well, but not about the scores. Actually, she was elated. What upset her was that the teachers had found defeat in the test results. The principal was aware of some data that the teachers also knew about but had not used in their evaluations of the test score. First, the composite measure of IQ for the group resulted in a score of 88, well below the fiftieth percentile mark and the lowest such measure the principal had ever seen at this school. This group also had 75 percent of students participating in the federal lunch and breakfast program. As first graders, their average attendance rate was only 86 percent. All of these indicators pointed to achievement rate that might have been well below average—a scenario not borne out in this year's testing scores. Second, the teachers had branched out and enriched the curriculum. Instead of emphasizing practice skills from worksheets, they had spent a lot of time on reading for pleasure, exploring in sciences and social studies, and using math calculation skills in a variety of school projects. Thus, the scores actually showed substantial gains from previous years. Third, absenteeism in the second grade was less than a third of what it had been in any of the last five years. Finally, PTA attendance and parent volunteerism were up, and discipline referrals were down. The principal recognized a dramatic success, whereas the teachers, who had put so much renewed effort into the year, only saw failure.

Aside from standardized tests, teachers can use other ways to assess student learning. For example, our discouraged second-grade teacher had tracked the number of books that each student had read and had managed to develop a series of "book conference" strategies in which she discussed the book with the student after he or she read it. Often, she discussed books while waiting in line for lunch, before and after school, and during recess. Students who had already read the book had "book conferences" with students who just completed the book. Sometimes, the children would develop "book advertisements" to solicit new readers. Each child kept an annotated reading list to which the book conference partner added comments. These assessment strategies and the resulting documentation are very plausible sources of data in determining whether the curriculum is successful in promoting reading for enjoyment, comprehension, and literary analysis.

The key to assessing curriculum is documentation, use of multiple instruments, and the consistent collection, use, and examination of data. Armstrong (1994) suggests the use of work samples, anecdotal records, class charts plotted for both skill attainment and completion of activities, checklists completed periodically (for example, at the end of a unit), and criterion-referenced assessments. Criterion-referenced assessments can be developed systemwide or be adapted from instruments provided as support to commercially published materials. Another assessment strategy includes teacher-made tests (particularly when those tests are developed at the grade level and represent common goals). Results and methods can be compared, effective and ineffective strategies identified, and student strengths and weaknesses communicated as part of a curriculum assessment program.

Assessing Students' Attitudes About Learning and Citizenship

Students' attitudes about learning and citizenship are proxies for future achievement and the ultimate success of the curriculum. Students who do not value learning eventually "vote with their feet" by leaving school or by being absent frequently. Even students who do come to school often "vote with their fingers" by not completing and returning homework that practices and demonstrates new learning. Students who do not come to school and who do not complete assignments are not being schooled effectively. This is not a condemnation of their teachers; it simply means that their work is not getting the intended results. When that disjoint between effect and result occurs, two choices are available: (1) The teachers' effort can change, or (2) the results continue as acceptable. Thus, the two proxies of students' attitudes in attendance and work completion are of critical importance to any teacher.

Other measures of students' attitude assist in assessing the curriculum. Incidences of vandalism, violence, disruption, and discipline referrals are proxy votes for assessing the success of the citizenship curriculum. If students are involved in ineffective or destructive school behaviors, the school must experiment with alternative methods to develop a curriculum that better meets the needs and characteristics of the students. The basic model that illustrates the dimensions in teacher decision making (Figure 2.10) illustrates that the interaction of teacher skill, intent, context, and student characteristics must match or form a curricular "fit" that optimizes students' success and positive outcomes. Unfortunately, teachers and school administrators often internalize criticism of unsuccessful curricula and are hurt or become defensive when students accept or reject their instructional strategies. Students can, and often do, make unreasonable demands and present outrageous challenges to schools and teachers. However, if the school is to develop an effective curriculum, the focus must be on alterations in the curriculum and the resulting potential outcomes, not on personal assessment of students or teachers.

Listening to students is one of the most valuable ways to gain information about students' attitudes about the curriculum. Care must be taken, however, to recognize that vocal students may have differing views of more reticent students. Providing formal and informal opportunities for students to express themselves and their views is an important strategy. Classroom meetings may be held to plan units and solicit suggestions about learning activities. A suggestion box or a "let's talk about" box can be used to solicit students' feedback regarding the curriculum.

Examples of the School Curriculum

With the curriculum being the primary guide for the school's efforts to deliver educational experiences to children, copious examples and excerpts of exemplary curriculum should be contained in leading texts and research encyclopedias on curriculum. They are not. What is found in published materials are descriptions of what curriculum should contain, how curricula is developed, histories of various subject curricula, program strategies for evaluating curricula, and leading criticism of current curricula. Few examples are found, and fewer are labeled as exemplars. The reason for this is that carefully developed curricula are tailored to the needs of students in a particular school, which probably would not work at another school.

The school's curriculum is typically codified in a curriculum guide. Curriculum guides have a variable number of components and may have radically different structures. However, curriculum guides typically contain the following:

◆ A mission statement or overall view of the purpose of the curriculum
◆ A stated sequence along with a reason for specified treatment (hierarchy of content)
◆ Specific outcomes (manner in which learning is displayed)
◆ Strategies, experiences, and activities recommended for inclusion
◆ Evaluation strategies

Examples for study can be obtained from your local school districts, your curriculum materials library at your university, or online at school district Web sites using the World Wide Web.

◆ ◆ ◆

Summary

1. Curriculum is a global statement of what is intended for students to learn while at school. Curriculum, therefore, is an expression of school values. The study of curriculum reflects this basis on values and, therefore, varies widely among schools.
2. Basic curricula are composed of an expressed intent ("what"), a rationale ("why"), a method ("how"), and results ("effects").

3. Curriculum can be directed toward planned aims but can also include the results of collateral learning experiences. Collateral experiences often determine the student's affective attitude toward learning and the use of knowledge.
4. Both what students learn and how they are taught have major impacts on instructional outcomes; therefore, both must be considered in designing the curriculum.

5. The primary vehicle for improving the curriculum is careful assessment of the results: intended, unintended, primary, and collateral.

6. Purposes, experiences, organization, and assessment form the basis of the Tyler rationale and is the dominant paradigm for curriculum development.

7. The curriculum has been expanded in recent years to include more than the traditional duo of moral development and economic enhancement. Today's curriculum includes such items as healthful living, tolerance, social improvement, creativity, interpersonal communication, and relationships.

8. By articulating the purposes of curriculum, better decisions can be made about support and direction for instruction, stronger learning environments, more focused attention on students' needs, and responsiveness to individuality.

9. Adding a variety of perspectives, purposes, and methods can enhance any school curriculum. Including models of student talents, taxonomies of objectives, and paradigms for constructive and creative

thinking strengthen the conceptual framework of the curriculum.

10. Common purposes of the contemporary curriculum include attaining basic academic skills, acquiring and processing information, fostering creativity, promoting citizenship, providing vocational education, sustaining healthful living, and developing positive attitudes toward living and learning.

11. Curriculum can be organized in a variety of ways including concentrations on subject matter, the needs of students, and central problems requiring student resolution.

12. The degree in which teachers' daily instruction reflects the established curriculum is called *curricular alignment*. Curricular alignment requires continued communication among educators and regular assessment of school experiences.

13. A number of strategies exist for assessing the effectiveness of the curriculum. Using singular approaches increases the likelihood of inaccurate conclusions about the appropriateness and effectiveness of the curriculum.

◆ ◆ ◆

Activities and Questions for Further Understanding

1. In "A Slice of Life," Donnie was able to make learning variables a reasonable and meaningful task. How would you make the following tasks meaningful?
   a. Recognizing nouns and verbs
   b. Adding a column of two-digit numbers
   c. Learning the basic rights provided by the Constitution
   d. Learning about chemical reactions
   e. Writing descriptive sentences
2. Develop a list of education aims that you think are essential to a good elementary

school education. Write a rationale for those aims.

3. Visit a public school or watch a videotape that shows the inner workings of a school. Identify the methods of instruction that you see. What will students learn, other than the actual content, from the methods used to instruct them?

4. Outline a unit of study that you might want to teach. Apply Tyler's rationale to evaluate its effectiveness.

5. What is your answer to Spencer's question, "What knowledge is of most worth?"
6. Describe how you would attempt to fulfill the needs identified by Maslow. Is it possible for schools to assist all children in each of the five areas?

7. What would you consider to be an appropriate social–moral curriculum for the elementary school? Share your curriculum (purposes, methods, results, and evaluation) with others. Compare your assumptions regarding basic purposes and methods.

◆ ◆ ◆

References

Armstrong, Thomas. (1994). *Multiple intelligences in the classroom*. Alexandria, VA.: Association for Supervision and Curriculum Development.

Binder, Frederick M. (1970). *Education in the history of Western civilization: Selected readings*. New York: Macmillan.

Bloom, Benjamin. (1956). *Taxonomy of educational objectives*. New York: David McKay.

Borich, Gary. (1996). *Effective teaching methods* (3rd ed.) Upper Saddle River, NJ: Merrill/Prentice Hall.

Broudy, Harry S., Smith, B. O., & Burnett, Joe R. (1964). *Democracy and excellence in American secondary education*. Chicago: Rand McNally.

Clandinin, D. Jean, & Connelly, F. Michael. (1992). Teacher as curriculum maker. In Philip W. Jackson (Ed.), *Handbook of research on curriculum*. New York: Macmillan.

Cruickshank, Donald. (1990). *Research that informs teachers and teacher educators*. Bloomington, IN: Phi Delta Kappa.

Dewey, John. (1916). *Democracy and education*. New York: The Free Press.

Doxiadis, Constantinos A. (1967). Life in the year 2000. *National Education Association Journal, 56*(8), 12–14.

Erickson, Frederick, & Shultz, Jeffrey. (1996). Students' experience of the curriculum. In Philip Jackson, *Handbook of research on curriculum*. New York: Macmillan.

Gardner, Howard. (1983). *Frames of mind: The theory of multiple intelligences*. New York: Basic Books.

Hunter, Madeline. (1994). *Enhancing teaching*. New York: Macmillan.

Jackson, Philip W. (Ed.) (1992a). *Handbook of research on curriculum*. New York: Macmillan.

Jackson, Philip W. (1992b). Conceptions of curriculum and curriculum specialists. *Handbook of research on curriculum* (pp. 3–40). New York: Macmillan.

Maslow, A. H. (1954). *Motivation and personality*. New York: Harper & Row.

Ornstein, Allan C., & Hunkins, Francis P. (1988). *Curriculum: Foundations, Principles, and Issues*. Upper Saddle River, NJ: Prentice Hall.

Piaget, Jean. (1973). Child and reality: Problems of genetic psychology. New York: Viking Press. (Translated by Arnold Rosin)

Pratt, David. (1980). *Curriculum: Design and Development*. New York: Harcourt Brace Jovanovich.

Raths, L. E., Wassermann, S., Jonas, A., & Rothstein, A. M. (1967). *Teaching for thinking: Theory and application*. Columbus, OH: Merrill.

Shepherd, Gene D., & Raga, William B. (1992). *Modern elementary curriculum* (7th ed.). Fort Worth, TX: Harcourt Brace Jovanovich.

Spencer, Herbert. (1894). *Education*. New York: Appleton-Century-Crofts.

Taba, Hilda. (1970). *Curriculum development: Theory and practice*. New York: Harcourt Brace Jovanovich.

Tyler, Ralph W. (1949). *Basic principles of curriculum and instruction*. Chicago: University of Chicago Press.

◆

CHAPTER 6

How Do I Get There?

Short-Term Planning for Teaching and Learning

Outline

We frequently fail to recognize that much of the material presented to students in the classroom has, for the student, the same perplexing, meaningless quality that the list of nonsense syllables has for us.

C. ROGERS AND H. J. FREIBERG

What does the child hear when he is called on? What does he feel? What does he think? What are his fantasies and wishes? What does he try to do? What kinds of habits is he developing?

JOHN HOLT

A Slice of Life

Mr. Brattain was ready to show his fourth graders a 16mm film on peristalsis, the wavelike motion that pushes the food from the mouth to the stomach. His introduction to the lesson had gone well. The children had just finished drinking ice-cold water, and most were sure that they could feel that first swallow of cold water traveling down their throats and to their stomachs. Mr. Brattain had introduced the vocabulary word "esophagus." Because of the ice water experiment, most of the children agreed that the esophagus must be at least a little longer than their necks. The team captains passed out slices of bread. The class chewed and paid special attention when they swallowed. Now, Mr. Brattain posed the real problem of the day: "Why does the food go down?"

The nearly unanimous opinion was "gravity." Mr. Brattain asked for any alternate hypotheses. Clement claimed the tongue pushed it down. Monica thought the stomach pulled it down. Others thought the throat squeezed it but weren't sure how it did it. Mr. Brattain smiled and told them that one of the hypotheses was very close. He told them he was going to show them a film about how the esophagus moves food to the stomach. Then they would go outside and hang upside down on the monkey bars. If the film is right about the esophagus, the food would go up, not down, to their stomachs. If the gravity theory is right, the food would just stick in their mouths (or perhaps slide out their noses). The children giggled.

Expect the Unexpected

"Lights out!" Mr. Brattain turned on the projector. Nothing happened. When Mr. Brattain checked the projector that morning, everything had worked fine. Right in the middle of the lesson! It never fails. Strategically, there were several choices he could make that would salvage the lesson; one was most fitting to the intent of the activity. He decided to do a little problem-solving. He asked himself, "There is a lesson in this . . . just what is it?" It occurred to him quickly. He decided to ask the children, "How would a scientist solve this problem?"

Mr. Brattain pursed his lips. "Well, children, I seem to be having a problem. Can anyone tell me what it is?" The children gleefully reminded him of the obvious—the projector did not work. Mr. Brattain wrote this on the board. Then he inquired more specifically, "I know the projector isn't working, but what is it not doing that I want it to?" The children asked for clarification. After his explanation, they began to make a list: "The reels aren't turning. The lights aren't on. It's not making sound. There's no picture. . . . "

"OK, but which of these best tells me what my problem is with the projector?" asked Mr. Brattain. To this question, the children hesitated, then protested: "It isn't doing nothing. It's broke."

Mr. Brattain replied, "What do you mean by doing nothing?" After some false starts and quizzical looks, the children protested once again. "All of those problems are problems. It isn't doing nothing."

Mr. Brattain scratched his chin and smiled. "Ah, but all of the problems together is different from having just one problem, isn't it?"

Jane looked at him seriously, "This way you don't know what's wrong with it. If it just did something but messed up, you'd know what's wrong with it." The other children saw Jane's logic but couldn't understand how that would help them to see a movie. Richard, always an enthusiastic student, volunteered to get the librarian. "She usually fixes things like this!"

Mr. Brattain interjected, "I think now that we know what the problems are, we might be able to solve the problem even if we can't fix the projector."

Richard was impatient. "What do you mean by that? How can you fix a projector without fixing it? That's dumb."

Mr. Brattain smiled. "It is certainly logically inappropriate!" He made a grandiose movement with his arm and continued, "Probably impossible. Let's try something. Tell me everything that you can think of that would cause all of these problems to occur at once. I'll write the list on the chalkboard."

"The machine is broke," they said almost in unison.

"Is it?" Mr. Brattain asked seriously. "If I try to start my car with the wrong key, is the car broken?"

"It means you aren't doing it right."

"Could 'not doing it right' be the problem here?"

The children laughed, "But you know what you're doing!"

Mr. Brattain scratched his chin again and said slyly, "Maybe I do, but do you know what to do? I bet you do." Mr. Brattain now made two columns on the chalkboard: one entitled, "The machine is broke," and the other, "Not using it correctly." They began to generate a list: Light bulb is out (false start, the reels would turn), the wrong switch was turned, a short circuit, no power, bad cord, bad circuit breaker, bad switch. . . . "This is a good list. Let's look at all of the problems. Let's list them from simple to complicated. What is the simplest explanation to the projector problem?" They all agreed that "no power" was the simplest. As they went down the list, decisions became progressively more difficult. Richard, who really wanted to see this film so that he could go outside and hang upside down, demanded that they should try the first things on the list and come back if they didn't work. The class agreed with his logic so the "no power" explanation was under scrutiny.

By now, all of the children had looked back at the socket to see if the projector was plugged in. It was. "I suppose that your first test is to see if it is plugged into the socket. Let me write that down. What other tests can we make to find out if the power is on?" The children decided that the power could be off, the cord could be bad, the switch in the projector was loose. . . .

Organizing Together

Mr. Brattain nodded in appreciation. "Let's order these the same way we did the earlier list. What tests can we try?" It was agreed that if the tape recorder worked on the cart socket, the projector was the problem. If it didn't, it was a power problem. The recorder wouldn't play. They decided to plug the recorder into the wall socket. Richard was selected for the task. It worked. Richard became excited. "It's the extension cord. It's bad!"

"Are you sure? What can we do to test it?" asked Mr. Brattain.

"Be sure it's plugged in good!" said Richard almost immediately as he began the test. One wriggle, and the projector began to whirl.

Mr. Brattain offered an explanation. "Evidently, someone stepped on the cord and pulled the plug out of the socket just enough to keep the power from making a connection without our being able to see it."

Jane scowled, "You could have told us that and saved 20 minutes. Now we won't get to go outside."

"But now you know how to find a problem, don't you?" countered Mr. Brattain. "And we'll get to go outside. I promise."

Planning and Instructional Facilitation

Curriculum theorists have long argued that planning is an integral part of teaching (Eisner, 1967; Tyler, 1950). What is accepted in theory, however, is not always accepted in practice. Extensive planning by teachers in public schools is not always possible. In successful classrooms, teachers must accommodate the needs of diverse students and modify instructional objectives to provide successful lessons appropriate to their instructional development. Optimal learning conditions require extensive analysis and environmental modification. The demands for individualized design and delivery of successful lessons present a formidable task to even the most talented teachers. Without question, problems exceed the very limited time allowed for their solution.

Teachers attempt to adapt to this time differential in several ways. Almost from necessity, teachers sometimes simplify the classroom by limiting the influence of the special needs of differing students. Harried teachers often require a class to adapt to their teaching style rather than adapting to the needs of students. Of course, this adaptive strategy usually does not lead to a successful classroom. Other teachers employ more successful strategies, such as "chunking" or generalizing the needs of students into more manageable units or groups. This permits the teacher to attend to many individual needs while bringing instructional strategies in line with the resources available in the environment. Many teachers develop elaborate routines that increase student responsibility for maintaining much of the classroom. These routines cover materials use, student movement, attendance to personal needs, obtaining and giving help, scheduling for special classes, and student conduct.

Time always remains in short supply. For example, if a teacher has a 50-minute uninterrupted period for planning, only seven minutes are available for each of the seven lessons to be taught during the day (spelling, language arts, reading, math, science/health, social studies, and physical education). Music, art, and special centers take additional time. In addition, the teacher must develop or assemble materials and analyze the results of previous lessons, which includes grading student work. This also assumes that no meetings, individualized instruction, or parent communication occur during the planning period.

Successful teachers, in spite of time issues, involve themselves in a critical analysis of classroom needs and activities. These teachers use analysis as the starting place of planning and believe that it is absolutely essential for implementing appropriate teaching strategies successfully and providing meaningful lessons. Although experienced teachers often use tacit or covert structures developed from countless experiences, all teachers, particularly novices, should critically examine their planned instructional delivery in detail before and after teaching. Without careful consideration of intended and realized outcomes, it is difficult for teachers to repeat successes and avoid duplicating failures.

Efficient Planning

Teaching is a task of intense complexity. Teachers typically respond to this complexity by attempting to simplify and control the instructional environment (Yinger, 1977). In short, teachers try to make an unpredictable educational environment into a more controlled predictable circumstance. They do this by planning. They group similar activities common to many lessons (such as distributing and collecting materials and work products) into an array of set procedures called *routines*. Thus, to plan all aspects of a lesson, teachers combine many of these rehearsed and reinforced behavior routines that fit the needs of a particular lesson.

When their routines not only work for the day-to-day events of the classroom but also accommodate anticipated but unpredictable emergencies, the teacher's classroom management style is elevated to its highest level. Planning for the day-to-day organization of the class also becomes less demanding and more covert. Thus, the best classrooms seem to "run by themselves." The children, not the teacher, appear to be responsible for the daily efficiency.

These successful teachers think critically about teaching during all phases of instruction, during planning, lesson execution, and post-instructional evaluation. They also look for new routines that have wide applicability. Teachers who constantly think about how to improve lessons and engage learners are also constantly planning. Planning is central to a deliberate improvement of student learning and is the first step toward systematic teaching success.

Tell-Tale Signs of Inefficient Planning

Unfortunately, efficient, successful planning does not always occur. When classroom routines are not sufficient for either the predictable events or the daily variations in the classroom, there can be unfortunate outcomes. General confusion and inefficient or purposeless movement of children in the classroom sometimes typify these classrooms. The teacher in these situations either tries to shout directions to inattentive children or creates a very restrictive, punitive environment.

Teachers with out-of-control classes often use overt signals such as rapidly blinking the overhead lights or blowing a whistle. Since activities in these classrooms are often boring and meaningless to children, external rewards become the primary focus of the classroom management plan. Thus, the teacher substitutes nonacademic time for lesson time as a reward for minimal compliance. External rewards such as comical stickers and food snacks often become central to the teacher's motivational strategies. Sometimes, when teachers are unable to direct the activity of the classroom toward educationally sound goals, the teacher attempts to slow the activity to a more manageable pace. In these classrooms, children may not talk to each other for any reason, even to help each other in learning. Children may not take care of personal needs such as getting a drink of water, sharpening a pencil, getting a tissue for a runny nose, or even looking at a reference book without the teacher's permission. Learning is impaired, boredom sets in, students act up in defiance, and learning suffers.

Teachers frequently report that they do not think about formal lesson planning before and during lessons. The results of their instruction often bear out this neglect. It is estimated that the average teacher spends about one-fourth of the lesson time in organizing and readying the classroom for learning. Successful teachers (those found to be effective in producing measurable learning gains) use only about one-tenth of lesson time in organizing for teaching. Successful teachers generally organize prior to the lesson or have carefully developed strategies that simply get more done in less time. Naturally, this saved time, if equated into active instruction, results in more learning. This prior planning activity and detailed mental planning result in more time for the teachers to develop additional effective instructional opportunities for the children. Without careful daily analysis and modification, classroom routines will never maximize the teacher's potential.

What Is Lesson Planning?

Teacher planning is the practical development of the "What," "How," and "Why" of instruction that leads to high levels of success and efficiency. The more deliberate and controlled the process is, the more likely the teacher will attain intended aims. In a stylized version of planning, the teacher should entertain a series of strategies. First, the teacher should tell the children what they are to learn (stating the objective), make them aware of what they will be expected to do, and prepare them for learning (introductory activities). The teacher then instructs the children in the most efficient manner possible (the dominant teaching strategy) and gives them ample opportunity to try out the new skill and begins to "debug" student learning (guided and independent practice). Developing these instructional components is more than just deciding what to tell children. Lesson development is a complex arrangement of verbal explanation, modeling, practice, observation, reiteration, and demonstration. The instructional component of planning occupies the greatest amount of time and requires the teacher to employ the skill of teaching most expertly. Finally, the teacher reviews the lesson to summarize what was learned (closure) and makes some assessment about whether the teaching objective was met (evaluation). This abbreviated explanation of the standard plan for a lesson simplifies a process in which steps can be added or deleted as necessary to meet the intended aims. Naturally, the steps of a basic lesson can be rearranged to meet the needs of learners and the teacher's strategy. The basic planning components shown in Figure 6.1 are described in subsequent sections.

Thinking About Purpose

The first component in skillful planning of instructional lessons is thinking. This thinking requires some very careful considerations regarding the substance of what is to be taught. Before putting pencil to paper, the teacher must ponder:

◆ "What do I want children to know when I'm finished?"
◆ "What do I want them to be able to do with this new knowledge?"
◆ "How can I teach them so they will understand?"
◆ "How will I know that they learned what I taught them and can do these things that I planned?"

FIGURE 6.1   Preplanning processes.

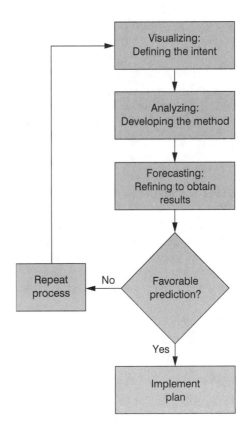

Careful attention to the intent of instruction provides the teacher with a focused direction to guide teacher thinking in purposeful, intentional ways.

Determining Activity

The second component of planning requires the teacher to analyze what he or she must do to actualize this vision. Will "telling" be enough? Is a demonstration needed? Should the children be given avenues and opportunities to explore? Will it take a single lesson or a series of lessons to bring about the change? What visual images will students need? Are concrete objects necessary for their developmental level? Is the goal substantive and worthy of attention at all? What will children be able to do with their new knowledge and skill? How will they be different after instruction? How will the teacher know students have learned? Analyzing the answers to these questions assists the teacher in selecting and refining the series of activities that are most likely to bring about successful learning. For the teacher to approximate the ideal lesson, the teacher must employ a special type of hypothesis testing in which the teacher predicts likely outcomes of various strategies. This leads to the third component of successful planning.

Forecasting

In lesson planning, teachers use forecasting to predict what will happen, what can happen, and what can go wrong. By thinking through each activity carefully, a teacher should be able to answer some of the following questions: How long will the lesson take? How will I break the lesson into manageable steps? How long will each step take? Which steps may cause the most difficulty? How will that affect the lesson flow? What supplies are needed? How do these supplies react to classrooms? (For example, open paint bottles love to turn on their sides in classrooms.) Who could be hurt? What can be harmed? What precautions must I take to safeguard the lesson and the children? By analyzing the answers to these questions, the teacher can develop a process in which his or her ideas about instruction are reconsidered, refined, and enhanced. If the forecast is not favorable, the process continues. The process stops only when forecasting predicts a favorable outcome or when it is clear that more information is needed about the goal and process. In either case, when the teacher proceeds from the intent-procedure-forecasting loop, planning results in a lesson design that is best considered an experiment. Although the teacher cannot be sure of the outcomes, he or she is able to come up with a "best guess" about the results using this deliberate planning strategy.

Writing a Plan

After visualizing the lesson through to a successful end, the teacher is ready to write the lesson plan. Essentially, the teacher has completed the plan. Many teachers complete all of the preceding steps but may not write any lesson plan in detail. The importance of an extensive lesson plan during the novice teaching period is to help direct the "debugging" process in which the teacher refines thinking and organization. Many issues must be resolved before any lesson can be taught consistently and effectively. Lesson plan formats, such as the one in this text, allow the teacher to leave a written path of thought processes and idea developments that can be shared with colleagues who can then make suggestions for improvement. No one outline for planning instruction has been found best for teaching. However, it is unlikely for a teacher to have consistently successful lessons unless he or she follows the steps outlined in this chapter.

There are no shortcuts to good planning. However, by carefully considering all aspects of each lesson before it is taught and by carefully considering its success after it has been taught, the teacher can begin to create generalizations and begin to chunk many small details into larger concepts. This allows much of what goes on in planning to become automatic, thus speeding the process and building the teaching repertoire of skillful strategies. As teachers gain experience, they establish routines developed from other successful lessons. The quickest route to successful routines and consistently effective lessons is to take the time to plan well, to analyze the plan to identify good practice, and to isolate and modify ineffective practice. This is precisely what the expanded lesson plan format attempts to help the teacher do: forecast effectively and reflect accurately.

Is Planning Important?

Each person's opinion of the importance of planning depends on his or her view of what planning is. If the focus is on the written plan, there is little to support planning as integral to effective teaching. If planning is viewed as extensive consideration and analysis of instructional aims and strategies and the cognitive alignment of learner, aims, and resources, planning is integral to intentional purposeful instruction (see Figure 6.2).

Yinger (1977) reported a view of planning that included three phases, roughly paralleling the process illustrated in Figure 2.1. First, the teacher engages in a "discovery cycle" in which the teacher brings together mentally all the various aspects of teaching. These include aspects of learners, resources available for teaching, and the teacher's understanding of content, students, and methodology. Second, a problem is formulated, and a solution is proposed. Yinger called this the "design cycle" and theorized that this cycle eventually becomes more complex and elaborate. Third, the planning model extends into the implementation stage (teachers think about teaching while teaching) and follows the teaching event with post-instructional evaluation, modification, and enhancement.

Yinger's argument is that lesson planning is an important contribution to thinking about teaching, not simply a pre-instructional exercise. Yinger's position is that teachers continually rethink and replan their activities. Successful teachers perform the following two activities during instruction: First, they continually assess the success of the lesson thus far through a variety of procedures that incorporate students' responses. It has been shown that teachers' instructional thinking is dominated by attention to student reactions and individual differences. Second, Yinger's argument suggests that the actual teaching act is an experimental laboratory in which teaching knowledge is created. It would be natural to conclude that the amount of teaching experience increases teaching effectiveness. This conclusion, however, is only partially true. Research indicates that after a brief period of growth in effectiveness lasting two or three years, teacher experiences cease to be a predictor of student learning and teacher effectiveness. Certainly, many teachers continually improve throughout their careers, but this appears to be the exception rather than the rule.

This chapter assumes that, during their careers, teachers underemphasize the process of knowledge creation through planning. Instead, teachers tend to attribute

FIGURE 6.2 Planning is the alignment of the major variables in instruction.

- Learner
  - Aims
    - Strategies
      - Resources
        - Teacher skill

changes in lesson success to unalterable differences in student attitude, ability, and motivation or in societal factors such as family values or income. To help novice teachers become more deliberate about the substance of an individual lesson and the creation of generalized knowledge about instruction, this chapter uses an extended overt outline to structure the types of tasks required for successful planning. This extended plan is remarkably resilient and responsive to the various views on planning.

Thinking Through a Quick Plan

Figure 6.3 shows a lesson plan developed by Amber, a preservice teacher, at the beginning of her teacher preparation program. In writing the lesson, Amber's overriding concern was that the students develop an accurate understanding of what composes a desert. As she formulated her lesson plan, she identified the following facts about her students: (1) A large percentage were new to the region and had never lived in a desert before, and (2) most of the children had never visited the desert but instead were surrounded by the irrigated lawns of suburbia.

Amber reasoned that if they were to visit a nearby vacant lot that was still in a somewhat "wild" natural state, the students could examine the terrain closely, find plant life, learn what the plants are called, and how pioneers used them. Her knowledge of the desert allowed her to identify three easily found, easily identified plants. Amber also hoped that the children might become better conservators of the region if their awareness of the delicate intricacy of the desert was increased. Being a desert dweller, Amber was well aware of the "desolate nothing" view that outsiders have of the Mojave Desert. She also knew from countless hikes and walks that the delicate desert biosystem is so rich that virtually every step you take in the desert, you step on some living thing. With this in mind, Amber concurrently began to think about three things: What can I do to help the children learn about the desert? What will I need to do it? How will I get them started?

Although the plan she eventually wrote puts "Materials," "Introductory Activities," and "Lesson Procedures" in a linear and specific order, it does not necessarily reflect the order in which Amber developed her lesson. Amber was quite perceptive in recognizing the potential of the vacant lot next to the school to conduct nature studies. Amber capitalized on a material availability and developed both her objectives and her methods based on a convenient resource. This resourcefulness is quite common among teachers. Although the logical sequence of planning always begins with determining the purpose, teachers commonly recognize certain fleeting attributes of special materials to prepare lessons. If, for example, Amber arrived at school on one of those rare occasions (for her region) when it was cold and the night's rain had formed a dozen short icicles on the window sill, Amber logically could have scratched her plant lesson and talked about how icicles are formed and about weather phenomena such as snow, sleet, and hail that many of her children had never experienced. Again, this illustrates that successful teachers are constantly

Grade 3   Time: 45 min.

Objective

Long term: Learner will be able to describe and explain a desert.

Short term: Learner will identify three common desert plants by sight and smell.

 1. Mormon tea
 2. Turpentine bush
 3. Creosote bush

Rationale: Viewing the desert as a living environment with a unique beauty will promote pride and conservatorship in their region.

Materials

 1. 31 small samples of each plant. These can be found in the desert area behind the school. Team leaders will distribute.
 2. 31 plastic sandwich bags.

Introductory Activities

We live in a desert. A desert has little water. All living things need water to survive. Plants are living things. What kind of plant can survive in the desert?

Lesson Procedure

 1. Smell all three plants. Which one smells the strongest? (2) Look at all of the plants. Which two look similar? *(1, 2)* How can you tell them apart? *(#2 has thorns and strong smell)* Which two smell alike? *(1, 3)* How can you tell them apart?
 2. Get with your tutor-buddy. One of you close your eyes while the other holds out samples to smell. Do this until the first one gets them right, then switch. Then name them by sight the same way.
 3. There are more than three kinds of plants in the desert. So, to find our three, we need to go on a treasure hunt. This is not a race. Slowly spread out and use your safety scissors to collect one small sample of each plant. Put the samples into your plastic bag. These treasures go in your "desert notebook." Work alone. Reassemble into your teams when you are done.

Evaluation

Children will be independently able to identify three types of desert plants and collect a sample of each.

FIGURE 6.3   Amber's first lesson plan.

thinking about a wide range of variables in determining their daily teaching schedule and strategies.

In this case, Amber took advantage of the vacant lot but decided that she needed to give her students some direction before she sent them out to the field. She determined that each child should have samples of the plants to view, touch, and smell prior to leaving the classroom. By the time the children were actually in the field, they had already almost accomplished her objective. She had also minimized the "risks" in teaching by keeping close tabs on student behavior. In her planning, Amber could have chosen other strategies for obtaining the same objective. For example, Amber could have had a brief introduction to plant collecting, had the students collect many plants from the lot, and then helped them to classify the plants they collected.

This method has several advantages over her original plan. First, the lesson is more discovery oriented, the children would be able to identify types of plants, and they would have an opportunity to construct and test strategies for identifying and classifying. This strategy, however, also has extra costs. Her students would be in the field with less direction and with an unfocused purpose (finding many plants as opposed to finding three particular plants). Amber had to weigh the costs with the benefits of each method. Since she was new at teaching large groups, she elected to provide generous external structure to the lesson. If she had more teaching experience and knew her students better, she could have altered her strategy and provided more freedom to the lesson. As it turned out, the children asked copious questions about things they found, brought extra plants back, and went to the fields again after school on their own time. Amber had introduced a lesson that increased, but did not satisfy, student curiosity.

Another issue that Amber had to face was that of taking children off the school grounds. Even though it was only next door, she had to obtain permission from parents. This meant that Amber must plan the lesson at least a week in advance. It also meant that she had an additional step to include in her lesson plan: a field trip permission slip approved by the school and signed by the parent of each child. If a parent denied permission, Amber had to plan an alternate lesson for that child and provide custodial care. If Amber had a child with special needs, she would have to accommodate those needs. For example, if Amber had a child in a wheelchair, she would have to examine the site access and determine if terrain and access was appropriate for this student without additional assistance. If modifications were needed, she would have to plan for additional assistance.

Amber was also accountable for the students' learning and welfare. Since she asked to leave the classroom and school grounds, she had to prove to parents and school officials that the added trouble of leaving the classroom would increase the learning opportunities for children. Amber's bigger concern, however, was determining if the children learned what she intended and if this strategy should be repeated. The evaluation strategy she used to test the success of her teaching was to examine the successful collection of the three plants studied during the in-class portion of the lesson. The evaluation strategy and her original objective matched quite well. Amber could easily assess whether her students could identify the three plants. Whether this was the best objective for the activity, whether more things were learned than intended or measured, and whether students made meaningful headway toward being desert conservators are important questions for Amber to consider. However, these three questions are not easily answered. Amber's activity was certainly successful and eagerly received by the children, but was that enough? After reflecting on the many aspects of the lesson and reviewing the day's events in her mind, Amber will develop stronger, more complex strategies and more important objectives in her quest to become a successful teacher.

Amber's planning began with a vague notion that the vacant lot, the desert, the children, and her love of nature could combine to make a meaningful contribution to education of the children. Sometimes, the objectives are prescribed by the written curriculum and can be very abstract and remote for children. Examples include learning to identify nouns in a sentence, adding unlike fractions, or describing the hydrologic cycle. These objectives, however, require the same type of associative thinking that Amber provided for her desert appreciation lesson: What are the abilities of the children? What skills and strategies do I have to help them learn? What resources do I have that can be used for this learning?

An Introduction to the Expanded Lesson Plan

Many formats for planning have been developed. Gagné and Briggs (1974) have a plan based on the following seven events of instruction:

- Gaining attention
- Informing the learner of the objective
- Stimulating recall of prerequisite learning
- Presenting the stimulus material
- Eliciting the desired behavior
- Providing feedback
- Assessing the behavior

Figure 6.4 provides the major headings and subheadings of the expanded plan created by combining many approaches to lesson development into a logical sequence. As mentioned earlier, this sequence is often radically altered during the mental design phase of instructional planning. When instruction is carried out in the classroom, this sequence can also be successfully altered into any number of patterns. Direct instruction most easily fits the conceptual sequence of the expanded lesson plan. However, inquiry-based approaches fit the basic design elements, although explicit statements of the purpose and process of learning are often omitted.

The keys to successful planning are knowing what is desired of the children at the end of the instructional sequence and having a systematic approach for achieving it. One student teacher, preparing a lesson plan for the first time, decided that her students should be able to recognize nouns used in their own writing. Her objective was: "Students will be able to identify each noun that they use in a short essay about what they like to do for fun." This seemed simple and straightforward. However, when queried about why she wanted students to learn to recognize nouns, she was somewhat uncertain. She decided that if students understood what a noun was, this would help them write better. However, the research on writing effectiveness minimizes the importance of studying formal parts of speech, diagramming sentences, and learning grammar rules on student writing skills.

Department of Curriculum and Instruction

University of Nevada at Las Vegas

Student Teacher: _____   Subject: _____

Date: _____   Approximate Time Planned: Begin _____ End _____

I. **Objective**
   A. Long-range aim:
   B. Instructional objective(s):
   C. Rationale for objective(s):

II. **Materials Needed for Lesson**
   A. Type   Location   Quantity
   B. Distribution strategy:
   C. Collection strategy:

III. **Introductory Activities**
   A. Reason for learning:
   B. Behavior and learning expectations for students:
   C. Focus and review activity (includes motivational strategies, anticipatory set and advance organizers, and so on):

IV. **Lesson Procedures**
   A. Dominant teaching strategy (teacher input):
   B. Guided practice:
   C. Independent practice:
   D. Closure:

V. **Evaluation of Learning**
   A. Evaluation instrument or strategy:
   B. Feedback vehicle:
   C. Provisions of informal (or ongoing) evaluation:

VI. **Post-Instructional Evaluation of Teaching Strategy**
   A. Present evidence that the objective of the lesson was obtained:
   B. Reteaching is an essential function. Explain which parts of the objective must be retaught (if any), how you determined this need, and indicate the strategy to be used:
   C. When teaching this objective again, explain what changes you would make in your strategy and why:

FIGURE 6.4   Expanded lesson plan format for student teachers.

The young teacher had fortuitously discovered one of the fundamental skills of teaching and learning: Always question what you are doing for value and effectiveness. The teacher finally decided that learning nouns may not help the students write better, but she still felt that it was unthinkable not to teach nouns to students. It seemed so fundamental, so basic, and so essential. When asked why she thought teaching nouns was essential, she stumbled into the obvious. Students must have a common vocabulary to talk about their writing and how to improve it. If a student's use of nouns was limited, the teacher had to have a term that they both understood to describe this part of the student's writing that needed attention. Teaching the concept of "noun" was fundamental to this end. Knowing why she was teaching this concept allowed her to achieve her objective systematically.

Being systematic in teaching allows the teacher to make instruction deliberate and intentional. Being systematic allows the teacher to convey to the students why what they are learning is important. In this case, the student's understanding of "noun" was necessary to help the student and the teacher communicate about writing. Knowing about nouns can be considered adequate when students can identify and modify nouns in their own writing. This young teacher also made some very calculated decisions about the amount of practice and drill associated with nouns. Rather than having students circle the noun or noun parts in sentences, she chose to embed the study of nouns in a context where they were used: the communication of ideas about one's writings.

Investigating before a field trip yields the best results.

Are Written Plans Valuable?

The question remaining is whether extensive *written* plans are valuable. This depends largely on the developmental level of the teacher. The complete novice, without experience in managing large numbers of children in a learning environment, finds that an extensive written plan is somewhat analogous to the training wheels on a child's bicycle: They are stabilizing, but there is a trade-off in maneuverability. Writing down instructional intents in detail forces teachers to make hard decisions and do precise thinking about their planning. This "forcing" of forecasting and rationalization can be very unpleasant, especially to inexperienced teachers. However, extensive written plans also allow other teachers and university instructors to evaluate the soundness of a novice's thinking about teaching and to give feedback on methods for enhancement. To experienced teachers, the time consumed by extensive writing may be more profitably spent elsewhere. Also, the experienced teacher may have several alternatives in mind, depending on how the lesson unfolds. Writing down this complexity may simply not be a possibility with existing resources.

Tyler (1950) developed a logical rational model of teacher planning. This model consists of four basic steps:

1. State the intended outcome of instruction in the form of an objective.
2. Select the learning activities that appear most likely to achieve the objective.
3. Organize the learning activity around available resources.
4. Determine the evaluation procedures used to test the success of the instruction in meeting the objective.

Central to this process is productive critical thinking. Tyler (1950) argued that a complex derivation process for determining learning objectives is needed to direct teaching successfully. Although a written plan is important, it is only a product of this process, not the process itself.

Teachers who are already burdened with too many tasks and too little time often find it easy to justify an objective and an instructional strategy simply because they are part of the stated curriculum. Teachers must pay close attention to the planned curriculum; however, curriculum guides vary in their appropriateness to all students. Too frequently, curriculum guides are only indirectly associated with the needs of students.

The length of the written plan varies with its intended use. In sharing and rethinking instructional strategies with others, the value of careful documentation of the intent, methods, and specific outcomes prior to instruction is unquestioned if a teacher's reflection is to be more than a rationalization of what just accidentally occurred. If the plan is to serve as a reminder of the predetermined guide to instructional effectiveness for the lesson, the mnemonic function of brief notes capturing the sequence and purpose of the lesson is sufficient. The written format of the plan should reflect the purposes for which the plan is to be used. Whatever written format is chosen, either by the teacher, the school administration, or the instructors in teacher education programs, the written plan is no more effective than the cognitive analysis, synthesis, and evaluation used in developing the plan.

Do Objectives Really Guide Planning Processes?

Truly purposeless activities are rare in society. Even the most mundane and unnoticed behavior has some type of purpose or intent. Although there are many specialized definitions, an objective is simply the intent or purpose of an activity. In teaching a lesson, the lesson objective tells what learning is to occur, how it is to be measured, and why the student needs this knowledge.

Objectives are necessary in the planning process. In fact, planning for instruction or the resulting instructional strategy cannot logically occur without objectives. Yet, research is showing that teachers often do not think about objectives or do so infrequently while they are teaching (Clark & Peterson, 1986). A study by McNair (1978–1979) found that teachers reported that less than 3 percent of their interactive thoughts during instruction were about objectives. Attention to the learner, with over 39 percent of interactive thoughts, occupied teacher thinking more than concerns about materials, content, facts, ideas, procedures, and instructional tasks. Overall, Clark and Peterson summarized the findings of the research on teacher interactive thinking by reporting that teachers' accounts of their interactive thoughts involved the learner in 40 to 60 percent of the reported incidences. This was followed by thinking about the instructional process (20 to 30 percent), content or subject matter (5 to 14 percent), with a relatively small portion of concerns with objectives (14 percent of the time or less).

The implication of this research is unclear. Do teachers not think about objectives because they are activity-oriented rather than outcome-oriented? Are teachers learner-centered rather than content-centered? Are objectives "standardized" (for example, children should learn multiplication tables in third grade) and so rarely questioned by teachers that the purpose of the activity is rarely considered? Do teachers so clearly have the long-range aims of instruction in mind that they need only concentrate on the activity of the learner? It seems basic to teaching that students have the right to know what the intent of instruction is and how that will assist them in preparing for adult life and a career. Teachers need to communicate this purpose explicitly. Knowing the instructional objective and informing students of the importance of the learning is more than common sense; it is integral to the democratic conception of education. Yet, teachers who reflect on the purpose of objectives and explain to students what the purpose of instruction is and how it can be used is a rare occurrence in American schools.

Unfortunately, the value of objectives is frequently debated. However, these debates tend to focus not on the fundamental purpose of objectives (to establish purposeful behavior) but rather on style considerations of written objectives. On one end of the debate are the behavioral objectives in which singular specific objectives are written explicitly, identify a specific observable act by the student, and define the conditions of the learning demonstration and a minimal standard of acceptable performance (Mager, 1962). On the other end of the debate is a view that the purpose behind even the most simple teaching act is never singular but rather an extensive interconnection of many short- and long-term intents. In this case, attitudes and personal esteem are as central to teaching as the observable skills specified in the objectives (Eisner, 1967).

The potential value of carefully developed instructional objectives is part of the controversy surrounding their use. Carefully developed objectives can provide a clear focus for daily activity and can communicate to teacher and student alike the expectations and benefits of working and learning together. These objectives can specify the performance and provide benchmarks for the inevitable assessment of learning success by carefully specifying the performances sought. By specifying the intent and the desired performances, objectives can enhance the teacher's and learner's effective use of time and improve task orientation. Finally, objectives that are carefully developed, clearly communicated, and fairly evaluated can provide a sense of progress to the learner and a sense of accomplishment to the teacher.

Writing a Lesson Plan

As stated earlier, the first activity in planning is careful thinking and mental testing of the purpose, method, and outcomes of a lesson. Once the teacher has generalized the plan, he or she can begin to create the plan in detail with the purpose of spotting any potential pitfalls and disasters in the prescribed course of action. Figure 6.4 outlines the basic components of any lesson. Each section is presented separately, its rationale discussed, and the criteria for successful planning at that stage described.

Objectives

Although the lesson is planned around the immediate objective, the long-range context of the objective must be understood, as well as the objectives that precede and follow the lesson. The long-range context of specific learning activities is embodied into directive statements called *aims*.

Guiding Function of Objectives. Children and teachers may not understand the significance of certain objectives. For teachers, not understanding why they are teaching something is a deadly mistake. Unless the teacher knows specifically what the child is to learn, teaching cannot be purposeful. Purpose renders meaning and substance to teaching. Without purpose, teaching is unintentional, inadvertent, haphazard, and random. All learners need to understand the significance of the learning objective, but this is impossible if the teacher does not have a clear, precise understanding of what the goal of the instruction is. Students make decisions based on their perception of the importance of an activity in which they are to participate. If the objective seems, at best, to be a dubious achievement, students rarely maximize their efforts toward realizing it. Likewise, teachers often fail to maximize their efforts at teaching toward objectives that do not appear to have significant aims or adequate rationales.

Aims, Objectives, and Rationale.   Following are examples of an aim, objective, and rationale that illustrate their relationship:

> *Aim:*   Students are able to buy small items at a store without supervision.
> *Objective:*   Students are able to count combinations of coins up to one dollar.
> *Rationale for objective:*   The first step in making a small purchase is to count money to see if there is an adequate amount.

This sequence proceeds from the global to the specific. Notice that the aim is the broadest statement of purpose, and its importance is usually self-evident. The example aim was to be developed with second graders. Notice that it is likely to take more than one lesson to achieve; if fact, it will take several lessons over a month or more. This aim connects individual learning activities that may have dubious value by themselves. For example, if the lesson objective is simply to count objects that represent different values, the motivation to do so may be lacking. Few children want to count the value of objects with arbitrarily assigned values (such as poker chips), whereas they like to count money (with its constant connotation of purchasing power). Because of this, the objective now has a structure that makes the value of this learning activity evident.

Notice, too, that the next lesson is indicated by the aim. After students can successfully count coins up to one dollar, the next activity may be to count a specific amount over a dollar. Another objective may be to compare coinage to a specific value to see if the coinage is less than, equal to, or greater than the amount specified. If the specific amount to be counted cannot be made with the given coins, the objective may be to count to the amount nearest to the value but higher than the cost of an item. The next objective may be to subtract the actual amount needed from the amount tendered to decide what change should be received.

Behavioral Objectives.   In the preceding example of counting money, the objective answers the question, "What is to be learned?", but the example did not specify the conditions under which the learning is to occur or the minimal criteria for successful learning. Some writers in instructional design (for example, Mager, 1962) expect that objectives should be written explicitly to contain the following: the performance (what a learner is expected to do), the conditions (the important circumstances under which the performance is to occur), and the criterion (a description of acceptable performance of the objective). The preceding objective, if rewritten to these specifications, might read as follows: "Given a pouch with less than one dollar in small change, the student will be able to count the money within one minute, accurately specifying the amount 90 percent of the time." In some specific instances, objectives written in such precise terms are valuable and necessary. For example, in writing a series of mastery learning lessons in which specified criteria must be met before advancing to the next lesson, such explicit objectives are demanded. Daily lessons do not normally require such precision, nor are all learners necessarily expected to meet the objective during the first session.

Each teacher should give careful consideration to each of the three issues: performance, conditions, and proficiency. For example, counting money using play coins could be a more difficult task than using real money. Altering the conditions (real or play money) can alter motivation. Having real money to count may be much more rewarding and motivating to a child than play money. The types of coins to be counted can illustrate another example of carefully examining the conditions under which learning is to be demonstrated. Counting large numbers of pennies may be easier for the child to learn to do, but counting large numbers of pennies, nevertheless, increases the likelihood of a counting error.

In practice, teachers are rarely expected to write all of their instructional objectives in behavioral terms, although writing some in this genre is certainly advantageous. Some objectives, such as those derived from very affective aims, seem to change both in quality and intent when converted to behavioral statements. In any event, to assess the learning of the child and the effectiveness of the lesson, teachers should always write objectives as explicitly as possible.

Criteria for Self-Evaluation of Written Objectives
◆   Objective is concise, legible, and easily understood.
◆   Objective is realistic considering time, student ability, and material resources.
◆   Objective has sufficient importance to warrant the expenditure of time and materials.
◆   The desired performance is identified in the objective.
◆   Objective reflects the general aim identified.
◆   Rationale justifies the objective.
◆   Objective answers the question, "What is to be learned?"

Materials

Remember the poem in which a disastrous series of consequences result from a missing horseshoe nail? The scenario begins with a missing horseshoe nail causing the loss of a horseshoe and, subsequently, the use of a horse. The domino effect continues as the missing horse causes the loss of a rider that, in turn, causes the loss of a message. The missing message loses a battle, and with the lost battle, a nation disappears. This sad—and unlikely—tale is a perfect analogy for the role of materials in instruction.

Efficient Acquisition and Handling of Materials.   Mrs. Conklin is excited about her unit on electricity. She has ordered new materials, and in this first lesson, all of the children are going to build a flashlight with a switch from tape, aluminum foil, paper clips, a battery, and a bulb. Handing out the materials, Mrs. Conklin finds that one battery is missing. Johnny, who didn't get a battery, is asked to share. However, Johnny objects with an unexpected outburst and causes a disruption. The teacher then sets aside the lesson to deal with Johnny's misbehavior, turns down an offer from Marie to share with Sue, while the rest of the class entertain themselves with the devices at hand. When the teacher reestablishes control of the class, the mood is lost—along with five minutes. The teacher rushes through the introductory material to make up for the lost time. Predictably, several students are having difficulty understanding the new material, and they start asking extensive questions, unnecessarily repeating the easier parts of the lesson. The poor, bedraggled teacher then blames the secretary for not buying enough batteries. Scenarios such as this can easily be prevented but, unfortunately, happen all too often.

Planning for the efficient acquisition, use, and storage of materials is certainly not a trivial activity. Anticipating the inevitable mishaps (the missing papers or extinguished projector bulbs) certainly illustrates the wisdom of a "stitch in time saves nine." Proper attention to materials and their use in the classroom can provide powerful methods for preventing classroom problems. However, the efficient use of a variety of materials provides even more robust avenues for engaging all of the students' learning abilities and styles. Using a complete range of materials allows students to use all five senses to collect information, and providing carefully selected materials offers more opportunities for students to interact, experiment, explore, and investigate.

When deciding what materials to use, consider where the material can be stored, how much is needed, and when it will be used in the lesson. Consider the plight of the teacher who decided that the children should draw objects from real life and decided to hand out cookies. She dutifully handed out the cookies and gave explicit instructions: "This is your cookie. Today we are going to draw cookies, and you may eat the cookie after we are finished. But first, let's draw the cookie. Let me tell you how it will be done." The teacher then capitalized on the intense attention directed at her cookie drawing lesson. But as the lesson proceeded, the inevitable nibble occurred, and a cookie was eaten. "Ah ha," thought the teacher, "I've planned for this one." From her bag, she pulled one of the five spare cookies and gave one to the errant little boy. Merrily back to her lesson, she had just gotten to explaining how to draw observed details when 20 cookies disappeared, each awaiting a replacement. The poor teacher didn't have a chance. What she needed was a distribution strategy that allowed children a cookie to view and, toward the end of the lesson, one to draw. At least, she should have talked faster and less. Preparing a distribution and collection strategy prevents mishaps, saves time, yields efficient results for irregular activities, and provides routines for repetitive operations.

Criteria for Self-Evaluation of Material Selection and Usage
- Materials are appropriate for the objective.
- Materials are appropriate for the student's age group.
- Materials are located for ease of use.
- Materials are safe for use with the maturity level of students.
- Distribution strategies minimize disruption and are suitable for the student's age group.
- Collection strategies minimize disruption and are suitable for the student's age group.
- Collection strategies are designed to collect all work easily so that the teacher is immediately aware of incomplete or missing work.
- Distribution and collection strategies appear efficient and routine.

Introductory Activities

Children can be cooperative, indifferent, passively aggressive, aggressively passive, stubborn, enthusiastic, smart, or slow. They can be anything they want when they want. The idea behind an introductory activity is to make them want to be learners. One of the best and simplest methods of introducing an activity is by providing a reason for learning that is meaningful and reasonable to a child. This knowledge reassures the child that the activity you propose has purpose and deserves his or her attention and effort. It is beneficial, for example, to assist children in understanding that today's lesson on multiplication helps them to solve a problem that is important and real. Helping them to see the similarity of today's multiplication-of-decimals lesson to their parent's problem of figuring wages earned when 12 hours of work is paid at $5.62 cents per hour is vital in establishing the purpose and value of learning. Providing purposeful and meaningful activity for children certainly holds their attention more than mindless and unfruitful endeavors do.

Developing a Reason for Learning.   A reason for learning is best when it empowers a child to perform tasks that he or she would like to do. For example, if the lesson is on measuring in cups, ounces, teaspoons and tablespoons, an excellent reason for learning can be that the children can then bake a cake. First, discuss the group's experience with various cake disasters and the results of measuring improperly. By emphasizing the necessity of measuring accurately when baking a cake, the lesson becomes more than an academic task in a math book. Giving children an introductory activity that discusses making a cake, followed by a culminating activity of accurately measuring the cake ingredients, motivates them more than simply giving them math workbook pages on which to circle the number of tablespoons indicated by the recipe. The workbook introduction is remote from the reality in which the child lives, but the cake-baking activity is precisely the skill that is to be taught and defines the reason for learning.

Communicating Expectations.   However, inherent motivation is not enough to ensure that everything goes smoothly. To develop proficiency in measuring, the children need much more practice than can be achieved in baking a single cake. The teacher must explain the behavioral and learning expectations for the lesson. Students are informed that they must practice measuring with sand and water before the teacher can take a chance with real ingredients. Explaining that all ingredients must go into bowls, not on the floor, on heads, or in pockets, states the expectation that learning must occur in a controlled and orderly fashion. Expecting each child to use the measuring devices appropriately and accurately defines the activity from free-form sand and water play. Thus, some inappropriate misinterpretation of the day's lesson is nipped in the bud.

Focusing and Reviewing.   Focusing on the reason for learning (baking a cake) and reviewing past experiences (discussing "cakes in our past") comprise the third logical part of the sample introductory activity.

Not all learning is as easily managed in an introduction as in our tidy cake example. However, all lessons can be greatly enhanced by introducing activity, addressing motivation, defining and explaining expectations, and remembering and reviewing past learning. Teachers should make every effort to connect the learning activity to an introductory activity that structures learning and lays out the "learning ground rules."

Criteria for Self-Evaluation of Introductory Activities
◆ Reason for learning is made apparent to children in terms that they are likely to understand.
◆ Reason for learning is made in concrete terms related to past learning or experiences.
◆ Behavior and learning expectations are made explicit.
◆ Behavior and learning expectations are reasonable for the age and maturity of the children, the objectives, and the activity.
◆ Focus activity is likely to increase children's attention to lesson activity and content.
◆ Review of material is structured so that it introduces new material.
◆ Attention to motivation is apparent.

Lesson Procedures

When using the expanded lesson plan format, the procedures component is the most important contributor to successful instruction. The lesson procedures are the culmination of planning—the focal point for teaching. As such, the lesson procedures must literally begin with a strategy as opposed to immediate implementation of some action.

Selecting the Strategy.   The teacher must understand and forecast the likely results of various methods of providing experiences to children that will realize his or her objective. After identifying the strategies, the teacher should specify the actual procedures. For example, the learning goal of one teacher is to assist young children in understanding that not all neighborhoods are similar to their own. There are many strategies to realize this goal. One strategy is for the teacher to read a different short story, deliberately selected for its cultural diversity content, to the children each day for a week. Each day after reading the short story, the teacher assists the children in comparing the home environment of main characters in the stories. Another strategy is for the teacher to select a series of contiguous states and examine each for similarities and differences with the children's home state.

No single strategy can realize the objective for all learners. Sometimes, for example, the differences among learners are so great that no single attempt at teaching can be successful. Because of this, the teacher may need multiple strategies to obtain a single objective.

To assist children in learning about neighboring states, the teacher may choose to first discuss children's trips to other states. Then, the teacher may point to these locations on a map. The teacher may discuss personal trips to surrounding areas, showing photos and other memorabilia collected. Finally, the teacher may show a film or video that features the business, industrial, and vacation highlights of a neighboring state. Some children will realize the objective just by being asked to recall their own travels and to point these out on a map that shows where the travel location and the school location are. Others may need more discussion or more extensive experiences since they may have had only limited experience from which to build the concept. These children are most likely to profit from visual strategies represented in the lesson by video or film. In any case, the variety of instructional strategies within a lesson generally ensures that more children are likely to realize the objective.

A second reason for having multiple strategies for obtaining the objective is the necessity of planning for what may go wrong. In the previous example, the projector may damage the film. In this case, the teacher (having her travel brochures at hand) can simply spend more time on sharing these experiences. She can divide the children into small discussion groups, have the children look at the pictures and text, and then follow up with a sharing session. This latter strategy, perhaps not as successful as the film strategy, could save the day and the lesson. In another scenario, the children may have already seen the film and want to look at the travel brochures and plan a fantasy vacation. Planning multiple strategies, even if the estimated time for all strategies greatly exceeds that time allotment, is good insurance. However, there is still another reason for multiple strategies.

It is often difficult to predict how children will respond to each experience planned. This is particularly true if the teacher is a novice or is not accustomed to the age or cultural group of the children. Having multiple strategies allows the teacher to have a backup just in case the "best shot" misses the mark. Comparing the relative effects of two different strategies designed and implemented around a single objective can add to the experiential knowledge base of the teacher. This knowledge will assist in planning and refining future lessons.

Each lesson should have a dominant teaching strategy that has many components and alternatives. The *dominant teaching strategy* is merely the sequence of events that occur during the course of the lesson. The strategy for teaching about neighborhoods, as noted earlier, may have several components, each designed to enlighten the learner from a different perspective. A sequence of strategies may also be indicated when the subject matter has a logical and sequential structure such as found in learning math algorithms. The precise selection and sequencing of the teaching strategy require a great deal of art. However, in general, there are a few guidelines that research has shown to be effective.

Matching Objectives and Instructional Procedures. The presentation should reflect the objective. If the objective is primarily one of information transmission, a lecture presentation or a video may succeed in presenting the greatest amount of information in the most effective and compact delivery mode. If the objective, however, is primarily affective in nature, other modes of instruction may be indicated. For example, the objective may be to assist children in understanding why story characters react to problems the way that they do. A discussion of how the children in the class have met and dealt with similar problems is more appropriate in meeting the objective of understanding than a lecture on how children react to problems.

Providing Clarity.   Clarity in any presentation is certainly essential. McCaleb and White (1980) identified five aspects of clarity:

◆ Matching the material to be learned to students' past understanding and knowledge
◆ Structuring the material to state the purpose of instruction, review main ideas, and provide transitions between strategies
◆ Sequencing to arrange information in an order conducive to learning; for example, increasing the difficulty of examples as the lesson progresses or providing a logical sequence of skills
◆ Explaining by providing examples, facts, or other information that relates the concept to be learned to facts presented
◆ Presenting in a skillful way by determining the amount of material to be presented, the pacing involved, and the speech mechanics in oral presentation.

Good and Brophy (1987) include enthusiasm as one of the procedural aspects that improve instruction. Teacher enthusiasm is helpful in capturing student attention, maintaining interest in instruction, as well as motivating students to achieve at a higher rate.

Including Practice.   Guided practice and independent practice is included in the expanded lesson plan because of its overall importance in completing skill-oriented lessons. In some lessons, guided practice or independent practice sessions may be unnecessary or undesired. If, for example, the lesson centered on a discussion of book characters and how they dealt with the problems in their lives, the teacher may not want any other follow-up to the discussion.

In one way, discussion can be viewed as a guided practice, but this distinction is more semantic rather than substantive. In any event, the purpose of guided practice is to provide experiences employing the new skill or information under the direction and supervision of the teacher. It is quite possible for the teacher to elect a guided practice function and ask students to write a one-paragraph reaction to the character's solution to the problem. Perhaps, as independent practice, the teacher may require the students to write a new solution to the problem presented in a story. These writing examples certainly provide important practice in communication. They also allow the teacher some substantive way to evaluate the more affective aspects of the lesson. However, these written activities may not be desirable as a follow-up to each discussion. In any case, the teacher should carefully consider the effects of omitting guided and independent practice aspects of the lesson.

Providing Closure.   Closure is often omitted because of a lack of adequate reflection, lack of planning, or lack of instructional time. *Closure* is simply the summarizing of the essential skills or information explored during the lesson. For example, students may have been working on simple two-place addition with some success, and the time allotted for practice has expired. To obtain closure, the teacher may simply work one more problem on the chalkboard as a summarizing example. In the previous example about story characters, the teacher may summarize a list of motives that students had reviewed during the lesson by writing them on the board and briefly identifying the significance of each one.

One last piece of information may be helpful in designing guided and independent practice and in obtaining closure. The success rates of various activities need to be considered. When students are learning a new skill, guided practice results should yield a success rate of 70 or 80 percent. Independent practice should yield a higher success rate because a greater degree of skill is involved when students are ready to do problems on their own. Independent practice on a newly acquired skill should reach 85 to 90 percent or higher. Independent practice of review material should approach 100 percent.

Criteria for Evaluating the Lesson Procedures
◆ Procedures reflect the intent of stated objectives.
◆ Procedures are appropriate for the maturity of the child.
◆ Procedures are sequenced in logical order.
◆ Procedures are likely to focus student attention and promote on-task behavior.
◆ Procedures reflect knowledge of learning and/or developmental theory.
◆ Procedures bridge past and future lessons.
◆ Procedures indicate strategies for smooth transition between activities and lesson components.
◆ Guided practice is appropriate to the objective, lesson, and evaluation procedures.
◆ Provisions for independent practice are appropriate to the objective, lesson, and evaluation procedures.
◆ Independent practice is likely to be completed successfully by most students.
◆ Provisions for student differences have been made.
◆ Closure activity summarizes the important points of the lessons.
◆ Questioning strategies are likely to give ongoing information to assist the lesson's development.

Evaluation of Learning

The evaluation of learning has two separate and distinct functions. First, evaluation should provide the teacher with information that assists him or her to determine whether the objective has been successfully obtained. From this point of view, the evaluation instrument should mirror the objectives as closely as possible. Second, the evaluation program should assist the teacher in diagnosing the common difficulties that students are having with the objective so that students may be regrouped for reteaching and should indicate what form the reteaching function should take.

Strategy. The evaluation instrument or strategy is simply the seatwork, scoring rubric, or observation strategy used in evaluation. If written work is not used, the teacher should indicate what strategy will be used to estimate the level of student achievement. Sometimes, an alternate evaluation strategy is the result of teacher-directed questions during the closure activity. On other occasions, the evaluation strategy may be the result of teacher observation of a skill that has been taught (for example, children successfully pantomiming various animals). Most often, the evaluation instrument is the guided practice function that can be analyzed for attainment of individual as well as class objectives.

Feedback.   The feedback vehicle for evaluation is a straightforward task. This planning function determines how the results of learning will be communicated to the student. Numerical percentages, although the most common feedback vehicle, are probably the least informative of the various feedback methods. If a student scores a 50 percent on a math homework, a "50" written at the top of the paper does not convey the source of the errors or indicate the method for remediation. In math homework, a typical feedback device may be a numerical grade with an encouraging comment for those students attaining an 80 percent correct or greater. Those attaining a score less than this may not be given a numerical grade but will receive a specific message such as, "Most of your errors were the result of regrouping." These children are then grouped for reteaching. A feedback vehicle may be a sticker, a written comment, a note home, a numerical or letter grade, verbal comment, a message about a new reteaching group, or displays of the exemplary work.

Ongoing Evaluation.   Providing for ongoing (informal) evaluation is a simple but essential concept. During the course of teaching a lesson, the teacher needs to assess the success of the lesson continually. If at some point in the lesson the teacher decides that students are not learning, the effective teacher alters the current course. Unless the teacher actively evaluates this information, he or she will probably not find out until the following day while grading papers.

Ongoing informal evaluation may consist of teacher questions to students, close monitoring of students' work during guided practice, requests for demonstrations by students, or solicitation of students' summaries of the discussion. Ongoing evaluation allows the teacher to make immediate corrections or alterations of both instructional strategies and pacing decisions.

The lesson plan should reflect concise and reasonable strategies for gaining immediate feedback on the lesson's effectiveness. "Teacher monitors student work during guided practice" or "Teacher records students' comments and questions on an alphabetical list of students indicating both frequency and accuracy of comments" are examples of preplanned strategies for ongoing evaluation. As teachers become more experienced, they typically develop a repertoire of these items. Some devices, such as inferences from eye contact, may take several years to develop. Such skills are very valuable, but such high-inference techniques often yield mistaken assessments. The teacher must concentrate and actively plan in this area to become skillful and to develop successful lessons. Effectiveness in maximizing instruction does not come without harmonious planning and evaluation.

Criteria for Self-Evaluation of Lesson Evaluation Procedures
- Evaluation strategy is appropriate for objectives.
- Evaluation is likely to provide diagnostic information.
- Evaluation is evident in each phase of the instructional plan (review, instruction, and guided/independent practice).
- Evaluation provides meaningful feedback to students.
- Evaluation provides meaningful feedback to parents.
- Provisions are made for informal evaluation.

Post-Instructional Evaluation of Teaching Strategy and Instruction

Post-instructional evaluation is always important but can only be completed after the lesson has been taught. This device assists the planning of future lessons by analyzing the results of current efforts. Collecting evidence that learning has occurred is essential for proper evaluation of teaching. Evidence that a lesson has been taught includes an analysis of the independent practice and examination of the class average or range of scores. Details are important in this area. For example, "Students had a post-instructional score of 86 percent on the spelling test with scores ranging from 64 to 100 whereas the pre-instructional average was 64 percent" is a different result from "Students had a post-instructional score of 86 percent." The first represents reasonably acceptable results from the week's work (assuming the appropriateness of the words and the philosophical orientation of the reader). The latter is vague and provides no direction. After all, it is possible that the pretest average was 83 percent, and the class has made virtually no gain. Without careful attention to the results of their efforts, teachers are likely to commit the same errors over and over. If the teacher can derive no evidence of learning over a series of lessons, he or she has no way of knowing whether the lessons are teaching, entertaining, or simply wasting time. Collecting evidence of teaching effectiveness is a primary avenue of teaching analysis and improvement.

Reteaching.   Reteaching requires the analysis of errors and grouping for appropriate instruction. Teachers always perform this function, although they probably do not write these plans in the plan book on a daily basis. Writing, however, always continues to be an instructional tool for teacher improvement if the teacher chooses to use it. An example entry in this area of the lesson plan may be, "Four children scored less than 70 percent on the basic facts worksheet and must have additional practice and explanation. This will be done with a parent volunteer. The remainder of class will continue with counters finding sums to 20."

The final issue, "What parts of your lesson should be changed?", may or may not have significance for a particular lesson. In the previous example, the parent volunteer was used to give immediate guided feedback to children who had difficulty, whereas more able children received the intermittent monitoring characteristic of whole-group instruction. At times, if most of the children fail to attain the goals, the entire approach may have to be scrapped. Other times, the procedure may only need to be modified in minor ways. Still other times, the question is superfluous because all of the children did well. In these situations, the teacher should carefully reflect on why the lesson went well so that he or she can repeat the performance.

Criteria for Self-Evaluation of the Rethinking Process (Single Lesson)
◆ Evidence is available that indicates the objective was attained.
◆ Diagnostic reteaching is indicated and explained.
◆ Teacher indicated reasonable strategies for improving the lesson when implemented again.

Criteria for Self-Evaluation of the Rethinking Process (Series of Lessons)
◆ Originality is evident in selection, development, and use of materials and procedures.
◆ Diversity of instructional approaches, procedures, and materials is evident.
◆ Attention to affective *and* cognitive domains is demonstrated.
◆ Use of direct and indirect instructional methods is evident.

Is Planning a Big Deal?

The expanded plan is carefully designed to help the teacher forecast and prevent many teaching problems. It also suggests that forecasting is the most effective preparation for the day's instructional effectiveness. As teachers repeat the planning process, they increase their knowledge base, and the planning process consumes less of their time. Writing excellent objectives is always a challenge, but with practice, the teacher's use of lesson procedures becomes more sophisticated and successful. Successful teachers develop efficient routines so that they can distribute and collect papers in seconds rather than minutes. They can establish motivation more easily and review student's understanding during lessons as well as at the beginning and end. They can begin to enjoy reflecting on the day's effectiveness and to find that grading papers yields few surprises because of the sophistication of their ongoing evaluation.

◆ ◆ ◆

Summary

1. Planning is the fundamental teaching activity in which the classroom is organized to construct the learning environment, to prepare learners to engage the opportunity successfully, to guide and direct the development of the class curriculum, and to accommodate unexpected or specialized needs and demands inherent in the educational enterprise.

2. Teachers tend to "chunk" similar requirements into routines or subroutines that can be interchanged among lessons and activities.

3. Some teachers are so successful in planning that these routines and incorporated classroom values appear invisible, giving the observer the impression that the classroom is "running itself."

4. Inefficient planning manifests itself in attempts to slow down the classroom pace overtly and increasingly to restrict student movement.

5. Teachers' views regarding planning vary with their interpretation of what planning is. Often, planning is viewed as the actual written plan in a teacher's plan book and is not often considered critical to successful instruction.

6. Many different outlines to guide planning exist. Most of the guides deal exclusively with the instructional procedures. However, students' motivation, students' movements, material use, time use, transitional activities, and maintenance of the psychosocial environment must also be planned if classroom learning is to be maximized.

7. Teacher planning is thought to occur exclusively prior to instruction. However, the activities of the teacher during and after instruction has a major impact on the classroom organization and, therefore, are recognized as planning activities.

8. The expanded lesson plan (see Figure 6.4) assists the teacher in developing a "whole classroom" approach to planning. It incorporates careful consideration of the physical aspects of the classroom, the motivation of students, and the cohesive delivery of a series of instructional activities as well as consideration of the instructional strategy for the current lesson. However, it is only one of many potential guides for successful planning.

9. Teachers have many options and alternatives in the planning process. They often create a dominant strategy but also consider variations if certain unpredictable (but anticipated) events occur.

10. Planning requires practice to develop skill. Post-instructional evaluation is not only a planning activity for subsequent lessons but also a vehicle for teacher growth.

11. Systematic planning in teaching allows the teacher to make instructional decisions deliberately rather randomly.

12. Teachers often do not understand why they teach what they teach. Their lack of understanding is passed on to their students, making instruction inert, meaningless, and lacking in tangible value.

◆ ◆ ◆

Activities and Questions for Further Understanding

1. The author claims that careful goal-directed planning and deliberate improvement of student learning are the same thing. Do you agree? Does accurate planning for specified goals always lead to student learning? Can sufficient student learning occur without planning? What arguments can you present to defend your views?

2. Can an elementary classroom "run by itself" in the teacher's absence? If so, how do you think the teacher accomplishes this task? If not, what limits children's skill in self-control?

3. Examine each component of the lesson plan. Develop plans for teaching children to perform the following:
   a. Walk a balance beam.

b. Capitalize proper names.

c. Describe honesty, its use, and to evaluate acts by their definitions.

d. Recognize and describe how chemical changes differ from physical changes.

4. Gather goals and objectives from curriculum guides and develop reasons for learning that you would give to children.

5. Write a lesson plan for Mr. Brattain's lesson in this chapter's "A Slice of Life."

6. Write objectives for lessons that you may teach. Share these objectives with a group of fellow students. The first participant is to read his or her objective. Then, each member of the group is to describe what he or she thinks the learner must do to demonstrate that learning. Questions for the discussion:

a. Are the perceptions of the members of your group similar to your perceptions of the learner's behavior?

b. Did group participants find it easy to describe a behavior that represents the learning that you specified in your objective?

c. Participants should share their view of the long-term aim that is represented by this objective. Was the long-term aim evident? Are these aims the same that you had in mind? Are children likely to find the learning relevant?

d. Did the objective specify what the learner was to learn? The conditions under which learning was to be demonstrated? The proficiency level (degree of accuracy)?

e. What suggestions can the group make to assist in increased specificity and clarity of the objective? Can they suggest ways to improve the significance of the objective to the learner?

◆ ◆ ◆

References

Clark, C. M., & Peterson, P. L. (1986). Teachers' thought processes. In Wittrock, M. C. (Ed.), *Handbook of research on teaching* (3rd ed., pp. 255–296). New York: Macmillan.

Eisner, Elliot W. (1967). Educational objectives: Help or hindrance? *School Review, 75,* 250–260.

Gagné, R. M., & Briggs, L. J. (1974). *Principles of instruction design.* New York: Holt Rinehart and Winston.

Good, T. L., & Brophy, J. E. (1987). *Looking into classrooms* (4th ed.). New York: Harper and Row.

Holt, John. (1964). *How children fail* (p. x). New York: Dell Publishing Company.

McCaleb, J., & White, J. (1980). Critical dimensions in evaluating teacher clarity. *Journal of Classroom Interaction, 15,* 27–30.

McNair, K. (1978–1979). Capturing inflight decisions. *Educational Research Quarterly, 3*(4), 26–42.

Mager, R. M. (1962). *Preparing instructional objectives* (2nd ed.). Belmont, CA: Fearon.

Rogers, C., & Freiberg, H. J. (1994). *Freedom to learn* (3rd ed., p. 35). Upper Saddle River, NJ: Prentice Hall/Merrill.

Tyler, Ralph W. (1950). *Basic principles of curriculum and instruction.* Chicago: University of Chicago Press.

Yinger, R. J. (1977). *A study of teacher planning: Descriptive and theory development using ethnographic and information processing methods.* Unpublished doctoral dissertation, Michigan State University, East Lansing.

Yinger, R. J. (1979). Routines in teacher planning. *Theory into Practice, 18,* 163–169.

CHAPTER 7

What Do Successful Teachers Do?

The Research on Effective Instruction

Outline

Then, my good friend . . . do not use compulsion, but let early education be a sort of amusement; you will be the better able to find out the natural bent.

PLATO

Sometimes one sees in the school simply the instrument for transferring a certain maximum quantity of knowledge to the growing generation. But that is not right. Knowledge is dead; the school, however, serves the living.

ALBERT EINSTEIN

◆

A Slice of Life

Mr. Pinion was beginning his fifteenth year of teaching in the same school. He knew the school had a history of producing good readers; therefore, it was odd that reading was the area showing the most improvement this year. Although math was always a problem, scores were getting better. But, he thought, the worst thing should be the easiest to improve. A series of teacher work groups had attacked the problem, and their first step was to align what they were teaching with what the district's curriculum guide required. Actually, the district guide in math had been changed to reflect the state guidelines and the suggestions published by the National Council for Teachers of Mathematics (NCTM). He had served on several of the committees and at first thought they were a waste of time. Like so many of his colleagues, he felt that he wasn't working if he was at school but not in his classroom with children. He changed his mind when he found that having a schoolwide plan in both curriculum and behavior expectations was paying off.

Mr. Pinion snapped back to the present when the bell rang for the first time this year. He got up and went to the door. Standing in the hall, he greeted former students with waves and some "high five's" and asked the name of each new student who entered. Actually, he knew most of them from cafeteria and playground duty. Each desk had a small placard with the student's name on it and a packet of papers lightly taped to the top. Mr. Pinion alternately greeted students, monitored the halls, and peeked inside to repeat the directions: "Find your seat and read the message taped to your desk. After that, chat with your neighbors." Normally, the process of getting students inside took only a few minutes, but the first day was always a little slow. Mr. Pinion looked around. All desks were filled.

A staccato of activity followed. Mr. Pinion double-checked attendance even though he knew everyone was here. He began his welcome speech for the fifteenth time. He introduced himself, told a little about his summer canoeing trip, offered to bring his canoe to school on hobby day, and asked when the class would like their first hobby day to be held. They decided on next Monday. Students would make exhibits of what they brought, each day five or six students would share, and they would take everything home on Friday.

Mr. Pinion asked if the children would mind writing an autobiography this week so that he could get to know them better. He picked up from his desk a small stapled book with his picture glued to the front. He read the title, "The Enviable Life of Troy Pinion. Best book in the room, I'd say." He read the homemade book quickly and discussed what might go into an autobiography. He reiterated that the students should pay careful attention to what they put in their outlines to be sure that their books would be interesting. He broke the class into groups of four and had them take turns telling facts about one another.

Mr. Pinion walked around the room as they chatted. Occasionally, he added a comment, usually an expressive "R-r-really?" followed by a wink. The wink was his trademark, and the children soon learned it was a sign of approval and support. Later in the day when he went over the rules, he would tell them about the wink along with the fact that if he leaned back, looked over his glasses, and crossed his arms, they ought to be thinking about changing something! He gave the children a three-minute notice, and soon all were making suggestions about what made facts about people interesting. Mr. Pinion wrote on the board, "Unexpected," "different from others," "exciting," "want to do the same things" . . . the list continued. "All right! Great! Now let's do a little quiet work. Begin a list of things about you that match each of the terms that we put on the board. Don't worry about order. Put more than one down if you can. Use the second page in your packet. It has the directions for your autobiography on it. I want you to share the whole packet with your parents tonight."

Research on Effective Teaching

During the past three decades, educational researchers have begun to verify certain teacher activities and behavior that have been found to be consistently related to desirable educational outcomes (Borich, 1979). These outcomes include, among other variables, student achievement, school attendance, on-task learning behavior, and student/parent satisfaction (Northwest Regional Educational Laboratory, 1990). A number of summaries have been developed that represent highly synthesized descriptions of what effective teachers do on a daily basis (Cruickshank, 1990). These behaviors apply to all subjects and generally are not age-specific, although many have been found to be more effective with certain subgroups that are related to economic status or age.

Many have accused the researchers of confirming "common sense" rather than really contributing to the body of knowledge about teaching. This criticism is both accurate and misleading (Gage, 1978). A large portion of the results of research on effective teaching is common sense. Further, the implementation of these behaviors does not pose particular problems and can readily be learned and practiced (Medley, 1977). However, for reasons that are hard to understand, teachers in a vast number of classrooms do not consistently employ teacher behaviors advocated by the research. For example, "starting on time" is not a radical notion, yet many teachers waste precious time unnecessarily by social chatting, verbal chastisements of miscreant students, and hunting for materials that are improperly stored. In short, effective teaching research may be common sense that is uncommonly applied.

Elements of Effective Teaching

One summary of effective teaching was briefly introduced in Chapter 1 when the role of the teacher was examined (see Figure 1.5) and will now be discussed in more detail. Of the eight functions listed in the North Carolina Teacher Performance Appraisal Instrument (TPAI) (North Carolina State Department of Public Instruction, 1986a), the first five—time use, management of student behavior, instructional presentation, monitoring student performance, and instructional feedback—are derived from effective teaching research. The remaining three—facilitating instruction, communication, and noninstructional duties—either have a shallower research base or are derived from nominal expectations of what a teacher's job in a public school entails. These variables have been reported in a number of studies and research summaries over the past three decades (Cruickshank, 1976, 1992; Emmer & Evertson, 1982; Good, 1979; Medley, 1977; Rosenshine & Furst, 1971; Stallings, 1982).

Use of Time

Time has been shown to be an important variable in schooling effectiveness. Teachers vary widely in what they accomplish with the time provided in school. Teachers have several strategies for effective use of their instruction time.

Have Materials Ready.   The first and simplest time-use strategy is simply to have materials and apparatus ready at the beginning of the lesson in proper quantity ready to be distributed. Effective teachers employ an idiosyncratic array of distribution and collection strategies. Some teachers have basic materials such as crayons, glue, scissors, rulers, pencils, sharpeners, and staplers in a crate-like "center" which is shared by four to six students. These students may share a single table with the material crate along with dictionaries, word books, and other materials. In some cases, stand-alone desks with separate chairs are clumped to form a larger table, and the crate is placed in the middle. Some classrooms have single desk/chair units, and materials are placed in containers such as potato chip tubes and tied to the chair backs. Still other teachers allow children to move freely around the room and have established a series of shelves for frequently used materials.

Some teachers employ combinations of all the systems. For example, they may divide the class into teams of four to six children who share most materials but also have private pencil boxes and storage areas inside their desks. These teachers may store art papers, paints, chalk, and books for the group on shelves painted in the team's color that matches their desks and chairs.

Store Materials for Easy Use. Storage sometimes takes on an inventor's ingenuity. One teacher drilled six small holes in a small wooden block painted in the team's color. Each pair of scissors, with handles painted with the corresponding color, was placed in the block with the nose of the scissors in the hole. The teacher only had to look at the desktop to see if each group's scissors was replaced and immediately knew if any pair was missing and, if so, which team must search for the missing pair. Time-saving methods for storage vary widely, and some methods that work for some teachers are much less effective for others. The goal, however, is the same: (1) Provide storage that is efficient, and (2) teach children to be responsible for the routines used to distribute and collect materials.

Create and Teach Routines. Another way that effective teachers use time wisely is to have established and practiced routines for handling the recurring business of the class. Tasks such as pencil sharpening, getting a tissue, going to the water fountain, and trips to the restroom need not be disruptive. Again, the routines employed vary widely with the context and students involved so that no single routine can be expected to work successfully for all teachers or even from year to year. However, carefully constructed routines do save time and minimize disruption.

Saving time and minimizing disruption are two criteria that often are at odds with each other. Some strategies for minimizing the possibility of disruption may actually take so much time that they are inefficient. Likewise, attempts to save time may increase disruptions by hurrying students beyond safety or decorum. Having rehearsed, clearly established routines allows the teacher to put routine activities on "autopilot" while the teacher attends to more important tasks. Time conservation is not the only benefit for teachers who use routines to get children to take care of their personal and learning needs.

By providing routines and placing the routine under the direction of the children, not only does the teacher save time for other classroom work, but the children are also provided optimal opportunity to exercise responsibility as well as achieve a sense of self-direction and freedom. This, of course, results in more cooperation which, in turn, minimizes disruptions and conserves even more time. However, having daily opportunity to practice responsibility can legitimately be considered a valuable learning activity in its own right, regardless of time management. Because of this, wise teachers often opt for maximizing the opportunities for developing responsibility even if disruption and time use are slightly increased when compared to more teacher dominated methods.

Use Task Orientation.   Effective use of time by teachers is also maintained by personal task orientation that includes prompt starts, avoidance of diversions, and concentration on learning activities. Task orientation by teachers is critical considering the semiautonomous nature of the profession. Only a small percentage of teacher work is supervised. However, some teachers, through either lack of knowledge, skill, or motivation, attempt to have children do "busywork" to fill their time.

Each activity that involves children should have a carefully articulated purpose that contributes to the educational mission. Obviously, teachers with higher levels of task orientation get more done, and what they do is directly related to learning. No wonder that teacher task orientation is consistently a strong predictor of teacher success (Borich, 1996; Cruickshank, 1976; Stallings, 1982).

Engage Students.   Similar to teacher task orientation is student engagement time. Teachers who manage to provide activities and instruction so that children use their time efficiently are more likely to realize substantial classroom learning gains. Student engagement time is not the same as allotted time; student engagement time is the amount of time that the student is actually working on the task. A teacher may provide 30 minutes for a 15-minute task. If the student works slowly with intermittent breaks and completes the task within the time provided, his or her engagement time is still only 15 minutes. Of course, the time needed by students to complete any task varies. Therefore, there will always be an imbalance between allotted time and engagement time. The goal is to have the greatest possible percentage of allotted time attributed to students engaged in meaningful learning tasks.

With 30 minutes of allotted time, most students can be fully engaged for the entire time by using that time to complete the task. Students who finish early can be involved in learning tasks that they can select from an array of self-directed experiences made available by the teacher. Such tasks may include silent reading or working at an investigation center. Maximizing student engaged time is the most complex of the time management tasks. Student variation in cooperation, motivation, and self-control obviously affect engagement time. However, teachers can radically influence the development of student cooperation, motivation, and self-control. Engaged time is affected by teacher planning decisions such as the amount of time allowed for practice, adequate preparation for practice, the sequence and comprehensibility of presentations, and adequate introductory activities that prepare students for the lesson and inspire them to perform at their best.

Management of Student Behavior

Few issues create as much anxiety in novice teachers as managing student behavior. Although teachers worry about how to get children to behave in appropriate ways within the classroom, they also have problems determining what those appropriate behaviors should be. To illustrate the dilemma, consider the issues surrounding student engagement time. If students are engaged in reading, must they be seated at their desks? Should students be able to select any seating location? Should students be required to sit at all, or can they be allowed to lounge on the floor or sit underneath a table (a particular favorite among children)? Are any of these sitting behaviors more likely to maintain student engagement? Are some behaviors simply expected, and must children be trained to behave in ways expected by the group? Unfortunately, as with so many educational issues, value assertions play a central role in answering these questions. Definite empirical or logical referents simply may not be available to guide the teacher. However, most teachers agree on the most basic expectations: work completion, task orientation, respect for the rights of others, and compliance with the legitimate commands of the teachers. In obtaining appropriate learning behavior and maintaining a socially stable environment, effective teachers have been found to display a general pattern of behavior even though the actual techniques may vary widely.

Have Clearly Defined Rules.   Effective teachers have an established set of rules that are clearly defined and thoroughly taught to children. Also, these teachers have established a set of routines for handling administrative matters, fulfilling students' personal needs, regulating verbal participation, and governing student movement. Effective teachers make explicit the requirements of the classroom and teach children how to fulfill those requirements.

Use Frequent Monitoring.   Frequent monitoring of students is characteristic of effective teachers and promotes positive behavior from children. Teachers who circulate around the room are able to provide assistance to children when seatwork is involved. When class discussions are in progress, teacher circulation provides each child with a "front seat" several times during the lesson. With frequent teacher circulation, students in remote corners of the room cannot hide behind desks and other students and, therefore, are more likely to pay attention to the discussion or presentation. Circulation also assists the teacher in stopping inappropriate behavior quickly, thereby minimizing the likelihood that severe misbehavior can occur.

Reexamine Time Use.   Saving time is also associated with better behavior from students. The two management areas—time use and student behavior—are closely interrelated. Teachers maintaining high levels of student engagement not only save time but also minimize student disruptions. Student engagement is also related to the success rates that children experience in doing their work. Teachers who vary the introduction and sequencing of new material have higher success rates. Their children cause less disruption, are happier in completing tasks, are more likely to finish work, and learn more successfully.

Children are like adults in that they like to have some control and influence in what they do. As expected, teachers who use student ideas in developing class rules and routines, in selecting learning activities, and in conducting presentations and discussions have children who are more attentive, comply with teacher requests more readily, and use time for learning more efficiently.

Presentation of Instruction

One of the most prevalent and consistent research findings is that effective teachers use a variety of instructional methods. Effective teachers vary their methods depending on the demands of the subject and abilities of students. A variety of methods minimizes the dangers of student satiation—that is, students do not tire of lessons as quickly, and their curiosity is not dulled by repeated familiarity. Variety of instructional methods has a strong consistent relationship with students' learning partly because the students are required to use a wider range of learning skills. This increases the likelihood that lessons inspire the students and use, at least once, the students' particular favored mode of learning. Although certain methods may be more effective than others, a wide repertoire of learning strategies is an absolute necessity for the successful teacher.

Begin with a Purpose.   Effective teachers begin lessons by stating the objectives or purpose of the lessons (Rosenshine, 1983). Having students understand what is to be learned serves as an advanced organizer and helps students prepare a mental picture of what they need to be successful in the lessons. When students know what learning is expected and what they must do to succeed, they are more motivated and work harder. The preliminary structuring provided by the teacher initiates a scaffold for building later concepts in the lesson. Certainly, if the student is convinced that the objective is meaningful and that he or she can succeed, motivation and effort are greatly increased.

Be Clear.   Instructional presentations that are clear and easily understood are also shown to be desirable by the research. Teacher clarity is consistently related to student achievement as indicated by repeated studies (Cruickshank, 1990). Teacher clarity is composed of several factors. Completing sentences before initiating another idea is a chief component of clarity. Using appropriate vocabulary easily comprehended by students facilitates their understanding. Sandwiching new vocabulary between more familiar words enables students to use context clues to unlock the meaning of the new words. Adding explanations and definitions of new or unfamiliar words also helps student comprehension.

Use a Variety of Questions.   Research also indicates that teachers who use a variety of questions and space them frequently throughout the instructional sequence are more successful. Effective teachers raise questions one at a time and solicit a response from the student before moving on. Probes are questions that are designed to expand the answers that students give. Teachers also use probes to elicit greater detail and enhance the accuracy of students' answers.

Use Summaries.   Effective teachers also summarize the content of the lesson prior to the end of instruction. Additionally, successful teachers summarize and review components of the lesson frequently. Successful teachers follow presentations with assignments that are clear, coherent, and well connected to the content of the lesson. Often, teachers assign practice activities that do not accurately reflect the substance of the lesson. For example, a lesson on writing descriptive sentences may be followed by an assignment to write a story. Writing a story requires many additional skills and only tangentially reflects the lesson's emphasis on descriptive sentences. Effective teachers find methods of practice that avoid incongruent strategies and integrate guided activity with the lesson presentation.

Make Clear Assignments.   Assignments that are clear, begin with a review of previous lessons, and have been checked for the necessary prerequisite skills for the current lesson are also characteristic of effective teachers. At the beginning of lessons, the teacher has the students focus on the lesson and makes them aware of the reason for learning. The teacher provides copious examples and broadly illustrates concepts and skills while maintaining a brisk pace, slowing as needed for comprehension and smooth transitions.

Monitoring of Student Performance

Many of the same research findings that were mentioned in the discussion on managing student behavior also apply to monitoring student performance. Teacher behaviors that promote task engagement and effective time use can be used to focus children on quality work products. In addition, the research shows that teachers who maintain clear, firm, and reasonable work standards have students who achieve more (North Carolina State Department of Public Instruction, 1986a).

Teachers who circulate among students during classwork are even more effective when they provide the student with encouragement, additional information or explanations, and quick checks of progress. Teachers who monitor student progress routinely with both oral and written work products are more likely to have students who achieve comprehension.

Feedback for Instruction

Students must be given information about their work if they are to make corrections that enhance the accuracy and quality of their efforts. Effective teachers provide feedback concerning correctness/incorrectness of students' participation in a variety of ways. While teachers who let the students know whether their responses to questions are correct and provide them with both appreciation and encouragement for their effort are more effective, many questions that teachers ask yield answers that are not subject to simple assessment formulas such as correct/incorrect. These situations require more sophisticated responses.

Responses to questions that ask for students' opinions or ask students to form an hypothesis need responses that clarify and assure the student that they are accurately understanding the material. Likewise, teachers may ask for additional clarification, explanation, or expansion of an idea contained in the response. Simple appreciation is almost always in order. For example, "I haven't thought about that," "That is a unique view," or "Very interesting approach!" conveys appreciation and provides the student with recognition that encourages them to contribute again. These assessments are equally appropriate in evaluating written work.

Be Prompt and Frequent with Feedback.   Effective teachers also give prompt feedback regarding out-of-class work. Although graded work is appropriate in many situations, other written comments may accomplish more in the long run. For example, grading written work in creative writing on an "A-B-C" scale while correcting grammatical and syntax errors may assist the child in assessing the quality of the work. However, teacher comments that convey strategies for improvement and acknowledge effort while encouraging the student is far more likely to promote student analysis and encourage continued refinement of the work.

Provide Wait Time.   Wait time is one of the more interesting findings of instructional feedback (Rowe, 1974). *Wait time* is the time between the teacher question and the teacher prompt for the student to respond. Optimal wait times vary with the question, but a general strategy is to give the student at least three seconds on straightforward questions where memory responses are expected. Wait time offers many advantages to the teacher. Wait time has consistently shown to improve the correctness of student responses, the number of volunteers to answer the question, and the elaboration and complexity of responses. For slower students, increased wait time is a true necessity if their repeated voluntary participation is sought.

Summaries of Successful Teaching Strategies

Fortunately, teachers are the beneficiaries of many summaries of effective teaching research. These summaries have basic characteristics in common but vary in many significant ways. In addition to the aging TPAI analysis examined earlier, three basic summaries are presented in this section. Reference charts that map the summary findings are provided to assist the teacher in a generic introduction to the research on successful teaching.

Research Is Subject to Interpretation

Since the research is varied and yields patterns subject to interpretation, several summaries are presented even though many of the findings are redundant. However, redundant treatment of successful ideas is itself an important predictor of successful teaching behavior. If a finding is reported repeatedly, pay careful attention to it. Certainly, findings that are consistently reported have a place in every teacher's repertoire. Many skills reflected in effective teaching research are general organizational and interpersonal skills that are used in many human endeavors. Individual teachers have already learned many of these skills outside of school. In developing plans for personal improvement, each teacher should carefully survey the findings and create their own summary carefully appraising his or her current skill level and areas for improvement.

Summary of the National Education Association

By employing a broader base of research and focusing particularly on novice teachers, the National Education Association (NEA) (1982) published a summary of effective teaching based on a teaching model with three basic teaching functions: (1) facilitating instruction, (2) managing the classroom, and (3) making professional decisions.

Figure 7.1 provides an outline of the major points within each function (NEA, 1993). Note that although many of these points are redundant with other summaries in this text, the unique structure of the NEA summary provides a different focus than did previously presented condensations. Also notice that "presenting subject matter" is only one of 24 primary functions provided in the summary. This is an important point for novice teachers who sometimes have a limited view of the scope of teacher responsibilities and skills necessary for effective classroom instruction.

Facilitating Learning

An intimate knowledge and understanding of students is the starting point for successful facilitation of instruction. This knowledge is of two types: (1) knowledge of students that is characteristic of their age, gender, development patterns, region, culture, ethnicity, economic status, and measured ability, and (2) knowledge of the child as an individual, including his or her personal likes and dislikes, the learning styles employed, personal challenges, personality, motivation factor, and attained skill level in basic academic areas. Knowing both the characteristics of children as they represent various groups and the unique characteristics of the individual provides the teacher with a rich resource of data from which to create hypotheses regarding the best strategies for instruction.

Teachers who have a broad knowledge about children and individual learners are more likely to provide appropriate motivating lessons. *Appropriate* concerns the ability and needs of students and the relationship of the instructional strategy to the proposed purpose of instruction and the learning characteristics of the intended students. *Motivation* reflects the estimated willingness of students to follow various proposed courses of action. By maximizing the appropriateness and motivation involved for a specific group of children and for the individual child, teachers obtain the best outcomes. In short, knowledge of teaching strategies is critical but must be combined with a rich understanding of the actual recipients of instruction—the children.

When strategies are selected and implemented, not all students learn as expected. Teachers must be able to diagnose learning problems of individual students and to use this understanding when creating and organizing learning groups.

1. In facilitating learning, teachers
   a. Know the unique characteristics of their students and draw on this knowledge to promote learning.
   b. Identify students' levels of achievement in subject matter and provide instruction and activities appropriate to those levels.
   c. Identify students' learning problems and provide instruction for overcoming them.
   d. Identify student interests and use them to promote learning.
   e. Work with students individually when appropriate.
   f. Organize groups that enhance learning.
   g. Draw on a variety of techniques, materials, and technology to accommodate different learning styles.
   h. Use questioning techniques and plan learning experiences that encourage thinking and problem-solving skills.
   i. Present subject matter.

2. In managing the classroom, teachers
   a. Organize the classroom to stimulate learning and to foster discipline.
   b. Evaluate classroom conditions and make adjustments when necessary.
   c. Provide opportunities for communication with parents and the community.
   d. Communicate with special service personnel and call on them when necessary.
   e. Refer students to community agencies when appropriate.
   f. Maintain student records for instructional purposes.
   g. Facilitate the work of classroom aides, volunteers, and paraprofessionals.

3. In making professional decisions, teachers
   a. Decide what to teach within and across subject areas within the context of available curriculum guides.
   b. Select and present/use materials and equipment.
   c. Plan priorities for the day.
   d. Reorganize activities as necessary.
   e. Use student assessment materials for instructional purposes.
   f. Anticipate the need for, and draw on the abilities of, special school service personnel such as school nurses, psychologists, social workers, librarians/media specialists, and guidance counselors.
   g. Decide how to deal with the external conditions that impact their role as teachers.
   h. Decide how to deal with political, economic, social, and professional factors that affect their ability to function in the classroom.

FIGURE 7.1 Major functions of teaching.

From "Excellence in Our Schools. Teacher Education: An Action Plan." Adopted by the NEA Representative Assembly, 1982. Reported in *Slices!: Juicy Facts from the NEA Student Program* (1993), Washington, DC: National Education Association. Reprinted by permission.

Making adjustments in instructional strategies and implementing those adjustments in efficient ways generally requires the use of specially organized groups. Since the number of children in a classroom can be quite large (many elementary classrooms have 30 or more students), this skill remains very important. However, if class size reduction efforts are successful among school districts, skill at providing individualized and diagnostic strategies may reduce the importance for skill in organizing groups. However, a teacher with skill in creating small groups for specialized instruction based on common elements of learner needs is certainly capable of adapting lessons to provide individually constructed learning experiences for students.

Questioning strategies, along with the use of a variety of instructional techniques to present subject matter, assist children in unlocking meaning and understanding. Questioning strategies fulfill a dual function: an instructional tool and a way to increase the teacher's understanding of the student's learning strategies, misunderstandings, and level of achievement. Employing a variety of instructional methods in presenting material and applying new skills is once again advocated as a critical component of teaching. Using a variety of strategies within this context is more than just rotating the types of teaching and learning activities. Teachers must calculate the inevitable interaction effects between lesson and learner to develop the optimal combination of subject matter presentation, its likely interpretation by students, a diagnosis of individual interpretations, and modifications for unique characteristics of students. Teachers must strive to develop skills simultaneously across a broad spectrum of specific proficiency domains.

Many independent groups work simultaneously.

Managing the Classroom

Within the confined space of the classroom, many human dynamics play out under the direction of the teacher. The classroom must provide for group learning needs but must also be organized to accommodate children's needs for comfort and protection. Space must be organized to house, store, and use the various materials for instruction. Storing microscopes, computers, and listening centers for both security and ease of use while maintaining the multifunctional floor space is difficult. Space management can present a significant challenge for teachers who often must use secondhand and makeshift furniture. The interaction between space management and student behavior must also be calculated, and adjustments continually made. As lesson topics and activities change, so do the space utilization strategies of the classroom. Transitions between space configurations save precious instructional time and permit a wider variety of instructional strategies.

The NEA view of classroom management also includes the use of resources located outside the classroom that have an impact inside the classroom. The use of ancillary resources such as curriculum support staff, health resource personnel, school counselors, and special education teachers places additional demands on the coordination skills of the teacher. Adding to the resource management formula are the contributions of paraprofessionals, volunteers, and classroom aides. Managing communication with parents can either realize support or materialize resistance. Parents need to understand the workings of the classroom, their child's functioning in that classroom, and be provided guidance in helping their children grow intellectually and emotionally. Adding to the melange is the challenge of coordinating the schedules of students who have special education opportunities and classes with curriculum specialists. Managing the classroom is ultimately a schoolwide affair.

Making Professional Decisions

Until a teacher is actually in charge, it is difficult for him or her to anticipate the barrage of decisions needed to conduct successful lessons with a roomful of children. Many of the most routine events in life become strategic planning exercises when those events include 30 six-year old children. Hanging up coats, putting on snow shoes, getting water, sharpening a pencil, or going to the restroom all become more complex if the teacher tries to have a classroom of children do them at the same time. If these common events are scheduled individually for each child, the length of time involved can create even greater problems. The teacher must decide what is to be done and how, or, more precisely, must convince the children to do appropriate things at appropriate times. Teacher decision making is a vast function that taxes even the most accomplished teacher.

Teachers must make decisions on what to teach, when to teach it, and how the lessons should be conducted. Although copious teacher guides are provided that incorporate hundreds of tips, hints, and ideas for governing daily classroom life, reality results in an rapid-fire array of daily decisions. Figure 2.10 displays a theoretical model illustrating the relationship of the basic variables in teacher decision making.

Although how teachers make effective decisions is not completely understood, it is very clear that successful teachers do make an incredible number of decisions during the day. In addition, teachers draw from a rich reservoir of information based on both generalized knowledge from prior learning about teaching and knowledge gained by observations of minute-by-minute classroom activity.

Cruickshank: A Summary of the Summaries

Our second summary is the result of an Association of Supervision and Curriculum Development (ASCD) book entitled, *Research That Informs Teachers and Teacher Educators*, by Donald Cruickshank (1990). The book is a highly condensed summary of the research considered contributing directly to successful instruction. Cruickshank identifies the major findings of thousands of research projects written over the past two decades. This summary, shown in Figure 7.2, lists the primary findings of ten massive research reviews.

The large number of items that were identified by only a single summary is of particular interest. Virtually no item was identified as being effective in one study and found to be ineffective in another, although "knowledge of subject" is an important and interesting exception. A substantial number of items were consistently identified by the summaries, although no single item was identified by all of the studies. Since the majority of these studies were published in the 1970s and 1980s, you might expect that more recent research has closed the gap and there is greater agreement on the major findings. This, however, has not happened. Research on teacher behavior and its relationship to specified outcomes has fallen into disfavor among many researchers. Currently, holistic studies using case study methodology are in vogue, but the success of these studies in providing instructional improvements is still under consideration. It is not unusual for a line of research inquiry to take a decade or more to influence practice. The comprehensive summaries identified by Cruickshank provide the best descriptors of effective teaching available to date.

Figure 7.2 presents a list of the major findings in the left-hand column, and each finding is coded according to its effectiveness in the right-hand columns. The right-hand columns contain the findings of one of ten reviews of the literature on teaching effectiveness. Items that have a series of "+'s" in the right-hand columns were found to be effective in more than one review. For example, clarity was found to be predictive of effective teaching in eight of ten summaries and was not reported in two studies. No study found clarity to be negatively related. By looking at the 85 listed characteristics in the chart, several important points are apparent.

Common Dominant Themes

A number of findings were consistently found by the reviews. These findings most often were applicable for all subject areas and student ages, although the findings were even stronger in some subject/age combinations. Again, clarity appeared near

| Key: + Support | – Negative support | | NS Not sure | | | * Contingencies affect the use | | | |

Effective teachers seem to demonstrate	Study									
	1	2	3	4	5	6	7	8	9	10
1. Clarity	+	+	+		+	+		+	+	+
2. Organization (clarity of)	+									
3. Enthusiasm (also valence-challenge arousal)	+									
4. Task-oriented, businesslike behavior	+		+				+			
5. Provision of opportunity for students to learn criterion material	+			+		+				
6. Variability/variety	+		+			+				
7. Criticism (negatively related)*	+	+	+	+						
8. Seatwork variety and challenge		+			+					
9. "With-itness"		+						+		
10. Smoothness (of transitions)		+				+		+		
11. Momentum (pacing)		+						+		
12. Overlappingness		+							+	
13. Group alerting*		+		+				+		
14. Accountability		+	+			+				
15. Praise*	–	+	+			+				
16. Use of material incentives		+							+	
17. Use of small groups*		+				+				
18. Use of more pupil participation/ interaction*		+	+			+		+	+	
19. Acceptance/support			+						+	
20. Attending/monitoring behavior		+	+		+	+	+			+
21. Awareness of and adjustment to developmental levels			+			+				
22. Consistency in controlling			+		+	NS			+	
23. Encouragement			+			+				
24. Tolerance/politeness/tact			+							
25. Optimism			+							
26. Equitableness of pupil participation			+		+	+			+	
27. Knowledge of subject	–		+							+
28. Structure*			+			+	+	+		
29. Ability to capture and use unexpected events (teachable moments)			+							
30. Warmth	–	NS	+			+				

FIGURE 7.2 Promising teacher effectiveness variables.

| | Study | | | | | | | | | |
	1	2	3	4	5	6	7	8	9	10
31. Wait time			+			+				
32. Individualization			+	+		+				
33. Less "busy work"			+							
34. Time-on-task persistence and efficiency			+		+	+	+		+	
35. Use of independent work*			+							+
36. Stimulation			+			+				
37. Use of feedback			+			+		+	+	
38. High expectations			+			+				
39. Awareness of and adjustment to pupil SES			+	+		+				
40. Use of open-ended questions*		NS	+							
41. Calling pupils by name			+							
42. Less recognition seeking			+							
43. Democratic style			+							
44. Flexibility-adaptability	−		+							
45. Ability to overcome stereotypes of particular pupils			+							
46. Acceptance of some noise			+							
47. Less caring about being liked			+							
48. Trust			+							
49. Less time consciousness			+							
50. Use of pupil peer teaching			+							
51. Use of programmed materials			+							
52. Use of manipulatives			+							
53. Immediate reinforcement		+	+							
54. Large-group instruction				+		+			+	
55. More seatwork				+						
56. More lower-order questions		NS		+						
57. Less use of pupil ideas or answers				+			−			
58. Less pupil-initiated talk*		NS		+			−			
59. Less complexity				+						
60. A repertory of control techniques		−		+						
61. Questioning of nonvolunteers		+		+						
62. Use of less traditional materials				+						
63. Use of independent work that is interesting, worthwhile, and able to be completed independently					+					
64. Use of mild forms of punishment						+				
65. Responsibility for pupil learning						+				+

FIGURE 7.2 *Continued*

	Study									
	1	2	3	4	5	6	7	8	9	10
66. Ability to provide information in small chunks						+				
67. Possession and use of factual knowledge						+				
68. Ability to minimize disruptions						+		+	+	
69. Provision of immediate help to learners						+				
70. Ability to maintain relaxed atmosphere						+		+	+	
71. Maintenance of pupil work and success standards						+				
72. Maximal content coverage						+				
73. Prompting								+		
74. Ability to express feelings								+		
75. Listening skills								+		
76. Organization for and from the first day									+	
77. Promptness in starting class									+	
78. Use of oral reading*									+	
79. Use of parent participation									+	
80. Planning expertise										+
81. Ability to show pupils relationship and importance of what is being learned to past and future learning										+
82. Metacognitive processes necessary for learning										+
83. Ability to anticipate and correct pupil misconceptions										+
84. Ability to select, use, enrich, and expand on appropriate instructional materials										+
85. Reflectiveness										+

FIGURE 7.2   *Continued*

From *Research That Informs Teachers and Teacher Educators* (pp. 57–61) by Donald Cruickshank, 1990, Bloomington, IN: Phi Delta Kappa. Reprinted with permission.

the top. Other findings, such as teacher use of time, were also key elements but were somewhat camouflaged. For example, teacher use of time reflects various elements including monitoring behavior, time-on-task, large-group instruction, task-oriented behavior, and the ability to minimize disruptions.

Cruickshank concluded that the findings broke into the following seven general areas:

- Teacher character traits showed that effective teachers were depicted as enthusiastic, stimulating, encouraging, warm, and task oriented. Effective teachers viewed students as individuals and felt responsible for student learning.

- Effective teachers knew the subject matter but also had a wide range of knowledge in many areas and possessed high skill levels in using knowledge. In short, teachers knew their subjects and possessed a great deal of factual information.

- Effective teachers ensured coverage of the criterion material and attempted to go well beyond the minimal coverage.

- Effective teachers used clarity, variety, effective use of time, and momentum (keeping the pace of instruction brisk). Also, they structured material, typically in small logical steps progressing to more complex and holistic concepts. They were also able to explain the meaningfulness and importance of the learning task.

- Successful teachers established clear expectations, communicated them to students, and held students accountable for attainment. They also encouraged parent participation in the student's academic performance.

- Teachers who were identified as effective were more supportive of student efforts, dealt with students in ways perceived as fair, and adjusted to student participation levels while encouraging equal participation by all students. Successful teachers also directed questions to nonvolunteers, prompted students to maintain high levels of engagement, gave immediate feedback to students about the accuracy of learning efforts, and displayed awareness and sensitivity to students' cultural and economic differences.

- Teachers who were consistently effective displayed excellent management expertise, particularly in planning the classroom curriculum, learning activities, and student movement. These teachers were skilled at handling more than two activities at a time, maintained activities so that students remained on task, and had a repertoire of control techniques for student behavior.

In closing, it is important to reemphasize that the research findings were rather consistent regardless of subject taught. Many educators have begun to look at teaching through generic strategies that are applicable across widely varying subjects rather than the more traditional view of "math methods," "language methods," "social studies methods," and so on. When novice teachers obtain their first jobs and launch their first year of practice, their self-improvement strategies can be greatly assisted by taking a generalized skill view rather than focusing on isolated skills contained within the subject-specific pedagogy traditions. The final decision, however, is up to the teacher. Developing a short- and long-term development plan is essential for teacher improvement and excellence in instruction.

Northwest Regional Education Laboratory: Classroom Characteristics

Another way of classifying and summarizing the effective teaching research is to look at characteristics of the classroom (see Figure 7.3). This analysis of the literature

- Instruction is guided by a preplanned curriculum.
- There are high expectations for student learning.
- Students are carefully oriented to lessons.
- Instruction is clear and focused.
- Learning progress is monitored closely.
- When students don't understand, they are retaught.
- Class time is used for learning.
- There are smooth, efficient classroom routines.
- Instructional groups formed in the classroom fit instructional needs.
- Standards for classroom behavior are explicit.
- Personal interactions between teachers and students are positive.
- Incentives and rewards for students are used to promote excellence.

FIGURE 7.3   Effective classroom characteristics and practices.

Extracted from *Onward Toward Excellence: Making Schools More Effective* by Northwest Regional Educational Laboratory, Portland, OR: Author.

examines what happens in an effective classroom rather than at what successful teachers do. This summary examines how the effective classroom functions and represents a much broader perspective than just focusing on singular teacher activity. A teacher can achieve a specific classroom characteristic by developing and considering a host of teacher behaviors that may accommodate the implication of the research finding. For example, instead of specifying that the teacher employ step-by-step instruction, the focus on the effective classroom specifies that "students are carefully oriented to lessons." The scope and nature of the orientation is then determined by the teacher in a way that best meets the needs of the students and the immediate objective.

Preplanned Curriculum

Instruction in effective classrooms is guided by a preplanned curriculum. The classroom does not operate in isolation when learning within the school is optimized. When instruction is guided by a preplanned curriculum, teachers coordinate efforts among many lessons spread over the years that a child is in elementary school. Further, a preplanned curriculum provides direction for acquiring appropriate materials in appropriate numbers. This may be a broad section of books in multiple reading levels regarding a particular subject in science or sets of math manipulatives that can be shared across grade levels. By coordinating efforts, materials are purchased so that they are used repetitively by a large number of classrooms. Additionally, prerequisite skills, advance organizers, and basic concepts are more likely to be present in students at the beginning of a new study because of a carefully structured array of prior experiences (Rosenshine, 1983).

High Expectations for Student Learning

In effective classrooms, there are high expectations for student learning. Teachers expect success, convey those expectations to students, and create corresponding experiences so that children can be successful. This is not the "think and grow rich" version of the Pygmalion effect. Instead, teachers establish reasonable expectations for growth, communicate those expectations for successful learning to children, and work very hard toward making that vision a reality. Teachers who minimize the expectations of children and underestimate their ability and willingness to learn usually fail to provide experiences that go beyond minimal expectations. The atmosphere of minimal success, minimal effort, and minimal results rarely brings about achievement. By the same token, unreasonable "pie in the sky" optimism that establishes activities beyond the scope of the children's skill and available resources likewise results in failure. Again, the "Goldilocks compromise" prevails. Finding the "just right" level of challenge is a difficult but essential task.

Successful teachers have high expectations, structure experiences for a wide range of student performances that can be considered successful, and provide generous praise for outcomes. Setting reasonable positive standards that reward performances above the standard is a common method employed by major businesses and also works well in the classroom (Berliner, 1979; Rosenshine, 1983). When employing rewards, the leading motivators are recognition, appreciation, and choice. Rewards may be material, but these should be ancillary rather than the major venue of success acknowledgment.

Careful Orientation to Lessons

Students in effective classrooms are carefully oriented to lessons. Many research studies, particularly those involving explicit (or direct) instruction, describe a careful sequence of introductory activities. The recommended introductory activities include a focus, a review of previous learning, communication of the objective to the learner, and a description of the behavior and learning expectations. This sequence is only one of many methods of orienting students to lessons. Implicit instructional strategies covered in a subsequent chapter include other carefully developed orientations. The use of *discrepant events* (in which a teacher provides a demonstration where the outcome is counterintuitive) is a strong orientation to an exploratory lesson. In these cases, a formal review rarely occurs in the beginning because previously learned information has already been employed by the student to form an incorrect hypothesis. However, all appropriate orientations to lessons accomplish three things:

◆ They obtain the attention and cooperation of students.
◆ They create an atmosphere of anticipation in which children expect to either learn something new or to practice a skill.
◆ They carefully orient students so that distractions are minimized and learning readiness is maximized.

Clear, Positive, and Focused Instruction

In effective classrooms, instruction is clear and focused, learning progress is monitored closely, and students who do not understand are retaught. Research summaries on instructional effectiveness uniformly list teacher clarity as a primary characteristic that forms an important component of effective teaching research. Regardless of the instructional strategy employed, digressions, scattered start-and-stop efforts, disruptions, and lack of focus on the objective are negatively associated with instructional success. Classrooms that provide guided and independent practice of new concepts, ask clear questions, obtain high participation among students in practice and questioning activities, and provide homework that can be completed successfully are characteristically more effective. Matching content, student ability, and practice exercises so that students continually experience high success rates are also characteristic.

Teachers monitor students' work in effective classrooms in a variety of formal and informal strategies that require students to be accountable for their work. Students are provided progress checks frequently, are given the results quickly, and are assisted in correcting errors. Teachers encourage parents to take an active interest and involvement in their child's success, and parents are provided tips on helping students learn. Teachers also provide additional lessons to children who have difficulty in learning. Successful teachers' methods are supportive rather than punitive and help to create classroom climates that promote excellence and a desire for content mastery.

Efficient Routines and Time Use

In effective classrooms, class time is used for learning. Time for learning is maximized by smooth, efficient classroom routines. The time use strategies that emphasize routines are cited as characteristic of excellent classrooms. Teachers in these classrooms follow a system of priorities for what is to be accomplished each day and allocate time so that class time is spent on all curriculum areas. Very little time is spent on noninstructional activities. Students are encouraged to monitor their work and pace themselves. When work is not completed during class, students manage to complete the task during lunch, before or after school, but not during other lessons.

Flexible Instructional Groups

Effective classrooms have flexible instructional groups formed to fit instructional needs. When introducing new skills or content, whole-group instruction is preferable. As students progress in learning, flexible groups are created using current measures of student success in mastering the skills currently being taught. These groups are reassessed often and are closely related to current achievement on specific instructional goals. Whole-group instruction for all lessons and grouping students by test scores for extended periods of time are not shown to be effective techniques.

Cordial but Businesslike Climate

The climate of effective classrooms is characterized by explicit standards for behavior that are reinforced with incentives and positive personal interaction between and among students and teacher. Effective classrooms have been characterized by the research as "businesslike." Students and teacher alike know the purpose of the classroom and work diligently together to obtain learning goals. Teachers let students know that there are high standards for behavior in the classroom. These standards, often written and posted, are taught to children and reviewed frequently. Conduct standards of classrooms tend to mirror schoolwide standards. Teachers pay special attention to student interests and work with the students to help develop positive appropriate social interactions in and out of the classroom.

Students are encouraged to develop independence and self-reliance but are supported by teacher attention as needed. Incentives are used, but the reward criteria are established by objective standards, not peer comparisons. Students are taught what rewards are available and how to obtain them. Teachers make great efforts to show students that they truly care about them.

◆ ◆ ◆

Summary

1. Four different summaries of effective instruction and successful classroom characteristics have been provided representing the views of a state education agency (Figure 2.10), a national teacher organization (Figure 7.1), a federally sponsored research clearinghouse (Figure 7.2), and a national organization for school improvement (Figure 7.3). All perspectives share many common elements, and each contributes a unique perspective about what composes successful classrooms and successful teaching. The teacher, however, must assimilate the information in a view that is directive and meets personal needs. In general, the research is very clear that successful teachers:

a. Have high expectations for students.

b. Take personal responsibility for their success.

c. Take personal responsibility for student learning.

d. Match the lesson difficulty to student ability.

e. Vary lesson difficulty when necessary to obtain moderate-to-high success rates.

f. Provide opportunities to practice new skills.

g. Provide feedback regarding the accuracy of student efforts.

h. Review previously learned material.

i. Maximize instructional time to increase content coverage.

j. Use a variety of questions and questioning strategies.

k. Structure materials, presentations, and practice for ease of comprehension.

l. Use probes to provide direction and control of student learning.

m. Use a variety of material and audiovisual aids.

n. Use student ideas in lessons.

o. Promote and maintain student engagement in the learning process.

p. Elicit responses from students each time a question is asked.

q. Present material in small pieces at a slow pace with opportunities for practice.

r. Encourage students to reason out the correct answer.

s. Engage students in verbal questions and answers.

t. Have instructional plans that are compatible with the school plan.

u. Use diagnostic information to guide/revise objectives/lessons.

v. Maintain accurate records.

w. Use the human resources of school and community.

2. Teachers also must employ "people skills" that encourage students to work toward a quality education and help them to develop sufficient confidence to attack difficult problems. Teachers who provide encouragement, teach with enthusiasm, and provide acceptance are typically more effective. It is also important to point out that criticism is negatively related to student achievement. Successful teachers are fair, treat children equitably, communicate with staff (faculty, parents, administration, and students), and adhere to school rules. Successful teachers also show respect for students and are available to help students at other than class times. The teacher who analyzes personal performance for professional growth is the teacher who is most likely to inspire students to seek more knowledge and to take an active role in their own education.

◆ ◆ ◆

Activities and Questions for Further Understanding

1. Prepare a conceptual web that chronicles the elements necessary to achieve each of the following:

   a. High student engagement rates

   b. Efficient distribution and collection of materials

   c. Routines for children to take care of personal needs without involving the teacher

2. Examine Mr. Pinion in "A Slice of Life." What do you think you would put in a "Beginning-of-the-Year" packet for parents and their child?

3. Think about the first day of school. What lessons and their objectives would you teach that day? Why? What unexpected events might you anticipate? How would you conduct routines for the first day?

4. Visit a school. Look at the various ways that teachers store materials. What are the most effective ways of storing materials for individual use that you see? Are materials that are used for group distribution stored differently? How are materials stored for safe-keeping until needed?

◆ ◆ ◆

References

Berliner, David. (1979). Tempus educare. In P. Peterson & H. Walberg (Eds.), *Research in teaching*. Berkeley: McCutchan.

Borich, Gary. (1979, Spring). Implications for developing teacher competencies for process-product research. *Journal of Teacher Education, 30*, 77–86.

Borich, Gary. (1996). *Effective teaching methods* (3rd ed.). Upper Saddle River, NJ: Merrill/Prentice Hall.

Cruickshank, D. (1976, Spring). Synthesis of selected recent research on teacher effects. *Journal of Teacher Education, 27*, 57–61.

Cruickshank, Donald. (1990). *Research that informs teachers and teacher educators*. Bloomington, IN: Phi Delta Kappa.

Einstein, Albert. (1974). *Ideas and opinions* (p. 60). New York: Wings Books. (Originally published in *Out of my later years,* 1950, New York: Philosophical Library)

Emmer, E. T., & Evertson, C. M. (1982, January). Synthesis of research on classroom management. *Educational Leadership, 38*, 342–347.

Gage, N. L. (1978, November). The yield of research on teaching. *Phi Delta Kappan, 60*, 229–235.

Good, Tom. (1979, Summer). Teacher effectiveness in the elementary school. *Journal of Teacher Education, 30*, 52–64.

Medley, D. M. (1977). *Teacher competence and teacher effectiveness: A review of process-product research*. Washington, DC: American Association of Colleges for Teacher Education.

National Education Association. (1982). *Excellence in our schools. Teacher education: An action plan*. Washington, DC: Author.

National Education Association. (1993). *Slices!: Juicy facts from the NEA Student Program*. Washington, DC: Author.

North Carolina State Department of Public Instruction. (1986a). *Teacher performance appraisal system: The standards and processes for use*. Raleigh, NC: Author. (ERIC Document Reproduction Service No. ED 271 453)

North Carolina State Department of Public Instruction. (1986b). *Teacher performance appraisal system training: A report of outcomes*. Raleigh, NC: Author. (ERIC Document Reproduction Service No. ED 271 452)

Northwest Regional Education Laboratory. (1990). *Onward toward excellence: Making schools more effective*. Portland, OR: Author.

Plato. *The republic,* VII, 537. [Benjamin Jowett, translator. (1937). Vol. 1, p. 796. New York: Random House.]

Porter A., & Brophy, J. (1988). Synthesis of research on good teaching. *Educational Leadership , 45*(8), 74–85.

Rosenshine, B., & Furst, N. (1971). Research on teacher performance criteria. In B. O. Smith (Ed.), *Research in teacher education*. Upper Saddle River, NJ: Prentice Hall.

Rosenshine, B. V. (1983, March). Teaching functions in instructional programs. *Elementary School Journal, 83*.

Rowe, M. B. (1974). Wait-time and rewards as instructional variables, their influence on language, logic, and fate control: Part one—Wait time. *Journal of Research in Science Teaching, 11*, 81–94.

Stallings, J. A. (1982). Effective strategies for teaching basic skills. In I. Gordon (Ed.), *Developing basic skills programs in secondary schools*. Alexandria, VA: Association for Supervision and Curriculum Development.

CHAPTER 8

How Do I Teach Factual Knowledge?

Explicit Instruction and Its Variants

Outline

Experience tells us what is, but not that it must be necessarily as it is. . . .

KANT

Only by starting with crude material and subjecting it to purposeful handling will he gain the intelligence embodied in finished material.

JOHN DEWEY

◆

A Slice of Life

Ms. Fong brought the children back from lunch on a beautiful spring day. "OK, children. It is time for language development. You know what to do." The children quickly settled into their desks and located a pencil and spiral-bound notebook with "Language Development" written on a gummed label. Each label also had the child's name on it and the number of the notebook. Some children had already filled four notebooks and were working on their fifth. "It's group work for today. We'll review yesterday's work first."

The children began sliding their one-piece desks into groups of three. One child from each group went over to a set of shelves next to the windows, retrieved an erasable board, picked up a felt-tipped pen, and returned to his or her team. Ms. Fong had turned on the overhead projector and was adjusting the focus and aligning it with the screen. The whole process took less than a minute. Ms. Fong stared at the second hand of the clock as it passed 45 seconds. "Thank you, children. It makes me feel very proud when you organize for language development so quickly. This afternoon, we are going to start with language development because I want to use our lesson today when you do your silent reading after science."

Review

"OK! I need a summary of yesterday's lesson." Ms. Fong glanced from side to side at a number of volunteers. "Mary, your hand isn't raised, but I bet you can tell us. What did we do yesterday?"

Mary blushed. Mary was attentive but quiet and rarely volunteered. "We read paragraphs and picked what we thought was the main idea from each one."

"That's right. Great! Now you said you picked the best. What were you picking from?"

"You gave us a list of ideas. We picked the best one you gave us."

Introduce New Material

Ms. Fong smiled. "OK. Today we are going to branch out. Look at the paragraph on the screen. Tom, will you read it?" Tom began reading aloud. "Thank you, Tom. Now, look at the four choices below." Ms. Fong called on a different child to read each choice and provide an opinion about how the summary statement of the main idea fit the paragraph. "OK, let's make a choice. Show fingers . . . now." The children raised hands showing one, two, three, or four fingers corresponding to the number beside their choice. One child provided a "wiggly wave" which indicated, "Not sure."

"All but five said number three. Damian, you liked number two. Why?"

Damian shied away from being different. "I meant number three."

Ms. Fong accepted his change without emotion. "OK, but if someone had chosen number two, what about number two would make them believe it was a good summary? Is there anything in number two that might be true?"

Damian replied without emotion, "It names the characters in the story. And they were playing the right game."

"Great. You're absolutely right! Number two mentions the characters and what they are doing. Then why isn't it the best statement of the main idea?"

Several students volunteered. Ms. Fong looked at Damian who instantly replied with a smile, "Number two said they were excited. They really were afraid. They were in danger playing near the pit."

"But weren't they excited, too?" Ms. Fong posed a possibility that maybe number two could be correct.

Damian replied thoughtfully, "Yeah, but number two doesn't give the whole picture. Number two doesn't say anything about danger."

Guided Practice

"OK, let's try another one." This time, Ms. Fong posed a situation in which none of the four solutions was particularly accurate. The student responses were split, and at least three students declared the problem was unfair. "Why do you think this one is unfair?" She addressed Shelley.

"I'm not sure it's unfair, but none of the answers fit well." Shelley thought a second and then volunteered, "I like the second one, but I'd want to change it."

Ms. Fong smiled. "Well, why don't we? Each group take what they think is a good answer and change it so that it really states the main idea. Everybody write the old idea and your new idea in your books."

Circulate

Ms. Fong visited the groups, nodding approval and posing an occasional question. The class then presented the new responses for the whole group, and the entire class voted on whether each was an adequate summary. Discussion ensued, and the statements were amended. Ms. Fong wrote each on the board until all were done. "What is the same about all of these?" Through a question-and-answer session, Ms. Fong led the class to conclude that a good statement of a main idea answered at least three and sometimes six questions: What was happening, who was doing it, and how it was happening were the most common. When, where, and why something was happening also were important. Ms. Fong reviewed yesterday's paragraphs, and students looked for the who, what, where, why, when, and how parts. Not one of the paragraphs had everything, but most had three.

Summarize

Ms. Fong put up a poster on the "Language Wall" entitled, "5 W's and an H Unlocks Meaning." The poster listed each of the words in bright red with a question written on either side of it in black. Under each question, Ms. Fong provided an explanation of each. Ms. Fong quickly went down the list, identifying each term, and then provided more paragraphs on the overhead. She asked them the "5 W's and H" for each. Usually, one or more were missing. Sometimes she had the groups work together to locate the information, and sometimes she asked them to write in their notebooks. Finally, she told them to draw a box and copy the wall chart into their notebooks.

Closure

"Wow, we've done a lot on main ideas. We know how to find them and what makes up the main idea. But can we write them without having answers to choose from? Can we write a main idea sentence and answer the '5 W's and H'? Remember most of our samples didn't have them all."

Damian volunteered, "But we wouldn't have to put them all into a sentence, would we? Maybe we don't know what the answer is from the paragraph."

"Damian has a good point. When writing a main idea or single sentence summary, what are we trying to do anyway?" Ms. Fong listened to various explanations and then asked each child to write what he or she thought went into a main idea. Afterward, she provided her own definition and explanation and asked the children to write those in their notebooks.

Independent Practice

"Well, I've checked everyone's notebook, and everything looks like a 'go' for doing it on our own. I have a sheet of five paragraphs. I want you to write a summary sentence that captures the main idea for each. You have time to do the first one or two, but you'll have to finish the rest for homework. It shouldn't take more than 20 minutes total. Most will finish in 10 minutes or so. OK! One quick review. Tommy, can you tell us what a main idea of a paragraph might contain?"

Ms. Fong quickly reviewed the main points in a terse question-and-answer session, lauded the children for their attention, and left them to begin work on the sample paragraphs as she began to assemble the apparatus for the science demonstration.

Types of Instruction

By oversimplifying a bit, all instruction can be viewed in terms of two overarching effects: (1) instruction that helps increase and elaborate existing knowledge, and (2) instruction that helps students increase their capacity to use and regulate thinking, deciding, and acting (Anderson, 1989). Some strategies have demonstrated exceptional success in increasing knowledge. These strategies are the topic of this chapter and are referred to as *explicit,* or direct, instruction. Strategies that increase the capacity and skill in using thinking and reasoning skills are referred to as *implicit,* or indirect, instruction and are covered in the next chapter. The terms *explicit* and *implicit* are very imperfect descriptors of two very different, yet highly interrelated, concepts.

Explicit Instruction

Explicit instruction refers to teaching strategies that are successful in helping learners acquire information that is "well-structured" (Rosenshine & Stevens, 1986). Well-structured knowledge is knowledge that is sequenced in a hierarchy of fact and principles that are logically related. Highly structured knowledge is easily generalizable in that it can be used repeatedly in recurring situations with little or no modification in application or understanding. Highly structured knowledge is, in general, relatively free of value assumptions and applies to a hierarchy of verifiable facts. Explicit instruction almost always deals with the material world or with definitions and descriptions of concepts and relationships. Because highly structured knowledge tends to be either concrete or logical, learning can be approached "directly" without requiring highly abstract inferences or substantive individual reconstruction of the concept.

Implicit Instruction

Implicit instruction refers to instructional strategies that are successful in assisting students to understand and resolve various problems in areas where knowledge is randomly related, loosely sequenced, or not sequenced at all. The learner, in order to accommodate the variances in each situation, usually must substantially modify knowledge that possesses low structure. Although it can also deal with the material world, implicit instruction more prevalently deals with nonmaterial reality in which learners face ethical considerations, values development, paradoxes, and dilemmas. Implicit instruction is involved when a learner has to make a "best" decision in a situation where applicable knowledge has low structure and the outcome requires compromise among competing effects. Implicit instruction requires substantial inferences from students as well as reconstruction of situations to fit the student's current knowledge and value.

Although very different, the educational results of explicit and implicit instruction are not dichotomous but rather form the endpoints of a continuum of effects. Further complicating the understanding of explicit and implicit instruction, any instructional approach may (and successful instruction usually does) include methods characterized by both strategies and obtain multiple outcomes.

Instructional Continuum

The process of determining the underlying structure inherent in an instructional goal and fitting it with the most appropriate instructional strategies is a basic teacher skill, albeit one of the most difficult to master. Finding the best methods for matching students with subject matter sometimes becomes focused on philosophical or value assumptions of educators. However, successful instruction is best obtained by selecting the instructional strategy from a careful matching of the needs of students, their demonstrated abilities, the intent of instruction, and the specific contextual traits of the situation (particularly time and resources).

To illustrate that most areas of study contain elements of both low- and high-structured knowledge, Figure 8.1 provides three examples of learning themes with four learning goals within each theme. The structure of the content areas permit the creation of four sample learning goals that range from highly structured sequential material to loose and poorly structured material. By going from the most explicit (on the left) to the most implicit (on the right), you can get an initial impression of the differences in the two and how no clear demarcation exists between them. Figure 8.1 oversimplifies the relationship of the instructional strategies to content structure in that the selection of methodology is associated only with the structured content in the lesson goal. By excluding considerations of student needs, contexts, and teacher skill, the relationship between content structure and method is more evident.

Special Considerations

The first example in Figure 8.1 describes various skills in personal grooming. When planning to teach a task such as learning to tie shoelaces, explicit instruction is an appropriate strategy. It provides a step-by-step demonstration and guided practice

Area	Explicit (Direct) ◄——————————► Implicit (Indirect) Continuum of Learning Activities			
Student dress and grooming (special education)	Student ties shoes.	Student selects and purchases properly fitting shoes.	Student determines the appropriateness of shoes for the occasion and use.	Student selects all personal clothing for purchase and daily wear.
Math (first grade)	Student provides sum of two single digits.	Student offers proof of the sum of two digits with object manipulation.	From a situation, student identifies appropriate information and combines digits to provide additional understanding.	Student calculates the sum of two digits in situational context (for example, cost) and includes additional criteria (value, appropriateness) in making a decision.
Geography (fifth grade)	Student can name the capital of the home state.	Student describes what a state capital is and why it is important.	Student provides analysis of the effects of the location of governmental functions on economic development.	Student provides an argument for or against diffusion of governmental agencies throughout the state.

FIGURE 8.1   Illustration of the instructional continuum.

and matches it to the general task of learning to tie shoes. For a child who is both eager and independent, this process may be unnecessary; simply setting aside time for the child's experimentation and self-teaching may be a totally satisfactory method. Although explicit instruction can be provided, letting this child construct the knowledge from raw experiences is appropriate, but most children would find such exploration needlessly tedious and frustrating.

Sometimes low-structured material can be treated as if it were high-structured to good effect because of special student needs. For example, with a student who has low esteem, who is not accepted readily by his or her peers, and who desires more attention, implicit instruction may not be successful for selecting clothes that express individuality if the goal is to develop social skills. If, for example, the child selects clothing that invokes ridicule, the generalizations of basic fashion and clothing conventions may not be developing in a way that fulfills the intent of the child.

Because the student lacks confidence and the basic tenets of fashion elude him or her, implicit instruction may not provide adequate guidance. A more explicit instructional strategy may be needed. This student may require direct instruction that assists him or her in selecting shoes and other clothing that "make a statement." In this case, the teacher should avoid telling the student how to dress but rather provide structured generalized information regarding dress and its potential social effects. The teacher may provide a chart of basic fashions and color coordination. The student who may not be able to generalize this information from a large body of experiences can benefit from a series of "fashion facts." Explicit instruction can provide an imperfect, but potentially effective, shortcut to a highly unstructured knowledge. However, such shortcuts have a price: The student has lost an opportunity to obtain skill in collecting and analyzing experiences that lead to social acceptance.

Combining Methods

Implicit and explicit teaching strategies are necessary to complement student learning from the experiences of others while increasing the student's ability to self-teach. Transmitting information from one generation to another is an important task of education. Earlier sections of this text have discussed the various philosophical issues involved. Explicit instruction usually should be used when the teacher can clearly specify what the child is to learn, how the child is to demonstrate it, and how that skill may be employed in typical applications. However, it is imperative that implicit instructional strategies be also used. Neither method should dominate the elementary school curriculum. Although a competitive debate between explicit and implicit instruction rages among educators, the successful teacher employs a variety of methods matching the instructional intent with student, context, and teacher skill.

Student-Structured and Teacher-Structured Concepts

The student must mentally process even the most well-structured presentation. It is a truism that students must construct knowledge. However, in this discussion, student-structured and teacher-structured knowledge are separated by the degree of effort necessary to learn information. Highly developed presentations of structured concepts can minimize both the necessary effort and time involved in successful learning. Those strategies that facilitate ease of learning and minimize the required time for mastery probably belong in the explicit teaching strategy group. When a teacher presents materials so that students must perform the majority of the structuring and even deliberately leaves out important facts so that students must discover the need for the missing information, implicit instruction strategies are most likely being employed.

When the material to be learned conforms nicely to an overt logical structure, teachers can carefully construct the lesson around the needs of students and the structure of the material. But if the material does not provide that structure, the

Teacher-Constructed	Student-Constructed
1. Teacher provides expository or didactic instruction.	1. Students discover or create.
2. The teacher is the primary source of (or guide to) information.	2. The teacher is a facilitator who creates and maintains an environment for discovery.
3. The teacher structures the material for ease of learning.	3. The students must structure the material.
4. Teacher provides examples, explanations, and opportunity to practice.	4. Students provide examples and explanations.
5. Teacher corrects students' errors and provides additional instruction as needed.	5. Students oppose or support ideas and provide additional information.

FIGURE 8.2   Instruction for teacher-constructed and student-constructed concepts.

teacher must rely on students to take an active part in engaging the material and constructing the concepts from a combination of experiences and associated data. Figure 8.2 outlines the basic differences between concepts that are structured by the teacher and those that the students are primarily responsible for developing.

Two important concepts are not apparent in the comparisons, however. First, two objectives are involved when implicit strategies are employed. The first concerns the mastery of subject content, such as learning about the processes of developing a city ordinance or the reasons for civil disobedience. The second objective, which is "hidden" or covert, is probably more important. Generally, implicit instructional strategies are used to develop the independent learning skills of students. These include creativity, hypothesis generation, experimentation, logical analysis, and intuitive reasoning. Again, a balance between methods is a responsible and effective approach to the classroom curriculum. Stormy debates surround the value of both strategic families. Again, the successful teacher should be prepared to provide for the intellectual needs of students by having an array of strategies appropriate for all students, subjects, and contexts.

Uses for Explicit Instruction

Before deciding on any course of action for teaching a specific objective, teachers must consider other factors, such as the entering behavior of the student. Thus, the activity of teaching is itself a low-structured task because many factors interact in a virtually infinite array of situations. Although learning about instructional strategies may be done explicitly, learning to use them cannot be described sequentially without the intervening cognitive interpretation and reconstruction of the learner. In many ways, selecting the course of action places more demand on the teacher than does implementing the actual strategies.

Explicit Instruction Aids Understanding

The discussions in this text about instructional strategies in the successful classroom attempt to provide information regarding the research, expert opinion, and consensus on the scholarship base of pedagogical knowledge. The explicit approach used includes a careful structuring and sequencing of that information and provides copious examples of how that knowledge is applied. In keeping with the spirit of explicit structure and to provide an example of explicit goal thinking, the following statements specify what you should be able to do after reading this chapter:

◆ Define and give examples of explicit and implicit learning objectives.
◆ Describe and outline the appropriate use of direct instruction.
◆ Compare and contrast student-structured and teacher-structured concepts.
◆ List and describe each of the seven instructional events.
◆ Describe the type of learning outcomes best achieved with direct instruction.
◆ Illustrate the major characteristics of direct instruction ("action teaching").
◆ Define the major components of direct instruction.
◆ Outline and illustrate the characteristics of effective demonstrations and lectures.

Necessity for Student Involvement

The goal statements of a chapter in a textbook focus on the act of understanding information given to the reader through the text narrative. The reader should be able to define, describe, list, compare, outline, contrast, and illustrate. These are important learning goals. However, there is more to a chapter's presentation than information. The goal is also that the reader will employ past learning, skepticism, critical analysis, experimentation, and a demanding evaluation of actual applications of the principles and strategies described. This may be difficult to achieve in written material such as a text. However, in a teaching situation where teacher-student interaction can occur, these more complex interpretations and understandings can and should be obtained. These latter purposes may actually be considered more important than the actual content of the material.

If the reader can be spurred to curiosity and his or her experimentation leads to effective application, learning comes to life. Normally, factual material, no matter how carefully constructed and skillfully presented, does not inspire this level of understanding. Interaction with the nuances of an area of study appears to be necessary for broad understanding and application. On the other hand, if the basic understandings are not present prior to using the information, many students are unsure, hesitant, and easily frustrated by the attempts to employ information in a meaningful way. Thus, for these learners, the information is discarded and shunted to the dustbin of the irrelevant. Successful application of learning is not likely to be facilitated by a muddled presentation that confuses the possibly already ambiguous relationships among the many instructional variables. Explicit and implicit instruction, using teacher-constructed concepts followed by student-structured concepts, effectively form the "one-two" punch that can knock out ignorance and misunderstanding.

Some Assumptions About Teachers

Two sayings illustrate the dilemma in advocating explicit instruction while acknowledging both its benefits and limitations. "Tell them what you are going to tell them, tell them, then tell them what you told them" is a well-known suggestion for those who are involved in public speaking. Another saying among teachers is, "If telling were teaching, we'd all be so smart we couldn't stand it." Although explicit teaching is more complex that just telling, the two sayings are still instructive. Presenting information in a highly consumable form is a valuable and important part of successful teaching. However, it is not likely to bring about the desired results alone. Providing maximized opportunity to learn for each student is critical but insufficient for success. Whether conveying information or assisting students in creating meaningful understanding, teachers must remember that many different desirable effects occur simultaneously if their teaching behaviors are carefully coordinated and orchestrated. Therefore, successful use of explicit teaching requires a context of teaching competence and the nurturing of a stimulating learning environment.

Explicit Instruction Requires Effective Teaching

Porter and Brophy (1988) provide a summary of the basic characteristics of effective teachers that is particularly applicable to explicit instruction and echoes the teaching descriptions of the previous chapter. Effective teachers who successfully employ explicit instruction do the following:

◆ Are clear about their instructional goals
◆ Are knowledgeable about their content and the strategies for teaching it
◆ Communicate to their students what is expected of them and why
◆ Make expert use of existing instructional materials to provide more time to practice
◆ Are knowledgeable about their students, adapt instruction to their needs, and anticipate misconceptions in their existing knowledge
◆ Teach students meta-cognitive strategies and give them opportunities to master them
◆ Address higher-level, as well as lower-level, cognitive objectives
◆ Monitor students' understanding by offering regular appropriate feedback

◆ Integrate their instruction with other subject areas
◆ Accept responsibility for students' outcomes
◆ Are thoughtful and reflective about their practice

If explicit instructional strategies are to be effective in daily instruction, these sustaining teacher behaviors must be consistently present in the background and characterize the teacher's interaction with students.

Basic Instructional Events

Explicit instructional strategies are based on the assumption that both the content and the learner's basic strategies for acquiring skill have an underlying structure that is generalizable across most situations. In short, the learner can readily understand the material without substantial reinterpretation. Also, the way in which material is taught mirrors the ways that students learn. If these assumptions are not valid in a particular situation, explicit instructional strategies are not appropriate.

Earlier discussions about content stressed that an assumed sequenced and ordered structure of knowledge is not to be made lightly. Even in areas of study where this assumption is valid, advanced study usually entails a randomness and lack of cohesive structure of knowledge. To enable learners to apply knowledge in new situations or enable learners to create new knowledge, explicit instruction is usually insufficient. Even when the structure and pattern of content knowledge does exist, the learner or the instructor may not know that structure, or its complexity mitigates the use of explicit strategies. However, a large important core of knowledge exists in most fields that needs to be conveyed effectively by employing the most efficient strategies. These strategies minimize both time involved in learning and the effort necessary from the learner. In explicit instruction, knowing what the learner must do with the information and experience is critical to structuring lessons.

Fortunately, the assumption that an underlying structure exists in the learner's basic strategies appears valid. A pattern of learner activity has been found consistently by cognitive psychologists in studying the learning strategies of children and adults. Cognitive psychologists have studied learning in a variety of situations and have developed highly generalizable findings that provide teachers with substantial direction in developing lessons.

Gagné and Driscoll (1988) provide a structured theory that outlines the processes involved in a human learning experience. The processes identified are presented in Figure 8.3 which also defines and illustrates each process area.

Although Gagné and Driscoll treat these processes as sequential, they note that some theorists consider the processes to be a single concurrent learner activity. They argue that once the processes of learning are established and understood, "planning a lesson is mainly a matter of taking care to assure that each of the internal learning processes . . . has been supported in an optimal fashion by external events" (Gagné & Driscoll, 1988, p. 118). To maximize learning effectiveness, they identify the follow-

Process	Definition	Description	Activity
Motivation/ expectancy	Learner seeks or is willing to receive a stimulus (learning experience).	Learner has a natural tendency to engage, manipulate, dominate, or "master" his/her environment.	Communicate the learning goal.
Attention/ reception	Presence assures that the learning experience is received with learner perceptual awareness.	Learner has a mental set or readiness to accept, embrace, or acquire a learning experience	Vary the stimulus.
Selective perception of features	A form or pattern is established from initially undifferentiated perception and stored in short-term memory.	Learner discriminates among many perceptual stimuli and selects only those of interest in making comprehension possible.	Point out or emphasize aspects of the event.
Short-term storage	What is perceived is transformed into a form recognizable to the learner.	Some detail is lost as the essential features are retained according to expected relevance.	Suggest the activation of rehearsal and chunking.
Semantic encoding	Information in short-term memory is ordered, prioritized, and organized to make memory storage possible.	New experience is classified and encoded to past learning and experiences to optimize meaning and retention.	Present encoding technique.

FIGURE 8.3   Processes of learning in sequence.

ing nine instructional events that correspond with the instructional processes shown in parentheses:

- Gaining attention (Motivation/expectancy)
- Informing the learner of the objective (Attention/reception)
- Stimulating recall of prerequisite material (Selective perception of features)
- Presenting stimulus material (Storage in short-term memory)
- Providing learner guidance (Semantic encoding)
- Eliciting desired behavior (Storage in long-term memory)
- Providing feedback (Search and retrieval)
- Assessing the behavior (Performance as the result of learning)
- Enhancing retention and transfer (Reinforcement)

Process	Definition	Description	Activity
Storage in long-term memory	The encoding transformation results in a familiar form that can be stored indefinitely; there is no evidence to say that the storage is limited by capacity.	Least understood of the processes, interference may occur where past learning or continued reception of information incapacitates or hinders storage processes.	Avoid interference; repeat rehearsal.
Search and retrieval	Recall requires the memory be searched and applicable information retrieved; related information may also be retrieved although not directly requested.	Retrieval is enhanced by external cues but sophisticated learners create and use their own cues.	Present cues.
Performance as the result of learning	A performance regulates the assessment of learning and provides evidence of what is and is not mastered.	Multiple performances are necessary for appropriate inference of learning; when previously learned material is merged with new, transfer of learning is said to occur.	Provide examples, practice.
Feedback	Information about the performance reinforces or modifies learning.	Learner expectations of performance are confirmed in successful learning.	Critique performance, pointing out improvement and suggestions for improvement.

Adapted from *Essentials of Learning for Instruction* (2nd ed., p. 118) by Robert Gagné and Marcy Perkins Driscoll, 1988. Used with permission of Allyn & Bacon.

These processes of learning have substantial parallels with the planning and effective teaching research discussed earlier. Teachers who want to be successful should use this basic structure in their fundamental planning strategy.

Gaining Attention

To gain attention, the teacher has the students focus on the task at hand and provides enough interest so that internal monitoring of attention is initiated. Simple activities may include directing attention to an object, a quick demonstration where the result is unexpected (a "discrepant event"), or a mental visualization of the consequences of an unlikely event. Gaining attention need not be elaborate but should provide a preliminary event that causes all students to be involved.

Informing the Learner of the Objective

When informing the learner of the objective, the teacher attempts to accomplish at least two goals. First, the teacher tells students what must be done to be successful in the lesson. Second, the teacher explains why that activity is relevant. Both of these acts, if completed successfully, increase the students' willingness to attend to the lesson. By informing the learner of the objective, the teacher attempts to establish in each student an intrinsic motivation in which the student takes responsibility for personally directing attention and reception. However, because children do not see instructional relevance in the same way and at the same time, the teacher needs to keep referring to repeated examples of the application of knowledge during the lesson.

Recalling Prerequisite Material

The connection between previous learning and the requirements of the current lesson is best accomplished by overt teacher direction that stimulates recall of prerequisite material. The purpose of this review is to pull previously learned concepts, information, and questions into short-term memory. The recall stimulation need not be elaborate. The teacher may ask a series of questions, present a situation to be explained by students, or simply recount a summary of previously learned material. Demonstrations of past learning are also effective in bringing the necessary prerequisite knowledge from storage. Demonstrations may include resolving math problems using basic information necessary for a new algorithm or asking students to write definitions for two or three special terms used in a social studies discussion. The key is to be sure that students have the prerequisite skills and their memories of those skills are refreshed.

Presenting Stimulus Material

The teacher is now ready to present the stimulus material. There are an infinite number of ways in which new information can be presented to students. When information is imbedded in experiences, however, learning outcomes are enhanced, and retention is more likely. The term *experiences* in this description is used loosely to include presentations that employ multiple senses and increase the likelihood of student interaction with the material. A lecture may be considered an experience. Likewise, a video presentation that provides visual and aural illustrations of the narrative content is considered an experience. The most powerful experiences occur when students have concrete opportunity to see and manipulate materials, events, and interactions. When the experience engages all of the senses, students have more opportunity to employ their particular individual abilities to the learning task.

Providing Learner Guidance

When students perceive the information, event, or experience, not all children attend to the same things. By providing learner guidance, teachers provide external cues to assist the student in sorting various information and separating the most relevant portion into "chunks" or cohesive patterns for comprehension. The most common external cue is the question. Questioning is a bewilderingly varied strategy and is covered in the next chapter. However, the relevance of questioning is instrumental in all types of instruction as well as informal learning situations. Other external cues include pointing to a particular detail in an object or picture, eliminating extraneous detail by drawing a model or diagram, and providing comparisons to more familiar objects, events, or relationships.

Eliciting Desired Behaviors

There is no way a teacher can understand what is occurring in the minds of learners without eliciting desired behaviors from students. If a question is asked, a student's answer provides a behavior that can be assessed. If the teacher has demonstrated shoe-tying, having children attempt to tie shoes provides the teacher with information about the effects of instruction. However, eliciting behavior serves a more fundamental purpose. By actually using the information or skill being taught, students intellectually act on the information more actively than if they were simply perceiving and encoding. This additional restructuring, testing, and refining of interpretations is as important to mastery as the original presentation of the stimulus material. In explicit instruction, a desired articulated outcome is always indicated.

Providing Feedback and Assessing Behavior

When observing the learning behaviors of children, teachers need to provide feedback. When critiquing the learning performance, the teacher provides the student with information that improves the student's demonstration. The teacher also begins to construct an assessment of the student's learning behavior. Although feedback and assessment are logically related, there are differences. The feedback function is designed to enhance learning immediately by providing a continual analysis of activity that assists the student in cueing on relevant information to improve performance. This type of feedback is called *formative* in that the criticism is provided to "form," or congeal, understanding, skill, and knowledge. Feedback on student performance assists the student in creating a more appropriate or a more elaborate response to the learning situation. It is not meant to be an evaluative judgment on the quality of student learning or a comparison to the minimum expectations for learning success.

When the student learning behavior is assessed formally, the student's performance is compared to a model of desired outcomes. This second type of assessment is called *summative*. It attempts to "sum" the successes of a series of learning demonstrations. Summative assessment should not be based on the practice performances in which feedback is used to help student improve skill and understanding. Instead, summative assessment should occur by evaluating repeated applications or demonstrations of the desired performance after appropriate practice has occurred. If the teacher were teaching basketball free-throw shooting in physical education, the teacher may provide feedback by letting the student know if the ball is being held too tightly, the feet are too close, or the ball is off center to the body. This feedback varies from throw to throw. However, the evaluation strategy to assess the skill is the degree in which students are successful in shooting the baskets at the end of instruction. Subskills are also used to direct learning and provide direction for the teacher. These subskills are considered a fundamental part of the activity and are important. However, these preliminary skills are only steps to a specified goal. That goal should be the object of assessment.

Enhancing Retention and Transfer

The teacher's efforts at enhancing retention and transfer are designed to assist the learner in retaining the knowledge so that they may apply it in the future under different contexts than those of the initial instruction. Periodic reviews assist the student in retaining learned skills and information. Providing students with ongoing experiences in using knowledge in a wide variety of contexts is the best assurance that learning can be generalized and internalized.

Although the terminology in Gagné and Driscoll's nine instructional events may be confusing because of overlapping relationships, it illustrates an important final point. Although a sequenced development of the nine events may characterize a lesson, the nine events are also repeated endlessly within lessons. In using explicit instruction, each small sequential step evokes a miniature application of the nine events, thus establishing a recurring cyclical application as well as a linear sequence.

Major Characteristics of Explicit Instruction

The premiere characteristic of explicit instruction is that it attempts to simplify the learning task for the student. Every effort is made to structure the material, the environment, and the experience to increase the ease, speed, efficiency, and power of student learning. Explicit instruction is delivered to the student "preanalyzed" in that the salient components of any task are analyzed so that the number of student errors during the learning process is minimized. Unfortunately, the fact that explicit instruction is designed to make learning as simple and easy as possible is the very point most overlooked when explicit and implicit instruction are compared.

Explicit instruction begins with a specific outcome in mind. If the outcome cannot be structured carefully or if the material to be learned is not highly structured, explicit instruction is probably not the best strategy to use in that situation. Explicit instruction can successfully obtain outcomes in low-structured content and in areas of affective development. However, in these cases, trial-and-error and copious individual experimentation are almost always beneficial. A harmonious fit is obtained if the methods used facilitate individualized expression and discovery. Trial-and-error and experimentation lead to discovery; improving students' abilities to discover, create, and expand knowledge are vital goals of public school. However, explicit instruction, by definition, is directed at mastery, not at discovery. Mastery requires the elimination (or at least the minimization) of error. Although explicit instruction does not view error with disdain (it is viewed as a natural development pattern), it does view error as something to be extinguished. Teachers must be very clear on this point when selecting the appropriate method.

Appropriate Use of Explicit Instruction

Because of its structure and the value placed on outcomes that can be specified, observed, and measured, explicit instruction is often lauded as the panacea for school problems. It is not. Explicit instruction has severe limitations for many instructional goals. However, explicit instruction does have wide application in the classroom.

Increasing Student Satisfaction

In addition to its success in attaining efficient outcomes in high-structured subject areas, explicit instruction is also entertaining and increases student satisfaction. This is contrary to many popular notions that portray explicit instruction as dry, boring, and rote. However, student satisfaction with skilled explicit instruction should not come as a surprise. Because of explicit instruction's emphasis on making learning efficient by obtaining the greatest learning gain with minimized student effort and time spent, students can be successful without suffering undue levels of failure and hardship. Further, students can clearly recognize when they have achieved specific learning goals and can demonstrate these to the teacher and others.

Success is almost universally appealing and motivating. Remember, however, we are describing effectively delivered explicit instruction. This does not include a "tell" session followed by a "worksheet" session, which, in turn, is followed by a "test." This meandering of teacher talk and "busywork" is not a method and should not be confused with explicit instruction any more than setting children down with a pile of counters and telling them to "explore" is discovery learning in math. These impostors are demeaning to students and are a drain on school resources, student initiative, and parent patience. When children attack a skill with carefully constructed strategies, their errors are minimized, and outcomes are attained quickly. Students infer that they are capable, bright, and successful.

Promoting Curiosity

Explicit instruction also plays on natural curiosity. Children and adults both enjoy finding out about new things, particularly if that learning is painless. With the advent of cable television, explicit instruction has found its way as a successful entertainment medium. The plethora of "how to" programs that enable viewers to build a garage or paint a landscape have emerged using the basic features of the explicit instruction methodology as an outline for script development. Explicit instruction can provide an easy portal to many knowledge areas, increasing both student interest and enthusiasm.

Overlearning Material

When students need to overlearn (learn something so well that it becomes automatic) a skill or a set of facts, explicit instruction is indicated. For example, if students need to recall basic addition facts, explicit instruction with its emphasis on practice and feedback is the simplest, most direct route to that objective. If students must experiment with various conceptual strategies and develop more intuitive understandings, inclusion of some implicit instructional strategies is indicated. If a skill sequence is structured (for example, tying shoes or landing an airplane), explicit instruction is appropriate. In explicit instruction, repeated trial-and-error is rarely beneficial and can retard learning.

Evaluating Appropriate Use of Explicit Instruction

Models and taxonomies can be used to classify curriculum goals to ascertain whether explicit instruction is appropriate. Figures 5.4 and 5.5 illustrate Rath et al.'s thinking skills and Bloom's taxonomy of cognitive objectives. The items at the top half of both lists indicate goals that can be readily accomplished using explicit instruction.

The thinking keywords in Figure 5.4—observing, classifying, comparing, summarizing, interpreting, collecting, and organizing data—are all indicative of material or skills that can be taught, or at least introduced, using explicit instructional strategies. Of course, other methods can be employed. Also, depending on how these thinking keywords are interpreted, any specific use of the keywords may not be applicable to explicit instruction. However, as defined in Figure 5.4, teachers can create explicit lessons that develop beginning skills in these areas. For example, by providing the classification scheme and key attributes, a teacher can teach students the meaning and use of the scheme and provide practice in their use. However, if the classification scheme is to be created by the student, implicit or inquiry strategies are probably appropriate. It is important to remember the purpose of the activity, the nature of the material, and the learner's skill in determining the appropriateness of the lesson.

In Bloom's taxonomy (Figure 5.5), knowledge, comprehension, and application objectives generally point to explicit instructional strategies. Explicit instruction is well suited to lessons in which the learner is required to remember facts; recall terms and procedures; locate information; demonstrate understanding by translating, paraphrasing and interpreting; change knowledge from one form to another; or predict outcomes and effects. In each activity, there exists a basic guiding structure to the task. Notice that some areas, such as locating information, vary greatly in structure. Locating information in an encyclopedia is very structured, yet may still need inferential and intuitive skill development that cannot directly be taught. Again, it is critical that explicit instruction be coupled with other strategies in the elementary classroom so that children can acquire and apply a variety of learning skills.

In summary, explicit instruction is appropriate when material to be learned is highly structured and learning outcomes can be carefully defined. Additionally, explicit instruction is appropriate when learning efficiency is desired, when students need or would benefit from a structured experience that minimizes errors during learning, or when heightened student interest or learning satisfaction is deemed important. Most importantly, remember that "telling and practice" is an inadequate strategy for almost any learning and that explicit instruction is much more sophisticated and involved.

Synthesis of Research on Explicit Teaching

Rosenshine (1986) provided a concise synthesis of the research on explicit teaching. He concluded that the research on effective teaching describes a pattern of instruction that is particularly useful for teaching a body of content or well-defined skills. This instruction consists of a systematic method for presenting material in small steps, pausing to check for student understanding, and promoting active and successful participation for all students. In general, researchers have found that when effective teachers teach concepts and skills explicitly, they do the following:

◆ Begin a lesson with a short statement of goals.
◆ Begin a lesson with a short review of previous, prerequisite learning.
◆ Present new material in small steps, with student practice after each step.
◆ Give clear, detailed instructions and explanations.
◆ Provide active practice for all students.
◆ Ask many questions, check for student understanding, and obtain responses for all students.
◆ Guide students during initial practice.
◆ Provide systematic feedback and corrections.
◆ Provide explicit instruction and proactive seatwork exercises and, where necessary, monitor students during seatwork.
◆ Continue practice until students are independent and confident.

Variants of Explicit Instruction

Explicit instruction has at its core an intent to convey a specified body of knowledge and skill to a learner with minimized effort and maximized success. Cognitive psychology has provided a pattern of activity that reflects an informed and reasoned interpretation of what occurs when students learn. In associating teacher activity with learners' needs, a pattern of activity emerges that composes the basic paradigm of explicit instruction. However, there are variants to the overall pattern, and these patterns provide some insight into the utility and power involved in explicit instruction.

Direct Instruction

Direct instruction usually implies that all of the characteristics of explicit instruction are applied in much the same sequence as outlined by Gagné and Driscoll in Figure 8.3. Although the direct instruction paradigm existed in one form or another centuries before cognitive psychology, only recently have comprehensive theories of learning emerged and currently guide the development and use of the paradigm. Rosenshine and Stevens (1986) provide a skeletal outline of direct instruction in six functions.

Review.   The teacher begins classes with appropriate reviews of homework and the prior lesson's activities and important points. Reviews of relevant previous learning and prerequisite skills and knowledge for the current lesson are discussed, presented, or solicited from students. Rosenshine and Stevens outline a number of ways in which the review function may occur in lessons:

- Asking questions about previously taught concepts
- Giving short quizzes at the beginning of a lesson
- Correcting homework, individually, in groups, or scoring each other's work
- Preparing and asking questions about the course of study thus far
- Having students prepare written summaries of class sessions

Although checking homework may be considered a standard instructional procedure, a math study by Good and Grouws (1979) revealed that teachers in the control group reviewed math homework only 50 percent of the time. Like so many components of direct instruction, one assumes by common sense that these events occur frequently. In reality, appropriately designed reviews that check for understanding of the previous lesson and prepare the learners for new learning are underutilized methods for improving instruction.

Presentations.   Numerous studies have confirmed that students who receive more extensive explanations of new concepts and material demonstrate learning at higher success rates. However, many teachers fail to provide substantial explanations of concepts. In one study (Evertson, 1986), effective teachers spent more than twice the time explaining material than less effective teachers did. However, there is a point at which additional time on a concept does not increase results, such as when students have obtained mastery or have begun to tire of the topic.

"Teacher talk" currently suffers a "bad rap" in that the present trend among many educators is to label teacher presentations as boring, unproductive, and minimizing students' opportunity to interact with the material. To be sure, "teacher talk" can be all of those things. However, a pattern of research findings indicates that teachers who clearly state lesson goals, provide conceptual outlines, teach in small steps, model procedures, provide concrete positive examples and negative examples, use clear language, and employ frequent checks for student understanding are consistently more effective. Likewise, teacher presentations that lack clarity, are illogically or randomly constructed, and are filled with digressions reduced student learning. These teacher traits are, at best, unproductive and, at worst, destructive of student motivation, interest, and confidence.

Guided Practice.   In the direct instruction model, the presentation is followed by student opportunity to practice or rehearse knowledge and skills. Teachers use guided practice to provide students with the first opportunities to apply new information and skill. During these student demonstrations, teachers can correct errors and reteach if necessary. With sufficient guided practice and subsequent provision of additional learning opportunity if needed, students are adequately prepared for independent work on the lesson objective. A high frequency of questions, reteaching demonstrations, and the provision of opportunity for student responses characterize guided practice. Guided practice is structured so that students obtain high success rates even though the material is new and unfamiliar. Criticism that is characterized by negative evaluations of progress, efforts, or ability is avoided and generally has no place in the direct instruction sequence. Teachers maintain high success rates by breaking up complex tasks into cognitively simpler components so that students can experience quick success. In the most complex situations, when student errors are likely to occur at high frequency, the teacher encourages, reteaches, and supports student efforts. Students continue to practice until they can provide fluid demonstrations of the new material.

There is something inherently logical with the proposition that as an individual performs a task repeatedly, the more likely his or her subsequent performances are to be successful. This is precisely what the research finds. However, there are a few caveats to remember. If students are practicing inappropriate strategies and those errors go uncorrected, students are likely to learn incorrect solutions and strategies. Appropriate learning in future lessons is actually made more difficult. There is also a point of diminishing return. Students may practice a skill to the point of satiation where interest and motivation are so eroded that further development of the skill is met with resistance. The teacher must discover the "Goldilocks' compromise" in which the teacher finds the amount of practice that is "just right."

Obtaining a high percentage of correct answers when teaching new material, particularly difficult material, can present substantial challenges to teachers. Immediate reteaching is essential when the error level is above acceptable levels. Also, providing students with frequent explicit demonstrations of the instructional skill decreases errors and improves overall performance. Interspersing questions between demonstrations or within components of an elaborate demonstration assists the students in focusing and attending to the most applicable aspects of the skills in relationship to their current performance. More experienced teachers can anticipate misconceptions and warn students about those false leads beforehand.

Guided practice allows the teacher to check for understanding. Frequent assessments of the students' level of attainment help the teacher to assess the success of the lesson. The teacher can employ corrective measures early in the learning cycle. Suggested strategies for checking for understanding include preparing a large number of questions beforehand, asking many brief questions on main points, calling on nonvolunteers, and asking students to provide oral summaries in their own words.

Teachers can also have students write answers on paper, the chalkboard, or on individual response cards. Response cards may be composed of three cards of different colors. A student holds up a green card if he agrees with the teacher's statement, a red if he disagrees, or a yellow to show he is not sure. Having students break up into pairs and have one student summarize to the other student while the teacher circulates and listens to student answers is also another excellent device for frequent checking. Students may be given a small chalkboard where the student writes the response and holds it up for the teacher to see on request. The variations are limited only by teacher imagination.

Correction and Feedback.   While logically a component of guided practice, providing correction and feedback is identified as a separate function. Providing correction and feedback is essential. Giving early direction in weak areas of a student's performance eliminates misunderstandings and performance errors. Feedback should describe the degree of accuracy of the work, not judge the qualities or efforts of the children. Corrections should be accurate and directive but not derogatory. Avoiding the natural tendency to be critical and judgmental in evaluating student work is an excellent skill to master first. Criticism is negatively related to learning success. That is, the more criticism a student receives, the less likely that student will achieve. Examined logically, this should not come as a surprise. When subjected to negative comments, students minimize exposure to the source of criticism in an attempt to minimize hurt. This has the de facto result of minimizing engagement time and thus a loss of opportunity to learn. With the resulting withdrawal, motivation and confidence are reduced, and the student simply tries less and less.

The teacher has several options when student feedback indicates that the level of understanding is below the level required for independent work. The class can be divided so that those needing independent practice are moved forward while students who showed mastery or near mastery during guided practice tutor those needing more. This peer tutoring is a valuable way to promote a number of classroom social goals as well as obtaining immediate progress toward the lesson objectives. The teacher can provide remedial instruction while others are engaged in independent practice or in another appropriate activity. If the learning progress has been minimal, the teacher may wish to assess the entire lesson and reteach with a new strategy.

Independent Practice.   When students attain rudimentary skills in the application of new knowledge, they are ready to operate independently. Generally, when a percentage success rate applies, students are considered ready for independent practice when they obtain correct responses about 80 percent of the time. In some situations, such as creative writing, percentages do not apply. Keep in mind that some independent practice activities for subjects do not provide the high levels of logical and sequential structure characteristic of direct instruction. Independent activity may be used in conjunction with one or more implicit instructional strategies for purposes separate from those represented by direct instruction. For example, students may be required to write a summary of a televised news story they have just viewed as an advanced organizer (a focus activity) for current events or expository writing.

In general, independent practice that is associated with direct instruction involves students who have met minimal standards in activities taught under the direction of the teacher. Independent practice is the first effort at practicing the skill without direct support from the teacher. Two purposes of independent practice emerge. First, students are expected to integrate the new information and skills with previous knowledge. Second, students are expected to become automatic in their use of the skills.

Samuels (1981) describes the two activities of independent practice as *utilization* and *automaticity*. In the utilization phase, students employ the new skills successfully making only a few errors, but their effort, time, and concentration is much greater than necessary. Through repetitive activity using a variety of settings and strategies, students develop an internalized repertoire of memory and meta-cognitive skills that permit high levels of success with minimal time and effort. In short, students no longer must think through each step. This automatic use of the new skill, or automaticity, is referred to as *overlearning*. Overlearning is appropriate for a wide range of goals, such as learning basic facts in mathematics, spelling of a fundamental vocabulary, decoding text in reading, and understanding materials that require a hierarchical structure to knowledge.

Weekly and Monthly Reviews. In addition to the initial review of material contained in the introductory activities of the lesson, weekly and monthly reviews of the material contribute to the overall mastery pattern of direct instruction. Periodic reviews provide students with opportunities to develop continuity among individual steps of learning a complex task and help them to see the "big picture." These reviews also provide additional practice and enable students to remember the relevant aspects of previously learned material. If the teacher is moving too quickly, the weekly and monthly reviews should reveal this weakness. These reviews also allow the teacher to disperse reinforcing practice over a period of time and act as a deterrent to satiation.

In summary, direct instruction, also known as "action teaching" because of the high activity level of the teacher and students, is usually characterized by the following:

- Providing full class instruction
- Organizing learning around teacher questions
- Presenting material in sequence
- Providing detailed and redundant practice
- Using formal arrangement of the classroom to maximize practice
- Determining instructional pace by the mastery of small steps in a sequence

Traditional recitations have an important role.

Mnemonics

Mnemonics refers to a family of teaching and learning strategies designed to help the student memorize material. It is common for educational goals requiring memorization to be disparaged and referred to as "rote" learning. Memorization is sometimes considered not only worthless, but also harmful to students because it wastes times and destroys motivation. As with other extreme statements in education, the truth regarding the value of memorization depends on the decision-making factors that include context, intent, students, and teacher skill.

Forgotten Importance of Memorization. An example shows the value of memorization along with the source of the vehement criticism against memorization. Imagine interviewing a potential teacher's aide by asking the applicant's home phone number and being told, "I don't remember, but I can look it up." This is a rather absurd scenario, but it does demonstrate that memory skills are essential. In fact, memorization is so fundamental that it is usually taken for granted until important information is forgotten. When information is forgotten, the consequences are often extremely unpleasant and bothersome. Consider a pilot who forgets the proper approach speed for his aircraft, the shopper who forgets the location of his car in the mall parking lot, or the child who forgets where she lives. It is quite clear that teaching memory skills is an important activity. Developing good memory skills is an ability that students can use for the rest of their lives. Memorization is important in daily living, but what are appropriate school goals that require teaching specific memory skills?

Each student needs to memorize school rules, personal schedules, the building layout, and daily routines. Many teachers consider basic addition and subtraction facts essential. These teachers argue that if information is used repetitively, students can develop instant recall. Other teachers, however, decide that basic facts can be located on a chart and need not be memorized. It is ironic, however, that the process of repeated use of the chart is a simple memorization skill. Unfortunately, as important as memorization is, frequent abuses of its use have diminished the recognition of its value.

Continued misuse of memorization activities can actually diminish the effectiveness of the total curriculum by reducing student motivation. Take, for example, the author's situation in high school where he was required to memorize passages of *The Canterbury Tales* in Old English. The exercise was totally meaningless to him. It was so objectionable that he developed a negative attitude not only about that topic, but also about the entire subject of literature. This type of memorization is what is meant by *rote work:* Rote work has no connection to past learning or does not lead meaningfully to a future line of knowledge. There are widely varying opinions regarding what knowledge is rote and what is valuable. Ultimately, what is rote or valuable is up to the student. For example, to those who have devoted their lives to emerging English literature, memorization of various parts of *The Canterbury Tales* is far from rote but integral to their profession and the source of many hours of entertainment and pleasure. When educators criticize memorization, they generally, but not always, are thinking about rote memory.

Six Mnemonic Devices. Joyce and Weil (1980) assembled the various paradigms of instruction and included an analysis of mnemonics (memory-assisting) devices. They identified six principle types of mnemonic devices: awareness, association, link system, ridiculous association, substitute word system, and key word. *Awareness* requires that the learner give careful attention to the thing to be remembered. All applicable senses are focused on the object to be remembered. For example, if a poem is to be remembered, it will be read orally as well as silently. The shape of the poem and the rhythm and rhyming patterns are noticed and sensed. Although this is essentially a readiness activity, it is often quite adequate for some memorization tasks such as telephone numbers or the basic anatomy of a spider.

Association is another memory principle that requires the new thing to be associated with something already learned. Joyce and Weil provide an example of how the musical notes "EGBDF" associated with the lines on the music staff associated with "*every good boy does fine.*" A second example is "a piece of pie" to help remember the spelling of piece, noting the "ie" in "pie" and "piece" are the same.

In the *link system*, two ideas are linked where the first idea triggers the recall of the second, more powerful and elaborate idea. This is the technique widely demonstrated by memory specialists who learn the names of entire audiences of people during a single session. Learning a list of words such as "table," "chair," "red," and "wet," the learner creates an image of a table with a chair on top dripping with red, wet paint.

Ridiculous association is another principle and is similar to the link system. In ridiculous association, an emphasis is placed on images that are ridiculous or impossible. If you were trying to remember that you parked your car in the "A" red section of the parking lot, you may imagine your car getting a diploma with straight "A's" wearing a red graduation gown.

The *substitute word* system suggests the substitution or replacement of concrete (or familiar) ideas with abstract ones. To remember the first four presidents of the United States, the student may be prompted, "The first thing you must do is *wash a ton* of clothes. Then take the clothes across *a dam* to Mr. *Jeffers' son* who lives on *Madison* Avenue. . . . " This helps the student to remember the names and the sequence: Washington, Adams, Jefferson, and Madison.

The *key word system* uses a central word that helps the student to unlock many phrases or ideas. This is helpful for students trying to remember speeches or presentations. An example might be the word "RIOT" used to help teachers remember the fundamentals of classroom affect. The word unlocks the saying, "To avoid a riot in the classroom teachers must treat students with *r*espect, *i*ntentionality, *o*ptimism and *t*rust." From this concept, an entire lesson on classroom affect can be reconstructed.

Although not included in Joyce and Weil's list, *repetition* is probably the most dominant and effective way to memorize. If repetition can be combined with other senses and a variety of activities practicing the same skill are used, the process of memorization is more effective. The author, while teaching in elementary school, desired quick recall of basic multiplication facts. A series of activities were used that, at first, may seem a bit bizarre. One of the children's favorites was to march back from the cafeteria in a mamba line shouting, "Two times three is six, huh! Six times two is twelve, huh!", following the lead of the teacher or team captain. For those unfamiliar with the mamba, each syllable is a step and the "huh" is a kick. Since all the children are in line, the entire class take steps in rhythm and move (albeit slowly) in line toward the destination.

Flash cards associated with traditional board games work well where each turn requires the completion of three correct flash cards in a row. Classroom games such as "Texas Pete" add a flair to fill in minutes before the end of school or a dead minute or two before lunch. The teacher requests the answer to a basic fact and mechanically begins to "draw down" on the selected student. If the gun (a cocked thumb with finger barrel) goes off before the student replies, the whole class has to recite the basic fact three times. If the student wins, the teacher must dramatically take a hit to the leg or arm, cry out in pain, and limp appropriately toward the next student where the battle continues. The same games can be used for an infinite variety of memorized information. Notice that humor, activity, and enthusiasm can take some of the drudgery out of an otherwise tedious activity.

Mastery Learning and Programmed Instruction

Mastery learning and programmed instruction may be misrepresented here as being considered a method of instruction. In one perspective, mastery learning is a philosophy underlying many instructional methodologies. The biggest differences between mastery learning and other methods are not with the actual strategies employed but rather in the assumptions about the abilities of children. On the other hand, mastery learning has developed elaborate extensions of existing methods and new variations of its own that warrant its inclusion as a variant of explicit instruction.

Competence versus Time. Mastery learning reverses the typical schooling curriculum from a *time-based* to a *competency-based* system. Current approaches, particularly in university-level instruction, are time-based. A specific amount of time is set for study, and the students then attempt to learn as much as possible in that set period. Those who learn the most are rewarded with high marks, and the learners who learn less receive lower marks. It is accepted that some students simply are not going to learn as effectively as others do within the time frame governing the school day. With this assumption, children are expected to have varying levels of understanding and skill in each instructional goal.

In a traditional learning system, time is held constant, and the level of mastery is left to vary among students. Carroll (1963) wondered what would happen if this process were reversed. Carroll started with the assumption that nearly all children can learn the basic material under consideration. However, he concluded that some learners may take more time than others. Carroll concluded that the time element of instruction should be manipulated rather than the varying the competency level of the student. If the body of learning is structured so as to make explicit instruction a good choice, the issue becomes not what percentage of the material is learned, but rather how long it takes for learners to master the material. Hence, the term *mastery learning* because all material to be learned is to be mastered. Mastery learning does not deal with "introductory explorations" or "appreciation development." Mastery learning is designed to achieve specific learning goals at specified competency levels for all students.

Goals and Mastery Learning. Although the focus is on content mastery among all students, designers of mastery learning programs claim a number of learning goals (Joyce & Weil, 1980):

◆ Enabling all students to work at their own pace
◆ Developing content mastery that can be demonstrated in predetermined ways
◆ Developing an internal locus of control for learning
◆ Exercising self-regulation of learning
◆ Fostering development of independence and problem solving
◆ Encouraging self-evaluation
◆ Developing personal motivation to learn

Mastery learning, like other explicit instruction strategies, is best suited to hierarchically structured programs and content. Instructional goals must be clearly identified in measurable terms, and instruction must be carefully focused and aligned with those goals. Diagnostic tests play an important role in mastery learning because it is through tests that the appropriate level of instruction is determined. Tests of one type or another are also used to demonstrate the outcomes of learning and determine mastery. Teachers must, therefore, be prepared to develop a series of short, specific tests to correspond with the sequence of development and learning inherent in the material. Should mastery on any test not be attained, the test should provide some indication about the missing concepts or skills and direct the learner to additional experiences.

Mastery learning materials may incorporate a wide range of teaching strategies so that a teacher's lecture, video, field trip, or whole-group activity may be an integral component of instruction. This is particularly true for the initial introduction of material. However, at some point, students must be provided with individually prescribed lessons that accommodate the inherent differences in students' progress. Between primary instruction and mastery assessment, children are directed to differing activities or "correctives" based on testing results. These activities need not be individual to each student, but rather should be developed to provide students with additional activity for advancing skills that need reinforcement or reinstruction. Children who master the material quickly are given enrichments or are allowed to pursue other instruction goals.

Primary Strategies of Mastery Learning. Some mastery learning programs have been adopted schoolwide and contain materials that are sequenced so that primary instruction using whole groups is eliminated. Instead, students complete a sequence of prescribed activities and tests. Commercial kits and programs are also available both for classroom and schoolwide use.

Bloom (1971, 1974) popularized the development of mastery learning strategies and materials. In general, mastery learning strategies are typified by the following:

◆ Focus on individual achievement at prescribed levels of mastery
◆ Presentation of learning material in a sequenced order
◆ Frequent individualized assessments of learning
◆ Multiple approaches to learn skills
◆ Reteaching strategies including self-instruction opportunities
◆ Opportunities for students to self-check and monitor progress
◆ Emphasis on progress and remediating learning difficulties
◆ Instructional modules that encourage individual progress and self-teaching
◆ Plotting and tracking progress so that each child is aware of personal progress

The research on various approaches to mastery learning in the elementary school has been promising. As a method, it has a proven track record, although it is important to recognize that mastery learning is not well suited to all learning goals.

Presentations

A *presentation* is both a component of direct instruction and an instructional strategy in its own right. As an instructional strategy, presentations mirror the components of direct instruction with the omission of practice activities and the evaluation that accompanies student demonstrations. Because there is no practice, effective presentations must be particularly clear and understandable. This includes anticipating student misunderstandings and confusion and building supplemental demonstrations and explanations into the presentation.

Presentations are becoming increasingly popular. The increased programming demands of cable and satellite television has spurred the development of "how to" programming in which presentations on a wide range of topics provide viewers with information in an enjoyable, helpful format. Presentations are the food for people who are hungry to know and understand. They are also utilitarian. Virtually any topic can be demystified, explained, examined, and described in a presentation.

Purpose of Presentations. Presentations can provide the needed instruction to initiate student activity that leads to mastery. However, presentations are also very useful when the skill display need not be learned by the students. Understanding of how a skill functions, but not being required to master the skills, can expand the perception and understanding of children. During the bicentennial celebration of the Declaration of Independence, one school brought in a complete textile production facility including cotton-carding equipment, spinning wheel, dye tubs, and looms. Operated by older citizens of the textile town, students were shown how cotton became cloth in the eighteenth century. It was not necessary for students to learn any of the skills. The purpose was to gain an appreciation of the time-consuming methods of manufacture that existed prior to the Industrial Revolution. Other demonstrations included musket firing, soap making, cooking, and baking. Although children were often given "hands-on" experiences, there was no attempt at developing a skill level. Mastery was simply not considered. It was thought by providing the information and experiences, students would have basic data in which to process other information.

Presentations are appropriate in many situations where careful transmission of information is vital, but practicing the skill is neither necessary nor possible. A teacher may wish to make a presentation regarding the events leading up to the Civil War and introduce information that may be needed in student debates or other activity contained in subsequent lessons. Or perhaps a teacher may make a presentation demonstrating the potential violence of a chemical reaction in which student participation may be too risky, supervision cannot be supplied, the chemicals are too expensive for individual use, or equipment is extremely limited. Although presentations may lack high levels of student participation, it is a mistake to label them as being necessarily passive. Good effective demonstrations can be as captivating, stimulating, and beneficial as any other type of instructional activity.

Procedures for Effective Presentations. Rosenshine and Stevens (1986) assembled the research that identified the characteristics of effective demonstrations and lectures. A summary of their findings is presented in Figure 8.4

Effective presentations begin with a clear statement of lesson goals. If a product is to be produced, for example, the presenter is shown the final product and the raw materials at the outset. This clear visualization helps the learners to form mental conceptualizations that assist encoding information from the demonstration. Often, the

1. **You clearly present goals and main points by**
   a. Stating goals or objectives of the presentation beforehand
   b. Focusing on one thought (point, direction) at a time
   c. Avoiding digressions
   d. Avoiding ambiguous phrases and pronouns

2. **You present content sequentially by**
   a. Presenting material in small steps
   b. Organizing and presenting material so that one point is mastered before the next point is given
   c. Giving explicit, step-by-step directions
   d. Presenting an outline when the material is complex

3. **You are specific and concrete by**
   a. Modeling the skill or process (when appropriate)
   b. Giving detailed and redundant explanations for difficult points
   c. Providing students with concrete and varied examples

4. **You check for student understanding by**
   a. Being sure that students understand one point before proceeding to the next
   b. Asking students questions to monitor their comprehension of what has occurred
   c. Having students summarize the main points in their own words
   d. Reteaching the parts that students have difficulty comprehending

FIGURE 8.4 *Characteristics of effective lectures and demonstrations.*

Adapted from Rosenshine, B., & Stevens, R.: "Teaching Functions" in *Handbook of Research on Teaching,* Third Edn., Merlin C. Wittrock, Editor, pp. 376–391. Copyright © 1986 by the American Educational Research Association. Used by permission of Macmillan Library Reference, USA, a Simon & Schuster Macmillan Company.

learners key in on specific issues that cause confusion and force mental questions, such as "How did he get it to do that?", thus sharpening students' perception and attention. If the concept is complex or multidimensional, the instructor may acknowledge these difficulties and then reassure learners that, if they concentrate on these specific points, they will successfully learn the concept.

During effective presentations, instructors focus on one thought (point, direction) at a time and focus attention on that thought so that its connection with previous thoughts is made clear. Attention is also directed toward providing a forecast of the substance and relationship to the next thought. Thus, the instructor reveals the major thoughts of the presentation one at a time in small steps that are clearly related to what has occurred before and what is to occur next. In classroom presentations where the size of the group permits, instructors check for understanding on one thought before proceeding to the next. However, that is not possible in many presentations because of the lack of a live audience, the size of the audience, or severe time constraints. Fortunately, these situations are not typical of the elementary classroom but do reinforce the importance of predicting beforehand possible areas of misunderstanding or resistance in the learners.

If the presentation goal is related to some activity that the student is to replicate at another time, the instructor gives step-by-step directions that provide a concise summary of the necessary events to replicate the performance. The instructor also models the behaviors by going through the directions. Finally, the instructor avoids digressions since that would destroy the logical sequence inherent in the prepared presentation. Again, the importance of being able to anticipate learner reaction and plan accordingly is critical to successful presentations. This applies not only in preventing digressions, but also in providing the highest level of clarity possible.

Presentations are dominant methods of conveying information either as factual information or as offering a point of view. Presentations are becoming more important instructional strategies because media has allowed individuals to capture presentations and disseminate them in a variety of formats. Future schooling may include presentations from teachers in space or under the deepest seas beamed via satellite into classrooms worldwide. Although they will never replace face-to-face communication, presentations, both live and by media, will increasingly have an even more prominent place in successful elementary classrooms.

◆ ◆ ◆

Summary

1. Instruction has two major purposes: to increase and elaborate on existing knowledge and to increase the capacity to create and use knowledge.

2. Explicit strategies are designed to help learners acquire knowledge that is well-structured with the primary purpose of increasing knowledge and understanding.

3. Implicit strategies are designed to help learners understand and resolve problems when knowledge is not well-structured with the primary purpose of increasing the student's ability in using and creating knowledge.

4. There is no clear demarcation between low-structured and high-structured knowledge, but rather the differences are endpoints on a continuum.

5. Teachers structure concepts for ease of learning and understanding when the information is factual and well-structured. Teachers structure knowledge for learning to increase student success, to improve learning efficiency, and to make learning as easy as possible.

6. Teachers assist children in creating and structuring concepts when the knowledge is heavily influenced by personal values, is poorly structured, or is used in ways that radically vary from one experience to the next.

7. Before using explicit strategies, the teacher must do the following:
   a. Be clear about instructional goals
   b. Be knowledgeable about the content
   c. Have a variety of strategies for teaching
   d. Communicate to students the learning expectations
   e. Make expert use of material
   f. Know the students well

g. Teach meta-cognitive strategies as well as content
h. Address a variety of cognitive skills
i. Monitor student understanding
j. Reflect on teaching practice

8. There is a pattern of basic instructional events that assists students in comprehending new situations and new information.

9. Explicit instruction is appropriate when the learning is sequenced, when skills are employed in standardized ways, or when overlearning is desired.

10. Explicit teaching has been extensively researched, and a primary set of characteristics has been disclosed. These include the following:
   a. Careful orientation of the student to the lesson
   b. Carefully sequenced instruction
   c. Active involvement of students
   d. Guided practice of the new skill
   e. Continued practice until mastery and intermittent practice thereafter
   f. Provision of feedback based on careful monitoring of student work

11. Direct instruction is a variant of explicit instruction composed of systematic review, presentations, guided practice, corrections, feedback, and independent practice.

12. Mnemonics are a group of strategies designed to enhance memory. The various strategies are designed to facilitate recall through the use of six principles: awareness, association, linkage, ridiculous association, substitute words, and key words.

13. Mastery learning is a constellation of basic strategies with the intent of learning to a preestablished standard regardless of the time involved. Mastery learning is, therefore, highly individualized and requires copious use of materials to support learning.

14. Mastery learning is based on enabling students to work at their own pace, developing content mastery, improving the student's internal locus of control, fostering the development of independence and problem solving, and encouraging self-evaluation.

15. Presentations are similar to direct instruction except that guided practice and the feedback role of the teacher is diminished or eliminated. Presentations are used to disseminate information, to increase awareness, or to demonstrate a concept or skill sequence.

◆ ◆ ◆

Activities and Questions for Further Understanding

1. Can you think of examples of skill and knowledge that would be dangerous to learn by individual exploration and trial-and-error? What methods would you use to teach these skills?

2. Information should be meaningful. Provide examples of classroom activities that employ direct instruction strategies that are not meaningful to children or to the school curriculum. What are the students' reactions to these activities?

3. If something is useful, is it meaningful? Describe several useful learning activities and then determine whether to use an explicit or an implicit strategy. What criteria governed your decisions?

4. Select several learning themes and develop a continuum of activities as is done in Figure 8.1.

5. Identify curriculum areas that are appropriate for teacher structuring of the major concepts. Do the same where it is best for

children to do their own structuring of the concepts. Interview children and find out which of the activities on the list that children enjoy more. Is "teacher-structured" or "student-structured" an instrumental element that predicts student enjoyment?

6. Develop a lesson using a direction instruction strategy employing the expanded lesson plan format presented in the text.
7. Watch television and find an example of each of the following types of shows: cooking, travel, arts/crafts, home repair, and history. What common basic elements do you find in each of these shows?

◆ ◆ ◆

References

Anderson, Linda M. (1989). Classroom instruction. In Maynard C. Reynolds, *Knowledge base for the beginning teacher*. Oxford: Pergamon Press.

Bloom, Benjamin. (1971). Mastery learning and its implications for curriculum development. In E. W. Eisner (Ed.), *Confronting curriculum reform*. Boston: Little Brown.

Bloom, Benjamin. (1974). An introduction to mastery learning theory. In J. H. Block (Ed.), *Schools, society, and mastery learning*. New York: McGraw-Hill.

Carroll, J. (1963). A model of school learning. *Teachers College Record, 64*, 723–733.

Dewey, John. (1916). *Democracy and education* (p. 198). New York: The Free Press.

Evertson, C. M. (1986). Do teachers make a difference? Issues for the eighties. *Education and Urban Society, 18*(2), 195–210.

Gagné, Robert, & Driscoll, Marcy Perkins. (1988). *Essentials of learning for instruction* (2nd ed.). Upper Saddle River, NJ: Prentice Hall.

Good, T. I., & Grouws, J. D. (1979). The Missouri mathematics effectiveness project. *Journal of Educational Psychology, 71*, 355–362.

Joyce, Bruce, & Weil, Marsha. (1980). *Models of teaching* (2nd ed.). Upper Saddle River, NJ: Prentice Hall.

Kant, Immanuel. (1966). *Critique of pure reason* (p. 1). Translated by F. Max Müller. Garden City, NY: Anchor Books.

Porter, A., & Brophy, J. (1988, May). Synthesis of research on good teaching. *Educational Leadership, 5*(8), 74–85.

Rosenshine, Barak. (1986, April). Synthesis of research on explicit teaching. *Educational Leadership, 47*(7), 60–69.

Rosenshine, Barak, & Stevens, Robert. (1986). Teaching functions. In Merlin Wittrock (Ed.), *Handbook of research on teaching* (3rd ed., pp. 376–391). New York: Macmillan.

Samuels, S. J. (1981). Some essentials of decoding. *Exceptional Education Quarterly, 2*, 11–25.

CHAPTER 9

How Do I Teach for Inquiry?

Questioning and Implicit Instruction

Outline

Knowing ignorance is strength. Ignoring knowledge is sickness.

LAO-TZU

He felt that in this crisis his laws of life were useless. Whatever he had learned of himself was here of no avail. He was an unknown quantity. He saw he would again be obliged to experiment as he had in early youth.

STEPHEN CRANE, *THE RED BADGE OF COURAGE*

A Slice of Life

"Who are you?" Mr. Stafford asked with a drawl. He was about to begin his all-time favorite lesson of his 32 years of teaching. "Now, that is a question, isn't it? 'Who are you?' Think about it for a minute. Now, let me ask you that question." Mr. Stafford waited a minute and suddenly looked at Bill and pointed, "Who are you?"

To Mr. Stafford's amazement, Bill answered, "I'm my daddy's son!" He had expected Bill to say "Bill," as almost everyone in the past 32 years had given their name as the first answer to the question. Mr. Stafford couldn't help but laugh along with the class. Bill looked back with some pleasure that he had stumped the teacher, or at least disrupted the dramatic flow. Mr. Stafford was delighted if a little perplexed.

"OK, try this one. Who are you?" Mr. Stafford tried again.

Bill didn't blink. "I'm a sixth-grade student at Aycock School. Captain of the football team and my mother's favorite boy."

"You're an only child," Mr. Stafford bantered back, hiding his enjoyment of the conversation.

"That's part of who I am, too, Mr. Stafford."

"OK, try this one. Who are you?" Mr. Stafford didn't know what might happen next.

Bill hesitated. A pause preceded his plea. "Mr. Stafford, I think that is too personal to ask in front of the class." He couldn't help chuckling and lost his dramatic edge.

In 32 years, the lesson had never happened this way. It had been a good lesson, one that was worth repeating every year. After asking the question, the children were assigned to read a selection from Lewis Carroll's Alice in Wonderland, *in which Alice meets the caterpillar smoking a hookah. The caterpillar asks Alice, "Who are you?", and Alice has difficulty answering the caterpillar's inquiry. The problem was that Mr. Stafford hadn't even had the children read the story yet. What was going on?*

To his surprise—and the children's delight—he was the victim of a practical joke. Mrs. Atwell, a fellow teacher for the last 20 years, had primed the children for the task. Knowing from conversations that the lesson was coming, Mrs. Atwell had taken some time to visit the class while they were with their music teacher and practiced some "appropriate" answers. Now that he knew about the joke, Mr. Stafford went around the class and gave all of the children a chance to give him their best punch line.

Mr. Stafford was immensely amused and impressed. "Well, I can see that you've given quite a bit of thought to the question already. I'm sure that these weren't your first answers, were they?" The class nodded in agreement. "Let me read the selection from Alice in Wonderland *that I assigned, the one in which Alice meets a caterpillar who asks her the same question." He had never read it aloud before, but he needed a little time to rethink his lesson.*

Mr. Stafford read the selection with expression, and the children listened attentively. When finished, Mr. Stafford asked what they thought Lewis Carroll was trying to say when he wrote it. Several children put forth some ideas. Mr. Stafford listened with care to each one, showed appreciation for the responses, but neither accepted nor rejected any answer. He paused and then asked very carefully, "Is there just one you? Think about it before you answer."

Mary was impatient. "There is only one me! Just one."

"When people look at you, do they all see the same person?"

Mary thought. "No, my mother sees me different than my brother does, but I'm still the same."

"Good point, Mary. You are a single person, but people look at you differently. You also look at yourself differently when doing different activities in different places. But when the caterpillar poses the question to Alice, she gets confused. Why?"

Several children argue that Alice feels like different people, and since she changes, she must be different people. At the very least, she isn't the same person all the time.

"Well, let's suppose that there is more than one you. If there is more than one 'you,' who are the 'you's' that make up you?" There was a smile and wink in Mr. Stafford's eyes. "Seriously, who are all of these 'you's'?"

Jane volunteered, "There's the 'me' that is a sister and a daughter."

"Then there is a 'you' that is a member of a family?" Mr. Stafford asked. Jane nodded. "Then let's put that one on the board." He wrote, "The Many Me's that

Make Me Whole," and circled it. Then he drew a line from the circle and wrote "Family Member" and put a circle around that. "What other 'me's' are there?"

"I'm the tallest one in class, and I'm a girl." Susie was proud of her height.

"Then we can compare the 'me' to other people by our physical bodies. That sounds like two 'me's' to me." The children chuckled on cue with Mr. Stafford's smile. "There is a 'comparative me.' That's when I look at myself compared to others. Then there is a 'physical me.' That's my size and hair color and what I look like. OK, are there other 'me's'?"

The children contributed, and Mr. Stafford wrote each on the board and webbed it back to the center oval. The webs included student, athlete, friend, comedian, and artist. It also included the "hidden me," the "private me," and "organism."

Mr. Stafford looked at the web. "Some of these seem to describe all of us. Which ones are they?" Mr. Stafford made a new web by including only those things that applied to everyone. "My, this is an interesting description of what makes up a person. You say that everyone has a family even though they may not live with the other members. You say that everyone has a 'physical me,' an 'emotional me,' and a 'learning me.' You didn't like my suggestion of a 'comparative me,' but I thought it made sense. You included a 'friend me,' although you thought it was possible not to be a friend or have one. You also included a 'personality me' that you say is the way a person acts around others. What you seem to be saying is who we are is really complicated with many views and opinions. Now, if we were going to write a story that was to seem real, our characters would have to be complicated, just like our web. Could we get into groups and create characters that have all the 'me's' that are on the board?"

What Is Implicit Instruction?

Like the question, "Who are you?", trying to define strategies for inquiry yields a number of answers depending on your perspective. *Implicit instruction* is a family of similar but loosely defined strategies commonly referred to as indirect instruction, inquiry instruction, experimentation, constructivism, and discovery learning.

Like explicit instruction, implicit instruction has a number of identified strategies that have been advocated, studied, and implemented. However, implicit instructional strategies do not share explicit instruction's emphasis on carefully structured presentations of subject matter. Instead, implicit instructional strategies are focused on the emerging understandings of students and on assisting students to construct concepts and to comprehend. Although student understanding can be predicted to some degree, it does not provide teachers with the sequential, orderly organization that explicit instruction and its highly structured content do. Since much of the lesson depends on how well students are able to structure concepts, implicit instruction must continually respond to a larger number of unanticipated events. Thus, implicit strategies are usually loosely organized and are often ambiguous when compared to explicit instruction strategies. Descriptions and interpretations of implicit instructional strategies are subject to wide variations, just as the concepts being taught using implicit strategies are subject to wide variations in understanding.

This "looseness" of methodology requires the teacher to be more thoughtful and more responsive during instruction. This intensity is a hallmark of successful implicit instruction. A second hallmark of implicit instruction is the high level of skill involved in providing questions that guide student development of understanding. Although both explicit and implicit instruction employ copious use of questions, implicit instruction must guide the student toward ordering a construct in which natural order may be elusive. Thus, the use of questioning strategies in the two methods varies greatly.

Questioning in Explicit and Implicit Instruction

A common misbelief is that if a teaching strategy involves many questions, it is implicit, or inquiry, instruction. Although this is often the case, it is still quite misleading. Both explicit and implicit instructions rely heavily on teacher questioning strategies. In explicit instruction, questions are used to illuminate the concepts that have been selected and structured by the teacher for the lesson. In implicit instruction, questions are used predominantly to assist the student in structuring information into self-developed concepts and abstractions. How questions are used in the two strategies differ in very subtle ways. Two short vignettes regarding lessons on Christopher Columbus are included in this section. As you read, note the purpose of each of the teacher's questions and the mental processes involved for students to answer successfully.

Vignette 1

TEACHER: *Last night you read about one famous explorer. Who was it?*

SHAUN: *(volunteering) Columbus.*

TEACHER: *Yes, Shaun, and what did he do?*

SHAUN: *Discovered America.*

TEACHER: *When he left Europe, what was he hoping to do?*

SHAUN: *Sail to China.*

TEACHER: *Was he sailing in the right direction?*

SHAUN: *No. . . . (hesitation) Well, he could have been.*

TEACHER: *Who can explain Shaun's answer? (Several volunteers) Allie?*

ALLIE: *He thought the world was round, and he could sail west and end up in the east.*

TEACHER: *Was this a common belief?*

ALLIE: *Yes, everybody knew the earth was round. Columbus thought it was a lot smaller than the experts did. He thought it was about seven or eight thousand miles around. The experts thought it was about 23,000. Columbus thought he'd only have to travel about 5,000 miles to China, but since he didn't have to go around Africa, it would be quicker.*

TEACHER: *Was Columbus right?*

ALLIE: *No, he was wrong. The world was much bigger.*

TEACHER: *Did he find land where he thought he would? Jack?*

JACK: *Yes.*

TEACHER: *We have a case here of an explorer making a discovery ... but the wrong one. Explorers are courageous people, but they do make mistakes. Look on the board, and you will see a list of traits that most explorers are thought to have.*

◆

Vignette 2

TEACHER: *Last night we read about Columbus and his voyage to America. We know there was an argument between Columbus and the expert navigators. Who can give a summary of the facts? Shaun?*

SHAUN: *Columbus wanted a quick and safe way to China. He thought he'd sail west across the ocean, and it would be shorter.*

TEACHER: *(interjecting) Great, but Allie, what were they arguing about?*

ALLIE: *The size of the earth. The experts thought it was three times bigger than Columbus thought it was.*

TEACHER: *Precisely. And that is a real problem. If you think you are traveling 5,000 miles and you really are going to have to travel 15,000 miles, you just might run out of food and water and be stuck. So, my question today is about all explorers, but we'll use Columbus. At the beginning of the journey, was Columbus excited or scared?*

ALLIE: *We don't know for sure. The book doesn't say.*

TEACHER: *Okay. If you were Columbus, would you be excited or scared? Think about it a minute. (five seconds pass) Allie?*

ALLIE: *I'd be scared.*

TEACHER: *Why?*

ALLIE: *I don't know what's out there. Nobody had ever done it, and Columbus was only guessing that the world was that small. He could certainly get stranded.*

TEACHER: *And you, Mike? How would you feel?*

MIKE: *I think I'd be scared, too.*

TEACHER: *Okay, then you both are saying Columbus was scared. But was he excited?*

MIKE: *Of course. He'd fought too hard to get the chance.*

TEACHER: *Then you are saying that most explorers would be both scared and excited about their journey? Shaun, what would an explorer do with his or her fear?*

SHAUN:	*Hide it.*
TEACHER:	*Why?*
SHAUN:	*If he showed he was afraid, nobody would go with him. Well, it would be harder to get people to go with him.*
TEACHER:	*Great! You are saying that explorers have to hide fear, be a leader, and show excitement and confidence. Let's write that on the board. Today we want to think about what characteristics and feelings an explorer might have. At the end of the period, I'll ask you all to write a short essay predicting whether you would make a good explorer of the unknown. Bill, what other traits would an explorer have to have?*

Differing Use of Questions

In both vignettes, the teachers start out with factual reviews of the material. In vignette 1, however, the questions represent a logical, step-by-step sequence of the basic factual theme of the reading. In vignette 2, the teacher asks for a broader, less sequenced summary of the facts. Early in the lesson, the teacher in vignette 2 completely abandons the discussion of facts and leads the children to speculate about the motives and traits of explorers although that material was not in their reading. Although both teachers employ consistent and copious questions, the purposes of the questions are quite different.

The first lesson employed an instructional strategy known as a *recitation*. In this version, recitation is an explicit questioning strategy based on a step-by-step sequential restructuring of the material that children had read previously. True to the complexity of most teaching strategies, recitation can also be used in implicit instruction. However, as used in vignette 1, the approach is considered to be an explicit strategy because the basic factual material as presented in the text was the focus of the lesson. The second lesson employed an implicit instruction strategy that is sometimes known as *constructivist philosophy*. In this case, the goal of the teacher was to get the children to examine the common context of exploration and to speculate on the skills and attitudes that an explorer must possess to overcome the barriers involved in all exploration.

In the first lesson, the teacher had structured the content of the lesson. In the second lesson, the content must be structured by the intellectual activity of the children. In the first lesson, the teacher provided the concept of exploration and the necessary skills to be an explorer, even though they were left open to interpretation. However, the second lesson required the children to construct an understanding of the traits that foster exploration and to evaluate the accuracy of those understandings.

Questioning serves different functions in explicit and implicit instruction but share many common elements. In explicit strategies, questions are usually used to check for understanding, whereas in implicit instruction, questions are usually used to develop or construct a concept. However, both purposes may appear in either type of lesson. For example, if in initiating a lesson like that represented in Vignette 2, the teacher discovers a lack of factual information in many of the learners, he or she may insert a brief recitation session to convey the basic facts to the uninformed children. Likewise, a teacher may find that lessons beginning like the one in vignette 1 may be totally unnecessary because of appropriate student preparation the night before. In that case, the teacher may easily refocus the lesson to build on the basic concepts that the learners have already acquired. In learning about questions and questioning strategies, the teacher must always remember that the appropriate and timely use of any technique depends on the teacher's ability to identify and combine purpose, students' needs, and emerging contexts.

Effective Questions

Effective questioning strategies are critical to both explicit and implicit instruction. Although questions supplement presentations and demonstrations in carefully structured explicit instruction, the question usually composes the heart and soul of implicit instructional strategies. For that reason, successful questioning strategies are contained in this chapter on implicit instruction.

MacDonald (1991) refers to the question-and-answer method of instruction as "interactive teaching." Whether the question has a known answer or the student must develop a hypothesis, speculation, or even a guess, students must process information in order to respond. Likewise, students' responses reveal much about what and how they are thinking so that the teacher can then tailor the lesson to increase the likelihood of student success.

The first rule of effective questioning is to make sure that the teacher obtains a student response to each question. When students respond, they must process information. Even if the student lacks the information to answer a question, a response such as "I don't know" provides the teacher with insight into the student's understanding. By employing probes (questions based on student answers), a teacher can further develop the lesson objective and his or her understanding of what the students are thinking. For example, the teacher may reply to the child's claim of inadequate information by simply asking, "What additional information do you need to be able to answer the question?"

Characteristics of Good Questions

Groisser (1964) lists the six characteristics of good questions as being clear, purposeful, brief, adapted to the level of the class, sequenced, and thought provoking. Wilen (1987) provides a thoughtful description of the effective teacher's questioning strategies (Figure 9.1).

Effective questions are clear and easily understood, but not necessarily easily answered, by the student. By phrasing questions carefully, students are provided with more time for developing a response and less time in trying to understand the question. Brevity usually assists clarity. Consider the following two questions:

FIGURE 9.1 Questioning behaviors of effective teachers.

From "Effective Questions and Questioning: A Classroom Application" by W. W. Wilen. In W. W. Wilen (Ed.), *Questions, Questioning Techniques, and Effective Teaching* (pp. 108–109), 1987, Washington, DC: National Educational Association.

- Ask questions that are phrased clearly.
- Ask questions primarily of an academic nature.
- Ask both low-level *and* high-level questions.
- Adapt questions to the age and economic/social background of the student.
- Provide three to five seconds of wait time between the question and the answer and between the answer and the teacher response.
- Obtain a response from a targeted student each time a question is posed to the student.
- Balance volunteers and nonvolunteers as the targets of questions.
- Ask questions that students can answer at a high rate of success.
- Help students with incorrect answers.
- Probe student responses for clarification, support, and extension.
- Acknowledge correct responses from students.

◆ When people are not sure of their abilities, what types of things do they do that telegraphs to others that they do not know precisely what to do to be successful in this situation?

◆ How do people act when they are unsure of themselves?

The first question includes unnecessary phrases and conditions, whereas the second is straightforward. The second would normally be considered the better question.

A Simple Question Sequence

Effective teachers ask a mixture of questions that require a variety of cognitive skills ranging from recall to speculation. Consider the following sequence of questions that the author routinely used when reading a story aloud to children. At any time, he would pose the questions in sequence:

◆ What is happening now?
◆ Why is it happening?
◆ What might happen next?

"What is happening now?" is a simple recall question and tests whether students are paying attention and understand what is occurring in the story. "Why is it happening?" usually requires some level of interpretation or comprehension for a student to frame an answer. Occasionally, the context of the story will have provided specific reasons for the current action so that no student inference is required. In that case, the question may be considered as a second recall question.

Generally, the question "Why is it happening?" requires a consolidation of past events that is antecedent to the current part of the story. "What might happen next?" requires the students to create a prediction. At first, the question may seem to be calling for wild speculation, but many stories have established patterns that foretell future events. Other stories provide enough information so that a logical conclusion can be predicted from the events already known. At other times, student creativity is required because of the unpredictable nature of the book. In any case, the sequence of these three simple questions moves from low-level recall to high-level interpretation, thus providing the desired mixture of cognitive requirements.

Include All Students

Students should never be allowed to "check out" of any lesson. The successful teacher uses questioning strategies that include nonvolunteers to maintain attention and promote student accountability. However, the use of nonvolunteers has a more fundamental purpose. By including nonvolunteers, children who are reticent to respond are included in the lesson. Effective teachers nurture the nonvolunteer by providing questions that permit success. They do this by employing a sequence of questions leading from simple to more difficult responses. Following is an example of teacher questioning that provides an initial safe setting, builds student confidence by a sequence of successes, and then culminates in a difficult question:

TEACHER: In *Alexander's Terrible, Horrible, No Good, Very Bad Day*, how did Alexander feel when he was riding in the middle seat of the car?

STUDENT: Bad.

TEACHER: You got that right! Alexander felt bad. Just how bad did he feel?

STUDENT: Terrible.

TEACHER: Okay. What do you think he was thinking about as he sat in the back seat?

STUDENT: He thought he was going to throw up.

TEACHER: Yes! He felt that way. But did he actually do it?

STUDENT: No. He just wanted to because he hated sitting between two girls.

TEACHER: Yep. But those kinds of things happen all the time. Has something like that happened to you?

STUDENT: Yes. (Teacher waits attentively.) I poured sour milk on my cereal this morning and took a bite. (Class moans; student smiles at the attention.)

TEACHER: Oooh. I bet that was unpleasant. My question is, "How should you react when things don't go your way?"

The teacher asked the reticent student a number of safe questions and offered encouragement before posing a more difficult question. In the example, students also encouraged the nonvolunteer by providing attention and sympathy. The final question requires considerably more thought and implies to the student that he or she may have to defend the answer. By this time, however, the student is involved in the lesson and is probably less hesitant about participating. Notice also that the questioning strategy set the stage for a number of volunteers to share their "bad thing" and their appropriate reaction.

Avoid "Yes-No" Questions

Generally, "yes-no" questions are not good questions because the options for response are limited to two choices and because there is little information gained as a result. If the student answers correctly, the teacher must recognize that the student had a 50-50 chance of answering correctly even if he or she knew nothing about the question. Likewise, if the student misses the question, the teacher cannot conclude anything about the student's level of comprehension about the concept. "Yes-no" questions are, however, appropriate in some instances. For example, the teacher may want students to take a stand on an issue and then defend their points of view. "Should we vote to end affirmative action when it appears on the ballot in November?" is an example of a "yes-no" question that is appropriate. The question oversimplifies the issues involved, but it is, nevertheless, presented in a form that students are likely to confront when dealing with the issue. However, to be an effective introduction, this question must be followed by a series of probing questions. When "yes-no" questions are used, probes are almost always necessary.

Questioning for Success

Students should view questions with optimism. If the teacher consistently uses questions to demonstrate how little students know or how limited their abilities are, students soon shy away from questions and instruction that is based on inquiry. Students should be given difficult questions, but in general, there should be a high probability of student success. When exceedingly difficult questions are asked, teachers can provide encouragement such as acknowledging the question's difficulty or recounting that the teacher is also unsure of the answer. In any case, questions should be posed so that student participation is consistently reinforced and that children are encouraged to think and take some intellectual risks.

Probing Questions

When students answer questions, asking follow-up questions, or probes, is usually, but not always, appropriate. Asking students to clarify their responses, provide defenses or explanations, or extend their answers reinforces their participation but also reveals much about how students derive specific answers. Often, the reasoning leading up to the response is far more effectual in assessing student learning than is a tally of correct and incorrect responses.

Effective teachers also use questions that do not have "right or wrong" answers. These types of questions are particularly important in certain areas of the curriculum such as social studies and literature. Having students entertain questions that are beyond their reasoning is also appropriate when the context is supportive. Asking students to predict the results of a demonstration is an example of questioning that sets the stage for learning. For example, a teacher may ask what will happen when two apparently identical rubber balls are dropped on the floor. Most students predict that they will both bounce the same. This is a logical, and usually accurate, prediction. Some students, however, answer a question with a question. They ask whether the two balls look the same or whether they are the same. This type of response is particularly encouraging to the teacher because it demonstrates that children are collecting all of the data possible before making a prediction. This is a premiere concept to be developed: The more data that the student has, the more likely that his or her prediction will be accurate. When the two balls are dropped and they actually respond differently, students have already begun an investigative analysis that is at the heart of every implicit instructional strategy.

Conditions of Effective Questions

Chuska (1995) describes four conditions for effective questioning. First, the stage must be properly set by having a topic in the form of a problem to be solved, an issue to be examined, a decision to be made, or an interest (or need) to be satisfied.

Second, a vantage point must be established. Are questions to reflect the views of the students, or are the questions grounded in previously learned facts? Are the answers to questions to be derived logically from an understanding of previous material, or is creativity and speculation needed? Students must be assisted in understanding the purpose of questions and how personal and group perspectives, prejudices, and biases affect the outcomes of the decision-making process.

Third, Chuska stipulates that ways of thinking must be taught in order to emphasize the differences in summarizing, analyzing, comparing, interpreting, speculating, and so on. Ways of thinking also include activities that help define the cognitive process.

Fourth, Chuska states that effective conditions for questioning must include meaningful reasons for thinking. Students must understand the meaning of the question and the potential for using the answer if they are to be motivated and encouraged to spend time and effort in answering questions.

Improving Questioning Effectiveness

Gaul and Rhody (1986) provide several suggestions to teachers for improving questioning effectiveness:

1. Ask questions frequently, but be careful not to ask them in such a way as to constrict students' thinking or to make them anxious. Also, be aware that extensive question-asking may become less necessary as students develop their own strategies for learning and reviewing.
2. Ask students questions before, during, and after instruction. Questions before instruction should be designed to get students to think about what they already know so that they can better assimilate new curriculum content. Questions during instruction should be used to keep students involved and provide a check on whether they are comprehending. And questions after instruction—in the form of seatwork, homework, review sessions, and practice quizzes—provide opportunities for continued practice and application of new information and skills.
3. During instruction, ask students questions about the facts, ideas, and thought processes that you think are particularly important. Students are likely to remember these facts, ideas, and processes better if you do so.

4. Ask lower-cognitive questions for your curriculum objectives at that level. Also, ask higher-cognitive questions if thinking skills are an objective of your curriculum. It is difficult to imagine how students will learn to think unless they have repeated opportunities to respond to higher-cognitive questions. Keep in mind that lower performing students may have more difficulty dealing with these questions than will high-performing students. (pp. 41–42)

Simply asking a good question—especially a good higher-cognitive question—does not guarantee a good student response. Therefore, use the following techniques:

◆ Provide controlled practice and remind students to listen in order to maintain a high level of on-task behavior.
◆ Phrase questions clearly.
◆ Pause at least three seconds after asking a question and after a student response.
◆ Give positive feedback.
◆ Ask probing questions.

Purposes of Questions

The versatility and utility of questions have made them a favorite teacher practice. Ross (1860) concluded a century ago that questions served two primary purposes: (1) Questions could be used by teachers to determine what children know, and (2) questions could provide children with an opportunity to apply their knowledge. A more modern examination by Clegg (1987) provides a plethora of historical reasons for why teachers ask questions. Teachers use questions to challenge students, to seek out alternate solutions, to pose problems, to review, to check on learning effectiveness, to diagnose, and to probe student thought processes.

In general, teachers use questions to promote students' discussion of what and how they are thinking. Effective teachers, however, understand that questions not only reveal the cognitive processes of students but also instigate students' thinking during learning activities. Ancient teaching methods exemplified by K'ung Fu-tse and Socrates, discussed earlier, capitalized on the power of the question to illuminate and to instigate student thinking.

Borich (1996) identified numerous reasons for asking questions:

◆ To arouse interest and curiosity
◆ To stimulate learners to ask questions
◆ To focus attention on an issue
◆ To diagnose specific learning difficulties
◆ To encourage reflection and self-evaluation
◆ To promote thought and the understanding of ideas
◆ To review content already learned
◆ To help recall specific information

♦ To reinforce recently learned material
♦ To manage or remind students of a procedure
♦ To teach through student answers
♦ To probe deeper after an answer is given
♦ To redirect or structure the flow of ideas
♦ To allow expressions of feelings (pp. 343–344)

Wilen (1991) also provides the following detailed listing of the purposes of teachers' questions:

♦ Stimulate student participation
♦ Conduct a review of previously learned material
♦ Stimulate discussion
♦ Involve students in creative thinking
♦ Diagnose student abilities
♦ Assess student progress
♦ Determine the extent to which objectives have been achieved
♦ Arouse student interest
♦ Control student behavior
♦ Personalize subject matter
♦ Support student contributions in class (p. 8)

A bewildering array of claims exists for the utility of questions. In general, Wilen's and Borich's lists can be divided into two classifications: (1) questions that promote student accountability, and (2) questions that stimulate learning. Students are held accountable when questions are asked, and the teacher can test the assumption that appropriate responses have been developed during the class session or in previous sessions. In short, the student should be able to answer the questions because of the extensive opportunity provided by the teacher.

Questions to stimulate learning, however, may require the student to assemble information in a new way or to attempt to resolve a problem without complete information. In stimulating learning, teachers ask students to take risks and to push beyond their comfort level of the familiar and the known. Because of the very real risk to students of answering incorrectly or providing an answer that is unpopular or novel, the teacher must provide a great deal of support. Thus, one of the most important purposes of questions is to build student confidence in their abilities and to develop coping skills for errors, oversights, and inaccuracies that occur during learning.

What can be achieved when asking a question? Chuska (1995) provides several basic results of effective questioning that include the following:

♦ Increased curiosity and interest
♦ Skill in developing and providing explanations
♦ Ability to explore dilemmas or problems in detail
♦ Intuitive reasoning that assists in examining discrepancies between new information and what is known or believed
♦ Increased capacity to deal with difficult or ambiguous information (pp. 10–11)

In implementing questioning strategies and in asking individual questions, effective teachers are always guided by purpose. Usually, teachers have many purposes for a single question. Sometimes, questions are developed for no other reason than to involve students who do not feel included. At other times, a difficult question is posed for the purpose of making the quick-witted child more reflective. In all cases, however, the purpose of the question entails an examination of the needs of the students who will be asked to provide answers.

Matching Students to Questions

Do teachers ask questions and then look for an appropriate respondent, or do they think of the students and then create a question? It seems that teachers do both. There is an array of student characteristics from which questions could be targeted. Matching questions to student willingness to participate and to student ability provides a solid foundation of consideration.

Why Do Children Not Respond?

Unfortunately, many children are hesitant to answer questions. Chuska (1995) provides a list of reasons why students are reluctant to answer questions:

◆ The student is afraid to fail.
◆ The student is afraid of ridicule.
◆ The student lacks confidence because of past failures.
◆ The student is unsure of the expected response.
◆ The student is afraid to speak in class.
◆ The student is uninterested in the topic or is apathetic.
◆ The student is unwilling to be labeled a "brain" by other students.
◆ The question is too complex or is unclear.
◆ The question is above the student's level of experience or is intimidating to the student.
◆ The answer is expected too quickly.
◆ The student does not know the answer.
◆ The student finds the answer difficult to express. (pp. 20–21)

Obviously, if teachers were to reverse these situations, more children may be more willing to volunteer to answer questions.

Students who are afraid to fail, are fearful of ridicule, and have amassed a rather dismal record of failure in the past are not likely to participate without encouragement. For these students to become regular participants in discussions, teachers must first alter the environment that has fostered these pessimistic views about participation. Teacher ridicule or student mockery adds to the reluctance of these students. The reasoning is clear and simple: "If the teacher or class laughs at any person, they will laugh at me." Therefore, the teacher must endeavor to change the climate surrounding student experiences with questions.

How Can Teachers Express Appreciation?

Successful teachers acknowledge responses with appreciation. If the answer is wrong, an acknowledgment of appreciation is helpful. Additionally, the teacher may wish to rephrase the question or follow up the student response with a probe. For example, to the student who answers the question, "How does food get into the stomach?" with "Gravity pulls it down," the teacher may respond, "That is very good reasoning since gravity pulls on everything on the earth's surface." Here, the teacher explains the reasoning of the response and accepts it as a natural, but incorrect, interpretation. The teacher may wish to rephrase the question. "Let me ask the question differently. If I were to hang upside down, would my food go to my stomach?" Another response to the student may be, "OK, but when I have water in my mouth, it just doesn't slide down to my stomach. What do I have to do to get it there?" Most children could now easily follow a line of leading questions:

STUDENT: You have to swallow for the water to go down.
TEACHER: Yes, can you describe what happens when you swallow?
STUDENT: A hole opens for the water to go down.
TEACHER: You're right there! But think about the tongue. When you swallow, what does the tongue do? (pause) Try swallowing and then answer.
STUDENT: My tongue goes back in my mouth.
TEACHER: Everyone try to swallow without closing your mouth and keeping your tongue still. (Children attempt, most laugh and make faces.)
TEACHER: Do you think the tongue is tied into other parts of your body that affects the way you swallow?

With this type of encouragement and support, most children will set aside a natural reluctance and join in class questioning voluntarily.

How Can Teachers Make Questions Meaningful?

Students who are bored, overchallenged, or underprepared also have a tendency not to volunteer or participate. It can be difficult for a teacher to overcome a lack of participation if the lesson is dull, lacking in relevance, or too abstract for students. Successful teachers continually attempt to make all lessons meaningful to children in ways that animate student thinking. When students do not participate voluntarily, teachers must begin to consider creating questions for particular student needs. Asking questions that apply to a particular student's interests or academic strengths is almost always an appropriate way to entice children into participation. Likewise, wording questions so that the chance of being "wrong" is minimized gives assistance to the slower child. Encouragement can come in the form of adding several possible answers to the question. "When we have lightning, is it usually windy or calm, clear or cloudy, getting warmer or getting cooler?" is an example of a question that provides support for the student who may need help in composing an answer. Compare that strategy with asking the child, "What are the atmospheric conditions that accompany lightning?"

FIGURE 9.2 Checklist for evaluating the quality of student experiences.

From *Making Connections: Teaching and the Human Brain* (p. 157) by R. N. Caine and G. Caine, 1991, Reston, VA: Association for Supervision and Curriculum Development.

- Are students involved and challenged?
- Is there clear evidence of student creativity and enjoyment? Are students dealing appropriately with dissonance?
- Are students being exposed to content in many ways that link content to life?
- Are students' life themes and metaphors being engaged?
- Are there "hooks" that tie the content together in a big picture that itself can make sense to students?
- Is there some sort of continuity, such as through projects and ongoing stories, so that content is tied together and retains interest over time?
- Is there any sign of continuing motivation or student interest that expresses itself above and beyond the dictates of the class?
- Is the physical context being used optimally?
- What do the setting, decorations, architecture, layout, music, and other features of the context actually "say" to students?
- What sort of group atmosphere is emerging?
- Are there any signs of positive collaboration, and do they continue after the lesson and after school?
- Do students have opportunities to reorganize content in creative and personally relevant ways?
- Are there opportunities to reflect in an open-ended way on what does and does not make sense?
- Are students given the opportunity to apply the material in different contexts?
- Do students consciously and deliberately examine their performances in those different contexts and begin to appreciate their own strengths and weaknesses?

Matching questions to students requires that teachers continually evaluate the quality of the student experiences. Figure 9.2 provides a reflective checklist for assessing the lesson and its effects on students. When children need a special challenge or need immediate success, careful targeting of questions can usually realize the desired effect.

Types of Questions

Not all questions have the same purpose or the same effect. Therefore, analysts who study questions and questioning have developed a number of strategies for classifying questions. Raths et al.'s "thinking keywords" (Figure 5.4) and Bloom's taxonomy of cognitive objectives (Figure 5.5) function well as ways of classifying questions. Both provide a basic structure for creating and analyzing questions so that a variety of questions is offered during lessons and the purpose of questions is more carefully understood by the teacher.

Figure 9.3 provides a model for creating questions using Bloom's taxonomy and provides examples of questions that may be asked in an elementary school. Instruction employing implicit strategies uses questions that are predominantly in the analy-

Question Type	Student Activity	Examples
Knowledge	Recalling facts or observations	1. Who? (is the main character) 2. What? (was the problem in the story) 3. Where? (did the accident occur) 4. When? (was the law passed) 5. Why? [if cause is given] (did it happen) 6. Define (the word *motivation*).
Comprehension	Giving descriptions Stating main ideas Comparing	1. Describe (what happened in our experiment). 2. What is the main idea (of this paragraph)? 3. How are (these two stories) alike?
Application	Solving problems that have a single correct answer using prescribed methods	1. Using the scales, how many paper clips does it take to equal a thimble? 2. Using the key, which seeds are monocotyl and which are bicotyl? 3. What city is nearest the mouth of the Amazon River?
Analysis	Making inferences. Finding evidence to support generalizations	1. Why? (was Alexander having a bad day) 2. Given the information in the story, what options did Alice have when confronting the Queen?
Synthesis	Solving problems Making predictions Producing originals	1. What solution can you derive for Alexander's dilemma? 2. How can we improve our routines for taking care of materials? 3. How can we improve (our experiment) communication?
Evaluation	Giving opinions about issues Judging the validity of ideas Judging the merit of problem solution Judging the quality of art and other products	1. Given that information, what was the character's best choice? 2. Do you believe that she acted properly? 3. Do you think that drivers should be required to wear seatbelts? 4. What is your opinion?

FIGURE 9.3   Questioning strategies based on Bloom's taxonomy.

Adapted from *Taxonomy of Educational Objectives* by Benjamin Bloom, 1956, New York: David McKay.

sis, synthesis, and evaluation categories. Instruction employing explicit strategies uses questions that predominantly come from the recall, comprehension, and application areas. Again, both instructional strategies should employ questions from all categories.

Using a taxonomy to assist in the planning and the development of questions and questioning skills helps assure that a broad range of student cognitive skills are used during each lesson. However, a number of other classifications provide

Function	Definition (Verbs)
1. Observing	Present an object such as a flower. Ask: • What does it smell like? • How is this smell different from the classroom? • What do you see? • How would you describe its shape? Its color?
2. Classifying	Present a group of objects such as a chess set. Ask: • How can you group these objects into groups? Into three groups? • How many ways can you group the chess pieces into two groups?
3. Comparing	Present two objects or events. Ask: • How are these two things alike? Different? • Which event is scarier? Why?
4. Summarizing	Read a story, listen to a presentation, or conduct an experiment. Ask: • What parts did you like best? • What is a good title for this summary? • How you would describe this story in three sentences?
5. Interpreting	Present a story or event. Ask: • What does the story mean? • Why did the character do that? • What could have happened but didn't?
6. Collecting and organizing data	Present a problem or task. Ask: • What information do we need? • How will we get it? • How can we organize it so that we can understand what it means? • How will we make sense of the numbers?

FIGURE 9.4   Twelve thinking operations.

broad support in understanding the many types of questions available for use in the classroom. Figure 9.4 provides a similar construction using the "thinking keywords."

Other strategies can be substituted for questions. This is particularly important when questions seem to multiply out of control or when children feel as if the lesson has turned into a mild form of interrogation. Dillon (1979) defines six alternatives to questions:

Function	Definition (Verbs)
7. **Imagining**	Teach a lesson on gravity. Ask: • What if gravity only pulled on living things? • What if gravity pulled heavier on small things than on big things? • What would happen if gravity went away during the night?
8. **Looking for assumptions**	Have students make a prediction about some event such as the teacher giving a pop test on today's math. Ask: • What are the grades going to be? Why? • What makes you think they will occur that way? • Do you know for sure? • What things could change so that your prediction is wrong?
9. **Criticizing**	Have children tell what their favorite subject in school is. Ask: • Why do you like it? • What could be done so you would like it more? • What could happen to make you dislike it? • How well do you learn in the subject? • What causes you to learn this way?
10. **Hypothesizing**	Perform a demonstration of a chemical reaction such as mixing baking soda and vinegar. Ask: • What would happen if I mix the two things again? • What if I added more vinegar to the solution? More baking soda? • What would happen if I put them in a corked bottle?
11. **Applying facts and principles in new situations**	Show children three different-sized containers after studying volume. Ask: • How can I found out which is larger? • Is there more than one way to compare the containers?
12. **Decision making**	Read a description of a playground incident. Ask: • What should happen to the students? • What could have been done to prevent the problem? • What other solutions could the students have used?

Adapted from *Teaching for Thinking: Theory and Application* by L. E. Raths, S. Wasserman, A. Jonas, and A. M. Rothstein, 1967, Upper Saddle River, NJ: Merrill/Prentice Hall.

- ◆ Declarative statements
- ◆ Declarative restatements
- ◆ Indirect questions
- ◆ Imperatives
- ◆ Student questions
- ◆ Deliberate silence

By using these alternatives interspersed with a variety of questions, student satiation can be avoided, and the questioning session made more cordial.

Creating and Asking Questions

Dillon (1988) presents a holistic view of question use by demonstrating that the foundation of any questioning sequence initiates with the purpose of the lesson and lesson component. The pedagogical purposes of any lesson contain not only the desired outcome (generally stated in the objective) but also the meaningfulness of the lesson (particularly as it relates to students). This view corresponds well to the planning strategies outlined earlier in this text.

Dillon emphasizes that the pedagogical purposes should not just influence the design of the lesson but should also guide each event in the lesson's implementation. Dillon states, "The teacher faces a hundred circumstances. These conspire with his hundred purposes. You will have to connect purposes and circumstances in order to choose the appropriate questioning strategy" (p. 56).

Such circumstances include an instantaneous assessment of the learner, the content under examination, the activities in which students are currently engaged, the specific milieu or context, the most recent results of the lesson, and the prognosis for future change. By combining purpose and circumstances, teachers' thinking about the appropriate questioning behavior is shaped and determined.

Teachers' questioning behavior contains 10 elements and forms both a development strategy for questioning sequences and an assessment tool for examining previously used strategies. Dillon suggests that the teacher consider the *usage* of the questioning strategy. Is a question appropriate here? Should a comment be made instead? Is this a time to summarize or to solicit new information? Additionally, the teacher must consider the *quantity* of questions asked. Are there enough questions to permit everyone to participate? Are there too many questions so that the feeling of interrogation is fostered? Are the questions and periods of summary appropriately matched?

The *kinds* of questions asked must also be considered. What is the mix between high-level and low-level questions? Should a probe be used, or should a new question be phrased? Should this question ask for opinion or fact? The *topics* of questions pose an additional area of planning for the use of questions. What should the question be about? Should the question introduce an idea for reaction, or should it solicit ideas from students? The *form* of a question determines choices of words, their order, and sequence. Does the question provide a choice of answers, or does it invite speculation? Does the question require prior understanding, or does it stimulate new thinking about previously presented information? The *addressee* is the person who receives the question. Should the question be framed for a variety of learners? Should the question be targeted to just a few? Should the question be developed for a specific child?

When questions are asked, *timing* is an important element in determining success for both the teacher and the learner. Is wait time provided? Are the questions sequenced so that the student has had an opportunity to learn the material requested by the question? The teacher's *manner* of asking questions also affects the outcome. Is the question posed in a supportive manner? Is the diction and volume appropriate for clarity? Questions also carry with them certain *presumptions* about both the answer and the student's knowledge. Is someone selected to answer a question because the teacher thinks that the student will provide a correct answer? Is someone selected because he or she is creative? Is a provocative question used because the students are thought to be lacking in attentiveness? *Purpose* composes the last issue suggested by Dillon. Purpose establishes the reasons for each question at any point in the lesson. Is a question posed to broaden the discussion? Is a question asked to bring new facts into the discussion? Is a question posed to force students to rethink their conclusions thus far?

At first, the number of variables to consider in selecting and developing questions may appear overwhelming. Many of these considerations occur naturally to most individuals as they frame questions in nonteaching situations. However, deliberate and thoughtful development of questions that respond to these issues increases the effectiveness of teacher questions.

Promoting Student Attention

Even the best question is ineffectual if it falls on deaf ears. Promoting student attention and participation during questioning periods is essential. Student attention and participation are mainly skills taught by teachers through careful use of questioning and appropriate support when questions are asked.

Wait Time

Rowe (1986a, 1986b) advocated the use of wait time to foster positive conditions during questioning that support and encourage children. As mentioned earlier, *wait time* is the time that a teacher provides between asking a question and soliciting an answer. Rowe described five teacher behaviors that interfere with the effective use of wait time and that minimize student participation.

- The teacher fails to think about the content of the question, the intent of the question, and the form and implementation of the question.
- The teacher mimics student responses by repeating the students' words.
- The teacher responds with "Yes," "But," and "Though" constructions that may imply a rejection of student responses.
- The teacher responds with "Isn't it?" and "Right" implying that students are being judged for compliance.
- The teacher responds with "Don't you think that. . . . ?"

Benefits of Wait Time

If these pitfalls are avoided and wait time is used effectively, several major benefits can be derived (Rowe, 1986a, 1986b):

- The length of student responses increases between 300 and 700 percent.
- Students are more likely to support inference statements by use of evidence and logic.
- Students do more speculating about possible alternative explanations.
- Student-initiated questions increase.
- Students' failure to answer questions decreases.
- Disciplinary moves decrease.
- Student-student exchanges increase as well as cooperation.
- The variety and number of students participating increase.
- Students gain confidence in their ability to construct explanations.
- Achievement on written measures improves.

Responses to Answers

When children respond to questions, teachers must display appropriate attending behaviors. MacDonald (1991) suggests eye contact, leaning, contemplating, and encouraging as helpful strategies for conveying teacher attentiveness. Eye contact requires looking directly into the speaker's eyes while avoiding the appearance of staring. The teacher should attempt to demonstrate undivided attention yet avoid intimidating the student. Leaning toward the speaker is encouraging and demonstrates not only attentiveness, but also a positive reception of the speaker's comments. Leaning away or turning the body at an angle to the speaker represents disinterest. Contemplating—actions that convey that the teacher is interested in, and attentive to, student comments—can involve simple encouraging gestures such as nodding the head up and down, touching the chin, and facial expressions. Encouraging—actions that entice students to continue their comments—can include verbal comments designed to facilitate additional comments from the speaker. "Tell me more," "That's interesting," or "What happened then?" all encourage the speaker to continue and to illustrate comments.

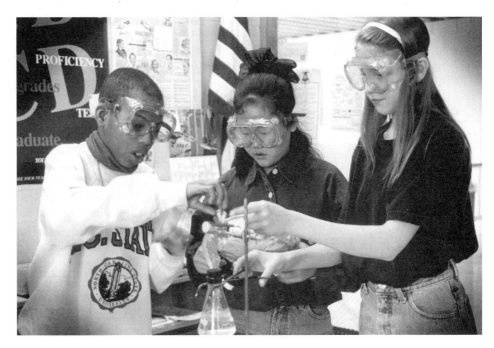

Students test hypotheses to generalize understanding.

Teaching Student-Structured Concepts

Questioning strategies are fundamental to most instructional methods in the implicit instruction family. By careful questioning, situations and information can be presented so that the student is compelled to act on the material cognitively to create order and to have experiences "make sense." In short, students construct concepts to provide relationships, order, and meaning to information.

Students Construct Knowledge and Understanding

There is no fine line between student-structured and teacher-structured concepts. In one point of view, often referred to as the *radical constructivist approach,* all knowledge is constructed by students, regardless of the type of instruction presented. By this view, any learner must construct an understanding of information, even if the material is carefully sequenced and presented. From a literal point of view, there is little doubt that the physiological processes and changes that permit memory and enhanced reasoning are totally independent of instruction and lie within, although not necessarily under the control of, the individual. However, constructing the neural network of proteins and acids necessary to remember one's telephone number is generally not what is meant by the constructivist view.

Constructivism is not a tightly defined school of thought but rather a loose confederation of beliefs about the purpose, process, and outcomes that should direct the work of the schools. Brooks and Brooks (1993) view constructivism as defining knowledge as "temporary, developmental, socially and culturally mediated, and thus, non-objective" (p. vii). They view learning within this context as a self-regulated process of resolving inner cognitive conflict.

Less radical views about inquiry exist in various taxonomies and dichotomies previously presented. These views acknowledge various forms and purposes of knowledge and, therefore, claim that there are various forms and purposes in teaching. This tradition describes a gradation of knowledge from totally trivial fragments of information available for recall (for example, former President Richard Nixon's middle name) ranging to broad overarching concepts (for example, equality under the law). The model on teacher decision-making presented earlier in the text represents a moderate constructivist view.

Matching Purpose and Method

Each type of knowledge has a different intent and use; therefore, instructional methods must vary to support the specific purpose of learning. This point of view recognizes that even the most trivial pieces of information can be critical when a learner is faced with certain circumstances and contexts. This broad conceptualization of knowledge supports the use of explicit instruction strategies as one of many viable strategies and maintains the value in fragments of information, such as a telephone number, not because of any contribution to understanding, but in its utility. However, not all information is trivial and limited to utility in specific circumstances.

Some information, such as the correct procedures for preparing an airplane for landing, has critical importance. Also, many learning objectives resulting from explicit instruction are considered essential for higher-level inquiry skills. In Vignettes 1 and 2 in this chapter, certain basic evidence or factual fragments were necessary to frame the discussion. However, not all information can be framed and structured in meaningful way. Instead, students must combine values, evidence, theory, skill, and imagination into increasingly complex cognitive structures. For example, learning how to participate in a democratic society demands the use of implicit strategies where the learner takes charge of understanding. Following are some questions that require intense examination using implicit instructional strategies:

- Does a business have a social obligation to communities, or is the purpose of a business to produce profit for owners?
- Can you steal (lie or cheat) for a good purpose? What "good purposes" (if any) can be supported by lying, cheating, and stealing?
- If your friend makes a mistake, do you protect him, or do you turn him in to face the consequences?
- If you only tell half of the facts about an event, you can get a reward. If you tell all of the facts, you get into trouble. Are you lying if you don't tell everything?

Although these questions rely heavily on value assertions of the individual, these values can often be in conflict or even inappropriate for certain contexts. Poorly structured problems abound even when values are not the central issue:

♦ How can you do your homework with the least time and effort and still learn the material?
♦ How do you arrange your furniture so your room is most comfortable and easiest to clean?
♦ Which story do you publish on the front page of the school newspaper?
♦ How will you make your story character interesting to readers?
♦ How can you express yourself so that everyone will understand?

These types of questions for students are representative of mission statements that advocate the school's role in helping students to become good citizens. To wit, students should contribute successfully to society while maintaining a healthy and happy independence in a democratic community. Teachers cannot possibly construct knowledge so that these questions are answered effectively for all children. Each individual must develop this knowledge by using his or her beliefs and values to provide significance.

Structure of Knowledge

There are any numbers of degrees on a continuum scale where knowledge is classified as either poorly structured or highly structured (see Chapter 8). Some questions lend themselves well to *either* explicit or implicit instruction because the knowledge in the study area is represented by a combination of both poorly and highly structured knowledge, for example:

♦ What are the characteristics of successful people?
♦ Why is the Bill of Rights so important to Americans?
♦ Why do the characters in a particular story behave as they do?
♦ What is the meaning of this poem? What does it mean to you?
♦ Why do some plants grow larger than others even when they are the same type?
♦ Why do we need police officers? What rights can police officers take away? What rights must they honor?
♦ How does a plant make food?
♦ Why does a bottle of soft drink fizz? (Remember, it doesn't fizz all the time!)
♦ What is good nutrition?

Any question can be a rote question if the teacher does not establish an appropriate environment. If the position of the teacher is made known beforehand, what appears as an earnest attempt to elicit a student's thoughtful response may be nothing more than a call for a restatement of the teacher's view. If the teacher has presented a structured lesson on homework completion that includes a three-step plan for completing homework successfully, the question "How do you do your homework most efficiently?" may be only a request for reciting the teacher's opinion. Teachers must be careful to avoid confusing attempts to foster student construction of concepts with attempts to test recall.

Meaning of Implicit Instruction

Implicit instruction is a constellation of loosely defined teaching strategies that focus on the student's construction of understanding rather than subject matter content as the central factor in structuring the lesson. In the previous chapter, a comparison of explicit instruction and implicit strategies was provided. Explicit instruction was presented as representing strategies for implementing lessons in which the teacher is responsible for the primary structuring of the lesson concepts. Implicit instruction, on the other hand, was presented as representing strategies in which students are responsible for the primary structuring of the lesson concepts.

Implicit instruction relies heavily on the active engagement of the learner to develop schema of understanding rather than to comprehend teacher-developed models and representations (see Figure 8.2). Implicit instruction is considered student-structured because of this central reliance on students' use of critical thinking and reasoning skills to engage the material actively. This strategy has a number of advantages but also has several distinct drawbacks.

When students are put in situations where understanding is created and used productively in a way that mirrors life's challenges, their learning is almost always more meaningful. Further, the development of independent thought is a primary function of the school's stated mission. Therefore, when students construct and guide the major concepts of lessons, there is strong potential for making significant contributions to the educational development of the child. However, just as in explicit instruction, implicit instructional strategies are often poorly used and implemented in an incomplete, piecemeal fashion. The result is unnecessary confusion and lost effort.

Confusion

Some confusion is fundamental to the early stages of most implicit strategies where early hypotheses are tested unsuccessfully. From this confusion comes more appropriate ideas, models, and hypotheses that more accurately represent the phenomenon under study. However, if basic factual knowledge is simply missing, students may become bogged down in acquiring information by fragmented methods that waste their time and energy. Even when students know where to get background information, the number of requests may exceed resources. In these cases, explicit instruction is a simple, straightforward way to develop prerequisite knowledge for more difficult lessons. Using implicit instructional strategies in these cases is generally not indicated.

Self-Reliance

Having students acquire basic facts on their own is a valued skill to be developed and practiced. However, the balance between the methods is critical. If students spend valuable time looking up information independently that could be provided to them through explicit instruction, they have less time for the critical aspects of implicit instruction, specifically the use of analytical and synthetic reasoning.

Constructivism

Before describing several implicit instructional strategies, it is worth examining the radical constructivist view one more time in order to highlight the considerable differences in the end purposes of explicit and implicit instruction. Brooks and Brooks (1993) provide a chart juxtaposing two views of school environments from a radical constructivist viewpoint(Figure 9.5).

Figure 9.5 illustrates the dichotomous thinking that often occurs when explicit and implicit teaching strategies are considered mutually exclusive activities. Forcing dichotomous choices on teachers in the classroom almost always leads to misleading

Traditional Classrooms	Constructivist Classrooms
Curriculum is presented part to whole, with emphasis on basic skills.	Curriculum is presented whole to part with emphasis on big concepts.
Strict adherence to fixed curriculum is highly valued.	Pursuit of student questions is highly valued.
Curricular activities rely heavily on textbooks and workbooks.	Curricular activities rely heavily on primary sources of data and manipulative materials.
Students are viewed as "blank slates" onto which information is etched by the teacher.	Students are viewed as thinkers with emerging theories about the world.
Teachers generally behave in a didactic manner, disseminating information to students.	Teachers generally behave in an interactive manner, mediating the environment for students.
Teachers seek the correct answer to validate students.	Teachers seek the students' points of view in order to understand students' present conceptions for use in subsequent lessons.
Assessment of student learning is viewed as separate from teaching and occurs almost entirely through testing.	Assessment of student learning is interwoven with teaching and occurs through teacher observations of students at work and through student exhibitions and portfolios.
Students primarily work alone.	Students primarily work In groups.

FIGURE 9.5   A look at school environments.

Reprinted by permission from *In Search of Understanding: The Case for Constructivist Classrooms* (p. 17) by G. B. Brooks and M. G. Brooks, 1993, Alexandria, VA: Association for Supervision and Curriculum Development.

or oversimplified ideas as opposed to the holistic inclusive thinking of the successful teacher. For example, according to Brooks and Brooks, traditional classrooms value strict adherence to a fixed curriculum in environments and students are viewed as having no prior learning, experiences, or viewpoints. There are very few, if any, elementary classrooms in which teachers do not take wide latitude in the interpretation of the curriculum. In fact, there are few curriculum guides written to the level of specificity that do not require copious interpretation from the teacher to realize any segment of the curriculum. A basic tenet of most classrooms is that students have a past and have knowledge that supports and scaffolds future learning; bringing that learning into memory is fundamental to good instruction. This is a fundamental proposition of direct instruction.

The view of constructivist classrooms in Figure 9.5 may also be misleading simply by the severity of the extreme positions posed. For example, the first tenet states that curriculum in the constructivist classroom is presented whole and then pared down to smaller components with an emphasis on big concepts. The difficulty with that view is quite obvious when contemplating the sum total of knowledge to be conveyed. What curriculum for any grade level can be presented whole without overwhelming learners with complexity? However, it is accurate that explicit instruction presents a lesson in sequential parts leading to a whole whereas implicit instruction starts with a much larger context. Additionally, almost all teachers value student interest and questioning even though Figure 9.5 indicates that this value is only contained in constructivist classrooms.

Combining Traditional and Constructivist Views

Whether various forms of classrooms are represented accurately or logically, Figure 9.5 demonstrates the dangers and misunderstanding that can occur if a curriculum is viewed from either endpoint of the continuum. Either extreme view will probably diminish students' success in the classroom. In this particular case, Brooks and Brooks (1993) go on to provide excellent descriptions of inquiry methodology and its beneficial effects. They also describe the following basic guiding principles of constructivism:

◆ Posing problems of emerging relevance to students
◆ Structuring learning around primary concepts
◆ Seeking and valuing students' views
◆ Adapting curriculum to address students' suppositions
◆ Assessing students' learning in the context of teaching

Although these propositions may represent constructivist philosophy, they represent many other teaching theories including many from the explicit instruction family. Hopefully, all teachers value these strategies. In implicit or constructivist strategies, these principles form the core values of the instructional strategy that supersedes serialized instruction, demonstration, skill development, and mastery that characterize explicit instruction. In reading about various forms of inquiry, successful teachers must always keep in mind the objective of these approaches: learning experiences that engage learners in developing understanding while fostering independence, critical perspectives, and experimental intellects.

Variants of Implicit Instruction

Although questioning forms the core of most implicit instruction strategies, implicit instruction differs significantly from direct instruction in important ways. First, implicit instruction utilizes areas of knowledge that are usually complex and multidimensional. Second, it emphasizes the individual's construction of understanding. Third, skill in inquiry and decision making usually takes precedence over content. Figure 9.6 describes three variants: discussions, inquiry, and investigations.

Discussions

Hyman (1987) defines a discussion as "an interactive endeavor with a set of defining elements or characteristics that distinguishes it from other teaching methods" (p.

Variant	Description	Primary Purpose
Discussions	Students exchange opinions, ideas, interpretations, reasoned explanations, and conclusions.	Gain insight into the perspectives of others, particularly about value-driven concepts and entities
Inquiry	Students develop hypotheses and defend or refute them by assembling and examining factual evidence from secondary sources (books, video, archives, interviews with experts, and so on).	Assemble information to support or refute a potential solution to a problem; also can be used to discover basic factual information in lieu of an explicit instructional strategy.
Investigation	Students experiment and manipulate the environment in order to develop, test, and evaluate hypotheses (students discover the needed information directly).	To gain experience with the creation and discovery of knowledge; to gain understanding about how knowledge is created; also to develop meta-cognitional skill and personal control over learning strategies

FIGURE 9.6 Three variants of implicit instruction.

136). According to Hyman, students participate in a social activity such as a discussion to examine (1) the facts of a situation, (2) the consequences and meaning of the facts, and (3) alternative perceptions of the situation. Effective discussions are cooperative, rational, purposeful, systematic, and creative. As may be expected, effective discussions are not easily developed and implemented and require considerable teacher skill.

Basic Phases of Discussions   Hyman does provide an outline of the basic phases of a discussion (Figure 9.7).

According to Hyman, in the beginning phase of a discussion, the topic is introduced, and the teacher (or class member) sets the limits for the discussion by clarifying the problem and its major components. This preliminary exploration establishes the intent of the discussion and provides students with the general information necessary to engage the problem thoughtfully. The group must then establish the procedure to be used. Will the group break into smaller groups and report to the total group after a specified period of time? Will the group simply answer questions provided by the teacher, or will students pose questions and create counterproposals? The exact procedure used varies with the group and the nature of the discussion. If many students want to talk, small discussion groups with their own moderator selected from their peers should be formed. If the problem is particularly difficult or if the group is tentative in its understanding of the facts, a teacher-led discussion provides more structure while still permitting free exploration. As the first phase of a discussion ends, the basic or primary assertions to be examined and debated are clearly established and put forward for consideration.

In the middle stage of the discussion, learners examine, modify, and restate initial assertions. Primarily, students provide perspectives, facts, or logical arguments either to support their point of view, to show shortcomings in a particular view, or to

FIGURE 9.7   General structure of all discussions.

Reprinted by permission from "Discussion Strategies and Tactics" by R. T. Hyman. In W. W. Wilen (Ed.), *Questions, Questioning Techniques, and Effective Teaching* (p. 137), 1987, Washington, DC: National Educational Association.

Beginning Phase
- Introducing and clarifying the question for discussion
- Setting procedure
- Making initial assertions on the topic

Middle Phase
- Examining the assertions made
- Using a variety of strategies to develop major ideas or a pro/con analysis

End Phase
- Drawing conclusions
- Recapitulating
- Launching new activities

propose alternatives to the points of view under consideration. This middle stage is an exploration of facts and opinions, and a preliminary examination of potential resolutions or hypotheses is conducted.

The final stage of a discussion involves a consideration of various potential consensual resolutions. The basic facts are reviewed, and the various approaches are summarized and critiqued. This stage should provide either alternatives to the original assertions or reasonable arguments for retaining those assertions.

Common Difficulties and Solutions.   MacDonald (1991) points out five common problems involved in question-and-answer periods or discussion: nonparticipation, overstimulation, conformity, teacher influence, and controversial topics. Figure 9.8 provides a description and potential remedies for each common difficulty. Every discussion, regardless of the skill of the teacher, is subject to participation problems. Teachers should involve all students by selecting topics carefully and by encouraging students when they participate. Some students may need encouragement over many class discussions before they feel comfortable. On the other hand, some students are very stimulated by class discussions and may tend to participate to the exclusion of others. These students should not be discouraged from participating, but they also should not be allowed to dominate the discussion. Breaking the class into groups is a simple strategy that permits a higher level of participation when students are particularly motivated. The reticent student and the stimulated student may be negatively affected when teachers "telegraph" the direction of the discussion. The teacher must always take special care to show respect for all participants and not to dictate the tone or direction of a discussion.

Discussions are used to stimulate students to interact with a topic from diverse points of view using higher cognitive skills (Good & Brophy, 1994). Although not necessary, discussions are usually easier to instigate and maintain if there is an initial question that presents a problem to students who do not have an immediate answer. Discussions may initiate from statements or demonstrations that pose unexpected results that are not easily explained using the students' current understandings. Consider the advantages and disadvantages of the following discussion topics:

1. The forest police arrest Goldilocks and the three bears in the woods. They are brought to you since you are the forest judge. Who has committed crimes? How will you deal with them? *(problem solving)*
2. We saw in the film that the Bill of Rights gives you free speech, but that doesn't mean you can say just anything. What are the limits to free speech? *(debriefing)*
3. There was very real talk about making George Washington a king. Instead, the nation created a Constitution and elected him president. How would the United States be different if he had been appointed king? *(predicting)*
4. The school cafeteria is concerned that students throw away too much food at lunchtime. The manager decides to fix only things that students like to eat. What will school lunches be like? If you have to make a choice between serving healthy food that goes uneaten or serving junk food that is eaten, what would you do if you were the manager? *(policy)*

Problem	Description	Remedies
1. Nonparticipation	Students fail to volunteer. When requested to contribute, students are hesitant or do not respond. Student gives a brief answer without details.	Provide encouragement to all participants. Call on nonvolunteers at random. Design questions for specific nonparticipants.
2. Overstimulation	Students shout out or speak at the same time. Certain students contribute continuously or monopolize the discussion.	Call on nonvolunteers. Break into small groups for discussion of the specific idea. Conduct a brainstorming session to collect a large number of responses quickly.
3. Conformity	Student contributions do not vary, are similar, and converge early on a single perspective.	Present stimulating questions that pose extreme or ridiculous answers. Encourage responses that are divergent or contain risks. Discuss with children the need for creative and original thinking.
4. Teacher influence	Teacher provides subtle "hints" as to the correct response. Teacher provides reinforcement to particular views while ignoring or discouraging others.	Be aware of teacher influence. Try not to form an opinion on the discussion. Call on students randomly. Provide encouragement to all students.
5. Controversial topics	Topic is emotionally charged, divisive, or inappropriate for the context of the lesson and class.	Carefully consider the purpose of any topic. Prepare students by acknowledging a wide range of views.

FIGURE 9.8   Problems associated with classroom discussions and strategies for overcoming them.

Summarized from *A Handbook of Basic Skills and Strategies for Beginning Teachers: Facing the Challenge of Teaching in Today's Schools* by Robert E. MacDonald, 1991, New York: Longman.

5. In the book *Amos Fortune, Free Man,* Amos (a slave) is treated well by his owners. Yet, it is very clear that the author thinks slavery is wrong. Amos also thinks it is wrong even though he buys four slaves in his lifetime. What makes slavery wrong? When is buying a slave the right thing to do? *(explaining)*

The preceding topics represent five types of discussions that include problem solving, debriefing, predicting, policy development, and explaining (Hyman, 1987). These are defined as follows:

◆ *Problem solving:* Students must seek answers to a dilemma or problem.
◆ *Debriefing:* Students must reflect on the facts, meaning, and implications of an event or proposition.

- *Predicting:* Students must go beyond data and propose probable consequences when antecedent events are altered.
- *Policy development:* Students must extract from situations the rules or guidelines that can be used in future situations as well as the one being considered.
- *Explaining:* Students must order facts and events into meaningful descriptions that show why an event occurred as it did and what it means to students and to others.

Each of these types of discussion also has a central purpose in which the teacher attempts to promote children's understanding rather than merely having children process information. For example, in question 1, the teacher may be attempting to have students solve a problem, but the major issue involved is how someone who violates the law is made into a heroine in the story. By combining purpose with various cognitive approaches and employing well-timed questions, teachers can enjoy vigorous and profitable discussions among children.

Inquiry

Barell (1991) offers a profound introduction to the study of inquiry:

> There are three questions we should ask ourselves as we work with the environment that invites thoughtfulness: What am I learning about my own thinking? What am I learning about my students' thinking? And what are my students and I learning about the change process in designing this environment? (p. 96)

Like discussion, successful inquiry usually begins with a problem, issue, or experience that creates confusion or dissonance in the child's mind. The student needs to reconstruct his or her understanding in order to accommodate the new information. Unlike discussions, however, inquiry does not depend primarily on the verbal interaction of a social group for data. Although inquiry includes many discussions, it usually entails additional data gathering that requires children to go beyond expressing reason and opinion. Inquiry is a very broad term and means many different things. Certainly, discussions as described in the chapter constitute a form of inquiry. However, for this discussion, the definition of inquiry includes a specific phase in which a hypothesis is formed and students then actively seek out facts and evidence to support (or refute) the hypothesis.

Social Inquiry Model. Joyce and Weil (1986) identified one form of inquiry specifically developed for the social studies curriculum that is equally appropriate in other areas of the elementary school curriculum. The social inquiry model described by Joyce and Weil has six primary phases:

- *Orientation:* Presentation and clarification of a puzzling situation.
- *Hypothesis:* Development of a hypotheses to structure an exploration or solution to the problem.
- *Definition:* Process of defining, clarifying, and understanding the hypothesis.
- *Exploration:* Looking for the assumptions, implications, and logical validity of the hypothesis.

◆ *Evidence:* Assembling relevant facts and evidence to support or refute each hypothesis.
◆ *Generalization:* Arriving at an acceptable solution based on evidence.

According to Joyce and Weil, social inquiry develops a reflective classroom in which the atmosphere of cooperation and collaboration are as important as the cognitive results of the inquiry process. Additionally, inquiry emphasizes the development and testing of specific hypotheses. Although a discussion may result in the creation of a hypothesis, inquiry requires the creation of a hypothesis early in the lesson. As the hypothesis is examined, the atmosphere of the classroom becomes "one of negotiation, and students are willing to modify their ideas in the face of evidence. Hypothesizing requires the skills of logic because the logical formation and implication of the hypothesis are as much a part of inquiry as are experimentation and observation" (Joyce & Weil, 1980, p. 312). The final characteristic of inquiry is the use of facts as evidence and the reliance on facts to defend and refute any hypothesis. Although opinion is valued in the inquiry model, opinions are best expressed as various hypotheses and are subject to testing and verification by using factual evidence as well as reasoned logic. This differs considerably from discussion in which reason and speculation are used and factual information may not be available or appropriate.

Usage of Inquiry Methods.   Inquiry teaching models vary but generally are used to teach children to reflect on explanations, models, or perspectives expressed through a hypothesis. Students test the validity of a hypothesis by first looking at it logically. Students should pose a number of questions when reflecting on a hypothesis:

◆ Is my hypothesis reasonable and based on evidence?
◆ Is the hypothesis a reasonable interpretation of known facts?
◆ If the hypothesis is true, does it provide a more effective understanding of a concept?
◆ Are the implications reasonable?

After logical examination, students verify the hypothesis with facts and evidence. This aspect fits traditional school approaches quite well because textbooks as well as school library resources are filled with factual information. The inquiry model presented here enables students to assemble the information so that students can create their own generalizations by examining the problem. In using the inquiry method, students learn how to define a problem, collect and assemble information leading to potential solutions, and work with others in examining many different ways that problems can be presented.

Investigation

Although discussions permit the exchange of opinions and perspectives, inquiry extends an examination of a problem by a formal process of gathering factual information. Factual data extends and illuminates the rational examination of a phenomenon. An investigation, under the nomenclature presented here, goes one step further. An investigation assembles data or evidence that was not available before the study.

Process of Investigation.   What if the factual data for a particular problem does not exist? Is it possible to gather data or create information from first-hand experiences? That is precisely what occurs when an investigation model is employed. Students are presented with a problem and an environment in which they may operate to obtain information directly from experience.

The process is not as difficult as it may sound. Suppose children are studying government in relation to taxes and expenditures. The teacher poses a basic idea that anything the government does has to be paid for with tax money. To illustrate the cost of government, the teacher poses a simple problem. How much tax money must be spent to construct the sidewalk that surrounds the school grounds?

Although a discussion permits speculation and shared opinions regarding the cost of the sidewalk, the question demands a more precise answer than can be derived by that method. Also, inquiry may fall short because the information is not easily located. Generally, the classroom texts and the library do not contain such information. The children may, however, have the creativity to call a private contractor or the public utilities office of the local government and ask for an estimate of the cost per square foot for constructing a sidewalk. However, even this is not accurate enough for computing the cost of the sidewalk around the school grounds. Additional information, such as the size of the sidewalk, is also needed and must be collected.

The students must take several courses of action to resolve this problem. First, the children must derive a strategy that will solve the problem. In this case, they decide that they can obtain a reasonable cost estimate for the sidewalk if they can get an estimated cost per square foot from a contractor and determine the square footage needed for the sidewalk. They find a contractor in the phone book and contact her. They then measure the length and width of the sidewalk to determine the square footage needed. They multiply the square footage by the estimated cost per square foot for sidewalk construction. However, they also include other expenditures such as site preparation, culverts, steps, and other features that require additional costs. The children can then provide an estimated cost for the school sidewalk.

In this case, the students created information where it did not exist prior to their investigation. In actual practice, the students became quite astounded at the cost of the sidewalk and began to calculate the costs of other things that they took for granted, such as the painted road markings separating lanes.

Benefits of Investigations.   Investigations are sometimes slow and tedious procedures, and the information gained is often not quite significant enough to warrant the expenditure of classroom time. Certainly, the knowledge of the estimated cost of the sidewalk is not particularly important to the students. However, investigations in elementary classrooms almost always have goals other than the information obtained by the study. The process of developing and implementing a strategy to acquire specific answers to questions is the top priority in investigations in elementary classrooms. Brown, Palinscar, and Armbruster (1984) identify six common benefits that result from cognitive strategy instruction such as investigations:

◆ Students have a better understanding of the purpose of the learning activity.
◆ Students' prior knowledge is activated in relationship to current problems.
◆ Student attention is focused on the *use* of content as opposed to *recall* of content.
◆ Students have opportunity to evaluate critical learning for internal consistency and compatibility with prior knowledge.
◆ Students monitor themselves to ascertain whether learning is occurring with their use of self-questioning and generalization.
◆ Students draw and test inferences through interpretation, prediction, and conclusions.

A simplified structure of an investigation is found in descriptions of scaffolding and mediated instruction. Langer and Applebee (1986) describe four general steps in scaffolding tasks such as investigations:

◆ The learner is informed of the goal and what it entails.
◆ The learner is made aware of the basic facts and missing data relevant to the task.
◆ The teacher arranges the environment in a way to help the learner deal with each step of the task separately.
◆ The teacher reminds the learner where he or she is in the solution of the problem.

The most difficult aspect regarding the implementation of investigations in the classroom is the construction of an environment that permits students to discover information. Many strategies have been developed to provide those environments, such as labs, centers, cooperative learning activities, projects, and simulations. Each of these strategies has four things in common:

◆ A principle or underlying concept that is comprehensible to students
◆ Repeated opportunities for experimentation and discovery
◆ Potential for immersion
◆ Safety

Special Considerations When Using Investigations.   Some principles are not likely to be discovered by elementary students during an investigation. Discovery of electricity and the behavior of electrons in an electric current are so abstract and complex that creation of exploratory activities are extremely difficult to engineer. Building electrical circuits or electromagnets with copious use of demonstrations is a more reasonable approach, on the other hand, offering broad opportunities for discovery.

A similar situation is found when studying magnetism: An explanation of the physics of magnetism is very abstract, whereas experimentation with magnetism and its effect on the physical world offers a plethora of investigative possibilities. By providing a collection of magnets in various shapes and sizes, students can begin to discover the relationships among magnets. By adding iron fillings in thin plastic boxes, students can discover the magnetic fields of various magnets and combinations of magnets. One caveat for the teacher, however, is needed. Since the subject matter of magnets at the basic level is highly structured, a well-sequenced, direct-instruction lesson is more likely to provide a systematic treatment of the properties of magnets. An investigation is likely to create misunderstanding as well as understanding. It also takes longer. Since the investigative lesson provides repeated opportunities for interaction with the materials, these misunderstandings can be reversed by further investigations, particularly demonstrations by the teacher, which correct the student's erroneous beliefs. Although it takes additional time to develop the concept of magnetism, this "testing of hypotheses" is the essence of implicit instruction and is fundamental to appropriate science curriculum.

When using investigations or any implicit instructional strategy, obtaining a concept is only part of the lesson intent. The underlying intent of all investigations is the development of meta-cognitional skill—that is, skill in controlling, directing, and understanding the learning and discovery process. Determining the type of lesson, implicit or explicit, to provide is a fundamental teacher decision. In this case, the ease in which investigations can be created and the high likelihood of student success provides a compelling case for a series of implicit instructional strategies. However, the final decision always lies with the teacher who considers not only the purpose of instruction, but also the students and the learning context.

Student safety in investigations is an important consideration and should always be central to development of student activities. Characteristics of safe materials and their use have previously been considered. It is sufficient to remind teachers that children need careful supervision in doing even routine tasks. Any type of investigation that deals with household chemicals, fire, the transport of breakable objects, and so on must be closely supervised.

Caine and Caine (1991) describe the goal of total immersion as "to take information off the page and the blackboard and bring it to life in the minds of students" (p. 107). They advocate experiences that are developed around curricular themes, pose complex but real problems of interest to students, and provide multisensory representations or involvement. The example of employing an investigation using magnets fulfills these requirements quite well. However, not all learning experiences do. Developing appropriate investigations remains a challenge for the teacher. Fortunately, many curriculum materials have been developed on a variety of topics that assist the teacher in designing appropriate experiences for children. It is unfortunate that many of these experiences are not offered in a vast number of elementary classrooms. Without using investigations, it is unlikely that any teacher can maintain the vitality and excitement found in the successful elementary classroom.

Combining Explicit and Implicit Instruction

Although pedagogical rhetoric claims singular methods as sufficient, none of the explicit or implicit instructional strategies can stand alone as the mainstay of the elementary curriculum. In fact, the most condemning criticism of either explicit or implicit instructional strategies is that there are substantive elements of the curriculum that each cannot sufficiently service. Fortunately, a substantial body of empirical research has accumulated that strongly suggests that effective teachers employ a variety of instructional techniques daily in the classroom. Unfortunately, developing a high level of skill in all of the various strategies is very difficult. Additionally, the number of things that must be done in the classroom is so great that teachers often attempt to limit their repertoire to two or three strategies and neglect the need for student learning from more diverse approaches. Limiting the number of strategies employed in classroom instruction is definitely a mistake.

The successful teacher actively develops skill in all of the strategies presented although such skills take time and practice to master. Because a variety of curricular materials are available to assist the teacher, the most important aspect of success for the teacher is a willingness to try new teaching strategies, to consider the advantages of the various approaches, and to persist in using and developing the strategies until they become part of the teaching repertoire.

◆ ◆ ◆

Summary

1. Questioning is a fundamental activity that supports virtually all teaching strategies.
2. Explicit instruction strategies use questioning to check for understanding. Implicit instruction strategies use questioning primarily to develop abstract knowledge.
3. Effective use of questions includes obtaining a response each time that a question is asked, being clear, being purposeful, asking brief sequenced questions, adapting questions to student ability, and stimulating thought.
4. A series of questions should include a variety of various cognitive levels and lead the student to a consideration of more difficult problems.
5. Reticent students can be encouraged by providing a safe environment, providing encouragement, phrasing questions to increase student success, employing a series of questions of increasing difficulty, and acknowledging responses with appreciation.
6. Many types of questions should be employed including the use of questions that do not have right or wrong answers.
7. Four conditions of effective questioning include (a) effective staging, (b) establishing a perspective, (c) teaching thinking strategies, and (d) providing reasons for thinking about and answering questions.
8. Strategies for improving questions include asking questions frequently, asking questions during all phases of instruction, emphasizing the importance of questions, matching cognitive level of questions to

purpose, and reminding students of question-answering strategies.

9. Questions can be used for an array of purposes including arousing interest, stimulating students to ask questions, focusing student attention, reviewing information, and holding students accountable for learning.

10. Effective use of questions results in increased curiosity, skill in developing explanations, and intuitive reasoning and other positive effects.

11. Students fail to participate for a variety of reasons including fear of failure, negative past experiences, fear of speaking in front of others, disinterest, and lack of understanding.

12. Questions can be improved in both variety and quality by using various taxonomies defining different levels of cognitive functioning.

13. Student attention can be improved by use of wait time, providing a positive reception to student comments, making eye contact with the speaker, and contemplating the student's answer.

14. Wait time is very beneficial to effective questioning and provides a broad array of advantages.

15. Student-structured concepts rely on the student's active participation in order to construct a concept or model from experiences.

16. Successful teaching requires a rich mixture of strategies that uses student-structured and teacher-structured concepts.

17. Implicit instruction is best used when at least part of the objective is to provide students with active engagement in developing a schema of understanding rather than on simple comprehension.

18. Implicit instruction is used to pose problems of relevance, structure learning around primary concepts, value the student's point of view, and adapt curriculum to student perspectives.

19. Discussions are used to examine facts, consequences, and alternatives involved in a problem employing the students' beliefs and opinions.

20. Inquiry is used to assist students in creating hypotheses to explain or resolve a problem or situation and gather evidence to support or refute the hypothesis.

21. Investigations are used when the assemblage of known data is inadequate. Investigations employ techniques in which student gather data from primary sources.

◆ ◆ ◆

Activities and Questions for Further Understanding

1. Select one of the questioning vignettes from "A Slice of Life" or the body of the chapter. Evaluate the questioning sequence with the checklist provided in Figure 9.2.

2. For one of the following concepts, write a sequence of questions going from simple to more cognitively complex.
   a. Why a shadow changes length during the day.

   b. Why $3 + 1$ is equal to $1 + 3$.
   c. Why a story always has both a character and a problem.

3. Using Figure 9.3 as a guide, write several questions from each of the six cognitive areas outlined in Bloom's taxonomy. Select a single topic for all of the questions so that they can be used in a single lesson.

4. Figure 9.5 poses a comparison between traditional and constructivist classrooms. Create a third category called "My Classroom" and complete a list of defining characteristics.

5. On a sheet of paper, label three headings with Discussion, Inquiry, and Investigations. Develop a list of appropriate topics for each strategy using each of the following subject matter areas: math, science, social studies, literature, and health.

6. Review the "Slice of Life" sections in this text. Classify the strategies as implicit or explicit. For each, determine what the main goal is and if it is appropriately represented by the teaching strategy used.

◆ ◆ ◆

References

Barell, J. (1991). *Teaching for thoughtfulness: Classroom strategies to enhance intellectual development.* New York: Longman.

Bloom, Benjamin. (1956). *Taxonomy of educational objectives.* New York: David McKay.

Borich, G. (1996). *Effective teaching methods* (3rd ed.). Upper Saddle River, NJ: Merrill/Prentice Hall.

Brooks, J. G., & Brooks, M. G. (1993). *In search of understanding: The case for constructivist classrooms.* Alexandria, VA: Association for Supervision and Curriculum Development.

Brown, A. L., Palinscar, A. S., & Armbruster, B. B. (1984). Instructing comprehension-fostering activities in interactive learning situations. In H. Mandl, L. Stein, & T. Trabasso (Eds.), *Learning and comprehension of text.* Hillsdale, NJ: Erlbaum.

Caine, R. N., & Caine, G. (1991). *Making connections: Teaching and the human brain* (p. 157). Reston, VA: Association for Supervision and Curriculum Development.

Chuska, K. R. (1995). *Improving classroom questions.* Bloomington, IN: Phi Delta Kappa.

Clegg, A. A. (1987). Why questions. In W. W. Wilen (Ed.), *Questions, questioning techniques, and effective teaching.* Washington, DC: National Education Association.

Crane, Stephen. (1895). *The red badge of courage.* New York: D. Appleton and Company. Reprinted by the Reader's Digest Association (1982, p. 13), Pleasantville, NY.

Dillon, J. T. (1979). Alternatives to questioning. *High School Journal, 62,* 217–222.

Dillon, J. T. (1988). *Questioning and teaching: A manual of practice* (p. 9). New York: Teachers College Press.

Gaul, M. D., & Rhody, T. (1986). Review of research on questioning techniques. In W. W. Wilen (Ed.), *Questions, questioning techniques, and effective teaching* (pp. 23–48). Washington, DC: National Educational Association.

Good, T. L., & Brophy, J. E. (1994). *Looking in classrooms* (6th ed.). New York: Harper Collins.

Groisser, P. (1964). *How to use the fine art of questioning.* New York: Teachers' Practical Press.

Hyman, R. T. (1987). Discussion strategies and tactics. In W. W. Wilen (Ed.), *Questions, questioning techniques, and effective teaching* (pp. 135–152). Washington, DC: National Educational Association.

Joyce, B., & Weil, M. (1986). *Models of teaching* (3rd ed.). Upper Saddle River, NJ: Prentice Hall.

Langer, J. A., & Applebee, A. N. (1986). Reading and writing instruction: Toward a theory of teaching and learning. In E. Rothkopf (Ed.), *Review of research in education* (Vol. 13, pp. 171–194). Washington, DC: American Educational Research Association.

Lao-Tzu. *Tao-te-ching,* bk. 2, ch. 71. [Translated by G. Feng & J. English. (1972, p. 142). New York: Vintage Books]

MacDonald, Robert E. (1991). *A handbook of basic skills and strategies for beginning teachers: Facing the challenge of teaching in today's schools.* New York: Longman.

Raths, L. E., Wasserman, S., Jonas, A., & Rothstein, A. M. (1967). Teaching for thinking: Theory and application. Upper Saddle River, NJ: Merrill/Prentice Hall.

Ross, W. (1860). Methods of instruction. Cited in W. W. Wilen (1991), *Questioning skills for teachers.* Washington, DC: National Educational Association.

Rowe, M. B. (1986a). Wait time: Slowing down may be a way of speeding up. *Journal of Teacher Education, 37*(1), 43–50.

Rowe, M. B. (1986b). Using wait time to stimulate inquiry. In W. W. Wilen (Ed.), *Questions, questioning techniques, and effective teaching* (pp. 95–106). Washington, DC: National Educational Association.

Wilen, W. W. (1991). *Questioning skills for teachers.* Washington, DC: National Educational Association.

Wilen, W. W. (1987). Effective questions and questioning: A classroom application. In W. W. Wilen (Ed.), *Questions, questioning techniques, and effective teaching* (pp. 107–134). Washington, DC: National Educational Association.

CHAPTER 10

How Do I Engage Children in Learning?

Seatwork, Centers, Cooperative Learning, and Technology

Outline

Their learning is like bread in a besieged town: every man gets a little, but no man gets a full meal.

SAMUEL JOHNSON

This isn't learning. This is work. Learning is when you don't know how to do it already.

BEN, 8, REGARDING BASIC ADDITION WORKSHEETS

A Slice of Life

Mrs. Chen and her parent volunteers had finished setting up the field kits for exploring the playground and surrounding school grounds. Each kit had three hand lenses, a small collection of various-sized "capture" jars with a magnifying lens molded into the cap, a field microscope, three notebooks, three pencils, a pencil sharpener, three spoons, several irrigation flags for marking special spots, a collection of self-closing plastic bags, a field guide to plants, a field guide to insects, a cloth measuring tape, and a ruler. Inside the notebooks were a map and a set of notes developed by each child. The map was of the playground and its important features. The notes included some special rules for the transect study, a list of things to do, and a description of how their findings would be presented to the class. Each kit was surrounded by a hula hoop. As the children returned from lunch, they were excited but well mannered. Today was the big day. They were going to divide into teams, and each team would then make a detailed inventory of a portion of the playground.

Mrs. Chen asked the children to get into their teams and sit at the table where their team's kit was placed. She then asked them to check the inventory and reminded them to be extra careful not to scratch the plastic lenses on the microscopes and capture jars. With one final summary, she reminded them of the mission:

"Find out what is in your transect area. Describe its appearance. List the plants and animals showing their number, shape, color, size, and anything else that you think is important. Mark any important discoveries. And handle any animal care-

fully and release it after examination." Finally Mrs. Chen added, "When in doubt, doubt!" which referred to the possibility that a mean millipede or stinging bug might pose a threat. With that, the children headed for the door and walked impatiently out of the building and toward the back region of the playground.

There the children found a rope with red flags tied to it every 10 yards. Each flag had a number. The rope started with a big oak tree that had a metal tag with the class's name on it: Chen's Fifth Grade, 1999. The rope pointed due north, and Jake was asked to check it with the compass that Mrs. Chen had in her transect bag. Jake declared that the rope was in line with the tag going due north. "Great!" Mrs. Chen shouted. "We can find the exact spot to study when winter comes and again in the spring. Okay, let's get started."

The children went to their assigned station finding the flag with their team's number. A buzz of activity followed. Children frequently ran to Mrs. Chen to show them their discoveries. The parents frequented each group and helped focus a microscope or helped children put a cricket into a plastic cylinder for observation. Mrs. Chen visited each group with encouragement. One parent had a video camera with a macro lens and took close-up footage of plants and animals. The class had a small digital camera and took close-up pictures for uploading to the computer. These pictures would be pasted into their word processor file and printed out (in color!) at the end of the study. This year they would also get to post their reports on the school's Web page. The hour passed quickly.

Mrs. Chen called time, and the children quickly assembled their materials. The parent helpers marked the end of the rope and moved the rope so that it started at the mark and headed due north, ready for the second round of investigations.

Independent and Cooperative Study

There is an array of teaching strategies available for use in the elementary classroom. The instructional strategies of the previous sections describe interactive instruction in which the teacher works closely with students, guiding and directing their learning. Both explicit and implicit instruction strategies feature student/teacher intercommunication where the active involvement of the teacher fosters the instructional development of the lesson. Sometimes, however, it is desirable for students to work with their peers or for students to work alone to practice a skill or to develop new knowledge. Seatwork, centers, homework, and cooperative learning round out a basic set of instructional approaches for the successful classroom.

Seatwork and Centers

Whether a teacher employs an explicit or implicit strategy during a lesson, children need to practice the new skill or use the new information in some fashion to commit it to long-term memory. Seatwork and centers are primarily practice devices for interactive instruction with the teacher. However, carefully structured seatwork and centers can be used for instructional purposes in introducing new material or concepts, but students need some prerequisite skills. *Seatwork,* in this discussion, is any work or activity that the child can do at his or her desk, such as writing a poem, reading a story, or memorizing spelling words. *Centers,* on the other hand, are areas of shared use elsewhere in the classroom, usually areas with specific materials and equipment that are dedicated to a special activity. Successful teachers have many varied ideas about the composition of effective seatwork and centers, but there are common elements.

Seatwork

The primary purpose of seatwork is to practice or employ skills and information taught during lessons. Seatwork is an essential aspect of classroom learning, yet it has a pernicious reputation among many educators. When students spend a majority of classroom time doing seatwork, that reputation may be well deserved. One of the basic characteristics of seatwork is that it should be brief and represent a minority of the time spent on any lesson (Good & Brophy, 1997; Northwest Regional Educational Laboratory, 1990). Seatwork should usually take no longer than 15 to 20 minutes during an hour of successful instruction. Overuse of seatwork is often a prevalent feature of classrooms (Good & Brophy, 1997):

> Process-outcome research suggests that *independent seatwork is probably overused and is not an adequate substitute either for active teacher instruction or for recitation and discussion opportunities.* This is especially the case when the seatwork emphasizes time consuming but low-level tasks that reinforce memory for facts and mastery of sub-skills practiced in isolation but do not provide opportunities to think critically or creatively about what is being learned or apply it in problem-solving or decision-making situations. (p. 381)

Types of Seatwork. Doyle (1986) identified two types of seatwork. The first type is work that students do independently at their desks with their own materials while the teacher is free to monitor the work of the entire class. This work permits the exchange of ideas between student and teacher with provisions for feedback, suggestions, and encouragement as needed. The second type is work that is done independently while the teacher is actively engaged in teaching other students and cannot provide extensive monitoring or feedback. When teachers use seatwork of the first type, they can use more challenging, difficult, and diverse activities because the teacher is ready to assist the child as needed. Teacher monitoring also increases the likelihood that the child stays engaged in the task. The second type of work is performed either independently or with the assistance of another student since the teacher is occupied in other lessons. This type of work must be more carefully aligned with the ability of the students and the lessons taught. It must have clear directions and be sufficiently motivating to maintain the student's interest and engagement. What constitutes appropriate seatwork in either category largely lies within the carefully constructed context of the lesson and the history of success and independence developed in prior lessons.

General Principles of Effective Seatwork.   A description of what constitutes effective seatwork has not been well developed in the literature (Brophy, 1992), neither has a good understanding of the effective monitoring processes required in seatwork (Doyle, 1986). Certain principles can, nevertheless, be gleaned from generalized research on classroom effectiveness. Seatwork activities share many of the characteristics of good lessons: Seatwork should be meaningful, build on previous learning, and have clear directions and expectations. Additionally, the work should be varied, challenging, interesting, and easy enough so that students will usually be successful (Good & Brophy, 1997). If students are required to do the work on their own without teacher assistance, success rates must approach 100 percent to assure engagement and completion (Good & Brophy, 1997). When creating assignments for mixed-ability groups, these requirements can pose significant challenges. Kounin (1970) discovered that the difficulty level of the material, the cognitive skills required, and the focal content also altered engagement and completion rates of seatwork. Evertson & Emmer (1982) found that successful seatwork also involves frequent monitoring, inspections of individual student work during the seatwork activity, encouragement to complete the work, and a history of praise for successful work.

Increasing Engagement.   Rosenshine and Stevens (1986) described instructional procedures that increase student engagement in seatwork:

- The teacher emphasizes the demonstration and successful use of the new skill before assigning work.
- The teacher makes sure that students are ready to work independently at success rates of 80 percent or higher.
- Seatwork immediately follows instruction.
- Seatwork is directly related with the teacher's instruction and practice learning as taught in the lesson.
- Teacher guides the students through the first seatwork problems to orient them to the lesson.

Additionally, students complete their seatwork when they know that they are held accountable, know how to get assistance, know when work must be completed, have their performance monitored, and are positively reinforced with praise, privileges, or token rewards (Brophy & Good, 1986).

Appropriate Seatwork Tasks.   The development of tasks for seatwork yields many varied activities. What makes a good seatwork activity relies heavily on the manner in which students are prepared for the activity. Specifically, students who know how to complete the work are more likely to learn from the activity than students who are confused. Many seatwork activities are predeveloped by curriculum specialists and accompany basal texts, teacher manuals, supplementary materials, and special unit packages. Good and Brophy (1997) summarize the research on seatwork to date and conclude:

◆ Seatwork should directly relate to current instruction although other content may be included as necessary.
◆ Seatwork should incorporate approximate review of previously taught skills to ensure prerequisites for the current activity are in place.
◆ The purpose of seatwork should be clear, made known to students, and emphasize critical lesson points.
◆ Instructions should be explained and be easy to follow.
◆ Student responses should exercise language skills (avoid underlining, circling, and so on).
◆ Cute, nonfunctional and time-consuming tasks should be avoided.

With appropriate teacher care, seatwork can be an effective and enjoyable aspect of student learning. It can be made more effective if it is not overused and if it includes the use of centers, cooperative learning, and technology-assisted independent activity. By developing a variety of approaches to independent activity, self-directed seatwork can substantially contribute to comprehension, student responsibility, confidence in learning, and higher-order thinking.

Centers

A center is a specific area of classroom devoted to special learning activities. Generally, a center contains learning materials that can be used independently, provides the necessary directions for student work, and has all of the necessary apparatus for learning.

Learning centers became popular in classrooms in the 1970s as a way of individualizing the curriculum. Centers are now frequently used to reinforce group instruction, similar to guided practice in direct instruction, and should generally parallel the academic work in teacher-directed activities. Centers are used to reinforce instructional concepts and enrich any area of the curriculum. As with seatwork, centers have a central purpose: providing independent learning activity under the dominant direction of the student. Teachers can provide structured activity in which students can work independently or interact with teachers.

According to Flemming, Hamilton, Hicks, and McKay (1988), learning centers should be designed so that children can do the following:

◆ Allow choices about learning tasks and how to complete those tasks
◆ Permit discovery through direct experience
◆ Employ skills in self-direction, self-confidence, and personal responsibility
◆ Develop skills in understanding directions and communication by using language, materials, and equipment
◆ Exercise critical thinking and problem solving using a variety of materials
◆ Assist social development by providing opportunities to relate to others and share responsibilities with the group

◆   Use materials independently
◆   Learn how to care for and use the materials and equipment

Godfrey (1972) argues that successful centers must start with a well-defined lesson plan with three components: self-direction for the child, provision for different ability levels, and some means of evaluation. A primary feature of centers is that students accept a large degree of responsibility for directing their own learning, both in practice activity and in exploring material for the first time. The center can be used to supplement activities for students who complete their work early, but it should also be part of the daily curriculum for all students. If centers are made available only to early finishers, some children never get the experience of working independently or cooperatively with other students (Petreshene, 1978).

Types of Centers.   Many types of centers are available: computational mathematics centers, independent reading centers, writing centers, spelling centers, listening centers, reading instruction centers, art centers, discovery centers, dramatic play centers, and readiness centers, just to mention a few. Centers are flexible tools that can be created to suit many varying instructional needs of students. Teachers, in general, must make decisions along five general dimensions:

1. Is the work at the center to be for individual activities or for students working in small groups or teams?
2. Is the center to be designed to support a specific subject, or is it to be developed around a topic to tie together study in different subjects by supplying a unifying theme?
3. Is the center to be set up for a short period of time to deal with a specific activity or designed to support continued study in a single curriculum area? For example, a center can be set up to explore properties of magnets with the goal of mapping magnetic fields, or it can be devoted to weekly writing experiences.
4. Is the goal of the center to reinforce cognitive learning or to provide outlets for the expression of creativity?
5. Should the center be designed to provide a carefully detailed sequence of activity or to provide low-structured experiences that provide many choices for individually determined courses of study?

These questions will help the teacher focus on the type of center best suited to his or her purpose and deserve considerable thought before the teacher begins assembling and implementing a center.

Developing Centers.   Flemming et al. (1988) describe a sequence of activity leading to appropriate development of centers that aligns with the classroom curriculum and provides meaningful learning for students:

1. Teachers employ a sound understanding of basic learning principles
2. The center provides the best conditions for learning by
   a. Promoting positive self-images among children
   b. Providing repeated opportunities to discover, explore, be challenged, and solve problems through direct experiences

   c. Providing diverse choices that can lead to independence, self-confidence, self-control, and a sense of responsibility
   d. Providing supervision that protects and ensures each child's opportunity to learn
3. The teacher includes a balance of activities among
   a. Structured/unstructured investigations
   b. Informative/creative content
   c. Observation/participation in demonstrations
   d. Individual/group activities
4. The teacher employs the wealth of human resources in the school and community
5. The teacher develops personal understanding of centers by
   a. Reading curriculum materials
   b. Visiting other classrooms
   c. Sharing ideas and problems
   d. Inviting resource people and parents into the classroom

Developing a center is a complex process in which there are many avenues for success. Forte and Mackenzie (1978) suggest five basic questions for developing and assessing the effectiveness of centers:

◆ What is to be done, learned, and mastered?
◆ What activities will obtain these purposes?
◆ What tools and materials will I need?
◆ What directions, guidelines, and explanations will be necessary?
◆ How will I know if, and how well, learning occurred?

A clear sense of purpose is a basic consideration for centers, just as it is in developing all classroom lessons. If the purpose is just to amuse the children while occupying their time, the center will not be successful. Centers must support the basic instructional purposes of the classroom. Once the purpose is established, strategies must be developed to realize that purpose and, in turn, materials must be assembled to support the intended instruction. The center must be structured so that students with minimal supervision can follow the directions and perform the activity. Although the whole class may need an introduction to the center, its use, and the proper care of materials, the center usually should provide for student involvement without the direct involvement of the teacher.

Implementing Centers.   Lloyd (1974) provides some extra considerations to guide the implementation of centers in the classroom. Although learning centers should be attractive and neat, specific criteria for the three different types of centers may vary.

Learning Centers for Practicing Something New
◆ Based on the apparent needs of the children
◆ Provide for practice of a particular learned skill recently taught or reviewed
◆ Include materials that are self-checking or quickly checked by the teacher

◆   Involve the child actively
◆   Are enjoyable and of interest to the child

Learning Centers for Learning Something New
◆   Describe the objective, identifying clearly what the children are to accomplish
◆   Make clear the purpose for learning at the center
◆   Emphasize only one new concept at a time
◆   Give multiple opportunities to practice the new learning

Learning Centers for Creating Something
◆   Provide the materials that foster creative expression
◆   Provide the opportunity for problem solving and critical thinking
◆   Provide an opportunity to use and extend skills and abilities
◆   Contain activities with many acceptable outcomes

Centers may take a great deal of experimentation before satisfactory results are consistently obtained. The effects, however, are cumulative. When students have had little or no prior experience in a learning center, the teacher must explain the purpose of centers to the children and why their self-direction and self-control are necessary. When students have had a great deal of experience in centers, the centers not only help them with the desired learning but also with their other lessons by increasing their ability to follow directions and resolve learning difficulties.

Cooperative Learning

Cooperative learning is a broad strategy with many specific teaching models. An exact understanding of what is meant by the term varies among authors. Most developers of cooperative learning activities view cooperative learning as being much more than children working collaboratively on a single project. Thus, two children who are editing a story together may be cooperating but may not be involved in a cooperative learning activity because they do not share common goals or share equally in the results. In this section, however, a more generalized interpretation is used. *Cooperative learning* is defined as any educational activity in which a group of students are engaged in obtaining a common goal, are required to use extensive social interaction within that group, and use student leadership and self-direction as the primary characteristics of the instructional environment.

Having a common goal requires that each student in the group works toward the same end as fellow members. Rather than comparative achievement among them (which would be competitive), students are directed toward simultaneous achievement of the goal by all in the group. This requires that students pool skills cooperatively to develop and implement a successful strategy. This cooperation requires extensive social skills if the group is to communicate effectively. Even if the task is to be divided, worked on independently, and the completed parts reassembled, communication is necessary for a delegation of tasks to occur. If the communication skills of the group are inadequate (even if they have the technical skills for reading, writing, construction, and so on), they will probably not complete the task successfully.

Goals of Cooperative Learning

Student leadership and self-direction are at the heart of all cooperative learning theories. If the task is structured so that there are few decisions and, therefore, limited alternatives, cooperation may occur, but cooperative learning will not. For example, consider a group of soldiers who are involved in precision drill. Although they have a common goal and have worked intimately together, the direction comes externally from the drillmaster. The same phenomenon occurs on most sports teams where the coach directs from the sidelines. This type of cooperative activity may be referred to as *teamwork*. In teamwork, the group sets aside individuality to carry out an orchestrated plan. Without question, teamwork is an essential social activity that has a place in the elementary classroom. It is certainly the heart of any classroom management plan. However, cooperative learning is thought to capture the spirit of self-direction and individual determination.

Cooperative Learning Is More Than Teamwork

There is no clear demarcation between teamwork and cooperative learning. In fact, teamwork may be considered a prerequisite skill for cooperative learning. However, most theories on cooperative learning tend to emphasize the higher-order thinking that is required when the group must first structure the task and then carry out the plans that are developed (Johnson & Johnson, 1989; Johnson, Johnson, & Holubec, 1991). If experiences in structuring tasks are omitted from the group activity, the likelihood of higher-order thinking being employed diminishes. These types of activities are more accurately described as teamwork where members cooperate, work together, and often share in the results. However, the planning, leadership, and critical thinking are not shared by group members.

According to Stallings and Stipek (1986), models of cooperative learning vary in two dimensions. First, the structure of learning tasks can vary. Tasks can be structured so that children must work together, whereas other tasks permit the group to divide the assignment into smaller pieces so that children can work as individuals or on subteams. Many advocates of cooperative learning, however, feel that an activity is only truly cooperative when the entire team works together. Others encourage the "divide and conquer" specialization if the strategy is developed by the group. The successful teacher, however, uses a variety of strategies.

Reward contingency is the second dimension of cooperative learning. A grade or reward is given that can either be contingent on all members of the group working together or be based on personal contributions. For example, if a report is the end product of a cooperative study, a group reward is given for the completed paper because all of the team members contributed and thus are all treated the same. On the other end of the continuum, individual rewards can be given by evaluating each student independently based on his or her achievement or activity; the reward is in proportion to the contribution of the individual. However, many designers of cooperative learning activities consider an activity to be representative of cooperative learning only if individuals in the group are evaluated based on the group's performance.

Grades

Assigning grades to an individual based on group participation must be handled carefully. When summary evaluations such as report cards are sent to parents, they assume that the evaluation represents the work of their child and not of others. It is extremely tenuous to hold any student accountable for the effort and activity of another student. For example, teacher associations have long opposed the principle that teacher pay should be contingent on student learning because student learning is highly dependent on student dimensions beyond their control. The student decides whether to read an assignment or do a piece of homework—not the teacher. Similarly, when a cooperative learning group has a member who fails to participate and the group has exercised good judgment, penalizing any student because of the errors of another can be difficult to defend. Fortunately, most models use group achievement to earn rewards—not grades—and that issue is a very significant contributor to the success of cooperative learning. When children are working cooperatively, the focus should be on group achievement—not grading.

Purposes of Cooperative Learning

Stallings and Stipek (1986) outline several established purposes of cooperative learning. They conclude that cooperative learning has been used to achieve the following:

♦ Raise academic achievement
♦ Encourage students to help and support peers
♦ Minimize competition
♦ Provide opportunity to learn from peers of mixed ability
♦ Pose an alternative to competition
♦ Provide a reward structure that motivates students by raising the likelihood of their success
♦ Improve race relations within schools

Early research tends to support the various cooperative learning models when evaluated against these purposes. There are some caveats worth noting. The research indicates that the incentive structure (rewards) is more influential in obtaining positive results than the opportunities provided for cooperation. Employing cooperative learning models without group goals, individual accountability, and the provision to earn rewards is not likely to produce the positive results found in appropriately implemented models. Another finding worth noting is that low-ability and minority students tend to achieve more in cooperative learning activities than other groups of children do (Stallings & Stipek, 1986), whereas high-ability children show few academic benefits from cooperative learning. Some studies indicate that students who were on teams that were responsible for other students' achievement were actually less successful than those students who were allowed to work independently (Johnson, Johnson, & Scott, 1978; Slavin, 1980). However, the potential contribution of carefully considered cooperative learning strategies to both academic achievement and affective development makes cooperative learning models an important tool in a teacher's repertoire.

Major Models of Cooperative Learning

By combining descriptions of cooperative learning models from Slavin (1995) and Furtwengler (1992), the characteristics of the most common cooperative learning models can be compared.

Student Teams-Achievement Divisions (STAD) (Slavin, 1986)
- Four-member, heterogeneous learning teams are designed for well-defined objectives.
- Direct explicit instruction by the teacher is followed by work in student teams for mastery.
- Students study together but take individual tests.
- Student quiz scores are compared to past averages, and points are awarded for improvements.
- Points are traded for team rewards.
- Learning teams can be used to support instruction in virtually any subject.
- Learning team concept readily integrates into traditional direct instruction strategies.
- Students utilize a vast array of strategies for study, completion of learning tasks, and test preparation.

Teams-Games-Tournaments (TGT) (DeVries & Slavin, 1978)
- TGT concept is similar to STAD, but it replaces quizzes with weekly tournaments of academic games.
- Team members play members from other teams at "tournament tables."
- Tournament table competitors are matched by ability so that high and low achievers have equal opportunity for success.
- Direct instruction by the teacher is followed by work in student teams for mastery.
- Students study together but compete against other teams for points which are traded for team rewards.
- TGT can be used to support instruction in virtually any subject.
- TGT readily integrates into traditional direct instruction strategies.
- Students use a vast array of strategies for study, completion of learning tasks, and test preparation.

Team Assisted Instruction (TAI) (Slavin, Leavey, & Madden, 1986)
- TAI combines cooperative learning with individualized instruction.
- Four-member, mixed-ability teams are used (designed for math but can be adapted for other subjects).

- Members of a team work on units of instruction based on personal ability.
- Team members assist each other and verify each other's work using check sheets.
- Teacher instructs homogeneous groups of students selected from all groups; students go back to teams to work.
- Individual unit tests are taken without team help. Weekly team awards are given.

Cooperative Integrated Reading and Composition (CIRC) (Madden, Slavin, & Stevens, 1986; Stevens, Madden, Slavin, & Farnish, 1989)
- CIRC is designed specifically for instruction in reading and writing in the upper elementary and middle grades.
- Four-member, upper elementary teams are divided into two or more ability levels.
- Basals or novels are used with or without traditional reading groups.
- Teachers instruct pairs of similar ability (reading, writing, and language arts).
- Teams are involved in a series of cognitively engaging activities, such as reading aloud to one another, writing responses to stories, or practicing vocabulary.
- CIRC is generally a sequence of teacher instruction, team practice, team pre-assessments, and culminating quizzes.
- Team scores are based on individual scores from work based on the individual ability level.

Jigsaw II (Slavin, 1986)
- Jigsaw II uses four-member, mixed-ability teams.
- Students learn common material, but each student is randomly assigned to become an "expert" on a subtopic.
- Experts meet with experts from other teams and then return to their original team to teach the material.
- Individual student quizzes are given with team results based on improvement, the same as in STAD.

Learning Together (Johnson & Johnson, 1987)
- The Learning Together concept uses four- to five-member heterogeneous groups in grades two to six.
- The teacher instructs the whole class. Student groups work on assignments.
- One final product is awarded a team score.

Group Investigation (Sharan, 1980; Sharan & Sharan, 1989)
- Group Investigation has two- to six-member student groups.
- Groups choose topic and then assign individual tasks.
- Groups make presentations to the entire class and receive a group award.

Cooperative Learning and Social Teaching

Most of the research on cooperative learning is based on carefully prescribed models of instruction that vary significantly. Implementation of most of these models requires considerably more information than is provided here, particularly in how scoring, point assessment, and rewards are managed. The types of learning out-comes must also be carefully considered. In most models, but particularly in models in which students are employed as "experts" or tutors for others, the material to be learned must be well within the grasp of most students in the group.

Information taught using cooperative learning instruction is generally well struc-tured and therefore amenable to direct instruction and testing where objective scor-ing (right-wrong) is possible. Extremely difficult concepts and low-structured topics may not fit well with the cooperative model, particularly when the requirements are not well matched to the group. For example, an objective may not be appropriate for all students in a group, and special instructional groups that do not have members of mixed ability are required. Although cooperative strategies can be employed in homogeneously grouped children, that is not their main purpose. When instruc-tional needs of individuals are radically different within the group, technological tools can be employed as aids.

Technology

In recent years, there has been an increasing tendency to couple the words *science* and *technology* (Fensham, 1992). However, in its basic form, technology is a collec-tive term for the tools that have been developed and the way in which they are used. With the advent of television and, more recently, the evolution of low-cost micro-computers, technology has emerged in the public schools as its own subject where the object of instruction is to learn technology rather than use it to support learning.

Goodson (1988) and Tickle (1990) describe how an area of the school curricu-lum often starts with a utilitarian intent only to meander into a high status academic subject with little utilitarian value. Technology may have already traveled a great dis-tance down that road. The danger of technology-the-subject overshadowing the actual use of technology-the-tool is very real. In many schools throughout the coun-try, children are scheduled for a one-hour session in the computer lab to learn about computers. They then leave the room and continue the business of learning for the remainder of the week totally unaffected by this once-a-week experience. The com-puter then has little or no place in student learning until the next week's computer class. Fortunately, the picture for the future is not that dismal as both the cost of computers and society's willingness to put them in schools are changing. One important aspect of technology that must never be forgotten is that access to tech-nology always precedes its effective use.

In this brief introduction to school technology, "low-tech" learning tools as well as "high-tech" computer and communications applications are discussed. The sheer number of technology tools available to the teacher dictates that this discussion can-not cover many important technologies. Fortunately, the principles involved in selecting and using one type of technology are generalizable to other types. In this section, technology is not viewed as an emerging subject matter area but as a mar-velous collection of tools to help teachers teach and students learn.

"Low-Tech" Tools

The contrast between "low-tech" and "high-tech" tools is a simple demarcation in terminology to reflect special characteristics of the vast variety of tools. *Low tech* implies technology that is simpler, older, and more thoroughly assimilated by the general population. Conversely, *high tech* implies tools that are complex, use the latest developments in science and engineering, and are not yet widely assimilated by the general population. By the very nature of the classification, low-tech tools are more common, more available, more assimilated, and therefore more frequently used in the classroom.

Low-tech tools should not be overlooked simply because they do not have the status and glamour of high-tech tools. One of the oldest teaching tools in American schools is the chalkboard. This single tool has had a prominent place in school classrooms for over 200 years. Although it probably will not be replaced in the foreseeable future, the humble chalkboard is currently undergoing a high-tech face-lift with the invention of "dry-erase" pens and white surface coatings. Another tool that has been used for many years is the chart stand. This free-standing rack enables teachers to prepare charts of information for children on large sheets of paper that can be seen easily by students and that provide the permanence that chalkboards lack. Although simple to use, chalkboards and charts require some careful considerations to use well. They also illustrate the questioning and reflection necessary for the successful implementation of all technology media.

Some low-tech tools today are really the high-tech tools of the previous decade. The overhead projector, television, videotape player, calculator, copier, and telephone certainly fall into the category of thoroughly integrated tools and are widely available although the simplicity of their use belies the complexity involved in their design and manufacture. These tools, like the chalkboard and the chart stand, are generally overlooked and, therefore, are almost universally underused and sometimes misused or abused. The following discussion about their effective use explains the contribution that these tools can make in the classroom.

Chalkboards, Charts, Projectors, and Slates. Most teachers never learn how to use chalkboards and chart stands during their professional training. The supposition is that since these are ubiquitous features of all classrooms and teacher candidates, having been students for at least 16 years, know all there is to know about these humble tools. This may explain why these tools are underused or misused.

Chalkboards and other presentation devices are often confined to their traditional uses:

◆ Draw attention to key words or phrases in a discussion
◆ Quickly present visual representations of objects
◆ Outline concepts as they are developed in the classroom
◆ Post reminders or directions

Although the chalkboard excels in these functions, many of these tasks can be accomplished through other means. Each type of presentation tool has certain advantages and limitations that need to be carefully considered (see Figure 10.1). For example, a visual representation of an object can usually be presented to the children more effectively through either a chart, which can be left for student view after the lesson is completed, or through the use of the overhead projector, which can provide more detail. The overhead projector provides additional advantages in that the pictures can be created in advance and stored conveniently in an ordinary filing cabinet. Also, in conjunction with the copier, transparencies for the overhead projector can be made from virtually any picture regardless of the artistic ability of the teacher. The chalkboard, however, provides for the spontaneity of the teacher, is readily available, never needs a replacement bulb, and always works. Additionally, for those teachers who have some artistic ability, students can be shown sequentially the components of an object as it is drawn. The difficulty is that this type of drawing can take time, perhaps requires some special talent, and often must be erased for later parts of the lesson. If the teacher wants the pictured object to be available to children after the lesson or during a seatwork activity, the chart stand certainly stands out with its advantage of permanence and ease of use. Charts can be flipped, rearranged by children easily, and available for reference indefinitely.

All of this information about display tools seems rather obvious once it is considered. However, it is not uncommon for teachers to fail to use one or more of these tools while overutilizing others. Also, each medium requires some time to master for its full potential to be used. The chalkboard requires gross-motor coordination for writing instead of the fine-motor coordination used in pencil-and-paper communication. Some teachers learn to write the necessary words and phrases over their shoulders, continually making eye contact with their audience, without ever looking back at the board. With the common use of overhead projectors, this art may be a fading one.

The most important key to appropriate use of these tools is thoughtful awareness of the advantages and disadvantages of each type of tool. The author has visited countless classrooms in which the teacher held up a book and the children strain and stretch to get a glimpse of the picture. Making a simple photocopy on transparency film would permit the teacher to both enlarge the picture and make it available to students more efficiently. When asked the reason for not using this tool, the teacher always answers with a variation of "I didn't think about it."

One of the oldest display tools is making a big comeback in classrooms around the country. The individual slate, or personal chalkboard, is a favorite among children. For whatever reason, children enjoy writing with chalk and writing in unusually large print. With the individual slate, children can perform math calculations, write short answers to group questions, and draw pictures to represent solutions to problems posed by the teacher. Individual slates have an added advantage because students who make a mistake can easily erase it. Students who do make mistakes are not constantly reminded as they would be if the calculations were written on a sheet of paper. Slates offer another advantage to teachers besides the general enthusiasm of students for their use. Teachers can obtain active participation from all students. By using slates as response devices, the teacher can check for comprehension of all students quickly.

	Advantages	Disadvantages
Chalkboard	• Prominent place in classroom • Easily provides for spontaneous use • Easy to use • Easy for students to see • Inexpensive	• Not permanent • Space is limited • Most teachers must turn their backs to students to write • Locations are predetermined • Color use is limited
Chart stand	• Permanent. Students can retrieve a chart for use after instruction • Inexpensive • Can provide for spontaneous use • Can have several for use in different subjects or by different cooperative learning teams • Can be moved to other parts of the room • Greater use of color possible	• Print is usually the smallest of the devices • Occupies valuable floor space • Usually has a lower line of sight so some students have obstructed views
Overhead projector	• Typically the largest print of all • Materials easiest of all to develop • Storage may be either permanent or temporary • Can be the easiest for students to view • Has highest line of sight for students • Best possible use of color • Copiers and computers can generate professional quality graphics and text • Teacher maintains constant view of students	• Noisy • Often needs darkened room • Transparency film is more expensive than other display devices, although still reasonably priced • Requires a carefully placed projection screen and, therefore, has limited portability • Fixed cost of projector and screen is expensive • Teachers complain of glare when writing on overheads while the projector light is on

FIGURE 10.1   Advantages and disadvantages of display tools.

Telephones.   The telephone is a technology tool that is often underused in the classroom. Unfortunately, the telephone is sometimes viewed as a business tool, and the school's telephone is often off-limits for student use. However, students are increasingly finding access to a telephone in the library/media center, in the office, and even in the classroom. A world of information is available to children through the telephone. The following illustrations help to demonstrate the use and versatility of this tool:

◆   Earlier in this text, an example explained how children worked through the process of calculating the cost of the sidewalk surrounding the school grounds. The telephone business directory ("yellow pages") assisted the children in locating a concrete supplier for a quote on the current cost of concrete and a concrete contractor who provided a square-foot estimate of labor for finishing concrete sidewalks.

◆ Children crowded into the principal's office to make a special telephone call to the author of a book that the class had just read. The principal arranged the call as a reward for a reading incentive program. Three students were selected to start the interview. The children had first discussed the questions to be asked and faxed those to the author.

◆ Children in one school were provided with the school intercom for four minutes each morning. Students could call listed numbers at the local telephone company for weather and local news headlines. These were then included in the daily "radio" update to the whole school.

◆ Children had visited a veterinarian's office and the local animal shelter. Having made friends there, some of the children with their parents had later participated in a weekend "spay-neuter" fund drive and awareness campaign. When an injured woodpecker was brought to school, the children called the veterinarian and the animal shelter for the appropriate first aid.

The telephone can connect children to the world. In these cases, the children used the phone in much the same way as they will as adults. Careful rehearsals and telephone etiquette lessons preceded the telephone access. Also, the use of residential and business telephone directories were taught along with alphabetical order and guide words. These lessons were much more meaningful and students more enthusiastic because of the application potential. Communication capabilities through telephones, computers, and the Internet are providing students with a vast array of information sources. However, even if a school does not have a computer or Internet access, children can still engage in meaningful research activities through the simple use of a telephone.

Television and Videotape.   Television and videotape players lie somewhere between traditional tools and emerging high technology. In recent years, this technology has increasingly been available in schools. Video players, in particular, have become so affordable that teachers often provide the video machine themselves. Television provides an interesting case of educational technology that has generally failed to meet expectations. The power of television to provide vivid images and sound is unquestioned. Early attempts to use television were difficult because of limitations in broadcast schedules. Programs had to meet wide-ranging curricular goals and even then generally appealed to only a small number of classrooms compared to the overall population. Even if the program was appropriate for the class curriculum, the teacher still had to deal with the restrictions of an inflexible broadcast schedule. Videotape eliminated those restrictions.

The explosion of cable channels and the inexpensive availability of videotapes have created a plethora of high-quality programming in history, geography, science, health, and literature. The previous problems of cost and availability have all but vanished. The problem now is almost the opposite: From the wealth of programming, the issues are now what is to be selected, what purposes will be accomplished, and how programming will be used.

The selection of material to be used in the classroom involves several considerations. Video materials can be purchased, or they can be recorded from broadcasts. The issue of copyright violations must be considered when using material taped from the broadcasts of TV stations. The school librarian can explain "fair use" of material taped from broadcasts and any specific district policies regarding taped broadcasts used as teaching tools.

The teacher also has to understand his or her purpose for using video materials. Materials can be used to convey information, demonstrate a phenomenon that is too expensive or too dangerous to show in class, provide a tour or visit, or compose a part of a series of lessons specifically designed for elementary children. Teachers should look for segments of video rather than limiting their search to entire works. For example, if a teacher was preparing for a play, video clips from a movie review may inspire children toward more expressive communication. Sometimes, a program segment provides a brief visual representation of an historical event included in a class discussion. The overall material in the video may be too complex for children to comprehend, but the visual images of certain sections may wonderfully illustrate the setting, dress, and action involved.

Teachers should always establish a direct link between the material to be viewed and curricular purposes and make sure that everyone understands the purpose for viewing. The TV should not be used as a pacifier; material should have educational purposes and should never be used to keep children occupied.

Teachers should consider developing strategies for the routine use of TV. Having a rehearsed plan for setting up the apparatus facilitates the successful use of TV in the classroom. Classroom arrangements vary. In many cases, the class must move chairs and pull the window shades to ready the classroom for viewing. These procedures should be rehearsed so that it takes a minimum of time and no disruption. The teacher should always be sure that everyone can see and is comfortable. Sitting on the floor for viewing may be comfortable for children at first, but often the floor is hard and the lesson long. Soon the children will be lying down, rolling, or simply wriggling for blood circulation. This is true even if they are totally engrossed in the video. If children must sit on the floor, the teacher should plan a short "stand and shake" circulation break or allow adequate room between students for movement.

TV/VCR's can be hooked up to listening centers so that a small group can watch without disturbing others. This is particularly helpful for students in cooperative learning groups or students doing special projects. Also, lessons designed specifically for the ability of a subgroup of children can be shown to the intended audience. For example, book review programs are often geared to specific reading levels. A single program may be presenting books that are either too difficult or too easy for various groups in the class. The use of a listening center provides much needed flexibility for TV use.

Teachers should remember to use all of the features provided on the VCR. The pause, slow motion, and replay features can be used to wondrous effect. Some things can be seen more effectively when viewed in stop frame or slow motion. The fast forward can be used to eliminate parts of the video that are not relevant to the lesson. The video counter helps to locate certain segments. Laser disk players and DVD technology provide for immediate random access to any part of a recording. With DVD subtitling ability providing multiple languages, the capacity to include mixed media, and the ability to interact with computer programming, this technology has enormous potential in the classroom.

During a viewing session, the successful teacher asks questions and conducts discussion during the video and during closure activities. Videos can be paused easily, student attention focused by a question, and any misunderstandings or questions from students answered. Videos can be used for purposes other than information transmission. For example, the beginning of a movie can be shown as an inspiration for writing. The teacher can use the TV to avoid satiation from continued use of pencil-and-paper activities. The TV can provide a pleasant diversion from more mundane aspects of the daily class work. On the other hand, the teacher should not overuse the TV and should vary the methods and purposes of TV use.

Other "Low-Tech" Tools.   The classroom is filled with a wide variety of other tools including audiotape, filmstrips, listening centers, calculators, microscopes, and hand lenses. For all equipment, several issues should be kept in mind as a guide to successful use:

- Know the proper use and storage of the equipment.
- Store equipment for immediate and easy access.
- Use variety in selecting instructional strategies that use the technology.
- Understand, anticipate, and accept that equipment sometimes does not work as expected. Be patient and have a backup.
- Teach children the proper care of equipment.
- Have children demonstrate, practice, and rehearse the proper use of equipment.
- Develop and practice routines for quick setup and breakdown.
- Whenever possible, have children operate the equipment so that they are involved and you are free to teach more attentively.
- Use your imagination; most equipment can be used in many ways.

"High-Tech" Tools

The most dominant of the high-technology tools is the personal computer. Like the emergence of television in the 1950s and 1960s, claims for the total restructuring of schools as a result of this technology is being touted. It is true that the potential of computers, like the underutilized potential of television, can radically alter the schooling paradigm (Blomeyer & Martin, 1991; Bork, 1985; National Science Board Commission on Precollege Education in Mathematics, Science, and Technology, 1983). In the meantime, extensive study must be done to understand how these technologies can help children to learn more successfully. This will require a great deal of experimentation from teachers as the patterns of computer use are established.

Computers as Teacher Workstations.   Although the focus on computers in school is on student use, the most immediate impact is the increased efficiency of teachers who use the computer as a work tool. Simply using the computer as an office tool to compose letters, to develop overheads for printing on transparencies, to develop worksheets/activities, and to record and average grades saves teacher time that can be used for instructional purposes.

The computer also affords additional opportunities. Macros, or short written programs, can make it easier for teachers to write personalized letters to parents. Macros provide the teacher with a list of issues involved and suggestions for remedies that he or she has developed. The teacher then uses the macro to write a letter quickly that addresses the specific concerns identified by the teacher. The name and address of the child's parents can often be obtained from a database and inserted into the proper location on the letter. Using a word processor, the teacher can then further customize the letter and print it using a printer hooked up to the computer. The result is a very carefully composed letter of concern or congratulations that is still personalized but that takes only a fraction of the teacher's time that a handwritten note might take.

Special software programs are available to track attendance, compute attendance reports, record grades, and compute grade averages. These programs can be quite sophisticated and permit weighting of individual work, dropping scores, and looking for patterns in student test results. Many of these programs perform a statistical analysis on a test, on a series of tests, or on the patterns of scores of a subpopulation within the class.

When connected by modem or direct line to the Internet, teachers can communicate with other teachers individually or through special issue forums. Teachers can retrieve lesson plans through Internet access using file transfers such as ftp, gopher, or the World Wide Web. Teachers can obtain instructional materials by visiting Web sites and downloading books, pictures, and activities. Because the procedures for accessing electronic mail and Internet web sites vary with the computer, the software, and the service provider, detailed information is not included here. The best sources for this information are the school's media specialist or the district's media supervisor, the computer "guru" in the school or district, and the local telephone company for information about Internet access. Most access providers provide simple-to-use software and computerized tutorials.

Parents who are knowledgeable about computers can provide a wide range of assistance to the teacher. Children are also great teachers of technology and enjoy showing teachers and fellow students how to use computer technology successfully. Most software providers include tutorials for computer applications. Supplemental tutorials on CD, text, and video are also available.

With such advantages, why are computers not a dominant feature in a teacher's work? A number of factors are involved. Often, the availability of the computer in a configuration that facilitates teacher work is the culprit. Unless a printer is attached, most of the teacher's work cannot be completed. Without a modem and a telephone line, the world of information is simply not accessible. Software costs for an appropriate array of programs can easily exceed the cost of the computer. The computer has to be customized to fit individual work patterns. In the past, the emphasis was exclusively on student use with little consideration given to modernizing the teacher's work environment. In addition, teachers simply may be not aware of how a computer can help them work more efficiently.

Teachers, however, are quickly overcoming these barriers. The future work of teachers will no doubt evolve to integrate the advantages of computers. First, however, teachers have to develop several skills and attitudes. Teachers must be willing to learn skills that may not be directly related to teaching. Teachers must also become more proficient in self-instruction. Many of the most powerful computing tools are simple productivity applications that can be employed in many creative endeavors. Learning to use basic computer tools may not appear at first to be appropriate to teaching. However, by speeding up routine tasks, teachers can release valuable time for instructional development. Teachers must also be willing to invest time up front for benefits that may take time to be realized. Finally, teachers must demonstrate that they can successfully use the equipment currently available to them before the public will spend additional money for more technology.

Computers as Learning Tools.   Computers can provide unique educational opportunities for students. Early computer use centered around learning tasks that employed the traditional classroom paradigm. For example, math programs simply presented a math problem, the student calculated the problem and entered the answer, and the computer evaluated the response. If the answer was correct, the computer made noise or showed a picture. If it was wrong, the computer provided a second chance. If the second answer proved wrong, the computer counted the problem as wrong and went to the next problem. At the end, a percentage score was presented. These simple programs were not capable of evaluating the source of error or providing any level of sophisticated interaction. In many ways, these types of programs posed no advantages over flash cards. The sophistication and power of current computers were lacking, and the instructional usage simply followed the capability of the machines themselves.

With the increased sophistication of the computer and the standardization of user interfaces (the commands used to direct the computer), computers are easier to use and are capable of very sophisticated activities. A modestly equipped computer permits a student to write, typeset, and print a story. The student can then convert the file to HTML (the language of the Internet) and publish the story or report to the world. The computer can show the student potentially misspelled words and make suggestions about what word may be intended. The computer can evaluate grammar, explain what is wrong, and tell how to fix it. The computer can also assist the student in improving the structure of the sentence. The computer can even read the story out loud to the student or write a story dictated by the student.

The use of spreadsheets and word processors for assisting students to complete high-quality work is referred to as *productivity enhancement.* Integrating productivity packages into routine learning tasks of students is a primary area of computer use in the elementary school. Two things are accomplished: (1) Students learn to use computers effectively, a skill that they can use in their nonschool lives and in a wide variety of jobs. (2) Students usually do better work. For example, the author visited a school where the school newspaper was published on a computer. The print was in columns with appropriate headlines and banners, just like in daily newspapers. Students had taken pictures with an electronic camera, uploaded them to the computer, converted them to black-and-white, and enhanced them so that they would look good after being photocopied. Of course, they had used the spelling and grammar checkers in the computer software effectively. The teacher had taught the process of writing a news story by conventional methods, and each child was expected to produce a news story sometime during the month. Each student had to find his or her own news story, determine what was newsworthy, and decide when to write the story. The production process using the computer was a strong motivator for the more traditional journalism exercise of writing a news story.

In addition to productivity management, computers can also act as research tools for students. With Internet access or the use of high-storage CD-ROM devices, computers can provide a potentially endless supply of information. In doing a report, students can access CDs containing an encyclopedia for general information or a specialized electronic book. Students can take notes directly into the computer memory, copy quotations, and even save electronic versions of the pictures. They can then assemble the information into a report and apply appropriate typesetting and other formatting. They can then print the resulting report for distribution, post it electronically on the school's Web site, or show it to other students through the use of a video projector similar to those used to show movies on airplanes.

In the near future, computers will have voice recognition capability so that they will be able to recognize a wide variety of voices without further program customization (called *training*). Children in kindergarten will be able to dictate stories, and the computer will turn the story into text and show it to the student on the screen simultaneously. Computers can already read stories to children including the stories they have written.

Students can send electronic mail to companies or individuals to obtain general information and to have specific questions answered. Many zoological gardens provide Web sites that not only provide information but also permit students to ask questions of the zoo staff and animal trainers. U. S. government agencies have been legislated to provide student-oriented Web sites. For example, NASA has provided a question-and-answer service for several years where children and teachers from all over the world can ask questions and get expert answers. NASA sites are particularly intriguing since they permit the downloading of graphical images from exploratory spacecraft immediately after the images are received here on Earth.

In addition to increasing student and teacher productivity, computers are reaching the low-cost, high-sophistication levels that permit their use to support the arts. Students can compose, play, record, and even print out musical scores from the computer. Computers can be used to simulate various instruments, record sounds, and even "create" unique instruments from children's voices or classroom noise. Computers have equally profound capabilities in the visual arts. In some schools, videotape, the computer, and musical interfaces have been combined so that students can create, edit, and publish their own documentaries or music videos. For the most part, computer applications to support the arts remain on the high end of the technology spectrum and are not yet part of mainstream computer usage in the elementary school.

Simulations have found a steady following among elementary teachers and their students. In a simulation, the student is provided a context, such as governing a city, and is then required to make various decisions about events occurring in the simulated world. Students must decide how much to tax, how to spend the tax money, what type of campaign to run, and how to get reelected. Other simulations permit students to command a space shuttle or to diagnose and treat electronic patients. Simulations truly extend the classroom walls to encompass the world.

More traditionally, computers are used for student instruction. In all of the previously described uses of computers, computer programs are available for teaching how to use the computer and the application. Software has been written that describes and explores a constellation of school topics, including basic magnetism, chemistry, historical events, and virtually any other topic. Programs have been devised to assist students in constructing a story, developing appropriate essays, and writing well-developed critiques of literary works. More sophisticated programs can record the sessions of each child so that it "remembers" what the child has completed and the level of success. Computers are "patient" in that they do not get discouraged if the child takes many repeated attempts to get a problem right. Some of the better computer-assisted instruction (CAI) can sense repeated errors and modify the instructional process to provide helpful hints or limit the child's choices so that, ultimately, the child successfully completes the task. The computer can assess the level of success, repeat the lesson for students who need additional practice, and provide more difficult lessons for those students who demonstrate mastery.

Considering the power of the computer as a teaching and learning tool, why are computers not a major component of the classroom? There are a number of barriers to the effective use of computers in the learning environment.

- Computer use depends on computer availability (a combination of number and access). In most classrooms, there are still too few computers in use for the number of students. Even with modestly priced computers available, providing several computers in a classroom is still very expensive.
- Students must have frequent, nondisruptive access to computer tools if they are to be integrated into daily work.
- Most school computers lack the power and software to perform many of the tasks just described. The computer's configuration (power, speed, features, and capability) determines its utility.
- The software installed on the computer is often inadequate for the needs of students. Software costs are grossly underestimated in the technology budgets of most districts. Generally, the software and hardware installation and maintenance costs for appropriately developed networks approach and can exceed the actual costs of the computers themselves. Without a variety of software, the variety of computer usage is minimized.

Eventually, classroom computer access will mushroom. New multimedia machines with the ability to use CD-ROM and DVD-ROM technology and supportive networking systems will pose innovative solutions to these fiscal and pedagogical problems. The general downtrend in costs of both computers and software will also lead to increased computer availability. In general, though, the computer's heyday in the elementary school is still somewhat in the future.

Other "High-Tech" Tools.   Video cameras, laser disks, electronic cameras, color copiers, laser pointers, and the like form a core of emerging technology that has yet to make its contribution to schools. Some of these tools, such as color copiers, were once quite rare but are rapidly becoming mainstream technologies. However, their major contribution is still well into the future. Other equipment, such as the video camera, is rapidly being incorporated into the elementary classroom. The exact use of each to support learning will probably be developed by the current generation of teachers.

An examination of the video camera demonstrates both the potential and the barriers of technology and illustrates the broad applications likely to emerge. Video cameras have passed from expensive devices into common household possessions in just a few years. Purchase costs are still quite high, but usage costs are extremely low. Currently, typical usage of the video camera extends to capturing school events such as plays, field days, and musical performances. There are many other ways to employ the video camera that can dramatically impact classroom lessons, yet are unused because teachers are unaware of the technology's capabilities. Careful consideration of how the technology can be used to support classroom endeavors is critical for teacher success. The underutilization of the video camera and TV illustrates this point quite well.

Most video cameras come with a capability to focus very closely on an object. This is called a *macro* capability. Even less expensive cameras can be focused so that the recorded image of a postage stamp can fill the entire picture format. These cameras can also be attached to TVs via a simple coaxial cable so that a live feed of that postage stamp can be displayed on the screen. The teacher can point at a feature on the stamp, and the image can be enlarged 600 or 700 times on the TV. If the stamp were replaced with a small beetle in a confined plastic bubble, the possibilities begin to emerge. An entire class of students can view the beetle at incredible magnification in a live in-class broadcast. A teacher can point out the characteristics of the insect's mouth (which can be as large as eight inches on a 25-inch TV), its legs, or its antennae. The same setup can be used to show parts of a plant, a dissection, a chemistry demonstration, or even to demonstrate how a human hair follicle reacts to cold. In short, the TV and video camera can be combined to provide the equivalent of a microscope for every student in the class.

Teachers, however, need to consider why technology tools, such as the video camera, are not employed more effectively to support instruction. When new tools become available, teachers must become intimately familiar with the capabilities of the devices and must think creatively about how those devices can be used to enhance teaching. Also, using most of these devices requires some familiarization with the use of the equipment, its care, and preparation for use. In the previous example, the coaxial cable that connects the TV and camera may not be included and has to be obtained prior to use. Also, the teacher must be familiar with the proper manner of plugging the cable into the two units. The length of the distance between TV and the demonstration may require long cable runs so that, typical of technology, there are many wires running in many places. This tangle of wires and cords must be thoroughly understood so that the time and effort to set up the activity is minimal. For example, one teacher simply left the cable plugged into the TV and looped around a bracket glued to the TV for just that purpose. An inexpensive "A-B" switch was attached so that the TV was ready at a click and the cable simply pulled out to the demonstration table. Even more clever, a fourth-grade teacher taught several of the students how to connect the devices (she color-coded the cable to the fitting) and how to set up the tripod.

Effective use of emerging or high technology depends on teacher willingness to develop strategies that employ technology and then develop standard routines to minimize the fuss. Teachers can use technology to get more done only if they develop their knowledge, practice the usage until the procedures are automatic, make creative adaptation to the environment to simplify use, and modify lessons so that technology is incorporated routinely.

Homework

Although there is probably no feature of public education in America that is more ubiquitous than homework, the procedure is not always given much attention. In the American Educational Research *Handbook of Research on Teaching* (Wittrock, 1986), homework is not even mentioned in the subject index. Homework is often ignored, maligned, used as punishment, cited as evidence of effective schools, and often required, not by the teacher, but by school board mandate.

◆

A Homework Vignette

Sammy was impatient. He had his third "homework/sciencework activity pack" in as many weeks. He couldn't wait until his mom got home to open it. His teacher had designed the activity packs to supplement the work at school and to involve the parents in the lessons. The routine was usually the same. The teacher provided a lecture and demonstration and then handed out a sealed packet with an activity to be completed with at least one parent or grandparent. The last one sent home had a magnet and an activity card. Sammy filled in a chart showing the things to be tested in the kitchen and whether the magnet would stick to it. He also got to put the magnet in a plastic bag and run it through the dirt. He was surprised at what he found. This time, the class had been talking about changes, and the teacher had told them that they were going to mix things to find out what happened.

Homework can be a family affair.

As soon as his mom got home, Sammy gave her the packet. "Now?" she asked. "Don't you want to eat first?" She opened the envelope and pulled out a carefully worded letter about what the children had been studying. There was a chart attached with a list of household things to mix in one column and a place to write down what happened in the other. Some of the combinations were vegetable oil and colored water, vinegar and baking soda, milk and chocolate power, and salt and water. There were squares left blank so that additions could be made. Sammy was ready to start, and his mom helped him locate the ingredients. Since Sammy was only in the second grade, his mom had to help him spell some of the words. After he wrote a new word, he also copied it into his "Word Book" which went home with him each afternoon and back to school again in the morning. The teacher wanted them to discover 10 new words each week for their "Word Book," but Sammy easily found 20 or more.

Sammy mixed the vegetable oil and colored water in a jar under his mom's direction. He was surprised that they just sat there, one on top of the other. His mom screwed the jar lid tight, and Sammy shook the jar. After the bubbles settled down, the oil and water separated. Sammy was intrigued. Next, he put baking soda in the saucer as directed, then poured a spoonful of vinegar on top. As Sam watched, he knew he had the "baddest" teacher around. His mom was also pleased.

What Can Homework Do?

Homework can be a blessing or a curse, and that determination primarily rests on the judgment of the teacher. From the previous vignette, it is evident that Sammy's teacher thinks that homework should help the home become a laboratory for learning. Sammy's teacher had constructed the requirements carefully, explained the purpose and meaning of the work thoroughly, and provided parents with an opportunity to explore with their child. Although every homework assignment cannot be as exciting as this one, all homework assignments can be carefully considered and have a clear, articulated purpose.

Payne (1963) suggests that homework should serve one of two purposes: (1) to practice a skill, or (2) to satisfy a child's intellectual curiosity. It has long been known that homework is used for less noble reasons. Over three decades ago, Payne wrote, "Any teacher who assigns homework as a disciplinary measure, exacting quantities of drill and meaningless busy work perpetrates an outrage on the teaching profession. This is not teaching but exploitation" (1963, p. 15).

Figure 10.2 lists some goals that homework can satisfy and gives some reasons and circumstances for not giving homework.

Benefits of Appropriate Homework

The U.S. Department of Education published a synopsis of school practices that have been found effective through multiple empirical studies. It concluded that student achievement rises significantly when homework is both assigned and completed (U.S. Department of Education, 1986).

Use homework	Do not use homework
• To expand the learning opportunities of the child • To employ devices and materials from the home • To involve parents in pleasurable learning activities • To review or practice mastered material • To stimulate or satisfy intellectual curiosity • To attend to individual needs of the student • To provide a worthwhile experience	• To punish students • To substitute for guided practice • To introduce new content or a new skill unless students are carefully oriented to these special requirements • When the required time becomes excessive • When there is no clear purpose or benefit to the student

FIGURE 10.2 Appropriate and inappropriate uses of homework.

Extra studying helps children at all levels of ability. One research study reveals that when low-ability students do just one to three hours of homework a week, their grades are usually as high as those of average-ability who do not do homework. Similarly, when average-ability students do three to five hours of homework a week, their grades usually equal those of high-ability students who do no homework.

There are definite benefits to having students do appropriate homework. However, the issue is not quite as settled as it may sound. As with all other issues in education, the benefits of homework and what defines appropriate homework is quite complex. One thing does seem clear: Older students profit more from homework than younger children do when the results of academic testing is the measure. However, with young children, the arousal of curiosity, the stimulus to explore the environment, and the potential to expand the child's learning opportunities in nonacademic areas seem to provide adequate defense for appropriate homework assignments.

Cooper (1989) provides an extensive analysis of homework and found, not at all unexpectedly, that homework has both positive and negative effects. A summary of those findings is shown in Figure 10.3. Cooper describes four types of effects from homework:

◆ Students who do homework have better retention of factual knowledge, increased understanding of material, better critical thinking, and concept formation.

◆ Homework benefits long-term academic performance by encouraging children to learn during their leisure time, improving their attitudes toward school, and developing their study habits and skills.

◆ Students with homework had greater self-discipline and self-direction, better time organization, more inquisitiveness, and more independent study.

◆ Homework helps parents become partners in the learning process, increases their appreciation of schools and the schooling process, and encourages them to emphasize learning in the home.

There is evidence to support all of these claims, but the final verdict on homework effectiveness depends on the type of homework required of children. Cooper surveyed 11 major summaries of the research on homework. Seven of the reviews concluded that the research on homework indicated that homework favors higher achievement, whereas the remaining five concluded that the research is inconclusive. None concluded that homework was harmful.

Like most instructional tools, homework can be abused so thoroughly that there is no doubt homework can become a tool of torment rather than a tool of learning. Parents recount cases in which homework failed to work toward learning success and promoting student motivation. For example, one parent recounted that his child was given 100 long-division problems to do in a single night because a large percentage of the class had failed to complete the previous day's assignment. Unfortunately, punitive use of homework exists, and children probably view homework negatively from the outset. Fortunately, such abuse is easy to avoid by several simple steps that compose the core characteristics of appropriate homework.

FIGURE 10.3 Positive and negative effects of homework.

Adapted from *Homework* (p. 12) by H. Cooper, 1989, New York: Longman.

Positive Effects
- Immediate achievement and learning
  - Better retention of factual knowledge
  - Increased understanding
  - Better critical thinking, concept formation, information-processing
  - Curriculum enrichment
- Long-term academic
  - Encourage learning during leisure time
  - Improved attitude toward school
  - Better study habits and skills
- Nonacademic
  - Greater self-direction
  - Greater self-discipline
  - Better time organization
  - More inquisitiveness
  - More independent problem solving
- Greater parental appreciation of and involvement in schooling

Negative Effects
- Satiation
  - Loss of interest in academic material
  - Physical and emotional fatigue
- Denial of access to leisure-time and community activities
- Parental interference
  - Pressure to complete assignments and perform well
  - Confusion of instructional techniques
- Cheating
  - Copying from other students
  - Help beyond tutoring
- Increased differences between high and low achievers

Characteristics of Appropriate Homework

Traditionally, homework has been used to practice a skill, prepare for instruction, or extend a lesson's content to develop individual skills and knowledge (LaConte & Doyle, 1985). However, many teachers use homework to reveal an otherwise hidden world of educational opportunity.

When homework is assigned for practice, it is imperative that the teacher has provided adequate instruction for the child to succeed. This usually entails sufficient guided practice so that the teacher knows what the results of the homework will be. If a child is having difficulty because the concept or general principles are not yet understood, independent practice that is typical of homework may not be indicated. If the teacher has established appropriate communications, a quick note can inform the parent of any special need for a student who has not yet mastered the skill and suggest that the parent help with the homework as necessary. If parental support is unknown or lacking, the practice work should be delayed.

Carefully Developed Activities.   Shockley (1964) suggests several positive criteria for appropriate homework that support the practice function. He suggests that homework should be planned (not hastily conceived at the end of the lesson) to accomplish something that cannot be done better by some other venue. He suggests that homework should reinforce lessons rather than attempt to teach something entirely new. Homework should be at each child's ability level but still should "stretch" the child a little. Appropriate homework requires modest time to complete, is matched to student ability, is designed to build study habits, and provides some room for student initiative, imagination, and creativity.

Applying the same principles necessary for appropriate seatwork, successful teachers design homework so that

- Children receive sufficient instruction so that they can perform the homework successfully.
- The homework has a clear purpose, and that purpose is communicated.
- The directions for homework are easily understood.
- The necessary materials for completing homework is available to the child.
- The homework can be completed quickly without undue anxiety.

Homework as Preparation.   Homework can also be used to prepare students for instruction. Often, this is a reading assignment in a novel or textbook that will be the topic of the next day's lesson. However, there are other types of activities that can be used to prepare students for future lessons and serve the purpose of advance organizers. For example, on a lesson describing the effects of technology on daily life, children could interview a grandparent or great-grandparent about what life was like in their childhood. The teacher may submit a list of questions to help the student conduct the interview. Questions appropriate for fifth graders may be as follows:

- What kind of games did you play?
- What did a telephone look like?
- How much did a calculator cost?
- What was the first video game you remember?
- What kind of computer did you use in school? What did you do with it?
- What did you watch on TV? What was your favorite video?
- What was your classroom like?

Children are often astounded to find their grandparent had no calculators, no computers, and no video games.

The teacher may alternately provide the student with a short letter to be given to the interviewee describing the purpose of the interview. With some coordination and timing, the teacher may be able to identify one or more documentaries that are being shown on TV that evening or weekend.

Documentation of Homework.   The teacher may be concerned that students will not complete homework activities unless there is some type of documentation created such as a written summary of the assigned interview. This documentation is appropriate, but not entirely necessary, for all types of assignments. When assigning homework to prepare students for lessons, several important points are necessary:

◆   All students must have access to necessary materials.
◆   The teacher must be clear with expectations and purpose.
◆   Evaluation procedures should not attempt to measure the degree of mastery. The appropriate time to measure mastery is at the end of instruction. Usually, the activity is measured as completed or not completed.
◆   If an activity employs a skill that students have not mastered, the teacher needs to acknowledge that in advance and reassure students that their effort toward the assignment is what is expected.

Extended Lessons.   Homework assignments can also be used to extend lesson content beyond the classroom treatment of the material and to provide individualized learning opportunities. This is perhaps the most exciting and least utilized form of homework. The types of assignments in this category are literally endless.

Often, homework assignments in this category differ from other homework in that the student is asked to work on the activity or project over a period of days or even weeks. For example, students may be writing autobiographies by interviewing their friends and family. Although they can practice interviewing their classroom friends, their journalism skills will be best developed by interviewing people outside the school. This type of activity provides a great deal of individualization in the knowledge employed in the activity and its content. Other creative examples of homework include developing a display and providing a written report of a hobby, writing a narrative describing a single day in the life of a pet written in the first person, presenting a photo essay about happiness and where it is found, or producing a short video describing the student's neighborhood.

Homework assignments to extend lessons and individualize the curriculum have some characteristics that the teacher needs to remember:

◆   The child should have a wealth of choices so that the assignment is of personal interest and relevance.
◆   The child's skills should be sufficient to complete the assignment successfully (or there should be a clear plan on how the child will obtain the skills).
◆   There should be clear expectations on what constitutes successful completion of the assignment.
◆   The child's and parent's perspectives must be kept in mind.
◆   There should be a high probability of success.

Overnight Homework.   Overnight homework can also be used to individualize the curriculum. Students can write several work problems using a particular type of math skill (for example, two-place multiplication) and then solve them on a separate sheet. The next day, the students break into teams and complete the problems. Scoring strategies from cooperative learning can be used so that a student earns a point for each problem written, one point for each solution developed during the class, and one point for each problem that stumps his or her competitor. Harmin (1994) provides four recommendations to assist teachers in developing homework that extends the curriculum and provides choices:

◆ Assign flexible amounts of homework: The child does as much as possible within a time or skill parameter.
◆ Assign homework that allows students to learn different material. Students self-select the material to learn, such as selecting spelling words, choosing their own book, or picking their own essay topic.
◆ Use a flexible time assignment. Set minimal time limits but encourage students to do more.
◆ Ask students to create their own homework assignments. Have students develop practice or extension activities with partners or individually.

Only the imagination and skill of the teacher limit homework use. Careful consideration of the purpose of the homework and appropriate attention to student motivation are essential for the successful teacher. Homework should not be a burden to the student or the teacher. Practice activities almost always result in success if appropriate instruction and guided practice have preceded the assignment. Preparation for learning should be motivating and create anticipation for the lesson. Individualization should be meaningful, relevant, and largely self-directed.

Homework Difficulties.   When homework difficulties arise, the teacher should carefully consider the possible origin. If a large percentage of students do poorly on practice homework, the teacher may conclude that the previous lesson was only marginally successful and institute reteaching with copious measures of encouragement. If large numbers of students do not complete the assignment, the teacher must carefully assess the meaningfulness and purpose of the assignment and try to view the assignment through the eyes of students. Did they understand? Did they know the purpose? Did they have sufficient time and were the materials at hand? Wood (1987) described a number of reasons why students do not complete homework:

◆ Child reads too poorly to understand the content involved in homework.
◆ The work was too difficult to be completed successfully without assistance.
◆ Instructional pace during instruction was too fast, and student lacked comprehension.
◆ Directions were not clear or not given.
◆ Resource materials were not available.
◆ Students lacked interest in the work. Students did not perceive the meaning or purpose of the homework.
◆ Students became frustrated when they did not understand or felt that failure was imminent.
◆ Students had poor writing ability.
◆ Teachers did not give feedback on earlier homework.

Students' failure to complete work may also indicate a lack of study skills. This is particularly true when substantial self-direction is required. The National Education Association (NEA, 1975) surveyed the research on study habits and made a number of suggestions to teachers about homework completion that are appropriate for today's schools:

- Use high arousal or high interest materials and topics.
- Explain why the activity is important. Do not depend on authority or coercion for obtaining completed assignments.
- Expect success. Communicate success.
- Make sure that the work is meaningful and contains a comprehensible sequence.
- Teach to mastery. Ensure that students obtain a sense of success through success.

Teachers must view homework as a cooperative endeavor between the child and the teacher. When things do not go well, teachers and children must communicate to find out why and to plan successful activities in the future. With this in mind, homework can be made to work in favor of learning.

◆ ◆ ◆

Summary

1. Seatwork and centers augment the interactive instruction of the teacher by providing opportunities to practice skills and to explore new areas of knowledge independently.

2. Seatwork is primarily used as a practice device for previously taught skills and knowledge.

3. Seatwork is best employed when the assignments are brief, clear, easily understood, and have high success rates for completion. Seatwork sessions should contain routines for obtaining assistance either from the teacher or from other students as appropriate to the type of activity.

4. Seatwork may be interactive (involving the teacher) or may be independent practice. Each strategy has varying requirements for appropriate use.

5. Centers may provide practice for previously taught skills or may introduce new subjects and topics for exploration.

6. Centers should be designed to provide for student independence, to be easily understood and self-directing, to provide experiences in problem solving using a variety of materials, and to allow students to discover and learn through personal experience.

7. The use of centers is flexible and can be applicable to a wide range of goals. Children may work independently or in groups, produce a product or read and study, visit once or many times, practice to mastery or learn new material.

8. Centers are best employed when children are challenged, have opportunities to explore, are accountable for their learning success, and solve problems through direct experience.

9. Cooperative learning includes any educational activity in which a group of students are engaged in a common goal, are required to use extensive social interaction within that group, and utilize student leadership and self-direction as the primary characteristics of the instructional environment.

10. There are a number of established models for cooperative learning that can be tailored to almost any instruction topic or subject and incorporate a variety of instructional strategies and learning goals.

11. The primary purposes of cooperative learning are to raise academic achievement, encourage children to work successfully with peers, minimize competition, and provide a group reward structure that aids in increased learning motivation.

12. Technology involves a full range of teaching and learning tools used in the schools. Simpler tools that are highly integrated are referred to as "low-tech," whereas more advanced and sophisticated tools are referred to as "high-tech."

13. Both low- and high-technology tools are underused because teachers lack awareness and reflection regarding their effective and creative use. Teachers' lack of skill in using the tools, integrative thinking about technology tools, and availability are the three primary barriers to effective use of technology to support student learning.

14. With careful consideration, most technology, particularly the low-tech tools, can be more effectively utilized. Teaching children how to use the tools and then allowing them to oversee the use of technology increases the teacher's instructional effectiveness and permits students to use technology tools in much the same way as they will in their work lives.

15. Homework can be a valuable tool in extending the learning environment and in promoting student independence and responsibility.

16. Homework is best when assignments are brief, easy to complete without assistance, reinforce previously taught concepts, and developed for student success.

17. There are a variety of purposes for homework and, therefore, a variety of appropriate strategies for the design of homework assignments. Homework can be used to expand the learning environment, involve parents in pleasurable learning activities, stimulate intellectual curiosity, and provide worthwhile learning experiences. When care is not taken in developing homework, it can be punitive, can be excessively used, and can demotivate students.

◆ ◆ ◆

Activities and Questions for Further Understanding

1. Reread "A Slice of Life." To assure student success in the outdoor lesson, what activities must Mrs. Chen conduct prior to the children's work on the playground? What types of homework, seatwork, and centers could she use to follow up on this activity? Evaluate Mrs. Chen's activity using the basic elements of a cooperative learning strategy.

2. Reflect on the type of seatwork activities you performed as a student. Were there activities that you enjoyed or disliked more than others? What are the characteristics that make work enjoyable? Unpleasant? Share your ideas with a group and develop a list of strategies for improving seatwork.

3. Arrange a visit to a school that uses centers. What are the key elements of successful centers for reinforcing previously taught skills? Providing exploration of new material? Promoting creative expression? What are the management challenges to centers? How are they overcome?

4. Design a center that provides extension activities for children who have just completed reading a fiction book. What will they do? What choices will they have? How is motivation developed? Where and how do they get help if needed? How is their work evaluated?

5. With a group, prepare an information guide about some aspect of teaching and present it to a group. What social interactions occur within the group? What rewards are expected? How central to the activity are the anticipated rewards?

6. With a group, design a cooperative learning activity for a specific learning goal. You may wish to use one of the models described in the text. What are the design difficulties involved?

7. What are the strength and limitations involved in the cooperative learning paradigm? Does it have limitations? What type of instructional objectives require the use of some form of cooperative learning?

8. Examine one technology tool (or cluster of similar tools) common in classrooms. What are its standard uses? What suggestion can you make to ensure the tool is used suc-cessfully? What are some additional creative ways of employing the tool?

9. Teaching children to use technology equipment, particularly high technology, requires thoughtful strategies. Consider the various ways to instruct students on how to use, care, and maintain technology tools using an implicit instruction strategy. Compare those ways to instruction using explicit strategies. What are the advantages and disadvantages of each?

10. Visit a computer lab on campus and ask users what types of computer activities assist their learning. Ask specifically about productivity tools, information retrieval, and tutorial usage.

11. Access is an important element of successful technology use. If access to computers were eliminated as a barrier, what resulting activities would you see in the classroom?

12. As a group, debate the issue of homework use and abuse. Are the abuses of homework so dominant or the value of appropriate use so critical that school districts should make policies regarding its use?

13. Develop a homework activity that introduces concepts that might be learned in a second-grade lesson entitled, "From Farm to Table: How We Get Our Food." Develop a homework activity that practices mastery of concepts in the lesson. Finally, develop a homework assignment that permits individual exploration of the topic.

References

Blomeyer, R. L., Jr., & Martin, C. D. (1991). *Case studies in computer aided learning.* London: Falmer.

Bork, A. (1985). *Personal computers for education.* New York: Harper & Row.

Brophy, J. E. (1992). *Advances in research on teaching. Vol. 3: Planning and managing learning tasks and activities.* Greenwich, CT: JAI Press.

Brophy, J. E., & Good, T. L. (1986). Teacher behavior and student achievement. In M. C. Wittrock (Ed.),

Handbook of research on teaching (3rd ed., pp. 328–375). New York: Macmillan.

Cooper, H. (1989). *Homework.* New York: Longman.

DeVries, D. L., & Slavin, R. E. (1978). Teams-Games-Tournament (TGT): Review of Ten Classroom Experiments. *Journal of Research and Development in Education, (12)*, 28–38.

Doyle, W. (1986). Classroom organization and management. In M. C. Wittrock (Ed.), *Handbook of research on teaching* (3rd ed., pp. 392–431). New York: Macmillan.

Evertson, C. M., & Emmer, E. T. (1982). Effective management at the beginning of the year in junior high classes. *Journal of Educational Psychology, 74(4)*, 485–498.

Fensham, P. L. (1992). Science and technology. In P. W. Jackson (Ed.), *Handbook of research on curriculum.* New York: Macmillan.

Flemming, B. M., Hamilton, D. S., Hicks, J. D., & McKay, D. K. (1988). *Creative teaching in early childhood education: A sourcebook for Canadian educators and librarians.* Toronto: Harcourt Brace Jovanovitch.

Forte, I., & Mackenzie, J. (1978). *Nooks, crannies, and corners: Learning centers for creative classrooms.* Nashville, TN: Incentive Publications, Inc.

Furtwengler, C. B. (1992). How to observe cooperative learning classrooms. *Educational Leadership, (49)*7, 59–62.

Godfrey, L. L. (1972). *Individualizing through learning stations.* San Francisco: Teachers Exchange of San Francisco.

Good, T. L., & Brophy, J. E. (1997). *Looking into classrooms* (7th ed.). New York: Longman.

Goodson, I. F. (1988). *The making of curriculum.* Lewes, England: Falmer Press.

Harmin, M. (1994). *Inspiring active learning: A handbook for teachers.* Alexandria, VA: Association for Supervision and Curriculum Development.

Johnson, D. W., & Johnson, R. T. (1987). *Learning together and alone* (2nd ed.). Upper Saddle River, NJ: Prentice Hall.

Johnson, D. W., & Johnson, R. T. (1989). *Cooperation and competition: Theory and research.* Edina, MN: Interaction Book Company.

Johnson, D. W., Johnson, R. T., & Holubec, E. J. (1991). *Cooperation in the classroom* (Rev. ed.). Edina, MN: Interaction Book Company.

Johnson, D. W., Johnson, R. T., & Scott, L. (1978). The effects of cooperative and individualized instruction on student attitudes and achievement. *Journal of Social Psychology, (104)*, 207–216,

Kounin, J. S. (1970). *Discipline and group management in classrooms.* New York: Holt Rinehart & Winston.

LaConte, R. T., & Doyle, M. A. (1985) *Homework as a learning experience.* Washington, DC: National Education Association.

Lloyd, D. M. (1974). *70 activities for classroom learning centers.* Dansville, NY: The Instructor Publications, Inc.

Madden, N. A., Slavin, R. E., and Stevens, R. J. (1986). *Cooperative integrated reading and comparison: Teacher's manual.* Baltimore: Johns Hopkins University, Center for Research on Elementary and Middle Schools.

National Education Association. (1975). *What research says to the teacher: Homework.* Washington, DC: Author.

National Science Board Commission on Precollege Education in Mathematics, Science, and Technology. (1983). *Educating Americans for the 21st century: A plan of action for improving mathematics, science, and technology education for all American elementary and secondary students so that their achievement is the best in the world by 1995.* Portland, OR: Author.

Northwest Regional Educational Laboratory. (1990). *Effective schooling practices: A research synthesis.* Portland, OR: Author.

Payne, R. S. (1963). The school's part in home study for intermediate grades. In M. Rasmussen (Ed.), *Homework: The home's part, the school's part* (pp. 12–26). Washington, DC: Association for Childhood Education International.

Petreshene, S. S. (1978). *The complete guide to learning centers.* Palo Alto, CA: Pendragon House.

Rosenshine, B., & Stevens, R. (1986). Teaching functions. In M. C. Wittrock, *Handbook of research on teaching* (3rd ed., pp. 376–391). New York: Macmillan.

Sharan, S. (1980). Cooperative learning in small groups: Recent methods and effects on achievement, attitudes, and ethnic relations. *Review of Educational Research, (50)*2, 241–271.

Sharan, Y., & Sharan, S. (1989). Group investigation expands cooperative learning. *Educational Leadership, (47),* 17–21.

Shockley, R. J. (1964). *Using homework as a teaching tool: Extending classroom activities through guided home study.* Upper Saddle River, NJ: Prentice Hall.

Slavin, R. E. (1980). Effects of student teams and peer tutoring on academic achievement and time on task. *Journal of Experimental Education, (48),* 252–257.

Slavin, R. E. (1986). *Using student team learning* (3rd ed.). Baltimore: Johns Hopkins University, Center for Research on Elementary and Middle Schools.

Slavin, R. E. (1995). *Cooperative learning: Theory, research, and practice.* Boston: Allyn and Bacon.

Slavin, R. E., Leavey, M., & Madden, N. A. (1986). *Team accelerated instruction: Mathematics.* Watertown, MA: Charlesbridge.

Stallings, J. A., & Stipek, D. (1986). Research on early childhood and elementary school teaching programs. In M. C. Wittrock (Ed.), *Handbook of research on teaching* (3rd ed.). New York: Macmillan.

Stevens, R. J., Madden, N. A., Slavin, R. E., and Farnish, A. M. (1989). Cooperative integrated reading and composition: Two field experiments. *Reading Research Quarterly, (22),* 433–454.

Tickle, L. (1990). Perspectives on design and technology. In L. Tickle (Ed.), *Design and technology in primary school classrooms* (pp. 12–28). London: Falmer.

U.S. Department of Education. (1986). *What works?* Washington, DC: Author.

Wittrock, M. C. (Ed.). (1986) *Handbook of research on teaching* (3rd ed.). New York: Macmillan.

Wood, J. A. (1987). *Helping students with homework.* Dubuque, IA: Kendall/Hunt.

CHAPTER 11

How Do I Know When I'm Successful?

Evaluation of Student Learning

Outline

Educational evaluation is useful only if it helps the educator . . . make sound educational judgments and decisions.

TERRY TENBRINK

You should be so lucky!

ABIGAIL, 12, AFTER HER FEMALE PE TEACHER SAID, "YOU RUN LIKE A GIRL."

◆

A Slice of Life

Mrs. Grant never liked report card day. No matter how good the work or how many "A's" were given, the day always seemed gloomy in the end. It never seemed to work out the way she wanted. Students who tried hard left feeling bad, and brilliant goof-offs left acting smug. But the big day had arrived and since this was the first report card of the year, she had set aside an entire lesson to discuss grades, grading, and report cards with her sixth graders.

"You all know that today I send home the first report card of the school year. I want you to know how the grades were determined, what the grades mean, and what to do if you disagree with the grade." Mrs. Grant always surprised herself that she listened to children who felt they had been incorrectly graded. In the past six years, she'd never heard a valid reason why the grade should be changed. She worked hard to prevent any surprises or errors. But when grades on report cards are given, nothing should be left to chance. Every opportunity for communication had to be used effectively. For Mrs. Grant, the development of the report card started two months ago.

A Careful System

Each week, Mrs. Grant sent out a progress report describing to the parents what was done during the week and what student work had been completed. She provided a short section describing the quality of the work completed by the student, whether work was missing or had to be redone, and the work habits displayed by the student during the week. For most students, there was an ongoing dialog with the parents, and a special work or study habit was targeted for extra practice.

Mrs. Grant sent a package of the work completed that week with the report. This way, parents could examine the work and make their own judgment about the learning successes for the week. When returned, Mrs. Grant would have students select certain pieces to go into a cumulative portfolio. Sometimes, she would tell the students which assignment would go into the portfolio. Often, she would let the children pick the best example of math or social studies and that would be included. Special projects were put into the portfolios as were all classroom tests.

Report Cards Distributed

"I have all the weekly progress reports stapled together. I want you to put them into your portfolio and take them home tonight with your report card. OK? I'm handing out a letter for you to give to your parents. It tells them that there should be eight weekly reports and at least eight pieces of work for each subject . . . that's math, social studies, spelling, reading, language, and science. They are to sign the note with any comments they'd like to make, and you are to return it on Monday. Bring the portfolios back, too! We'll keep them until the end of the year."

There was not a lot of cheer in the classroom, and Mrs. Grant felt the tension. "Well, let me tell you once again how I computed your grades. Remember, I don't give grades; I compute them from your work. For all subjects, tests count for one-half of your grade; completed classwork and homework count for the other half. If you tried hard, completed, and returned all your assignments and progress reports, I added up to three points to your average." As Mrs. Grant handed out report cards, there were expressions of elation and muffled moans of disappointment.

"Geez, Mrs. Grant. A 'B+'? That'll cost me my bonus! Can't you give me an 'A'? I did everything you asked for and made 'A's' on everything else. If I make all 'A's,' I get an extra ten dollars! I'll do an extra credit report." Jeremy was a wonderful kid, but his timing was sometimes not quite the best.

"Jeremy, let's talk about it later, OK? I need to give out the rest of the report cards." Mrs. Grant handed out the last of the reports and reminded the children again that she only computed the grades from work they did. "Remember, children, if you want a better report card, you'll need to work harder every day. Each assignment contributes in some way to your grade. I'm also very proud of you. There is a lot of hard and wonderful work that went into earning these grades. Look at your portfolios and progress reports and see if you don't agree that you've done some fine work. What we need to do is be sure that every day is our best work

day." Mrs. Grant knew that each portfolio contained a sample of excellent work, and she had written special comments regarding the quality of work each child was capable of doing. Her motto was to point out the best and expect it every day.

A Collective View

At the sixth-grade meeting after school, all of the teachers felt about the same. No matter what they did, reports cards always seemed like a firing squad to someone in the class. Mrs. Adams, however, did express a bit of thanks for the current situation. "At my last school, teachers couldn't give grades, and the kids wouldn't do anything. As bad as they are, it is one way to hold children accountable. There's not a kid in the sixth grade who got a bad grade that didn't have plenty of offers from us to provide some extra help."

Mrs. Grant agreed. "I know that, Trudy, but it still doesn't seem right. I had a boy today that looked at his report card as income. He didn't care about learning. He just wanted money."

Mrs. Huskins offered the final comment. "Well, if you know what works better, let everyone else in on the secret. I've been around a long time and have gone through lots of report card fads. Parents want grades, everyone understands them, and it makes most kids wake up for at least a week afterward."

Mrs. Grant found herself nodding in agreement but left for home still wondering about report cards, grades, and what they contributed to learning.

Ancient Tradition of Testing and Grading

The earliest known program of testing began in China over four thousand years ago (Robinson & Craver, 1989). From around 2300 to 1100 B.C., successive Chinese dynasties administered formal examinations to civil servants every three years. After three tests, civil servants were either promoted or dismissed.

Testing has continued throughout the millennia as a fundamental measure of learning, knowledge, and work effectiveness. During each millennium, tests have been subject to harsh criticism. Even though few express enthusiasm about testing and grading, the practice is almost ubiquitous in every conceivable school setting. With all its copious shortcomings, testing and grading still find the widest acceptance for student and teacher accountability.

Formal testing of students in the United States became widespread at the same time that common schools were developed. Horace Mann advocated switching from oral examinations to written ones because of the abuses, limitations, and inefficiency of the existing oral examination system. By the early 1900s, significant work began on developing written tests so that the results of tests could be interpreted uniformly, thus ensuring fairness to test takers and comparability of results across institutions (Robinson & Craver, 1989). Harsh criticism of these new tests began almost immediately, yet the idiosyncratic grading practices of individual teachers posed no real alternative. This status quo, a distrust of both systematic testing or idiosyncratic grading, continues today. Is the standardized test or the report card the best indicator of student learning? Does either system actually communicate the level of academic achievement of students? If not, why are they so prevalent? Although all current strategies for evaluation have flaws, the greater and more pervasive fear has been that of no accountability at all. Thus, teachers must give grades, and students must take tests. As limiting as the practice may be, the alternatives have not found widespread acceptance.

Teachers, like our Mrs. Grant, have made excellent progress in making the grading process fairer, albeit a system far from perfect. However, even the most fair and most comprehensive procedures are continually subject to criticism and limitations. The single most important improvement for giving school grades is the development of *evaluation systems* that employ multiple measures of a broad spectrum of outcomes. Rather than relying on tests alone, evaluation systems are designed to use a range of assessment measures including actual demonstrations of skill, checklists of observable behaviors, and formal questioning of students on lesson content.

Teachers are generally required to fulfill a broad range of evaluative roles using a multitude of strategies. Two goals, however, remain constant and are consistent concerns for teachers: (1) the accuracy of the measure, and (2) the fairness of its use. To obtain accuracy and fairness, a teacher must understand the development and use of fundamental components of an evaluation system.

Basic Parts of an Evaluation System

An effective evaluation system for student learning is similar to all well-developed evaluation systems in that five core areas form the basic structure of the process. Evaluation systems include a carefully articulated purpose, measurable objectives, instruments capable of measuring the objectives, a process of interpretation, and a method for communicating the results. Although each of these areas are discussed more fully later in this chapter, a short description of what is meant by each will serve as an introduction to the complexity of what is seemingly a simple process.

Purposes: Accountability and Instructional Improvement

Two broad purposes of accountability and instructional improvement govern the development and implementation of an evaluation system for school learning. Although simple in concept, many, if not most, evaluation systems do neither. Accountability has two types: (1) The student must be accountable for successful learning, and (2) the teacher must be accountable for teaching effectiveness. Most measures include an element of both types of accountability, although students are held accountable for learning more frequently than teachers are held accountable for effective instruction.

If accountability is to be obtained, the evaluation system must contain both measures of student learning and a description of the activities and efforts provided by the teacher to bring about that learning. Without understanding the methods employed, knowing the results may not carry sufficient meaning to help parents improve the educational attainment of their children.

Improvement of learning is the heart of any evaluation system. If students and teachers are held accountable, both student effort and teacher effort must be applied to shortcomings identified by the evaluation system. It is important to point out the subtle difference between assigning blame and providing remedy. Although it would be naïve to assert that evaluation systems should focus only on providing remedy, it is destructive if the system puts an emphasis on blame. Improvement of instruction requires teamwork from parents, students, teachers, and administration. The purpose of an evaluation system is to see what all parties are doing and what is most constructive to successful learning. With that focus, an evaluation system is an essential core force in improving learning success in the elementary school.

Objectives That Can Be Measured

In addition to the long-range goal of improving accountability and instructional effectiveness, evaluation of student learning also has immediate purposes in the form of short-term objectives. For example, prompt completion of work is an objective that represents a strategy toward improving learning success as well as more effective social living. Therefore, evaluating students on prompt work completion on a daily basis is both appropriate and helpful. Objectives guide and direct the assessment process by directing the evaluator-teacher in determining what is to be measured and what is to be omitted from consideration. In grading a specific piece of work, the objectives can provide guidance in assessing the success of the work. When a number of pieces are being assessed simultaneously, such as the case with a report card grade, objectives may be more like goals in that a number of specific objectives must be represented by a single judgment. Clearly developed objectives that describe the type and extent of learning to be measured must be communicated effectively if the assessment strategy is to be meaningful.

Instruments

The development of an instrument to provide accurate measurement is a challenging task. In the elementary school, many student activities can be used to assess student learning. Daily work, projects, homework, activity from centers, and unassigned activity all can be used efficiently to assess learning progress. These tasks serve dual duty as vehicles for developing learning skill and for evaluating the success of student learning. However, instruments that fulfill the most stringent measurement requirements usually do not fall into this category. Homework success may be heavily influenced by parental assistance or through the expediency of copying other students' work. Some students have difficulty in learning new tasks; therefore, early trials result in poor work although the task may be mastered in the appropriate amount of time. Thus, if scores from early trials are averaged with later trials, students are measured not only on learning success but also on the speed in which learning occurs. Tests, although not popular among students and many teachers, minimize these extraneous influences and provide the most controlled view of student learning. Although often viewed as external and artificial, tests can be constructed with skill and care so that most negative consequences are either eliminated or their effects neutralized. A wide variety of instruments besides tests and teacher records of daily work exist. Teachers use checklists, observations, demonstrations, portfolios, presentations, performances, and special projects to assess student progress.

Interpretation

Once collected, information from various forms of instruments must be combined to establish patterns of skill attainment or deficits. The process of collecting information is much simpler than interpreting the data and making judgments to guide further instruction. The simplest is a system in which each piece of work is assessed and a numerical representation (often the percentage of items correct) is computed. These numbers are averaged or combined in some fashion to provide a single point estimate of the student's learning. Almost everyone is familiar with a graded test yielding a percentage score that in turn is averaged with other percentages. The resulting average is used to determine a letter grade. There are a number of advantages to such systems that account, in part, for their popularity. Such systems also contain serious flaws by making many assumptions that usually are unexamined. For example, it is assumed that tests are created so that someone who has learned the material taught in class can successfully complete all items. Often, tests or other written activities do not appropriately reflect that assumption.

Teachers have developed an array of strategies for dealing with violations of these assumptions. These strategies include curving (adding points so that the highest score becomes a perfect score and all other scores are moved accordingly), "extra credit" items, weighting, or dropping the lowest score. Other assessment instruments, such as anecdotal comments, checklists, and scales, can also be used. However, most interpretation strategies attempt to simplify the data for ease of understanding and communication.

Communication

Evaluations must be communicated to others if they are to influence future events. In schools, evaluations of student learning must be provided to students and parents on a regular basis. For students, evaluations of work should be frequent and helpful. How learning effectiveness is communicated to students, however, can be destructive as well as helpful. A student who has a particularly difficult time in comprehending math problems presented in situation form (word problems) may be overly discouraged by an inability to comprehend what information to use and how that information is to be computed. Communicating the success of the student's effort with a "45% . . . careless!" may not be sufficient to correct that specific learning difficulty. In fact, such treatment may make future learning even more difficult.

Consider the potential effect of one alternative in this situation. The teacher circles the incorrect math problems and puts an "=" mark beside those that were set up properly but computed incorrectly. The teacher then writes, "In the circled problems, you got the right information and set the problem up correctly . . . but you computed wrong. Why don't you do the computations again? Save the others for class discussion." In this communication, the teacher made at least one suggestion for future improvement, proposed a process for improvement, and extended an invitation for future learning. When the student removed the careless errors, the teacher returned the resubmitted work with the comment, "Much better! With careless mistakes removed, 80%!"

Errors and Values

Because errors can occur in each of the five phases of evaluation, it is easy to understand why current efforts to assess student work result in such misunderstanding and gloom. Even when great care is taken, the appropriate development and implementation of a system of evaluation for student learning and teacher instruction are fraught with difficulty. The following sections attempt to deal with the major issues and provide some guidance for their resolution. However, it must be remembered that evaluation is a process of placing value on outcomes. Since values, particularly as they relate to education, vary widely among parents, teachers, and children, there will be substantial disagreement about the effects and success of various approaches to evaluating student work even when the technical requirements of various approaches serve as exemplars of excellence.

Basic Evaluation Concepts

Merwin (1989) outlines the basic key concepts of evaluation as including an understanding of what composes the following:

- Evaluation
- Individual differences
- Assessment
- Tests
- Validity
- Reliability
- Relevance
- Objectivity

Merwin acknowledges that evaluation is widely defined and carries a number of differing connotations. In general, *evaluation* is establishing the worth or value of an activity usually by careful processes involving the assembly and analysis of data and its comparison to a variety of criteria. Criteria can be absolute (as when the specific level of mastery is defined) or comparative (as when the performance of an individual is compared to that of others). Absolute criteria are typically referred to as *criterion-referenced* because the student's work is compared to an absolute standard independent of the work of other children. Relative standards are usually referred to as *norm-referenced* because the work is compared to that of other learners in the group. Norm-referenced and criterion-referenced evaluation should not be confused with *standardized testing*. Standardized tests can be referenced to norms (generally an age or grade population) or to criterion standards such as elaborate constructs defining mastery or basic competency. The term *standardized* applies to the quality and professionalism that goes into the extensive research and development involved in test development. Standardized tests differ substantially from teacher-made tests. *Teacher-made tests* usually are developed with a specific population in mind and generally do not undergo rigorous examination for validity and reliability.

Validity and Reliability

Validity refers to the appropriateness, meaningfulness, and usefulness of an evaluation approach. There are many types of validity, each with a specific definition. In this text, validity means the degree of alignment of the test, assessment, or judgment with what is supposedly being measured. In short, if a test measures what the test claims to measure and only that, the test has validity. *Reliability,* on the other hand, refers to how stable the results of the evaluation are in repeated measures of the same child or how the score remains constant when different evaluators are used. Although validity determines how reasonable an inference from a test or observation instrument is compared to what is supposedly being measured, reliability refers to how accurate those scores are when compared to the vagaries of examiners, scoring, timing, and other circumstances. A test without validity or reliability is subject to charges of being arbitrary, unfair, or inaccurate.

Assessment

Assessment is a broad term that is generally limited to the process of collecting information about a student's learning. To wit, assessment does not make an inference or judgment about the quality or value of a student's work. However, in education, the term is used rather loosely regarding evaluation purposes of individual work. Data collection (assessment) and data interpretation (evaluation) are not always considered separate processes. For example, in *authentic assessment,* data is collected and interpreted by the student and the teacher. In general, teachers use the same concepts (such as evaluation, assessment, validity, and reliability) as do the psychometricians, but more broadly and more informally. However, because of the vast differences between the two occupations, the precision employed by teachers during instructional evaluation does not warrant comparison to operationalized definitions in the field of psychometrics.

Relevance and Objectivity

Relevance is similar to validity except that relevance is related to the appropriateness of the use of data whereas validity is related to the instrument's congruence with the stated content domains. Objectivity is similarly related to reliability in that the stability of an assessment across multiple observers is of primary interest. *Objectivity* refers to the ability of two or more raters to obtain similar descriptions of the same phenomenon because the measure does not appeal to the predispositions, emotions, or tastes of the raters. This is also referred to as *inter-rater reliability.* Usually, raters are trained in the use of a scale, rubric, or other form of description so that words or numbers have very precise agreed-upon definitions.

Tests and Testing

Finally, the last of the basic evaluation nomenclature refers to the various conceptualizations of a test. Although a test can be a pencil-and-paper activity, this definition is far too simple to be useful. A *test* is "a systematic procedure for observing a person's behavior and describing it with the aid of a numerical scale or a category system" (Cronbach, 1970, as cited in Merwin, 1989, p. 185). Watching to see if a child can stack six specific blocks within a given time limit is a test as much as when a student writes answers to history questions after a week's study. Unfortunately, tests and testing are viewed in some educational circles with a great deal of disdain. However, appropriate use of tests with fair and appropriate testing practices are critical to systematic evaluation of student learning success.

Purposes of Evaluation

Why grades are given is a topic of heated debate and one that reveals many differing views about the nature of children and why children do what they do. A common belief is that grades are children's "pay" for their work—that is, children do work and receive grades. Grades, in turn, have an extrinsic value in that good grades can be exchanged for attention, praise, privileges, toys, activities, money, and even the love and affection of parents. Bad grades, of course, usually earn condemnation and restrictions for the child. Since families differ in many significant ways, it is difficult to ascertain just what part grades play in student motivation. It is clear, however, that children need a sense of success to sustain motivation.

Perceptions of Grades Vary

Teachers are confronted with an array of family values regarding the importance of grades, the consequences of both good and bad grades, and how grades are to be determined and interpreted. In some cases, grades do act as motivators for children. In many cases, grades probably detract from the school experience. For some children, grades are a source of torment. In still others, grades are nothing more than a rite of passage and a way of learning to deal with the world of authority. In the classroom, however, grades and grading must be subject to continuous and careful consideration. Successful teachers should not assume that grades are positive motivators for all children. Instead, successful teachers should subject grades and grading to continuous rigorous scrutiny.

Dual Purpose of Evaluation

An implied hidden purpose of evaluation is the sorting of students. However, there are reasons for evaluation other than obtaining comparative information from students. Slavin (1986) reports a number of reasons for evaluating the extent and quality of student learning. He claims that evaluation, if properly conducted, can motivate students extrinsically by providing tangible acknowledgments of success such as grades. Evaluation of learning provides feedback to children about the quality of their work and how they can improve. Evaluation provides feedback to teachers about the success of lessons in achieving long-range goals as well as on efforts to instill an ethic of quality work in each child. Evaluation can provide parents with a description of how their child is progressing in several important areas. Finally, evaluation provides teachers with measured characteristics of learning so that students can be grouped for instruction that is most appropriate for their immediate needs.

Accountability

School, student, and teacher accountability is fostered by careful evaluation of student progress. Resources can be used more efficiently if the effects of resource allocation are known and understood. Evaluation also is a primary and fundamental method for teachers to assess the success of the instructional program. Teachers must teach for success. If the evaluation and grading program indicates that students are not succeeding, the instructional program must be carefully scrutinized so that appropriate modifications can be made.

Whatever evaluation program the teacher uses in the classroom, it should support multiple purposes because it will be viewed variously by the many individuals affected by the system. As with most educational policies, the actual evaluation plan employed in the successful classroom reflects a compromise that accommodates student needs, institutional policies, parental wishes, and teacher judgment. Such a compromise is not easy to develop successfully and requires diligence, analysis, reflection, and effort.

Sources of Comparison and Standards

Inherent in every evaluation strategy is the assumption that there is some standard from which measurement is to be assessed. Building on previously discussed concepts, there are three primary reference points for evaluation: comparisons to others, comparisons to standards, and comparisons to past performance of each individual.

Norm-Referenced Evaluation

Comparisons to others are called *norm-referenced criterion* and are relative. Student standing is relative to the specific group; therefore, student assessment of achievement may change with the characteristics of the group. For example, a student may be the most fluid and most skilled reader in his class at one school but may only be average if transferred to another school. National norms are often cited when standardized tests are administered, but local district and state norms are often used.

Criterion-Referenced Evaluation

When a standard is established and student learning compared to the stated standard, a criterion reference is being made. *Criterion-referenced evaluation* compares students to a clearly established set of competencies that are the objective of the instruction. The student should be aware of the requirements of learning and how to demonstrate them. Criterion-referenced tests and assessment are *absolute* standards in that the comparison is made to a standard that does not change regardless of the group in which the student is placed or any specific traits that the student possesses.

Personal Best Evaluation

When students are compared to their own past learning behavior, comparisons to others or to absolute norms are omitted. Student learning is based on *personal bests* (PB), and student work is evaluated on improvement rather than on competition and external standards. Sports have used PB systems in marathon races and in golf by establishing a rating, or "handicap," system. Thus, in practice, PB systems usually permit comparisons to others by virtue of the scale used to establish the baseline standard and incremental improvements.

Comparing the Reference Points

Figure 11.1 outlines the advantages and disadvantages of the three reference points. In the classroom, teachers often use all three systems for different purposes. Within the classroom, the least desirable reference point for formal evaluation is any norm-referenced system. This is particularly true when the teacher predetermines an arbitrary number of high marks and low marks to be assigned regardless of the work quality of students. However, the standardized testing that is mandated by state legislatures and district school boards are generally (but not always) norm-referenced systems. Teacher-developed learning evaluation systems usually use a criterion system. In this approach, teachers attempt to describe the standard of performance expected of a student and how that standard will be measured. Unfortunately, this system provides more able students access to high evaluations with less effort than is

FIGURE 11.1   Reference
points for learning evaluation
strategies.

Norm referenced: Comparison against others in the group
- Establishes a sense of accomplishment as compared to others
- Can identify excellence and exceptionality
- Can be used to calculate predicted developmental norms
- Can encourage overly competitive attitudes
- Can be discouraging

Criterion-referenced: Comparison against an independent standard
- Establishes a common standard
- Has success expectations for all
- Exceptionally bright students may be underchallenged
- Slow students may find the standards too high

Personal best: Comparison against individual's past practice
- Emphasis is on progress and achievement
- Standard is appropriate for all
- Bright students are challenged
- May establish modest achievement for bright children
- Requires previous measures for comparison
- Does not establish clear expectations and goals

required of less able students. Overcoming these barriers has increased teachers' interest in PB systems, although few are currently using these promising systems.

PB systems have several drawbacks that generally arise from a lack of carefully established standard measures from which to track progress. For example, if a student makes a 75 percent on a spelling test in week 1 and an 80 percent in week 2, does it necessarily mean progress? Were the words from week 1 more difficult than those from week 2? Of course, this particular situation can be resolved by a pretest–posttest system. This method involves testing a student on the words prior to study and after study. A comparison between the scores is then used to describe the learning. Students, however, quickly catch on to the pretest strategy. To manipulate the grade with minimal effort, students may deliberately do poorly on the pretest to assure learning "gains" on the posttest. In short, there are no simple, error-free, comparative systems. Teachers must carefully weigh the advantages and disadvantages of each type of reference system and determine the method or methods that best meet the needs and purposes of evaluation in the context of each classroom.

Tradition of Letter Grades

Letter grades are used in a vast majority of American schools. Dissatisfaction with letter grades is historic, but a less controversial replacement has not been forthcoming.

Letter grades have been under serious attack from school reformers for at least four decades. Letter grades are used in two different ways: (1) Teachers may indicate their interpretation of the quality of an individual piece of work with a grade. (2) Teachers may indicate the cumulative quality of student work over a period of time through the combined inferences of many work products, observations, and estimates of attainment gained through interaction with the student.

Although letter grades are used almost daily in schools, teachers favor a number of alternatives. A National Education Association teacher poll revealed that most teachers considered a parent-teacher conference to be the best method of reporting pupil progress (Evans, 1976). That belief has continued until today despite the difficulties involved in conferences. Among elementary teachers, only 16 percent felt that letter grades were among the best ways to report student achievement. Robinson and Craver (1989) acknowledged the widespread criticism of grades as an evaluation practice. The range of criticism is vast. Grades have been accused of maintaining a racist, elitist, and sexist educational system (Bellanca, 1977) and of rationalizing poor work (Glasser, 1969). Robinson and Craver (1989), in their extensive review of grading practices, note that much of the criticisms ignore substantive issues involved by focusing on the symbols used in grading rather than on the assessment needs of schools and the limited options available to teachers.

Anticipated Functions of Grades

Although grades are an easy target for critics, finding workable substitutes is more difficult. The difficulty in finding a substitute for a system of letter grades is partly because of the expectation that any evaluation system must serve many diverse functions. For example, Wrinkle (1947) reported four functions of school grades:

◆ *Administrative functions* provide designations of whether students have passed or failed, whether they should be allowed to pursue the next level of studies, how they are rated when they transfer from school to school, and how they are judged for college or other advanced study.

◆ *Guidance functions* use grades to identify areas of special study, student ability (or inability), decisions on enrolling students into certain courses, keeping students out of courses, and determining the number and difficulty of the course of studies.

◆ *Information functions* serve to inform parents of the student's achievement, progress, and success in schoolwork.

◆ *Motivation and discipline functions* serve to stimulate students to make greater effort in their learning activities and to determine eligibility for academic honors, participation in group activities, and membership in selected groups.

Wrinkle, surprisingly, did not identify grading practices as a way of increasing student learning or stimulating the most effective teaching. With such broad anticipation, there is little surprise that grading practices continually fall short of expectations.

A summary of the most powerful argument outlining the limitations of grading is by Combs (1976) who wrote:

Any information will have an effect upon the behavior of an individual only to the degree that he or she has discovered the personal meaning of the information for himself or herself. . . . The principle has vast implications for all aspects of education. It means that learning happens inside people; it is a subjective experience. The behavior we observe is only a symptom of that which is going on within the individual. An educational system preoccupied with behavior and behavioral change is a system dealing with symptoms. . . . (pp. 6–7)

Four Questions for Effective Evaluation

Combs (1976) suggests that grading, as with all of evaluation practices, must answer four questions:

- ◆ Is the objective measured a truly important one?
- ◆ Is the grading practice employed the best way of achieving the objectives?
- ◆ What are the effects on the teacher?
- ◆ What are the effects on the student?

Combs and many others have noted that what is measured in schools is what we know how to measure. What we know how to measure often is not the most important aspect of learning or the objective of the classroom instruction. When teachers measure what Combs calls the "symptoms" and inadvertently ignore what is truly important, the grading function departs from its role in an effective evaluation system. Hayman and Napier (1975) conclude:

Understanding the possible injury grading might inflict on anyone but especially a vulnerable child, the educator might investigate the differences between grading and evaluation. The latter is definitely essential to any educational process; the former is not. Grading implies a limiting process through which the individual is forced into some artificial category for the sake of efficiency. Evaluation, on the other hand, implies a discovery, an application of some value to a particular behavior. (p. 24)

Despite the inappropriate use and frequent abuse of grades and grading practices, the system is widespread, and few teachers are free of its requirements. Fortunately, careful attention to the practice issues involved in grades can minimize the difficulties and, at the same time, provide at least nominal contributions to the overall purposes of accountability and improving learning success.

Self-Evaluation and Grading Practices

Gronlund (1974) suggests that teachers ask themselves a series of questions regarding their grading practices:

- ◆ Should the grade represent achievement only, or should it also include the student effort and work habits?
- ◆ What evidence will be included in the grade? What combination of tests, written work, performances, and teacher observation will be used?

◆ What evidence will be the most important indicators of learning? How should the various elements of achievement and development be weighted?

◆ Will the grade represent norm-referenced or criterion-referenced achievement?

◆ What distribution of grades (that is, "A, B, C, D, F") will be used? How should this distribution be determined?

Persistence of Grades

With so much criticism of grades and grading practices, why do they persist? First, moving from letter grades to other types of evaluation measures does not reduce the need for, and use of, teacher judgment. Often, the same problems exist with the new scheme as with the old; the only change is in the wording of the grading scheme. For example, changing letters to words is a common strategy that is usually only superficial. In these attempts, letter grades are eliminated for a scale of phrases such as "well above expectations, at expectations, below expectations" or "utilizing, emerging, developing." Children quickly figure out the relative rank of each phrase. Most of the substantive issues in assigning phrases are identical to those of assigning letter grades. When new phrases confuse parents, the alternative scale can create problems that are even more detrimental to effective communication of learning success and need.

The problems and issues involved in grading have sparked criticism but have resisted substitution by viable alternatives. However, teachers can, and do, employ a variety of practices that mitigate many of the more onerous aspects of grading.

An Analysis of Current Evaluation Practices

A wide array of evaluation and reporting practices exists in elementary schools. Gronlund (1974) identified several alternatives to letter grades: pass-fail marking, checklists of goals, individual letters to parents, and parent conferences.

More recently, teachers have started to give parents more information about their child's learning success, thus shifting at least part of the interpretation and evaluative responsibilities to parents. Cumulatively, these methods are referred to as *alternative assessment*. Assessment practices vary as widely as the traditional grading schemes. Assessment in its broadest application is less preoccupied with assigning a judgment to learning demonstrations as is typical in other grading schemes. Instead, the central foci are what is being assessed and how meaningful demonstrations of learning are obtained. Robinson and Craver (1989) describe the differences between assessing and grading student achievement. They argue that assessment includes the measurement, interpretation, and evaluation of student learning, whereas grading is a communication function in which symbols are used to inform parties of the results of the assessment. Figure 11.2 is adapted from Robinson and Craver's presentation on homework and has been modified to include additional measurement, evaluation, and communication functions.

Assessing Functions		Grading Function
Measurement	**Evaluation**	**Communication**

• *Testing:* A series of questions, problems, or physical responses designed to determine knowledge, intelligence, or ability
• *Observation:* The act of noting and recording something, such as a phenomenon, with instruments
• *Demonstration or performance:* Activity that shows, or makes evident, skill and knowledge in a particular area
• *Scoring:* Determining the correctness or appropriateness of a response
	• Comparing to a reference point
	  • To others in a group
	  • To an established performance standard
	  • To an individual's previous demonstration
	• Assigning value or interpretation to gather information
	• Relating the evidence gathered and synthesizing a summary view establishing the importance of various aspects of data
		• *Symbolizing:* Presenting an estimate of performance along a continuous scale from ineffective to most effective learning
		• *Reporting:* Presenting an official, formal, or regular account of the evaluation of learning; relating the results of considerations concerning student learning

FIGURE 11.2   Assessing and grading student achievement.

Adapted from *Assessing and Grading Student Achievement* by Glen E. Robinson and James M. Craver, 1989, Arlington, VA: Educational Research Service.

Alternative assessment places great emphasis on the process of assessment while downgrading the communication issues. Advocates of alternative assessment argue that communication is best served by involving students and their parents in the evaluation activities, thus minimizing the need for symbols or formal representations involved in the communication.

Regardless of the strategy used, no strategy is without its limitations. Each strategy attacks the dual purposes of accountability and improving learning in different ways yielding certain advantages while entailing some disadvantages. Because no system seems to be adequate by itself, many teachers use a combination of strategies. Therefore, it is important to take a summary look at the various methods so that the established purposes for any evaluation activity in the classroom has the greatest chance of success.

Traditional Letter Grades ("A, B, C, D, F")

The critique of traditional letter grades presented earlier in the chapter indicated serious weaknesses in the process. However, when grades are used with skill and in conjunction with other forms of communication, traditional letter grades can have their advantages. Letter grades are easy to use and convenient in maintaining school records. By using various conversion scales, letter grades can also be averaged easily for administrative purposes and provide a point estimate of student learning success. Grades are easy to interpret and provide fairly good predictions of future achievement. Letter grades, while easily understood, also convey different meanings in different contexts. Because teachers often include estimates of student behavior other than learning in the determination of letter grades, these grades may represent achievement, effort, personal behavior, or various combinations of the three. Letter grades can become ends in themselves, producing harmful side effects such as anxiety, cheating, and poor self-esteem (Gronlund, 1974). However, the successful teacher uses effective communication and a caring heart to minimize the harmful effects.

Pass-Fail System

Pass-fail systems are not too different from grading scales. Instead of a four- or five-point scale, a two-point scale is used. However, since that minimizes the distinctions among achievement differences of students, pass-fail systems generally lower student anxiety about the grading practice. Pass-fail systems are also easy to use and record. However, this strategy provides little information about student learning and may encourage students merely to pass rather than work toward levels of excellence.

Checklists of Objectives

Most of the advantages and disadvantages of checklists depend on the items identified on the list and the training that teachers have had in understanding what is meant by the items. If checklist items are carefully developed to correspond with the classroom curriculum, a checklist can provide a detailed analysis of learning strengths and weaknesses. If the items are carefully worded or if there is a guide to the meaning of each item, students and parents can obtain a comprehensive view of the instructional goals of the school. Teachers who receive competent training in the use of checklists can provide a detailed assessment on how successfully the student achieves each goal. Although there are some limitations in the method itself, most limitations of checklists are a result of implementation issues.

Checklists are time consuming in maintaining data collection procedures and in preparing the reports. If checklists are poorly worded or use educational jargon, parents may not readily understand the statements of objectives. Since instructional goals will change during the year and certainly will change as the child progresses through subsequent years at the school, the reporting system must either be changed periodically, or there must be multiple forms. This entails reteaching parents about what goals are measured as well as retraining teachers on how to identify characteristics of mastery for each item. The biggest difficulty in creating a checklist lies in choosing item goals that represent what is important in the educational setting and then determining how to measure those goals. However, since checklists can be changed periodically, these probably will yield more truly meaningful information than simple grading practices do.

Letters to Parents

A note to parents from school historically has meant trouble. However, that is changing rapidly. Successful teachers are increasingly communicating with parents using form letters, personalized notes, and letters regarding student achievement and behavior. Letters to parents may be systematic (a part of a regular evaluation program) or intermittent (written on an "as-needed" basis). Letters to parents are particularly potent vehicles for notifying parents of positive changes in student effort and of particular achievements.

Letters are representative of a host of communication devices available to teachers, including e-mail and telephone calls. These means of communication can provide the teacher with a highly individualized way of reporting learning strengths and weaknesses. Systematic approaches to evaluation through letters permits teachers to focus on those learning areas that are most essential to student progress at a particular time. Teachers can describe in detail the student's learning strengths, types of learning activities, and classroom behavior. Intermittent letters can supplement other modes of communication, serve as significant representations of teacher concern, and express appreciation for students and parents. However, what is gained in detail and personal communication comes at a significant cost in time. This time may be spent more effectively in planning and developing enhanced lessons that increase student opportunity to learn. Students and parents can easily misunderstand a letter unless particular care goes into developing it. When student misdeeds or intellectual challenges are included in the letters, an extensive narrative may be necessary to report and explain any deficiency tactfully. Probably the most difficult aspect of letters is that they tend to be generalized and do not provide easily comprehended analyses of student strengths and weaknesses. This is particularly true when subsequent teachers try to assess past learning successes to assist them in developing appropriate instruction.

Parent-Teacher Conferences

Many of the same advantages and disadvantages of letters to parents are representative of conferences with parents. The major improvement of conferences over letters is that two-way communication occurs. Also, a teacher who can show the parents their child's work samples while they are discussing the child's successes and needs can make communication both easier and more meaningful. Many misunderstandings can be avoided in face-to-face communication, and those problems that do occur can be resolved on the spot. A real advantage is when the parents and teacher choose to develop a cooperative plan for improving the child's development and share information about the child that can be used to the child's benefit.

Parent conferences can be extremely time consuming; teachers have little time set aside for conferences. Likewise, many parents have difficulty in finding both the time and the transportation to school for the conferences. Having to conduct conferences before and after school for 20 to 30 sets of parents, each on a difficult schedule of their own, can be a daunting and tiring task regardless of the messages to be conveyed. Conferences also leave no written record of student performance for other subsequent school personnel. Subsequent teachers will lack adequate information about past student performance to assist them in interpreting student behavior. However, when parent-teacher conferences are used in conjunction with other evaluation processes, there is no better method for informing parents of the child's learning patterns and successes.

Authentic Assessment

Authentic assessment is widely considered to be a major improvement in the use of evaluation systems to improve student learning and the teacher's teaching effectiveness. According to Fischer and King (1995), the greatest difference between authentic assessment and grading is that *authentic assessment* focuses on a performance-based demonstration in which the student's answer and the processes involved in deriving the answer are considered in the evaluation. Fischer and King (1995) state, "Students do something other than the traditional norm-referenced or criterion-referenced paper-and-pencil measurement, requiring students not only to respond but also to demonstrate knowledge and skills" (p. 2).

Unfortunately, testing is viewed by most advocates of authentic assessment as being an artificial and weak predictor of student learning, a position that is valid in many situations. However, this view of testing is extremely narrow and can lead to a belief that systematic testing and authentic assessment are incompatible. Regulatory agencies have for many decades provided tests that measure technical skills in the armed forces, airline industry, and business with full context demonstrations of skill. Schools, particularly in vocational education and in physical education, have incorporated tests into the curriculum that require demonstrations of knowledge and skill. However, proponents of authentic assessment are arguing for more thoughtfulness in all areas of evaluation; thus, a reduced emphasis on tests is certainly justified.

Authentic assessment and the more generalized areas of alternative assessment argue that what a student does, how he or she completes a task, and why he or she selects particular courses of action can yield a wealth of important information about his or her learning. Authentic assessment must be given careful attention since it represents a potentially superior evaluation strategy when compared to current models that collect data primarily from tests and pencil-and-paper classwork. For some, the differences between testing and authentic assessment may be in the degree of emphasis placed on various aspects of learning rather than on the kind of instrument. The teacher must continuously monitor the balance between the knowledge-and-skill sampling techniques involved in well-developed tests and the creativity, spontaneity, effort, and personal responsibility demonstrated in alternative assessments.

There are limitations to these broadly based systems. Teacher skill requirements for sophisticated evaluation systems are quite high. Additional time to collect a variety of work products is needed as well as alternative assignments to produce that work. The amount of data is difficult to manage, and a collection of student work is often hard to interpret. Communicating the information to parents can be unwieldy because parents usually expect a point estimate represented by a grade rather than a representative sample of current work.

Enhancing Evaluation Systems

Regardless of the evaluation system used, some general suggestions can help enhance any evaluation system:

◆ *Use multiple measures.* Formal reporting of student progress is more stable when several measures are used. This is true for the types of activity that students perform as well as the number of activities employed. By providing multiple opportunities to demonstrate skill, the relative importance of any one activity is diminished, thus lowering the stress for students.

◆ *Use clearly stated goals.* Be sure that students understand what is expected of them and how they will demonstrate their learning. Clear communication of expectations provides students with appropriate guidance so that they can do their best.

◆ *Cooperatively develop the reporting system.* Teachers, parents, students, and school administration should be included in developing the reporting system to incorporate as many viewpoints as possible. By working with others, potential biases and misunderstandings are minimized.

◆ *Keep the report form brief and compact.* Students and parents alike distrust what they cannot understand. By keeping reports short and straightforward, central ideas are presented more forcefully and are more easily understood.

◆ *Limit judgments to what can be done with validity.* Teachers are not capable of making some types of judgment and should not do so. To infer that children who are completing assignments but are having difficulty succeeding need only try harder is generally not an inference that teachers can make. Careful attention to evidence that supports any judgments must be a constant vigil.

◆ *Evaluate the reporting system.* The evaluation system should be evaluated regularly. The needs of students and parents are not constant, and the purposes of any one system may not be appropriate for continued use. Teachers should subject any evaluation to extensive scrutiny. A professional responsibility of teachers is to endeavor to be as fair, accurate, and helpful as possible. Continued reevaluation of any assessment or grading program is a minimum expectation.

Assessment of Multiple Intelligences and Cognitive Dimensions

Students have many skills and abilities that can be developed in the elementary school years. Schools have a preoccupation with cognitive skills in what is variously referred to as *recall, comprehension, linguistic demonstration,* or *verbal information.* Looking for information about a student's other abilities usually leads to greater understanding of how that student learns. In turn, that information can be used to enhance various instructional strategies and to introduce new approaches to learning in the classroom. Two approaches—one examining multiple intelligences and the other focusing on learning outcome domains—can assist the teacher in developing an awareness of the student's rich resources of skills.

Multiple Intelligences

Cognitive psychologists such as Guilford (1967) and Gardner (1983) have continually argued that intelligence was more complex than simply recalling information and enacting skill sequences. To provide students with opportunities to develop all of their skills, teacher instruction and student work should entail a wide range of activities. Armstrong (1994) provides an extensive list of sources for assessing student work: anecdotal records kept regarding important accomplishments, work samples, audio cassettes, videotape, photography, student journals, student-kept charts, sociograms, informal tests, informal use of standardized tests, student interviews, criterion-referenced tests, and checklists.

Armstrong (1994) suggests seven ways in which students can demonstrate learning based on Gardner's multiple intelligences:

- *Linguistic demonstration.* Student provides oral or written narratives describing what was learned.
- *Logical-mathematical demonstration.* Student develops a comparison of events to theorem or formula.
- *Spatial demonstration.* Student illustrates learned concepts through visual presentations such as drawings, photographs, and video images.
- *Bodily-kinesthetic demonstration.* Student communicates through movement in dance, acting, or pantomime.
- *Musical demonstration.* Student creates a representation of concepts using vehicles employing melody or rhythm.
- *Interpersonal demonstration.* Student uses relationships and experiences with others to communicate concepts and ideas.
- *Intrapersonal demonstration.* Student demonstrates an understanding by relating information to his or her own life experiences.

Jarolimek and Foster (1993) identify a number of evaluation procedures used by elementary school teachers that employ or incorporate multiple intelligences. These strategies include participation in group discussion, teacher observation of student dramatic performances or skill demonstrations, checklists specifically developed around special talents and modes of expression, individual conferences with students including oral examinations and debates, as well as teacher-made tests.

Five Types of Learning Outcomes

Gagné and Driscoll (1988) identify five learning outcomes of instruction: verbal information, intellectual skills, cognitive strategies, attitudes, and motor skills. Verbal information composes the most familiar type of learning outcome. Gagné and

Driscoll also refer to *verbal information* as declarative knowledge or "knowing that." This type of learning outcome takes the form of facts, names, principles, and generalizations representing scholarship from organized bodies of knowledge. Verbal information is particularly important because it is prerequisite to other types of knowledge, provides labels for concepts, and provides a vehicle for thought processes so that concepts can be manipulated and meaning created and understood. This type of information is quite important and justly deserves a prominent place in the elementary curriculum. Unfortunately, other forms of learning outcomes have been neglected in the school curricula, while verbal information is increasingly being questioned regarding its value. Again, the problem for teachers is one of creating balance among many important aspects of student learning rather than on an overreliance on verbal information. If an evaluation program almost exclusively focuses on the assessment of students' verbal information, it is possible that the evaluation will be skewed, inaccurate, and of limited value.

Intellectual skills form a second category of learning outcomes. *Intellectual skills* are simply "knowing how" and extend the "knowing what" of verbal information to include useful utilization of circumstances. Intellectual skills involve the ability to carry out actions indicated by information and are the building blocks of sophisticated intellectual activity. Gagné and Driscoll (1988) identify a number of intellectual skills, including discriminations, concrete concepts, defined concepts, rules, and higher-order rules.

Generally, grading and student evaluations rarely go beyond assessing a student's acquisition and recall of verbal information. The better systems extend their scope to include intellectual skills, but very few evaluation programs extend to the other three areas. *Cognitive strategies*—the ways in which learners guide their attending, learning, remembering, and thinking—are rarely the object of teacher evaluation. Teachers may assume that study skills or learning strategies are indirectly measured when intellectual skill or verbal information is assessed. To wit, students who acquire and recall verbal information and use it in its basic forms have adequate cognitive strategies. However, when students fail to demonstrate verbal information and intellectual skills successfully through teacher-made tests and other assessments, teachers have little information to support any suggestions other than to "try harder."

Cognitive strategies are a powerful force behind student success. Learners who are routinely successful have strategies for isolating important parts of material that they have read, for establishing what is important for them to pay attention to most carefully, and for remembering what they have read. Cognitive strategies are also behind setting aside time for study, deciding on what types of note taking to use, and other strategies that guide and direct students' thinking and learning activities. Teachers' assessment of these strategies and their helpful feedback can greatly increase student success in other learning outcomes.

One basic cognitive strategy used by successful learners is the development of self-assurance that the effort placed into study and other learning activities will yield results. Glasser (1992) provides a simple explanation of the importance of the evaluation of student work:

In school what we have to do is devise a way to get the students to do some work so we can give the input that they are doing something that is worthwhile. If I tell any of you, "I think you are pretty smart, pretty worthwhile, and I think you are proceeding in the right direction," there is a good chance that you will at least listen to what I have to say. This is basic to the whole procedure. This is what you must do with students.—Get involved with them; help them become friendly; create some warmth and some interaction in the classroom. This is a basic minimum for getting them to listen to you and then, hopefully, to listen to what you are attempting to teach them. . . . We ought to make it impossible for children to fail in school. Let me define failure. Failure occurs when the options are closed. That's what failure is all about. (p. 102)

When students have limited cognitive strategies, they have no options for doing other than what they have done in the past, and that past is filled with failure. Hence, teachers must carefully assess student strategies for learning if learning successes are to be increased and enhanced.

Another area of student outcomes is *student attitudes*. Teacher assessment of student attitudes not only includes attitudes toward learning but also toward other life skills. Attitudes such as tolerance, kindness, helpfulness, and thoughtfulness are important learning outcomes in the elementary school. Additionally, attitudes about positive preferences for activities such as reading, healthful play, and physical exercise are fundamental to successful social living. Attitudes toward citizenship and its responsibilities are also included in this area.

Motor skills are the final area of learning outcomes that deserve attention of the successful teacher. Motor skills are fundamental to handwriting, to operating a computer, or to manipulating equipment in a science or math demonstration. Motor skills are essential to many basic learning achievements such as swimming, dancing, and active play.

Using Tests

Although the limitations of tests have been pointed out, it is important to remember that tests do have important uses in schools. Careful and thoughtful development of tests can eliminate much of the stress and anxiety associated with testing. Because much of the criticism regarding tests are the result of test abuses, poor execution of testing strategies, and a failure to employ other methods, teachers can avoid many, if not most, of the negative outcomes of testing by informed test construction and use. This use of tests can provide clear and reasoned guidance for the teacher in assessing both the accomplishments of the children and the success of the instructional strategies. When teachers construct and use tests, a series of questions need to be considered:

◆ What is the purpose of the test?
◆ How will the test contribute to improving learning?
◆ How will the test contribute to accountability?
◆ What will be learned from the test?
◆ Is the information from the test valuable?
◆ Will the results of the test be useful to children, parents, and the teacher?

◆ How important will any single test be in the evaluation scheme?
◆ How will the results of a test be communicated to the students?
◆ Have all students been appropriately prepared for the test?
◆ Are other options available for administering the test that would serve the educational purposes more appropriately?

By considering each of these issues, teachers can find alternatives to test administration. When tests are used, it is more likely that tests can and will perform the intended function if these questions have been carefully considered. Lastly, by carefully answering each question, teachers can avoid test abuses while promoting a positive view toward quality teaching and learning.

Guidelines for Test Construction

Test construction need not be an elaborate affair. Simple tests specifically designed to collect carefully defined information are generally best for young children. For example, after instruction and practice, a group of kindergartners can be tested for attainment of basic number concepts by having each child create a block train with the teacher specifying the number of blocks to be used. Such tests should be frequent and routine. Older children can give a demonstration of the proper operation of a microscope and orally designate the basic parts. In such cases, the teacher may test a few of the children, and then these children can watch others to see if the operation is appropriate. If shortcomings exist, these children can become tutors and provide the additional instruction needed. The teacher can then have the students who have been retaught demonstrate the skill at a later time.

Seven suggestions for text construction can help the teacher navigate the maze of difficulties:

◆ *Clearly know the purpose of the test.* Although it is customary to test at the end of a unit of study, that is insufficient reason to guide the construction of a test. The test should reflect the most important themes of instruction and provide students with multiple opportunities to demonstrate their understanding of those ideas. Constructing tests simply to sample content covered on a random basis reflects a purpose limited to simple recall. Testing recurring themes in a unit of study permits the teacher to develop items that measure major themes of learning and provide more guidance to instructional success of the teacher and the learning strategies of the student.
◆ *Clearly know the purpose of each item.* Test items should also have specific purposes. Far too many test items measure simple recall. Instead, the teacher can develop additional items that permit students to predict outcomes, make evaluative judgments, and demonstrate skill in sequenced problems that require a succession of reasoning and decision making.
◆ *Use a variety of item types to assess knowledge.* Because the purposes of items vary, the type of items should also vary so that the purpose is best represented. Also, the cognitive style of each child is different. By varying the type of items in a test, students are permitted to use an array of skills.

Tests can be demonstrations of learning.

◆ *Keep items simply stated.* Simple language and syntax provide better assurance that all students will understand an item. Items should reflect the same type of characteristics as a good question used during classroom instruction.

◆ *Test for success.* A test should never be used as a punitive measure. Designing tests specifically so that students fail in order to point out their limited efforts is a strategy that is likely to backfire. Although students always reserve the right to fail, to avoid effort, and to limit commitment to learning, teachers should make every effort to ensure that students understand test items and how to succeed in the test. Development of careful objectives that are shared with children is a first step. Strategies that heighten student chances of success include providing sample test items during various phases of instruction or including test items that employ the same type of learning strategies used during instruction. The duty of each teacher is to provide each child with the opportunity to succeed, regardless of his or her entering ability.

◆ *Test what is important.* Do not include trivia items. Each test item should reflect important concepts that have been carefully developed during instruction. Inclusion of items just to make the test hard or to keep the brightest children from a perfect score demeans the purpose of the test. Tests should indicate whether students comprehend the information, skills, and significance of material presented in class. Be sure that the test aligns with stated aims and with material taught in the preceding classes by developing test items directly from the lesson objectives.

◆ *Remember validity and reliability issues.* Validity (does a test measure what it purports to measure?) and reliability (is it measured consistently?) must always be kept in mind. Although developing tests with high levels of documented validity and reliability is an extensive and difficult task, teachers should never lose sight of the goal.

By following the preceding recommendations, teachers can work toward maintaining exemplary levels of accountability and learning improvement. Perhaps more importantly, by carefully considering the types of tests and the evaluation measures that they administer, teachers can treat children fairly.

Types of Test Questions

When developing a test, a variety of item formats can be used. Each type of item has advantages and disadvantages. The selection of the item format must match the purpose of the item. Following are the most common item formats:

True-false.   A statement is made, and the student ascertains if the statement is true or false.
◆ *Pros:* Short; large number of items; easy to score; tests very specific; inferences, particularly recall, can measure student ability to discriminate.
◆ *Cons:* Easy to misunderstand; difficult to construct; provides no information about student reason for selection (correct or incorrect); often are trivial; highly influenced by guessing; not effective in testing understanding or high cognitive functioning.

Sentence completion.   A sentence is constructed leaving blank key ideas or phrases.
◆ *Pros:* Short; large number of items; relatively easy and quick to score; controls for guessing; measures recall effectively.
◆ *Cons:* Not effective for high cognitive functioning; little understanding provided for student responses; can be ambiguous or confusing; answers may have appropriate responses other than that intended by the test constructor.

Multiple choice question.   A question is asked, and the test taker is given a selection of answers.
◆ *Pros:* Quick to score; can be constructed to reflect a number of cognitive functions; can test for specific reasoning processes; relatively short; many items; can be statistically corrected for guessing.
◆ *Cons:* Student guessing still an element; students can misunderstand the context of the question; very difficult and time consuming to develop; little or no understanding of the students' thinking is revealed.

Matching items.   Two lists of items are provided, and the test taker determines which items are appropriately related.

◆   *Pros:* Short; easy to score; tests a large number of associations quickly.
◆   *Cons:* The relationship between items may not be clear in all instances; missing one item may influence success in other items; guessing still possible; measures only lower-order recall or comprehension.

Short answer.   A question is asked, and the test taker writes a short phrase, sentence, or paragraph in response.

◆   *Pros:* Can measure higher-level thinking processes without the investment of the time required by essays; provides opportunity for self-expression, allows construction of responses that demonstrate sources of understanding or misunderstanding; allows for originality.
◆   *Cons:* Students can write thoughtfully on the subject while not answering the question; difficult to score; final score can vary with different graders; time consuming to score; students who write with difficulty may be at a disadvantage whereas less knowledgeable students with a flair for writing may do better; few items can be developed during the testing period.

Essay.   Student is requested to provide an extensive analysis regarding a situation established in the question. Essay questions can vary greatly in purpose; therefore, essay questions often state the test taker's requirements for an appropriate response.

◆   *Pros:* Can measure higher-level thinking processes; provides opportunity for self-expression; provides extensive opportunity to demonstrate understanding; allows for originality.
◆   *Cons:* Students can write thoughtfully on the subject while not answering the question; difficult to score; score can vary with different graders; time consuming to score; students who write with difficulty may be at a disadvantage whereas less knowledgeable students with a flair for writing may do better; few items can be developed during the testing period.

Demonstration/performance.   Student demonstrates a skill such as a recitation of a memorized piece or completion of a problem that requires demonstration of a specific skill.

◆   *Pros:* Most naturalistic of testing procedures; provides students with appropriate context for display of learning.
◆   *Cons:* Difficult to score when task is done partially correct or done with errors; time consuming; can require the attention of the teacher to the exclusion of others; limited to performances or skill demonstrations.

When developing and implementing tests, the successful teacher will be vigilant in monitoring student reaction, involvement, and motivation. Using a variety of tests, carefully preparing students so that they know how to succeed, and providing lots of encouragement are some of the ways to provide fair and effective testing.

Using Portfolios

Portfolios have been used in many professions, but their systematic use in the elementary school is fairly recent. In its simplest form, a portfolio is a collection of student work. From that perspective, elementary teachers have used portfolios for years. However, the use of the portfolio as an evaluation tool is more than a collection of work. If portfolios are to be used in evaluation, the design must be deliberate and structured. The first element of designing a portfolio program is to consider a series of questions:

◆ How will the portfolio be used?
◆ How will it be organized?
◆ What procedures will you use in placing items in the portfolio?
◆ What will the portfolio look like? How will material be arranged? Who selects the work?
◆ Will the portfolio be evaluated? Who will evaluate it?
◆ What criteria will be used (amount, appearance, theme, improvement, overall quality)?

Purposes of Portfolios

Portfolios can have many evaluation purposes but are also instructional tools in their own right. Therefore, the use of portfolios in the classroom can fulfill many instructional goals. However, portfolios have limitations, particularly with young children, in that many learning experiences are hard to document efficiently. For example, cooperative play is an important instructional goal in kindergarten and can be documented with videotape. However, making the tape, editing it for the student's portfolio, labeling it for the parent or portfolio reviewer can be cumbersome.

Portfolios can be used to organize a particular course of study, such as independent or team projects. They may be used to document the student's learning in a particular subject or skill area, such as a series of poems, essays, and stories representing the development of his or her writing skill. Portfolios can be used to track total intellectual development across a variety of subjects, for example, in a classroom that uses an integrated curriculum.

Likewise, the time period of a portfolio can vary from just a few weeks to the entire school year. In some schools, annual portfolios are kept for a student's entire elementary school years, thus chronicling his or her intellectual development during these years.

Portfolios are rarely used strictly as an assessment tool but as a vehicle for giving congruence for a wide range of instructional activities and learning experiences. As a snapshot of a child's activity, portfolio materials can be selected somewhat randomly. Some teachers select only the child's best work. The purpose of this portfolio is to chronicle the child's achievements. Another teacher selects specific assignments for inclusion regardless of the quality of the student's work on that particular item. The purpose of this portfolio is to give a cross-section of the child's work that typifies day-to-day achievement. A different teacher may ask children to assemble their own portfolio and request that the children include their best work, work that shows early work on a skill and later mastery, and work that is most meaningful to them. Each teacher has a different purpose for the portfolio and, therefore, the structure, content, and interpretation of the portfolios will also differ.

What Should a Portfolio Contain?

Armstrong (1994) provides a comprehensive list of suggested materials to be included in a portfolio using Gardner's multiple intelligences as a basic design element. This type of portfolio adapts well when the portfolio is to be used to demonstrate a wide array of student achievements in an integrated curriculum. The type of materials is quite extensive. Teachers who assist students in assembling this type of portfolio must provide the students with an enriched curriculum full of many different opportunities for learning.

◆ *To document linguistic intelligence, include notes and preliminary drafts of writing projects as well as best samples of writing.* Although activities cannot be included, written descriptions of those investigations and the student's interpretation and personal evaluation of the results can be. Final written reports and copies of group reports can also be included. Audiotapes of debates, discussions, individual interpretive reading, and story telling provide alternatives to paper documents.

◆ *To document logical-mathematical intelligence, include the best samples of math papers demonstrating both computation and reasoning skills.* Math skills checklists can be completed by the teacher. These checklists provide estimates of the level of mastery of specific skills and indicate the level of instruction provided during the portfolio development period. Final write-ups of science lab experiments, photographs of those experiences, and lab notes can also be included.

◆ *To document spatial intelligence, include photographs of projects, pictures, sculptures, and three-dimensional models.* Diagrams, flow charts, sketches, concept maps and webs, photos of collages, drawings, and paintings illustrate both activity and achievement in spatial intelligence. Videotapes of the student in action are also recommended along with the student's notation on the material that shows what was done and what was accomplished.

◆ *To document bodily-kinesthetic intelligence, include videotapes of projects and demonstrations as well as samples of projects actually made.* Videos may include students "acting out" thinking processes and displaying dramatic interpretation and dance.

◆ *To document musical intelligence, include audiotapes of musical performances and compositions.* Samples of written scores (performed or composed), lyrics of raps, songs, or rhymes written by students can illustrate activity and achievement.

◆   *To document interpersonal intelligence, include correspondence with others (for example, a letter requesting information from someone), group reports, and written feedback to and from peers regarding student work.* Any type of communications display is appropriate, including teacher-student conference summaries written by the student. Photos, videos, or write-ups of cooperative learning projects or documentation of community service projects round out the list of potential items.

◆   *To document intrapersonal intelligence, include selected entries from the student's journal and reflective essays written by the student about the student's learning and development.* For younger children, teacher checklists, student drawings, and samples of self-reflection exercises can be included. Simple questionnaires, attitude surveys, and interest inventories can also provide revealing information.

Composition and Portfolios

There are, of course, many rubrics from which to construct the purpose and structure of the portfolio. What types of work and other types of evidence to include in a portfolio varies with the purpose. The decision of which particular work samples are included and which are excluded also is affected by the overall purpose of the portfolio and how the portfolio will be used. In general, portfolios will reflect some combination of the following:

◆   Classroom tests and quizzes
◆   Observations of student work
◆   Group evaluation activities
◆   Class discussions and recitations
◆   Homework
◆   Notebooks and note taking
◆   Reports, themes, and research papers
◆   Discussions and debates

Using these ideas, well-developed portfolios can provide students, teachers, and parents with an excellent alternative to grades when desiring to communicate learning results.

Using Observations and Checklists

Teacher observation can yield important inferences about student learning. There are a number of advantages in using guided observation tools for evaluation. Teacher observation can work well in a variety of circumstances. It is efficient in that the teacher is already a party to the education event. Teachers can be trained to observe details in learning that tests are not likely to describe. However, teacher observation has some substantial limitations. Observation is a perceptual tool and, therefore, subject to great variations among observers. Although careful training and well-constructed checklists can help control these variations, they are never eliminated. Another problem is the hidden biases that inevitably occur during the interpretation of the observed event.

Bias

Bias is an element of all observations. There are deliberate biases when individuals feel so strongly about an issue that they deliberately twist events to accommodate their needs. This type of bias, while onerous, can be controlled and is not the primary difficulty. Hidden biases in observations come from what the teacher perceives to be important about an instructional event. It is not intended to be deceiving or to hurt. However, a teacher, like all of us, does have a predisposition to see certain events in a particular way. For example, as a child reads, he or she begins to sway with the rhythm of the words. One observer records that the child accentuates the melody of the text with body movement. A second observer writes that the student distracts from the meaning of the text with unnecessary movement. Both have observed the child's movement as he or she reads, but both have interpreted the movement differently.

Bias can be controlled to some degree by careful consideration of what is to be observed and why. In our example, if the criteria in the observation protocol specifically excluded the use of body movement to enhance the meaning of the text, our second reviewer is not biased. Instead, the reviewer would have made a judgment in accordance with the guidelines. Of course, the question becomes whether the guidelines are biased in favor of one interpretation or another. Teachers can be certain that any guide to evaluation, whether checklist, test, or observation scale, contains a bias of some sort. The key, however, is to make those preferences explicit and known to the observer and the student. The successful teacher is constantly open and receptive to other interpretations. Observations and most other judgments that teachers make about children's learning must be tentative and focus on the well-being of the student to be helpful.

Informal Observations

MacDonald (1991) describes several types of informal observations. Teachers can observe and note the amount and quality of student participation in activities, the kinds of questions that a student asks during and after class, and the cooperative skills that the student demonstrates while working. Teachers can comment on how a student receives and follows directions, responds to teacher questions, and completes tasks. These types of work habits are important to student socialization and success in dealing with the world outside school.

Formal Checklists

Herman, Aschbacher, and Winters (1992) identified six characteristics of alternative assessments that highlight the characteristics and uses of checklists:

◆ The student must do something that can be observed or that results in an observable product.
◆ The purpose of using an alternative form of assessment is to gain insight into higher-level thinking or problem solving. Therefore, higher-order thinking must be included in assessment activities.
◆ The tasks used must represent meaningful instructional activities.
◆ "Real-world" applications must be invoked.
◆ People use their judgment, which is subject to variation, when they do the scoring.
◆ New instructional and evaluation roles are created for the teacher.

Using Observation Successfully

At least three types of observations are employed in elementary classrooms:

◆ Informal ongoing observations of a general nature
◆ Formal guided observation using a checklist or written protocol
◆ Formal observation of a general nature

By far, the most common observation is the informal ongoing observation. Generally, after a period of interaction with the student, the teacher completes a checklist or writes a summary statement of his or her observations. This has a very naturalistic flavor, and very profound understandings can often be achieved. However, memory is a very fragile thing, and this form of observation is probably subject to the greatest inconsistency and error.

Formal guided observations use a written checklist or observation protocol that instructs the teacher to look for specific events. If the student is to demonstrate a particular skill in a particular way, this type of observation is most appropriate. The student, as well as the teacher, should have access to the judging criteria. Formal observations, in which no guide is provided to direct teacher interpretation or to inform the student of what is to be measured, is also common. With undefined criteria, the likelihood of the student demonstrating exactly what the teacher hopes to observe is greatly diminished. If this type of observation is used, the teacher must be very open-minded about interpretation, and judgmental inferences should be minimized. This type of observation results in descriptions of how the student performed, but since no preset standard is communicated to the student, a teacher risks being unfair or misdirecting if, after the performance, the student is judged by an implicit scale.

To avoid implicit scaling, a checklist can be created and shared with students and parents. Checklists are not difficult to develop although careful consideration of the items should occur. The teacher should have in mind what the correct action or product should be for each item. This information must be carefully communicated to students prior to their preparation for the demonstration or their development of the project or work product.

Examples of Observation Checklists

Figure 11.3 is a checklist for a simple generic report. In this example, the teacher has placed considerable emphasis on work effort by including promptness, completeness, and neatness as criteria. This is an appropriate expectation because development of work skills is an important part of any project or report for young children in elementary school. The teacher also indicates that there should be a title for the report, an introduction that explains the topic, and at least one illustration. The item entitled "Report provides a description of important parts of topic" is shown to be double value ("× 2"), indicating the special importance of the item. The scale for the checklist is a simple "yes" or "no." However, the teacher can place a "check plus" in the "yes" column to note exceptionally well-done material.

The teacher also includes an area for comments and for computing a total for the columns. In this case, the teacher is computing one point for each "yes" and zero points for each "no." The special boxed item counts double. The teacher has communicated to the students the minimum number of points required to complete the assignment. Whether the teacher provides a letter grade or a pass-fail mark or simply includes the report and the evaluation in a portfolio is a final decision made by the teacher. In this case, a letter grade was computed based on the total number of

Report Criteria	Yes	No	Comment
Prompt (work handed in on time)			
Complete (all requirements fulfilled)			
Neat (easy to read and interpret)			
Accurate (information is factual)			
Report has a title			
Report starts with an introduction to topic			
Report contains an illustration			
Report provides description of important parts of topic (× 2)			
Totals			

FIGURE 11.3 Checklist for a generic report.

points. The scale was 9+ points equaled an "A" and went down a letter grade for each point lower than nine. Thus, a student who satisfactorily completes each criterion will receive an "A." A student who does one part poorly but another section exceptionally well can still receive an "A" since a "check plus" in the "yes" column counts for two points. Although the grade is certainly not the important part of writing a report, the teacher has clearly explained the expectations and has a reasonable system for ensuring success. Note, however, that there can still be great variation in the quality of the report because only one item in this particular assessment truly reflects quality as a criterion. Additional lines are provided so that the teacher can maintain the basic pattern of expectations during the term, yet increase the expectations for each ensuing report.

Figure 11.4 provides a checklist for an active performance of a student. In this example, the activity is a dramatic reading. The activity has been described to the children, and special lessons on the use of voice have been given. Otherwise, the checklist would not be measuring lesson objectives and probably would be measuring the students' natural talent in interpretation. The teacher has probably had students select a passage. The teacher may also suggest that the children practice for the dramatic reading as the culminating activity for a series of lessons.

The teacher has been quite clear about the expectations. Since the reading is a practiced piece, smoothness and pronunciation are appropriate criteria. Also notice that because many different text selections are available to the student, a selection can be made that matches the ability of the student. In this example, all students have an opportunity to read with smoothness and pronouncing words correctly. Expression, loudness, rhythm, and tone are terms used in the development activi-

Item	Always	Most	Some	Never	Not Observed
Pronounced words accurately					
Read with a smooth rhythm					
Used voice for expression					
Varied voice loudness					
Varied voice rhythm					
Varied voice tone					
Totals					
Comments:					

FIGURE 11.4   Checklist for oral dramatic reading.

ties. If students understand and have developed skill in their use, they should be able to employ these skills in an oral reading selection. Notice that this demonstration is far more relevant to students and to the objective than a test may be. The rating scale indicated in the checklist demonstrates that the teacher expects varying levels of implementation. Although the scale means little to an outsider, the teacher has probably given positive and negative examples showing the gradation in each task. In this example, the teacher has decided not to give a letter grade but instead has the student complete an evaluation after the presentation. The teacher will complete one, and both evaluations will go home with a suggestion that the child be given the opportunity to present the reading at home.

Using observations and checklists can greatly expand the teacher's alternatives in assessing and evaluating student work. Although no system is perfect and observation and checklists can be misused, the shortcomings are easy to avoid. When used to help children expand their opportunities to demonstrate their learning, observations and checklists are sophisticated tools deserving a place in every classroom.

Conducting Parent-Teacher Conferences

When assessments are made, they must be communicated to parents, students, and school personnel. Ornstein (1990), Gronlund (1974), and Ahmann and Glock (1959), representing several generations of researchers, provide suggestions for guiding the assignment and explaining the student's grades to parents:

- Focus on student achievement and enhanced learning.
- Explain what grades mean and how they are computed.
- Have a set of written standards for basing grades.
- Be positive and remember that students need appreciation and dignity.
- Use a variety of work products to determine grades.
- Keep records that support teacher decisions about grades.
- Have work products available for parents to view.
- No surprises . . . students and parents should be continually informed.
- Have a purpose for the conference.

Preparing for the Conference

Gronlund (1974) suggests preparing carefully for the conference (see Figure 11.5). Prior to the conference, the teacher should have a specific idea about what he or she wants to accomplish. The teacher should have appropriate materials ready so that the parent has time to review the materials and can gain an understanding of what they contain. The teacher should have specific and limited expectations of what can be accomplished in a conference. Simply exchanging telephone numbers with a promise to contact one another when questions arise is often one of the very best outcomes of a conference. The teacher should be prepared to receive a parent who may not want to be at school and do everything possible to make these parents feel comfortable so that they will want to come back. He or she should be prepared to listen to parents. If the child has problems at school, there may be a source or influence other than the classroom that can be either a cause or a cure. Although teachers should not pry into a student's private life, they can appropriately ask about the child's behavior and happiness when out of school. The teacher should be prepared to ask specific questions and then listen attentively without making judgments.

Conducting the Conference

During the conference, the teacher must remain positive, regardless of parental behavior. If the parent is hostile, aggressive, or angry, the teacher should attempt to listen attentively to their complaints and save his or her comments for a later time. Providing an angry agitated parent with more bad news rarely achieves anything positive. If the only thing that can be accomplished during the conference is that the teacher demonstrates a willingness to listen and be positive, the conference is a success.

Usually, parents are apprehensive rather than angry. The teacher should be positive and act positively about the child. It is often best, after brief introductions, to ask the parents if they have any concerns, questions, or comments they wish to be addressed and deal with those first. One important thing to avoid in a conference is

FIGURE 11.5 Planning tips for teacher conferences.

Adapted from *Improving Marking and Reporting in Classroom Instruction* by N. E. Gronlund, 1974, New York: Macmillan.

Before the conference
- Know the purpose of the conference.
- Review student's work and behavior records.
- Have student work on hand.
- Have materials organized systematically.
- Have questions ready to ask parents.
- Anticipate parent's questions.
- Provide a comfortable setting.
- Prepare to be positive and supportive of the parent, regardless of reception.

Conducting the conference
- Create a friendly atmosphere.
- Maintain a positive attitude.
- Use language that is understood by parents.
- Listen to parents.
- Be honest and sincere.
- Describe student strengths.
- Describe areas needing improvement.
- Avoid advice giving; ask parents questions instead.
- Have parents assist in planning a course of action.
- Review what you understand to be the areas of agreement.
- End positively.

insisting on specific remedies to be conducted at home. Instead, it is usually best to gain the confidence of the parents so that the child's educational opportunity can be maximized. When parents do ask for advice, the teacher should suggest but never demand. He or she should attempt to create a friendly, positive atmosphere.

When talking to parents, the teacher should try to avoid using educational jargon and use lay language and a conversational vocabulary instead. The teacher should be honest and sincere while listening closely to parents. Parents who are unconvinced about a teacher's interest and sincerity are unlikely to act on any suggestions that he or she makes. The teacher should work toward establishing rapport with the parent by describing the student's strengths. If the student has weaknesses that need to be reported, he or she should attempt to describe them in terms of strengths. For example, if the child's work is often incomplete or undone, the teacher should not attack the child as lazy, inconsistent, or uncooperative. Instead, he or she should point out those parts that are completed, comment on the strengths demonstrated in the completed parts of the work, and suggest that it would be best if this ability were used to complete the assignment.

When making a request for a behavior change from the child, the teacher should point out the child's strengths in prior activities and avoid offering criticism of some weakness. The teacher should provide parents with evidence that a more favorable state of affairs is possible. He or she should always work toward progress and remedy and never permit a conference to become a session for teacher complaints and blame.

Ending the Conference

In ending the conference, the teacher should have parents assist in developing a plan of action that is clearly intended to benefit the child. He or she should quickly review what was said and what goals have been set. A summary of what both parents and teacher have agreed to do to improve learning is necessary. The teacher should then end the conference positively and always invite the parents to share other ideas by notes, calls, or conferences and offer to do the same.

Encouraging Student Self-Evaluation

Glasser (1992) states the relationship among self-evaluation, motivation, and self-concept:

> Everyone has a basic concept of himself, whatever that concept may be. Each of us not only has such a concept, but we are continually evaluating ourselves. This ongoing process is true of all of us. It is as though, over our heads, we have a little radar that is constantly passing back signals to us. If the signals come back continually: The *work you do is no good. You are not worth very much. I don't care much for you,* one's self-concept is bound to become a concept of failure. (p. 101)

Every teacher can ask children to participate in self-analysis activities as did Mrs. Grant in the vignette at the beginning of the chapter. In reality, the student's personal assessment is most likely to affect whether he or she has the desire to improve or becomes so frustrated that he or she just gives up. Providing students with opportunities to determine what quality work is and to establish pride in self-control is always difficult, always contains risk, and always is fundamental to successful teaching.

◆ ◆ ◆

Summary

1. Evaluation programs such as testing and grading have existed as long as formal schooling; however, formal evaluation remains problematic and unpopular.
2. Evaluation must be accurate and fair if it is to contribute to the benefit of students and the learning climate.
3. Evaluation systems include an articulated purpose, clear objectives, instruments for measuring learning, a process of interpretation, and communication vehicles.
4. Two broad purposes of evaluation are accountability for learning and instructional improvement.
5. By measuring a variety of student outcomes, an evaluation system typically increases its validity, reliability, and usefulness.
6. Understanding evaluation requires knowledge about individual differences, tests, measurement concepts such as reliability and validity, and relevance.
7. Student performance can be compared to others, to preestablished standards, or to personal bests.
8. Letter grades have a long tradition and their use is often a matter of district policy. Letter grades have severe limitations, but replacement systems, suffering from equally distressing problems, have not received widespread acceptance.
9. In grading, the teacher must always consider whether the measurement is impor-

tant and necessary, whether the grading practice leads to achievement of stated objectives, and whether the likelihood of student learning is increased.
10. Current evaluation practices include letter grades, pass-fail systems, checklists of objectives, letters to parents, and parent-teacher conferences.
11. Authentic assessment attempts to alleviate an overdependence on tests and grades and provides performance examples for parental review as an evaluation tool.
12. Evaluation can be enhanced by using multiple measures, clearly stating goals, cooperatively developing the reporting system, keeping the report brief, and limiting judgments to what can be done with validity.
13. The use of tests can be enhanced by teacher activity that clearly delineates the purpose of the test, considers the purpose of each item, uses a variety of items types, keeps items simple, and tests with success in mind.
14. Portfolio development offers an avenue to reduce the dependence on tests and grades. Portfolios should be used only with specific purposes and with clear directions on its development and external assessment criteria.
15. Observations and checklists offer the teacher an opportunity to broaden the data

collection process although they are subject to hidden biases from judges.

16. Parent conferences offer the best opportunity to communicate a child's learning successes and learning needs.

17. Self-assessment must be taught over the entire school career and is the only true avenue to develop life-long learning and quality work habits in children.

◆ ◆ ◆

Activities and Questions for Further Understanding

1. Design a general report card that you think would be appropriate for your class. Determine the intended age and grade for the report card or state if it is an omnibus instrument. Consider the inclusion of skills, subject, and attitude measures.

2. Develop a weekly progress report that may improve on Mrs. Grant's design in "A Slice of Life."

3. What is your experience with report cards? Did they assist or detract from your interest in learning?

4. If there were no grades or tests in your class, how would that affect your motivation to read this text?

5. Role-play with a fellow student the following scenario: One of you is the teacher, and the other is an angry parent. The teacher failed to include grades on the nine weekly progress reports but had listed a number of missing pieces of classwork. The completed work averaged near 100 percent, but when the missing work was included in the average as zeroes, the grade fell to below 70 percent. The teacher gave the student a "C," and the parent expects much better. The parent's reasoning is that the child learned how to do all the work but was tired of the senseless repetition. What does the teacher do?

6. Develop an observation checklist for the student's use of cooperative research activities while using resources in the library. What are the barriers involved in using the checklist? What are the best strategies to integrate the checklist into student assessment of research skills?

◆ ◆ ◆

References

Ahmann, J. Stanley, & Glock, Marvin D. (1959). *Evaluating pupil growth.* Boston: Allyn & Bacon.

Armstrong, Thomas. (1994). *Multiple intelligences in the classroom.* Alexandria, VA: Association for Supervision and Curriculum Development.

Bellanca, James A. (1977). *Grading.* Washington, DC: National Education Association.

Combs, Arthur Wright. (1976). *Educational accountability: Beyond behavioral objectives.* Washington, DC: Association for Supervision and Curriculum Development.

Cronbach, Lee J. (1970). *Essentials of psychological testing* (3rd ed.). New York: Harper & Row.

Evans, D. M. D. (1976). *Special tests and their meanings.* London: Faber.

Fischer, Cheryl F., & King, Rita M. (1995). *Authentic assessment: A guide to implementation.* Thousand Oaks, CA: Corwin Press.

Gagné, Robert M., & Driscoll, Marcy P. (1988). *Essentials of learning for instruction* (2nd ed.). Upper Saddle River, NJ: Prentice Hall.

Gardner, Howard. (1983). *Frames of mind: The theory of multiple intelligences.* New York: Basic Books.

Glasser, William. (1969). *Schools without failure.* New York: Harper & Row.

Glasser, William. (1992). *The quality school: Managing students without coercion* (2nd, expanded ed.). New York: HarperPerennial.

Gronlund, Norman E. (1974). *Determining accountability for classroom instruction.* New York: Macmillan.

Guilford, J. P. (1967). *The nature of human intelligence.* New York: McGraw-Hill.

Hayman, John L., Jr., & Napier, Rodney N. (1975). *Evaluation in the schools: A human process for renewal.* Monterey, CA: Brooks/Cole Publishing Co.

Herman, Joan L., Aschbacher, Pamela R., and Winters, Lynn. (1992). *A practical guide to alternative assessment.* Alexandria, VA: Association for Supervision and Curriculum Development.

Jarolimek, John, & Foster, Clifford D. (1993). *Teaching and learning in the elementary school* (4th ed.). New York: Macmillan.

MacDonald, Robert E. (1991). *A handbook of basic skills and strategies for beginning teachers: Facing the challenge of teaching in today's schools.* New York: Longman.

Merwin, J. C. (1989). Evaluation. In M. C. Reynolds (Ed.), *Knowledge base for the beginning teacher* (pp. 185–193). Oxford: Pergamon Press.

Ornstein, Allan C. (1990). *Institutionalized learning in America.* New Brunswick, NJ: Transaction Publishers.

Robinson, Glen E., & Craver, James M. (1989). *Assessing and grading student achievement.* Arlington, VA: Educational Research Service.

Slavin, R. E. (1986). *Using student team learning* (3d ed.). Baltimore: Johns Hopkins University, Center for Research on Elementary and Middle Schools.

TenBrink, Terry. (1990). Evaluation. In J. M. Cooper, *Classroom teaching skills* (4th ed., pp. 337–376). Lexington, MA: D. C. Heath and Company.

Wrinkle, William L. (1947). *Improving marking and reporting practices in elementary and secondary schools.* New York: Rinehart.

CHAPTER 12

What Classroom Climate Should I Build?

A Review of Current Theory and Research About Management

Outline

Nothing you do for children is ever wasted. They seem not to notice us, hovering, averting our eyes, and they seldom offer thanks, but what we do for them is never wasted.

GARRISON KEILLOR

What the vast majority of American children needs is to stop being pampered, stop being indulged, stop being chauffeured, stop being catered to. In the final analysis it is not what you do for your children but what you have taught them to do for themselves that will make them successful human beings.

ANN LANDERS

A Slice of Life

Mrs. Donald was losing patience with the situation. She and the other three fifth-grade teachers had classrooms in an annex separate from the rest of the school. The situation was almost ideal having both large classrooms, private halls with no traffic, and large restrooms centrally located from the classrooms. This gave the teachers the luxury of providing extra freedom for the students to work in the carpeted halls for quiet projects as well as providing ease of access to the restrooms for children to take care of personal needs.

The problem was that a handful of children in each of the classrooms seemed to be ignoring the extra responsibility that came with the freedom. The restrooms, particularly the boys' facility, were spoiled with littered tissue, graffiti, and poor toileting practices. It seemed unfair to the fifth-grade teachers to restrict the activity of everyone, but catching the culprits presented some special problems, particularly because all of the teachers were women and the boys' restroom was the central focus.

388

At the fifth-grade meeting, Mrs. Donald suggested that each class have a class-room meeting regarding the problem. She suggested putting the problem directly to the children. The teachers took pictures of the restrooms at the beginning and end of the day for a week. The "before" and "after" pictures were quite revealing. It clearly showed the litter and poor hygiene habits of some of the children. Mrs. Donald was still a little nervous showing a slide of toilet fixtures, graffiti, and the like. However, all of the teachers agreed that a direct, candid approach to the problem was necessary if the children were to accept the responsibility for solving the problem. By now, the teachers were quite tired of "preaching" and playing police officers.

Mrs. Donald called the meeting to order and put Martha, the class president, in charge. Martha announced that the teachers had approached her and the other fifth-grade class presidents about the restroom problems. She had seen the pictures and agreed with the teachers that the class could do better. Martha then asked Mrs. Donald to present her view of the problem.

Mrs. Donald asked the children if restroom activities of her class and the other fifth-grade classes were acceptable. The class was quiet. Mrs. Donald was quiet, too. After two minutes of silence, which seemed much longer, Mrs. Donald asked the children if they would like to see the slides of the restrooms at the end of the day from last week. To her relief, the children quickly giggled and replied in a vehement negative. Mrs. Donald laughed with them and quickly added, "I guess from your reaction, that you believe there is a problem in the restroom?" The children giggled, and several held their noses, which only brought more laughter. Mrs. Donald smiled, "Great, I see you have an idea of the problem in hand! But let's use this class meeting to list what the problems are and then make a list of how to solve them. Martha, if you will take the ideas from the class, I'll do the writing on the board."

Charles immediately blurted out, "It stinks in there!" The class broke into laughter. Mrs. Donald wrote, "The restroom has a bad odor." She paused and then rewrote the comment, "The restroom stinks!"

The children laughed, but Charles was the first to notice. "Look, Mrs. Donald's red!" It was true. Mrs. Donald was not enjoying this meeting. She was embarrassed but was determined to bring the children around to accepting some responsibility for remedying the problem. Martha and Mrs. Donald conjured a list of problems as viewed by the class.

Charles was first to suggest a remedy, "If everyone would just quit being dumb, it would be OK!"

Mrs. Donald winked at Charles, "You're right. But that isn't working now. Maybe we should post reminders?"

Charles nodded, "Yeah, let's put up some signs."

Martha called on the students as their hands were raised, and a list of more remedies began to emerge. Mrs. Donald was a little surprised at the student's insistence on harsh punishment for offenders. With Martha's permission, she interrupted the session to ask how the students proposed to catch the offenders, particularly in the boys' restroom. "Should I only allow you in the restroom when I'm there to watch over you?" Her voice was irritated, and no one laughed. "That's not what this meeting is about. I don't want to watch over you or to catch you messing up the restroom! I want the messing around stopped!" With that last comment, Mrs. Donald unloaded a lot of the frustration and anger that had been building up. It also stopped the meeting.

After a moment, Mrs. Donald regained her voice and said, "I didn't mean to be hateful. But this isn't funny, and it isn't pleasant for me. I want you to act responsibly without my having to play cops and robbers. Are there any other ideas?"

Mrs. Donald looked at the list of helpful suggestions. The class determined that this would be their plan of action:

- *Post reminders.*
- *All students act responsibly.*
- *Remind others to act responsibly.*
- *New paper towel holders that didn't "dump" the towels.*
- *Additional trashcans.*
- *Soap dispensers rather than bars of soap.*
- *Report any mess immediately.*
- *Don't go inside if restroom is noisy; report it.*
- *Anybody caught goofing off in the restroom cleans the restroom.*
- *Class monitors to inspect the restrooms periodically.*

The plan was announced to the children, and all agreed it was reasonable. For the next few days, the plan steadily improved the restroom situation. A special squad volunteered to scrub the graffiti off the walls. By the end of the second week, the improvement was so great that the principal decided to have all the stalls painted and to go along with the new paper towel holders and soap dispensers. Less than a month after the plan had been enacted, the children returned from a weekend to find both restrooms entirely repainted with the added bonus of new mirrors and ventilation fans.

Teachers' Attitudes and Classroom Climate

A teacher's attitudes and beliefs greatly influence the climate of the classroom. Whether the teacher has high expectations or low, views children with trust or suspicion, nurtures personal responsibility, practices forgiveness, and provides support and encouragement—all combine to establish the atmosphere in the classroom. Among the most influential elements of climate are the teacher's views on behavior management. Although behavior management in elementary classrooms remains one of the strongest concerns of beginning and veteran teachers alike, the research offers only general assistance. This research also has a great deal of appeal in that it supports many different perspectives of the ideal classroom. Each perspective has a different set of values and leads to differing climates and mechanisms for governing the classroom activity.

At the center of the debate on classroom management are the wide variances of values held by teachers, administrators, and parents about the behaviors and learning activities that should exist in the classroom. If a teacher values free expression, self-determination, and individual learning goals, he or she will not like solutions that suggest restrictive behavior codes.

Review of Classroom Management Research

Evertson and Harris (1992) published a review of the research on managing classrooms. They noted a trend developing that abandons the focus on student conformity through coercion and embraces a strong emphasis on managing learning climate. Because of this extended focus on learning environments, their summary reflected much of the research on effective teaching presented in earlier chapters of this text. Evertson and Harris found six primary areas of focus, summarized in Figure 12.1.

Evertson and Harris were optimistic about the quality of the generic information about effective classroom management. However, fitting generic strategies to specific contexts still needs more exploration. Evertson and Harris were also optimistic about teaching teachers to employ more successful strategies to manage their classrooms. They concluded that research findings can and do influence teachers' decisions about management practices. Management practices, in turn, compose the essential elements of the classroom climate.

Combining Research and Philosophical Beliefs

What is acceptable behavior is embedded in our values, our social perspectives, tradition, and context. Likewise, what is acceptable in managing students' classroom behavior is also embedded in values, social perspectives, tradition, and context. The first section of this text examined the many perspectives on education, social outlooks, and individual differences. It was noted that, in a democratic society, certain unifying factors guide our schools. One of the most important factors is individual determination and the right to individuality. This, in turn, puts inordinate responsibility on teachers to accommodate an array of parental expectations regarding the behavior of their children in school settings.

When parents give supportive nurturing guidance to the child, the school's job is to extend the development of social maturity and provide a relevant academic curriculum (Black, 1994; Freiberg, 1996). However, when parents do not give appropriate guidance or the child's expression of individuality is characterized as socially limiting behavior, the school has difficulty in providing the academic curriculum and

Time management
- Amount of time students spend learning varies. Less than one-half of the school day is generally used for learning.
- The amount of time spent learning is associated with achievement.
- Time use (time management) is a critical factor in student success.

Group management strategies
- Teachers can and do elicit high levels of work involvement.
- Teacher behavior is associated with student task orientation.
- Student task involvement is inversely related to student misbehavior (involvement decreases misbehavior).

Lessons that engage students
- Frequent seatwork lowers on-task behavior.
- Changing activities frequently maintains interest.
- Engagement in seatwork varies among teachers while engagement rates during recitations are similar.

Classroom communication
- Teachers use verbal and nonverbal communications to communicate norms, rules, and expectations.
- Students need to understand rules of participation in order to engage lessons successfully.
- Management systems need to be visible, established, monitored, modified, refined, and reestablished.

Beginning the year
- Proactive programs that prevent misbehavior or more effective strategies for stopping misbehavior are needed.
- Beginning-of-the-year strategies for teaching rules, routines, and expectations are critical.
- Rules and procedures need to be planned in advance.
- Communications must be communicated clearly.
- Feedback regarding academic performance and behavior promotes positive growth.

Handling misbehavior
- Carefully planned and enacted management plans will not stop all misbehavior.
- Physical proximity and eye contact can usually handle most situations.
- Punishment is best left as a planned response to repeated misbehavior.
- Interventions depend on orderly structures already being in place in the classroom.

FIGURE 12.1 Highlights of classroom management.

Summarized from "What We Know About Classroom Management," by C. Evertson and A. Harris, 1992. *Educational Leadership, 49*(7), 74–78.

associated experiences in social maturation. In these situations, teachers look for strategies that either assist the child in developing self-control behaviors or that externally impose behavior limits on the child. Research and theory exist that support and advocate both views (Educational Research Service, 1996; Morris, 1996).

Theorists classified as *instrumentalists* have a central belief that certain acts have determined predictable results. In other words, a teacher may choose behavior that directly influences a child's conduct in a predictable way. These teacher behaviors need not be punitive; most theorists readily recognize that punitive behaviors typically do not provide the desired results. Instrumentalist behaviors are based on common student reactions to specific teacher activity. A teacher who looks into a child's face from less than 10 inches away usually invokes discomfort in the student. A "pat-on-the-back" when the student is trying something difficult usually is interpreted as supportive and encourages the student to continue trying. Instrumentalists usually have their foundations in behaviorism, although most would not advocate a dominant use of stimulus-response conditioning in classroom management plans.

Instrumentalists are also pragmatists. For example, if a teacher gets the desired results by acting in a certain way, he or she expects that similar results occur with each repetition of those actions. However, there are limits to teacher actions that are sanctioned. Hurtful teacher acts are not advocated, and induced physical or emotional pain is universally condemned. Instead, instrumentalists capitalize on natural responses of students. For example, students are less likely to misbehave if the teacher is watching them. Therefore, instrumentalists advocate looking directly at misbehaving children, prompting them to stop. Instrumentalists want to establish a climate that is open and free where children act responsibly to further their learning. However, when things go awry, the teacher is always prepared to step in and enforce the rules with teacher behaviors that bring about predictable student responses.

Theorists classified as *developmentalists* believe that certain teacher acts are appropriate and valuable because they allow children to develop responsibility, self-control, and morality. The short-term results are less important than the cumulative effect of repeated treatment and experiences designed to develop internal controls. Developmentalist views are very similar to psychological developmentalists because both believe that child behavior and perceptions are influenced by changes in cognitive and physical abilities caused by natural growth processes. Thus, children are treated differently than adults and are subject to different expectations.

Developmental theorists in student behavior management are primarily concerned with providing experiences that provide optimal opportunity for the student to assess and regulate their own behavior. For example, rather than issuing the command, "Stop that!", a developmental theorist may advocate the question, "What should you be doing now?" The idea is to have the students identify and correct their own behavior. Developmentalists also want a classroom climate in which children act responsibly to further their learning. However, when children misbehave, developmentalists eschew direct intervention in favor of soliciting children's personal judgment of their behavior and promoting self-correction.

The views of instrumentalists and developmentalists are not antithetical or mutually exclusive. They do have different foci from which to develop models and programs in classroom management. For example, "looking on" and "making eye contact" would be advocated by an instrumentalist because of the immediate changes in a child's behavior that results. However, a developmentalist may use the same process in hopes that the child will assess his or her behavior and modify it appropriately. In the developmentalist view, children do not change their behavior because they fear teacher-imposed consequences, but because these behaviors are not in their best interests.

Some instrumentalist views do contradict the developmental position. Contrived consequences for misbehavior (for example, keeping a child after school for excessive talking) are instrumental in generally diminishing, at least in the short term, the misbehavior. Developmental views advocate more student participation in recognizing and solving the problem and a logical connection between student behavior and consequences. For example, the child concludes that moving to a new seat with different neighbors may minimize the temptation and thus improve his or her class behavior. The latter strategy emphasizes growth; the former emphasizes compliance. Both are generally considered necessary in today's classrooms, although there is strong debate on this issue. Although it is always preferable for children to self-correct and govern their own behavior, there are circumstances when it does not happen. In those situations, teachers need to have instrumental strategies that maintain and restore order efficiently so that the day-to-day business of learning can continue successfully.

Instrumentalists

The three instrumentalists presented in this chapter vary widely in their assumptions about children and school. Their acceptance among scholars and teachers also varies. Jacob Kounin studied teachers in classrooms in hopes of identifying teacher behavior that correlated with high levels of positive student behavior and low levels of negative behavior. Fredric Jones studied teachers in a similar fashion and extended the basic work of Kounin by identifying teacher "body language" that facilitated teacher "with-itness" and overlapping. The most controversial of the three is Lee Canter whose packaged discipline plans, workshops, and videotape materials are used in a vast number of public school districts in the United States. His management plan reflects many of the practices of the common school movement during the first half of the century and focuses on the teachers' "right to teach" and the students' "right to learn" in an orderly structured environment clearly under the control of the teacher.

Jacob Kounin

Jacob Kounin was born in Cleveland, Ohio, in 1939 but did not publish his major work *Discipline and Group Management in Classrooms* until 1977. His description of the traits of an effective classroom manager is discussed earlier in the text. His observations of teachers in the classroom and their use of what he termed the "ripple effect" stimulated these conclusions. Kounin (1977) noted that when a teacher noted and commented publicly on one student's behavior, other students responded by changing their behavior usually in the direction desired by the teacher. In short, when a teacher told one student to stop talking other students who were not addressed by the teacher but were also talking stopped, too. The ripple effect also works in the opposite direction. If a student misbehaves and is not monitored by the teacher, other students are aware of the misbehavior and assume that it is sanctioned. Thus, the misbehavior spreads through the classroom. Kounin wondered if the ripple effect could be managed and used deliberately by teachers to alter the behaviors of groups of children indirectly.

Use of Desists. Kounin argued that teacher interventions to stop misbehavior should occur soon after students initiate off-task or disruptive activity. Kounin called these early interventions "desists." A desist appropriately timed and publicly administered had two benefits: (1) The student was made aware that the teacher had observed and disapproved of the behavior, and (2) other students were made aware that their behavior was subject to teacher scrutiny and their compliance was required.

Kounin went to great lengths to help teachers understand that, although almost all desists create a ripple effect, desists that are perceived as threatening by students do not bring the desired changes in behavior as much as they contribute to a demeaning, uncomfortable classroom climate. Supportive desists are consistently more influential in bringing about desired improvement both with the student under consideration and indirectly with others. Figure 12.2 provides examples comparing the two type of desists.

Kounin was able to identify three qualities of a desist and describe the typical effects of each quality. The first quality, *clarity,* describes how readily the student can comprehend the meaning of the desist. Kounin described this desist as containing a short description of the unacceptable behavior, the name of the student under observation, and a redirection pointing the student toward the appropriate task for

FIGURE 12.2 Examples of two types of desists.

> **Threatening Desists**
> - Teacher's voice is loud and speech is fast: "Stop it! I'll not have this in my class!"
> - Teacher stares with hand on hips showing exasperation: "Why are you not doing your reading?"
>
> **Supportive Desists**
> - Teacher's voice is firm but low: "You need to stop talking and read silently."
> - Teacher approaches student and makes eye contact with a smile: "You must finish your story today. Please use this time to do it."

the moment. Desists provided with clarity also increased the conforming behavior of those who witnessed the desist.

The second quality, *firmness,* describes how the desist is delivered. Firmness describes more than just the words spoken, but also the way in which words are delivered, the body language of the teacher, and the teacher's history in dealing with this type of event. Firmness was described as sending a serious message to the student that a modification of behavior is imminent and required. Firmness should not be confused with hostile, aggressive, or even assertive behavior. Firmness simply means that the student is aware that the teacher will no longer tolerate the current behavior. This desist brought about an increased conformity only in students who were misbehaving; the degree of firmness had little effect on children who were not misbehaving.

The third quality, *roughness,* involved statements made in anger, threats of physical punishment, or negative sanctions with restrictions of freedom. Roughness did not bring about sustained improvements in student behavior directly or indirectly.

Kounin described many of the teacher traits that led to success in managing student behavior. These characteristics are summarized in Figure 12.3.

Kounin's Management Goal.   Effective and efficient learning is central to Kounin's view of effective classroom management. By keeping students busily and happily involved in learning activities, Kounin thought teachers could reduce behavior problems to a minimum. Systems of rewards and sanctions were considered less effective measures of effective classrooms than were the teacher's ability to provide vibrant, meaningful lessons to students and to monitor the inevitable misappropriation of

---

With-itness: Knowing what is going on in all parts of the classroom at all times

Smooth transitions: Moving between activities while maintaining consistent flow in learning activities

Group alertness: Holding every student accountable for the content of a lesson when working alone, in small or large groups

Avoiding student satiation: Preventing boredom by providing a variety of activities that provide a feeling of progress

Overlapping: Attending to more than one thing at a time without becoming frustrated, confused, or ineffective

Momentum: Pacing lessons quickly, avoiding diversions or unnecessary delays, maintaining a focus on learning

Accountability: Knowing the learning successes and limitations of each student by using a variety of assessment activities

---

FIGURE 12.3   Kounin's characteristics of effective managers.

Selected from *Discipline and Group Management in Classrooms* by Jacob Kounin, 1977, Huntington, NY: R. E. Krieger Publishing Co.

time and energy on students who were immature and not ready to accept adult responsibility.

Kounin's view was optimistic. He believed that if teachers were to concentrate on their teaching behavior, student behavior would align with their expectations. He also believed that teachers could learn the skills necessary for effective classroom management, although some would have less difficulty than others would. This optimism is at the core of the current belief that teachers' management skills can be improved if they concentrate on reflective decision making over a number of years. Improving management skills will equate into better-managed classrooms with more learning from happier children. Kounin demonstrated that the teacher's ability to manage groups and lessons was as important to successful learning and effective classrooms as the entering behavior of the students. Therefore, according to Kounin (1977), the teacher must learn to do the following:

◆ Know what is happening in every area of the classroom and to communicate that to students.
◆ Be able to deal with more than one classroom event at a time.
◆ Provide clear redirection to students before misbehavior escalates.
◆ Carry out smooth transitions when changing from one activity to another.
◆ Maintain the group's focus on learning, using alerting and accountability events.
◆ Teach with activities that provide tangible progress, sufficient challenge, and appropriate variety for students.

Additionally, Kounin suggested that teachers establish an awareness of the nuances of student behavior and classroom conduct that allows quick processing of clues. For example, students who sit up rapidly and look particularly busy are possibly, if not probably, hiding an event from the teacher. For example, one teacher found an injured bird in the lap of a child who had brought it in from the playground only because the child was sitting hunched over trying to protect the bird from view.

Kounin also proposed that teachers should not dwell on misbehavior but take appropriate action and move on to the next situation while always emphasizing learning over student disruption. Teachers also must be flexible in routines so that student needs are central to decision making rather than focusing on the routine itself. Kounin reiterated the need for the teacher to focus attention, to appeal to student curiosity, to use practice activities and closure techniques, and to develop positive attitudes toward the lesson by employing a multisensory approach to learning.

Kounin also suggested that teachers carefully avoid and eliminate unproductive teacher behaviors such as directing desists to the wrong students when disruption occurs. Additionally, teachers should avoid focusing or dwelling on minor misbehaviors, particularly in the presence of more serious behaviors. Finally, teachers should not allow inappropriate behaviors to spread or intensify before intervening.

Fredric Jones

Fredric Jones's work (1987) is a complementary extension of Kounin's findings in that "with-itness," overlapping, and momentum are revealed in more detail. Jones was concerned with identifying effective management behaviors and also with strategies for developing those skills. Jones provided copious descriptions of specific management skills and how teachers can develop and use these skills in classroom settings.

Jones was one of the first to create "packaged" programs for teacher workshops and personal professional development. In packaged programs, research and theoretical findings are combined with practical instructional strategies and are made available to school districts through videotapes, pamphlets, and workbooks.

Jones's findings are still quite pertinent to today's teachers. Jones, along with others studying teacher behavior during the 1970s and 1980s, found that teachers commonly spent less than 50 percent of student contact time on instruction. Not only did teachers spend large blocks of time on noninstructional activities, they also lost time dedicated to lessons because of off-task behavior of students. This lost time was due largely through students talking with other students about topics other than the lesson.

Jones, like Kounin, had an optimistic outlook and demonstrated that this lost time could be salvaged. He believed that three teacher skills were essential to reclaiming lost time and putting it to use effectively: effective body language, incentive systems, and efficient help to students (see Figure 12.4).

Body Language.   A person's posture, movement, and gestures convey messages to others, a well-known fact. Jones isolated certain gestures and sequences of gestures that he felt best assisted the teacher in managing student behavior. Valued above all behaviors is calmness. A teacher whose posture conveys confidence, calmness, and restraint possesses increased power in the situation. When a teacher shows strong emotions such as bursts of anger, hostility, remorse, or hurt, he or she has established a posture of weakness. Being calm is possessing power, and power is necessary to influence children who choose not to control their behaviors appropriately.

Like Kounin, Jones emphasized that teachers should develop and use their ability to monitor, or "track," activities in the entire room. Jones also emphasized that teachers should make students aware of this monitoring ability and use it to prevent or stop misbehavior. Students, when misbehaving, tend to track the teacher to conceal their misbehavior. When the teacher scans the class and finds inappropriate behavior, the teacher stares at the student, waiting for him or her to look back.

Body language: Messages are sent nonverbally that communicate your intents.

Incentive systems: External rewards can direct and create positive behaviors.

Efficient help: Teacher has developed routines that permit students to get quick assistance and experience success when they try.

FIGURE 12.4   Main focus of Jones's ideas.
Selected from *Positive Classroom Discipline* by Fredric H. Jones, 1987, New York: McGraw-Hill

When the student looks, the teacher makes eye contact in an attempt to make the student recognize the unacceptable behavior and self-correct. This eye contact, or "locking eyes," makes students realize the teacher is continually noting all student behavior.

Proximity control refers to the teacher's use of physical presence to minimize negative behavior and promote positive ones. The teacher constantly moves about the room, taking note of student work, making eye contact, and commenting on progress. Even during whole-group discussions, moving about the room makes students aware that the teacher is watching, thus minimizing the likelihood that student misbehavior will go unobserved. Physical proximity is an excellent tool that teachers can use to avoid entanglement in a verbal interaction (and disruption). Teachers can use movement that decreases the distance between teacher and student to communicate teacher's awareness of students' activities.

Facial expressions can convey many important messages from teacher to student without disrupting the learning of others. A smile and nod almost universally express acceptance, whereas slightly squinted eyes and pursed lips send a message of disapproval. Thus, teachers who use facial expressions can encourage positive behavior and discourage negative behavior without delaying the task at hand.

Signals and gestures in the classroom also extend nonverbal methods of communication and make a valuable contribution to the classroom management repertoire of the teacher. Hand and arm signals can communicate quickly and accurately without disrupting other classroom tasks. Wagging an index finger while making eye contact accurately tells a student that the behavior has been noticed, is not acceptable, and must stop. Often, a smile can accompany a signal to imply that the teacher assumes the negative behavior is a result of the student's enthusiasm and energy while conveying an understanding that the student is not deliberately trying to cause mischief. Hand signals can direct movement, provide or deny permissions, regulate the volume of student talk, govern participation, or encourage patience.

Of all the body language messages, the most important to master is the posture that conveys, "I mean business." "Meaning business" was how Jones described credibility. The teacher's conduct must portray confidence, strength, and earnest intent. Teachers should clearly describe the acceptable and unacceptable activity to students, implicitly set behavior and learning goals, and strenuously monitor all activity that promotes or detracts from these intentions. Again, "meaning business" is not an expression of threat but a confident posture of goal-oriented, businesslike teacher activity.

Incentive Systems.   Incentive plans have been used in business management for years. Generally, these plans work to provide individuals with tangible rewards for achieving specified goals. Teachers have used incentive plans of various types for both individual and group goals with mixed results. Jones argued that incentive plans work, but they must be used properly.

Incentive plans fail to improve student productivity, according to Jones, when the incentives are too elaborate, erratic, or appeal to only a few children. Figure 12.5 provides some characteristics of effective incentive plans.

- Use of incentives must be systematic.
- Rewards must appeal to many students at modest (preferably no) cost.
- Goals established by the incentive plan must be attainable by all.
- The incentive plan should have academic merit/educational value.
- Plans must be simple to implement.
- Grandma's Rule (do what I want first to get what you want).

FIGURE 12.5 Jones's ideas regarding incentives and incentive programs.
Selected from *Positive Classroom Discipline* by Fredric H. Jones, 1987, New York: McGraw-Hill.

Jones acknowledged that incentive plans are not popular among many teachers. The cost and time involved in implementing the plan are cited by some teachers as reasons for not using incentive plans in their classrooms. Others point out the conflict in value structures. Many teachers feel that incentive plans "buy" behaviors that should be freely given by children. Effort, manners, and social responsibility must be valued in their own right and should not be "bought."

Incentive plans in schools and businesses have their supporters, and strong evidence shows achievement of immediate short-term goals. However, incentive plans have hostile critics such as Kohn (1993). Kohn claimed that the cumulative effect of incentive plans is to destroy the internal locus of control of the student. Further, incentive plans misdirect student and teacher attention from the importance of socially responsible and individually controlled behavior. Instead, incentive plans promote a "What's in it for me?" attitude.

Incentive plans can be formal plans with prescribed goals, behaviors, and rewards. Common among these plans are group-alerting techniques that track the time spent on off-task behavior. For example, when students are off-task, noisy, or not following the routines appropriately, a teacher may open a music box. The music is a signal that tells the children that the current classroom status is unacceptable and alerts them to monitor not only their own behavior but also those of their peers. If at the end of the week, music is still unplayed in the music box, the class gets a prescribed reward, such as time for academic games or a free reading period.

Simple informal incentives can be rewards of appreciation to groups or individuals. Usually given for academic productivity, incentives may also be given for positive personal behavior and effort. Informal incentives include positive acknowledgment, small tokens of recognition, selection for special jobs in the classroom, or a short period of special activity.

Efficient Help.   Jones advocated a classroom program that maximizes students' opportunity to learn. More opportunity to learn equals more opportunity for success which, in turn, leads to student satisfaction. Students who are taught how to complete daily assignments easily and successfully will be less motivated to misbehave and even have less opportunity to do so. Efficient help from a teacher encourages students to work independently instead of misbehave. .Figure 12.6 provides a short list of efficient help guides and activities.

> - Provide graphic aids for students.
> - Praise, prompt, and leave technique provides students with quick, clear assistance.
> - Efficient help combines challenge with security.
> - Goal is to get students to work independently without misbehaving.
> - Key to corrective feedback is positive, helping interaction.
> - Contact of needing student should be 10 to 30 seconds in duration.
> - Focus on being positive.
> - Don't develop student dependency.

FIGURE 12.6 Jones's suggestions for effective management.
Selected from *Positive Classroom Discipline* by Fredric H. Jones, 1987, New York: McGraw-Hill.

When students are working, the teacher must not become overly involved with a single student. Focusing on a single student for an extensive period of time minimizes the monitoring activity of the teacher and increases the likelihood of other students' off-task behavior. Jones developed the following procedure for delivering positive effective help:

- *Praise*. Praise students for what they have completed correctly.
- *Prompt*. Tell students what you want them to do in a clear and simple manner.
- *Leave*. Walk away instead of watching students carry out the instruction.

A "praise, prompt, and leave" session should last no longer than 30 seconds. If a student needs more assistance than can be delivered in that amount of time, the teacher should provide the help in a series of short staccato visits or establish a peer-peer tutoring arrangement for more thorough explanations and guidance.

Jones argued that if a teacher watches the student after a help session, the student may interpret this as mistrust or expectation of failure. Continued monitoring may even give students an incentive to fail. The recommended action is for a teacher to tell the student that he or she will be back shortly to check on them, move on, and then come back in a minute or two to check for progress. The teacher need not interrupt the student on the follow-up but may wish to give verbal encouragement, such as "Great," or a signal, such as a wink and a smile.

Jones provided some helpful reminders for teachers in developing and maintaining an effective management plan:

- Catch misbehavior early and deal with it immediately.
- Use body language instead of words.
- Use physical proximity.
- Use group incentive systems.
- Provide individual help efficiently.
- Do not use threats. Establish rules and attend to misbehavior.
- Arrange furniture for quick and easy movement toward any student.
- Use graphic reminders to guide behavior.
- Spend as little time as possible dealing with individual students. Be positive, be brief, and be gone.

◆   Develop a management program that is economical, practical, simple, and easy
    to use once mastered.

The purpose of a classroom management program is to reduce the teacher's
workload and free the teacher for teaching. Jones's suggestions for a classroom management program help the teacher to set limits and build cooperation while maintaining a program of successful and satisfying learning.

Lee Canter

Few individuals in classroom management literature are as controversial as Lee Canter. Canter (1979, 1992) began work on a program he describes as *assertive discipline* in 1976, which led to the founding of his publication and consulting company,
Lee Canter and Associates. This organization has published extensive books, worksheets, and videotapes on assertive discipline (Canter, 1979, 1992; Canter & Canter,
1989a, 1989b). In some ways, Canter's approach is similar to that advocated in the
normal school movement of the early 1900s: in charge, intolerant of mischief, and
ready to dole out reward and punishment so that everyone understands that the
teacher is "boss." Yet, Canter has been uniquely successful in obtaining and maintaining the blessings of school districts across the nation. Elements of his management
program can be found in most schools throughout the country.

Although popular among many school districts and teachers, Canter's
approaches have come under severe criticism from other management researchers
and theorists (Curwin & Mendler, 1988). Canter's programs are sequential, straightforward, and easy to understand. In short, assertive discipline is a simple solution to
student misbehavior; however, critics claim its simple negative reinforcements are
counterproductive.

Canter built his program on a series of assertions regarding the role of teachers,
students, and learning in schools. Canter believes that teachers should insist on
decent, responsible behavior from their students. Teachers must exercise firm control that sets clear limits because students both need and want external controls.
Canter believes firm control and instructional success are synonymous with successful classroom management. Although students have the basic right to choose how
they will behave, they also have a right to know and understand that certain consequences will follow.

Canter is not bothered by a strong dependence on the teacher's use of external
devices for regulating student behavior. He claims that everyone needs discipline for
psychological security to prevent us from doing things that we would not be proud
of later, to allow us the freedom to build and expand our best traits and abilities, and
to maintain an effective and efficient learning environment.

Canter further argues that teachers have the right and responsibility to establish
rules and directions that clearly define the limits of acceptable and unacceptable student behavior and to teach students to follow these rules and directions consistently
throughout the school day and school year. Canter believes that teachers can expect
both parents and administrators to support the teacher's handling of student behav-

ior when the teacher makes rules that are clear and uses procedures for administering consequences that are fair.

Canter also argues that students have a right to a teacher who sets firm and consistent limits, who provides them with consistent positive encouragement to motivate them, and engages them in activities that enable them to succeed in the classroom. Canter believes that student self-responsibility is an important goal of an effective management plan. Children are entitled to a teacher who shows them how to manage their own behavior.

Expectations of Teachers. Canter clearly expects teachers to be in charge if they are to be successful managers. Being in charge is not an arbitrary use of power but requires the teacher to accept a great deal of responsibility for personal conduct in the classroom. Canter suggests that teachers must identify expectations clearly and communicate them to children in terms that are easy to understand. The teacher must be willing to say, "I like that" or "I don't like that." The teacher must be persistent in stating expectations and feelings by using a firm, yet respectful, tone of voice while maintaining eye contact. Again, hostile, hurtful, or sarcastic treatment is inappropriate and brings about the worst results in all situations.

Canter believes in negative consequences for poor behavior. These consequences should be determined by the teacher in advance and communicated clearly. Canter advocates posting rules and the consequences for rule violation in the classroom as a constant reminder. Teachers must consistently follow through with their consequences for unacceptable behavior.

Summary of Canter's Plan. Teachers must assume an assertive attitude in the classroom by thinking, "I am the boss. I have a right to teach. My students have a right to learn. No student will stop me from teaching or another student from learning."

The teacher must develop a discipline plan by carefully planning the consequences of student misbehavior. The plan consists of (1) clearly stated rules, (2) disciplinary consequences for rule violation, and (3) positive reinforcement for acceptable and exemplary behavior.

If students are to fulfill teacher expectations and accept the plan, teachers must carefully explain and teach the plan to students. To prepare students for successful implementation of the classroom management plan, teachers must do the following:

- Carefully explain all rules and strategies for obeying rules.
- Explain disciplinary consequences.
- Establish the positive reinforcements that students will receive when they conform.
- Make sure that students understand each of the rules and consequences.
- Explain, rehearse, and practice.
- Provide disciplinary consequences consistently according to the plan.
- Use positive reinforcement by giving prizes, privileges, coupons, or progress measures leading to more substantial rewards.

Assertive discipline evokes strong emotions, both positive and negative, among educators. Even though dealing assertively with student misbehavior has inevitable dilemmas attached, Canter is adamant that teachers must not tolerate inappropriate behavior from students in any circumstances. Misbehavior must always be addressed. However, teachers must always have time to deal with appropriate behavior after dealing with inappropriate behavior.

Developmentalists

Developmentalists display a different, but not generally contradictory, orientation to the management of student behavior. Rather than concentrating on the coercive and reward power of the teacher, developmentalists believe the key to classroom success is engaging students in repetitive encounters where students have opportunities to recognize and evaluate the appropriateness of their own behavior. Central to these beliefs are assumptions about children's misbehaviors. Developmentalists claim student misbehaviors are inadequate attempts to deal successfully with events with which students have yet to develop adequate coping mechanisms because of a lack of maturity.

Haim Ginott

Haim Ginott was an elementary school teacher in Israel who turned to child psychology when he emigrated to the United States. In his clinical practice, Ginott (1965, 1972) found lack of effective communication skills to be the source of many of the problems that occur between parents and children. Ginott's solution was to turn to a language of acceptance and compassion. Ginott's view of language was built on common understandings about human individuals—for example, individuals prefer to be understood than misunderstood and prefer acceptance to rejection. Ginott found language that conveyed feelings also heightened understanding between individuals who had competing interpretations about their relationship. Ginott argued that adult responses to children that change moods, invite goodwill, bring insight, and radiate respect were more effective in regulating children's behavior than were forceful measures based on an adult's more powerful position.

Ginott's View of the Teacher.   Ginott viewed the teacher as a powerful force in a child's life. Teacher actions toward children must be carefully considered so that children grow intellectually, emotionally, and morally in the desired direction. Growing toward responsibility and kindness almost always rules out coercion. Ginott (1972) wanted teachers to have a thoughtful outlook on the long-term effects of daily activity in the classroom:

◆   The teacher is the decisive element in the classroom.
◆   The teacher's personal approach creates the climate.

◆ The teacher possesses tremendous power to make a child's life miserable or joyous.

◆ The teacher can be a tool of torture or an instrument of inspiration.

◆ The teacher can humiliate or humor, hurt or heal.

Congruent Communication. The heart of Ginott's classroom management strategy is the use of words that communicate feelings rather than words that pass judgments. Ginott felt that language often does not match intent when children and adults try to communicate. For example, when a teacher says roughly, "I told you to get to work!", her intent may be to help the child, but her language is that of dominance and power. To align language with intent, Ginott said that people should rethink the use of words that judge. In the previous example, the teacher could have approached the student and said quietly, "When you just stare into space rather than do your work, I feel that either I haven't explained the material well or that you don't care. Both concern me." The teacher still expressed disapproval, but she emphasized learning and purpose rather than compliance and power. When teachers align the intent of communication with the actual language, they are more likely to be understood by children. These teachers are using *congruent communication.*

To speak congruently, a teacher must have the ability to discipline without humiliating the child. Therefore, the teacher must express disapproval of the behavior—not of the child. Criticizing the behavior while using language that values the child and conveys acceptance preserves the child's self-worth. The teacher has several strategies for accomplishing this. The teacher must find ways of praising a child without judging the child. For example, "You had the best paper in the class" judges the child. "I laughed myself to tears about the antics of Johnsie in your story!" conveys acceptance and interest. It is up to the child to judge the work. Negative communications can occur similarly. A teacher judges when he or she says, "I told you it had to be two pages. You didn't include enough detail." Congruent communication guides the teacher toward the true goal of the interaction: The teacher wants the child to use more imagination and creativity. A congruent statement may be, "I really wanted to know more about the Johnsie character. Is he made up or do you know someone like him?"

Congruent communication must also align strong teacher feelings, such as disgust or anger, with messages that focus the child's attention on the behavior but do not hurt or threaten. Ginott's solution was to suggest statements that convey the feeling without using the child as a target. "You make me sick!" is different from "When I see this mess, it makes me feel sick." Likewise, Ginott reverses the process by acknowledging feelings without arguing whether those feelings are appropriate. When a child expresses his or her displeasure with the current assignment, a teacher's best move is to reassure the child that his or her message was understood. When a child says, "I hate reading this book. Why do you make us read it?", the teacher replies, "You obviously do not enjoy reading this book." Rather than engaging in a debate about the book, the assignment, or the teacher's right to give the assignment, the teacher simply accepts the feeling.

It is troubling to many teachers to accept the feelings of anger and hostility from students, particularly when their questions both challenge authority and insult the teacher. Additionally, this acceptance does nothing to direct students back to the task. In practice, one of the following generally occurs: (1) Having been understood and accepted, children generally accept the situation and go on with the task. (2) When teachers model acceptance, children learn first-hand about acceptance. By eliminating the use of harsh judgments, the teacher demonstrates that there are other ways to express displeasure that promote and develop intellectual and emotional maturity. Ginott argued that the teacher's response enables children to learn to trust their "inner reality" and develop self-confidence, thus reducing the need for socially aggressive behavior. Because this is not the dominant method of communication in our society, most teachers must experiment with these strategies over a period of time to test their validity and results.

Management Goals. Ginott asserted that the goal of education is to help children grow to maturity as decent human beings who are compassionate, show commitment, and act responsibly. *Learning efficiency* (obtaining the most learning while consuming the least resources in the smallest amount of time) is only credible as a goal if classroom life and the children's lives are tangibly improved. Simply put, to teach children's minds, a teacher must capture their hearts.

A belief that children assimilate the character of their surroundings led Ginott to conclude that teachers must discard the language of rejection. They must learn to use the language of acceptance if children are to learn to trust themselves and to have faith in their ability to accomplish self-established goals. Teachers need to use language that protects the feelings of children. Ginott suggested that teachers treat children with the same respect, dignity, and kindness as they would a guest. In this way, schools will have children that incorporate kindness, caring, and accomplishment into their lives.

"Childrenese." Discovering and using creative tools to establish a positive, civilized language for communicating successfully with children is a true challenge for teachers. Ginott (1965, 1972), however, provided some general guidelines for teachers in developing a communication style. This style is referred to as "childrenese." Teacher language should be calculated to generate affection rather than hate. "Childrenese" is language that encourages and is characterized by the following:

◆ Efforts to diminish dissension
◆ Efforts that preserve the student's desire to learn and succeed
◆ Statements that acknowledge feelings
◆ Emphasis on solutions and deemphasis on blame
◆ Responses to complaints without defensive statements
◆ Questions designed to illuminate points of view

The best way for teachers to handle a problem with a student is to have the student evaluate the situation and develop the most appropriate course of action.

Teachers can do this by addressing learning and learning activities in the present tense and avoid bringing up past events into present discussions. When children are upset, even if they are upset with the teacher, the teacher should offer warm words and empathy. When discussing behavior and emotions with children, the teacher should talk succinctly, listen carefully, and provide reflective statements that acknowledge the meaning of the children's words. Teachers who spend more time listening than talking always communicate more effectively. Teachers must be flexible and convey empathy for the plight of students. When students express complaints, such as "It's not fair. I do the work, and you get the pay!", teachers are more effective with empathetic responses. When teachers respond with "You want pay for your work now, not when you grow up" rather than "That's silly. You don't do anything worth pay. I'm the one who really works!", they are communicating congruently.

Teachers who remain solution-oriented when students lose self-control are focusing the children's attention on emotional growth. Teachers who judge the child's behavior, impose external controls, or demean the child are focusing the children's attention on defensive self-preservation conduct. Teachers must help students regain self-control. For example, when the teacher is faced with a shouting match between two children, conveying respect for the children while sending a message that the behavior is unacceptable is essential to "childrenese." An appropriate teacher response may be, "You are both very angry at each other. I think you might even want to hurt each other. But this is a classroom, and this time is devoted to writing. I'll try to give you time after lunch to sort out your disagreement."

Ginott's View of an Effective Teacher.   Teachers do become angry with students, and expressions of anger are both appropriate and necessary. However, teachers must express anger without insult and must focus on helping children regain control and growth in emotional maturity. Effective classroom managers are aware of their own feelings and respect those feelings. However, teachers must always model appropriate language. When angry, the cardinal principle for the teacher is to express indignation, not indignity. The primary role of the teacher in behavior management of students is always to protect the child's dignity while directing the child toward more appropriate activity.

The teacher's classroom management role is also defined by his or her attention to eliciting cooperation. Rather than forcing a confrontation, providing an invitation for cooperation in a supportive environment offers children the opportunity to make rational decisions regarding the appropriateness of their conduct and to consider alternative courses of action. Ginott (1972) provided some suggestions on how to invite cooperation:

- Diminish hostility in voice, gesture, and demeanor.
- Give children a choice in school matters.
- Avoid commands.
- Convey respect.
- Safeguard self-esteem.

Strategy of Compromise.   Because of their greater authority, independence, and maturity, adults have a different status than children, granting them privileges and credibility that children generally do not have. This differentiated status does not apply to children and adults in their need for acceptance, respect, and belonging. Just as when adults relate to each other, children must negotiate and compromise when obtaining and maintaining acceptance, respect, and belonging. Continual denial of feelings, of needs, and of respect lead both adults and children toward isolation and hostility. Ginott (1972) developed several strategies that allow teachers to compromise with children while maintaining appropriate work and learning environments.

The first strategy is to grant children in fantasy what they cannot be given in reality. When a child is angry with another child, the teacher may say, "You are angry at Steve, and you wish you could hurt him." The child's feelings are acknowledged, and his or her outrage is communicated. This reduces the child's need to act on the impulses because the message is already conveyed. A student who receives a disappointing score in a test may be told, "You wish you could make a perfect score without having to study." In both cases, the teacher leaves the child with the responsibility for his or her own life.

A second strategy is to use nonjudgmental praise. Praise consists of two parts: (1) what the teacher says to the child, and (2) what the child says to himself or herself. In nonjudgmental praise, the teacher expresses appreciation so that the child is assisted in making a personal assessment of progress. For example, "Your story made me smile. I liked your character, Marcie" is nonjudgmental, whereas "This is a very good paper" is judgmental. Ginott claimed that there are very real dangers in judgmental evaluations. If the teacher praises the child in a way that is not valued, the child may reverse his or her actions. For example, "Marcie, you are a wonderful teacher's helper" may be interpreted by Marcie as implying she is a "teacher pleaser" when she really thinks of herself as "tough." To prove the teacher wrong, Marcie acts out, thus invoking confusion and often resentment from the teacher. A nonjudgmental expression of appreciation such as "You have saved me a lot of time and effort. Thank you!" leaves Marcie free to make the judgment about the quality of her work.

A praise statement that is not judgmental is constructed from a brief description of the behavior, a simple factual statement of the result of the behavior, and, if desired, a simple statement of how it made the teacher feel. When Bobby helps Timmy, a first grader, pick up his papers and books after a collision, the observing teacher may say, "Bobby, thank you for helping Timmy pick up his papers. You kept them from blowing away. I enjoy seeing students help each other." However, "You are such a good boy!" is an unnecessary and unhelpful judgment. Regardless of the syntax of appreciation, Ginott suggested that the teacher leave self-evaluation to the child.

Ginott's View of Discipline.   Ginott's foremost advice to teachers regarding discipline was to find alternatives to punishment. To Ginott, misbehavior and punishment were not opposites that cancel each other. Instead they bred and reinforced each other. This view is held by many and has excellent foundation in works by other researchers such as Kounin (1977); however, it is quite contrary to popular opinion and perhaps is counterintuitive. Ginott flatly stated that punishment fails to achieve its goal of promoting positive behavior. However, teachers must have some alternatives. Ginott (1972) suggested that when faced with misbehavior, the teacher do the following:

◆ Attempt to handle incidents with humor.
◆ Ignore a small problem if it is likely to correct itself with no further disruption.
◆ Remain calm; keep composure.
◆ Write a note to the student requesting the student's cooperation.
◆ Have students write down problems and conflicts.

Ginott's Suggestions for Classroom Success. Ginott had a number of suggestions for teachers who want their classrooms to be more successful. Teachers who encourage children to ask questions will have students who are more involved and learn more successfully. When students ask questions or make other comments, the teacher must focus on the students' words and the various meanings behind their words. To promote the belief in all children, Ginott suggested that teachers should have underachieving students be tutors in their areas of strength in their own class and in their area of weakness with younger children whose information needs are within the level of the tutor.

Students whose needs are satisfied are happy learners.

Ginott advocated pairing children for learning activities that typically have been done alone. The teacher can also involve children in determining the classroom operation, routines, and even the sequence and topics in lessons and the curriculum.

Teachers can promote positive successful classrooms by listening and taking time to know students. Teachers can give children "time to grow" and provide support for "learning and growing by littles" instead of expecting radical changes in small periods of time. Successful teachers find ways to make children feel important and create a pleasant atmosphere in which student imagination is valued and students understand and appreciate the connection of effort and learning success.

Rudolph Dreikurs

Rudolf Dreikurs (Dreikurs, Bronia, & Floy, 1982) is known for his program of student behavior management called "discipline without tears." Born in Vienna, Austria, in 1897, Dreikurs obtained a medical degree from the University of Vienna before emigrating to the United States in 1937. Dreikurs' main focus was on children's needs and how they go about fulfilling them. At the heart of Dreikurs' works (Dreikurs & Cassel, 1974; Dreikurs & Grey, 1968; Dreikurs & Soltz, 1964) is the assertion that all students want recognition, and most misbehavior occurs from their misguided attempts to get it.

Because children have limited power and other resources needed to achieve their needs, students often turn to four mistaken goals that teachers must be able to recognize: attention, power, revenge, and inadequacy. Children must be taught new skills in dealing with day-to-day social situations to replace these mistaken goals. Dreikurs argued that a democratic classroom environment was the perfect laboratory for students to learn social skills for fulfilling their personal needs.

Dreikurs (Dreikurs & Cassel, 1974) outlined three alternatives for classroom governance. First, the teacher can choose *autocracy* in which the teachers and school administrators determine and enforce school rules and policies. Teachers can also choose *anarchy* in which the teacher exercises minimal control over classroom events. Finally, the teacher can choose *democracy* in which teachers and students negotiate to obtain the greatest amount of freedom while fulfilling the obligations required of teachers and students. Autocracy provided order but limited freedom. Anarchy provided freedom without the necessary order in the classroom so success could be obtained. Only democracy provided a balance between the need for order and need for freedom.

Autocratic teachers act as bosses, give commands, and use power and pressure to force students into learning activities. These teachers employ sharp voices, demands for cooperation, and frequent punishment when students do not comply. Anarchical teachers do not accept responsibility for student actions and learning in the classroom. They are permissive, offer few or no limits, and are unclear about the goals of the classroom. Democratic teachers value a balance between order, freedom, rights, and responsibility. Democratic teachers work toward establishing both order and freedom and making flexible compromises in response to students' emotional and learning needs.

Teachers are responsible for establishing the conditions that foster a democratic classroom. Teachers must be both firm and kind and explicitly discuss with students the procedures for establishing order and limits while teaching students to accept the responsibility that comes with freedom. A major tool for the teacher in establishing a democratic classroom is involving students in establishing and maintaining rules through the use of classroom meetings. Although classroom meetings may require extensive leadership from the teacher, the success of meetings requires the full participation of each student.

Discipline Is Not Punishment. When Dreikurs spoke of discipline, he referred not to an external requirement for order but rather an internal freedom of choice and the understanding of the consequences of the choices that students have. To Dreikurs, authority figures should not impose discipline, but rather individuals must make deliberate choices to impose limits on themselves. This view fits quite nicely with general definitions of social maturity and good citizenship. Dreikurs felt that when individuals choose to behave in certain ways, they gain acceptance from others and progress toward fulfillment of basic needs. Dreikurs and Cassel (1974) described four basic concepts that define discipline in classrooms:

◆ Students are responsible for their own actions.
◆ Students must respect themselves and others.
◆ Students have the responsibility to influence others to behave appropriately.
◆ Students are responsible for knowing what the rules and consequences are in their classrooms.

Four Mistaken Goals of Misbehavior. Dreikurs and Cassel (1974) described four mistaken goals of misbehavior that he thought illuminated the incentive behind student disruption.

◆ *Getting attention* is a source of motivation for students who feel neglected, ignored, or lonely. Misbehaviors for getting attention include making noises, asking questions unrelated to the lesson, repeatedly making the same comment, making faces, or acting out. These misbehaviors call attention to the student while often making fellow students laugh and irritating the teacher. Dreikurs noted that if the student's behavior annoys the teacher, the student is attempting to get attention.
◆ *Seeking power* is the impetus behind behaviors that emphasize conflict. Students who contradict, argue, deliberately continue prohibited acts, show aggression toward others, or damage property are seeking power. If a teacher feels threatened by a student, the student is exhibiting power-seeking behavior. Students who feel powerless or alienated by the events in the classroom may seek to assert themselves to validate that they are important and worthy of recognition.

◆   *Seeking revenge* is caused by a student's perception of unfairness and poor treatment from the teacher or other students. Revenge-seeking behavior can be displayed by a full gamut of misconduct. These behaviors, however, are almost always directed at hurting someone, either physically or emotionally. Revengeful behaviors may involve thefts, physical aggression, name-calling, gossip, damage to materials, or attempts to embarrass others. If the teacher feels hurt by the student's actions, the student's motivation is probably revenge.

◆   *Displays of inadequacy* often appear as immaturity, silliness, or withdrawal. Students motivated by inadequacy stop trying, employ self-defeating behaviors, and belittle themselves and their efforts. Behaviors designed to obtain pity are displays of inadequacy. If the student's behavior leaves the teacher feeling powerless, the student is displaying inadequacy. This behavior is the most problematic for the teacher because it is based on a breakdown in the student's self-esteem and often is imbedded in a deep sense of failure, worthlessness, and hopelessness. These feelings are not easily altered and require a consistent, deliberate treatment plan designed to help the student recognize self-worth and personal success. Direct approaches, including demonstrating to the child that his or her perceptions of inadequacy are wrong, generally are not effective.

Strategies for dealing with specific sources of misbehavior have been developed by Dreikurs (Dreikurs, Bronia, & Floy, 1982; Dreikurs & Grey, 1968). Figure 12.7 shows a sample of these strategies.

Dreikurs also outlined several treatments that apply to most forms of misbehavior. These include the following:

◆   Help students to discipline themselves rather than immediately attempt to suppress the student's misbehavior. When a student is misbehaving, either by withdrawal or aggression, the teacher may approach and ask, "What can I do to help?" or "Are you getting the situation under control?"

◆   Identify the student's mistaken goal and confront the student with it. If a student refuses to do an assignment, the teacher may ask, "Are you refusing to do the work because you think it is too difficult for you?" If a student is aggressive, the teacher may ask, "Are you hitting because someone threatened you?" Other questions may include, "Could it be that you want me to pay attention to you? Could it be that you want to prove that nobody can make you do anything? Could it be that you want to hurt me or others?"

◆   Follow misbehavior with reasonable logical consequences. Dreikurs goes to great lengths to emphasize that a failure to govern personal behavior appropriately should be followed by consequences. To be instructive, these consequences should be logically associated to the misbehavior. For example, if a student fails to hand in homework, having to write "I will remember to do my homework" is not logically attached to the omission. Instead, Dreikurs suggested that the teacher require the student to complete the work using time forfeited from activities that the student ordinarily enjoys, such as free time after eating lunch.

Appropriate Action for Attention-Getting Behaviors
- Ignore the misbehaving student.
- Be firm, not annoyed.
- Give lots of attention at other times.

Appropriate Action for Power-Seeking Behaviors
- Admit that the student has power ("Of course, I can't make you do this.").
- Ask for the student's aid ("I really need your help in this. I hope you will help.").

Appropriate Action for Revenge-Seeking Behaviors
- Apply natural consequences.
- Do the unexpected.
- Avoid deciding for the student; get the student to own personal behavior and consequences.

Appropriate Action for Displays of Inadequacy
- Encourage the student when effort is made.
- Avoid supporting the student's feelings of inferiority.
- Offer constructive approaches.

FIGURE 12.7 Appropriate action for attention-getting behaviors.

Compiled from *Maintaining Sanity in the Classroom: Classroom Management Techniques* (2nd ed.) by Rudolf Dreikurs, Grunwald Bronia, and Childers Floy, 1982, New York: Harper & Row, and from *Logical Consequences: A Handbook of Discipline* by Rudolf Dreikurs and Loren Grey, 1968, New York: Meredith Press.

◆ Provide helpful suggestions and encouragement to students so that behavior improvement is facilitated. The best time to reinforce appropriate behavior is when misbehavior is not occurring. By genuinely demonstrating an interest in the success and well-being of students, teachers can head off misbehavior by filling the day with successful learning and satisfying social interaction.

Support and Encouragement. Teachers should always provide a supportive and encouraging environment. Teachers should always be positive toward students and avoid negative comments. Troubled students do not need additional obstacles to overcome. Teachers should advocate effort toward improvement instead of toward unrealistic goals such as perfection. Teachers should note a student's effort and emphasize his or her strengths while minimizing the weaknesses.

Teachers can teach students to learn from mistakes rather than grieve over them. Students should be taught that mistakes are not failures but unsuccessful attempts to achieve. Teachers can stimulate internal motivation by providing meaningful instruction and discussing the purposes of classroom activities. Teachers should avoid exerting pressure by promises of rewards or threat of sanctions. Finally, a teacher should encourage independence and let students know that the teacher has faith in their abilities.

William Glasser

William Glasser published his book *Reality Therapy: A New Approach To Psychiatry* in 1965. In reality therapy, Glasser advocated that, when dealing with individuals having emotional or behavioral problems, help providers must focus these individuals' attention on carefully analyzing their choices. Glasser continued his study of individuals and the role of choices in their development with a special interest on students in public school. Subsequent books both developed and altered his initial ideas (Glasser, 1968, 1990). Glasser continued his work for over 30 years and provides the most comprehensive analysis of all of the theorists.

Glasser's Views on Students.   Glasser's approach to behavior management was methodical. Glasser carefully delineated a set of assumptions about students and student behavior. The first of Glasser's assumptions is that students are rational beings and are fully capable of controlling their own behavior. Further, Glasser argued that students choose to act the way they do, and student misbehavior is a result of bad choices.

Students, according to Glasser, attempt to satisfy their needs and, therefore, tend to do what is most satisfying. Because all students have the same basic needs, teachers who help students satisfy those needs have students who are more capable and willing to learn. If learning activities assist students in satisfying those basic needs, students control their own behavior in positive ways.

Students' basic needs are fundamental and include a sense of belonging, a need for power, freedom of self-determination, and fun. Student pleasure results when needs are met; frustration (stress) results when needs are not being met. In schools with good discipline, students' and teachers' needs are being met.

Glasser's Views on Teachers.   A teacher's primary classroom management role is helping students to make good choices. If students are to make good choices, they must have good information and process various courses of action to fruition. Using excuses to avoid responsibility or to rationalize poor performance is always a bad choice. A caring teacher does not accept excuses for bad behavior or poor performance.

Teachers also are governed by the same needs as students (belonging, power, freedom, and fun) and also need to make good choices to obtain positive outcomes. The position that excuses are always bad choices applies equally to teachers. Teachers' behavior, as well as students' behavior, is nothing more than their best attempts to control themselves to meet their needs.

Glasser's Management Strategies.   Because teacher and student behavior is governed by attempts to fulfill fundamental needs, only a discipline program that is concerned with classroom satisfaction will work. For students to produce quality work representing successful learning, students must experience a sense of belonging, some sense of empowerment, certain feelings of freedom, and fun along the way. If teachers desire to promote positive behavior in the classroom, teachers should actively provide appropriate activities for self-determination and develop a class culture in which all students belong and are valued. Additionally, teachers should give students choices in some areas and negotiate in others—all within a spirit of seriousness as well as fun.

Glasser advocated classroom meetings to develop and regulate rules, behavior, and discipline policy. Class meetings are arenas for students and teachers to talk with equal standing about all facets of the classrooms. The curriculum, student behavior, learning activities, maintenance of classroom spaces, trips, and schedules are all topics of the classroom meeting. Class meetings provide teachers and students time for questions, answers, and problem solving. Appropriate classroom meetings assist the teacher and students in communicating goals, expectations, needs, and accommodations that lead to student success.

Success was the hallmark of Glasser's program. He disagreed with the popular notion that success must always be preceded by failure. According to Glasser, failure does not help people develop and learn; only success does. Therefore, the school environment, lessons, and learning activities must be carefully planned and sequenced so that any student who chooses to do so can succeed. Blame for school failure cannot be placed on the home and community. Regardless of background, each student is responsible for his or her own needs and bad choices. However, if the teacher does not provide appropriate opportunity for successful learning, students do not have the chance to learn and can never compensate for the lack of opportunity they may have at home. When students are equipped to make better choices, success follows. The teacher's primary management responsibility and challenge are to see that students have good choices available to them.

Success for most children requires a supportive but orderly environment. Therefore, class rules are essential. Rules mirror everyday situations and are a natural part of social life. Rules, however, should be cooperatively developed, and students should know and understand behavioral expectations. However, the teacher's emphasis should be on quality learning—not on rules. Rules are only vehicles for clarifying expectations and establishing an environment in which everyone can cooperatively work together. However, Glasser disagreed with those who consider rules to be the central element of a student behavior management plan.

Instead of focusing on rules, Glasser (1990) proposed three alternative areas for teaching concern:

- "What do I teach?"
- "How do I teach it?"
- "How can I best help my students?"

By focusing on successful instruction, teachers avoid misguided emphasis on managing student behavior in which controlling student conduct becomes an end in itself. Managing student behavior, according to Glasser, can never be separate from effort to realize the learning success of the students. By focusing on student needs and successful learning, teacher energy is expended on meaningful activity that benefits students. Although students need assistance in developing appropriate behavior strategies, they must first realize the need for learning and how it permeates successful living as an adult. Additionally, students need to ask how this knowledge affects their lives, and teachers must be able to provide succinct and plausible responses. When students know how they can use the knowledge, learning has purpose. The central element in successful teaching is consistent purposeful activity in which students can discern serious knowledge from "nonsense."

Reality Therapy.   Reality therapy was Glasser's attempt at emphasizing that individuals are not bound by past experiences. Instead, an individual's future is heavily influenced by the choices he or she makes today. Glasser argued that people who rely on emotion are more likely to fail. Individuals must collect good information, assess an array of options, and critically consider the logical outcomes of various decisions. Glasser maintained that a central role of school is to breed values that foster success and self-responsibility. Students must make the choice to control their behavior; no one else can. Any effective attempt to control behavior must be an attempt to convince the student to control his or her behavior in a certain way. Therefore, successful behavior management leads students to see the consequences of choices. Reality therapy, therefore, stresses self-discipline and self-appraisal. Figure 12.8 shows Glasser's 10-step plan for guiding students to accept and exercise personal responsibility.

Reality therapy suggests that teachers ask students questions that lead them to identify and assess their personal behavior. When approaching a student displaying unacceptable behavior, the teacher's first task is to get the student to identify the current behavior realistically and to make a judgment about its acceptability. The teacher may do this quite directly by asking the student, "What are you doing? Is it against the rules?" The key to this interaction is getting the student to determine if his or her behavior is beneficial and appropriate. Glasser cautioned teachers never to label the behavior for the student. If the student fails to answer or answers without

FIGURE 12.8 Glasser's 10 steps to positive discipline.

Developed from *Managing the Disruptive Classroom: Strategies for Educators* [videorecording] by William Glasser and Robert E. Wubbolding, 1994, Bloomington, IN: Phi Delta Kappa.

"What am I doing?"

"Is it working?"

Ask the student, "What are you doing?"

Get the student to make a value judgment about his or her actions.

Ask the student, "What should you be doing?"

Require a student to make a plan.

Let natural consequences follow.

Isolate the student but do not punish.

The student must leave the room until a plan is made.

Seek professional help.

due seriousness, the teacher can then describe the behavior and state that it is unacceptable.

In most cases, recognition of misbehavior is all that is necessary for the student to choose to correct it. However, if further involvement is necessary, the teacher may help the student make a plan to improve behavior. The plan should emphasize realistic approaches. In the case of severe or persistent difficulties in student self-control, Glasser suggested that the teacher emphasize a written contractual plan. The plan should accurately describe the needed behavior and contain strategies for obtaining those behaviors. The plan should increase student motivation by outlining the consequences of the student's personal control of behavior leading to the fulfillment of the contract. It is important for the teacher to focus on the student's ability to control his or her actions. Therefore, teachers should not accept excuses for misbehavior. The teacher should always place the responsibility for student behavior on the student.

Control Theory.　　Control theory is Glasser's (1986) most recent analysis of the issues involved in teaching students to control their own behavior appropriately. Control theory is in many ways an extension of reality therapy but is different from it in many important ways. Control theory attempts to explain a person's constant attempt to control himself or herself and others, although, in reality, people can only really control themselves. People try to control their behavior and the behavior of others in ways that attempt to satisfy their own needs. In control theory, however, the focus is not solely on the teacher's duty to create an environment that meets students' needs but also to help students develop a personal lifestyle that successfully meets their needs. By assisting students in developing plans for improvement, the teacher places primary focus on helping students make better choices. The teacher also is directed by a careful consideration of students' needs that are not being met and assists them in identifying what they need to meet these unfulfilled needs. By helping students make a plan for producing positive quality work, teachers can help students fulfill personal needs and feel better about classroom instruction. In doing so, teachers can become more influential with students.

Boss Management in American Schools.　　Glasser's most recent work (1990) focuses on the management of American schools that result in quality work from students. Glasser argues that quality work by students is mitigated by the dominant use of *boss management.* Boss management sets standards without consulting others, and students have to adjust to the job as the boss defines it. Boss management tells students what to do rather than showing students what must be done. Boss management evaluates and judges work. Students respond to boss management by settling for "good enough." Boss management punishes students who resist. This punishment breeds resentment and further lowers quality work.

Lead management is the alternative to boss management. In lead management, the teacher engages students in a discussion of the purpose, processes, and resulting quality of their work. Teachers help students to determine what they must do to meet learning goals, which activities are to be used, and how much time is required to do it. In lead management, the teacher attempts to tailor the learning activities to the skills and needs of students. Teachers attempt to provide visibility and purpose for students' work by using or showing work products. Students are involved in assessing and evaluating the quality of their work. The teacher facilitates the students' work by providing the best environment and tools to do the job.

Lead management is necessary for schools to remain viable institutions for today's students. By focusing on students' needs, stressing students' responsibility, and establishing rules that lead to success, lead managers emphasize the students' ability to determine outcomes by personal effort. By refusing to accept excuses and having students make value judgments regarding the appropriateness of their behavior, teachers focus student attention on personal responsibility. Teachers may suggest suitable alternatives and invoke reasonable consequences when students do not accept the invitation to responsible learning. Glasser encourages teachers to be persistent, regularly review the successes in the classroom, and involve students in assessing classroom accomplishments. Teaching, according to Glasser, is the most difficult job there is. Quick fixes, simple solutions, and packaged plans will not work. Only focusing on the needs of students in obtaining meaningful learning can promote a responsible classroom environment.

Planning Teacher Responses

When attempting to understand the research in behavior management and examining the articulated theories of the best scholars in the field, teachers can be overwhelmed by many conflicting and competing views and interpretations. Shrigley (1985) approached the problem of overwhelming information quite systematically and created what he labeled a "ladder of alternatives" to student disruption. His premise was simple: Teachers must have a ready-to-use array of strategies to deal with misbehavior. However, these strategies must be developed from an understanding of students and result from a continued critical analysis of the overall classroom management plan. Reliance on single strategies or singular approaches to misbehavior weakens the teacher's management program when children do not respond.

Shrigley's "ladder of alternatives" to student disruption starts with the weakest response using the fewest teacher resources and leads to successively stronger responses using increasingly more teacher resources. The goal is to choose from the ladder of alternatives with a sufficiently strong response so that the behavior is corrected, but not so strong that it wastes teacher time and diminishes student cooperation.

Nonverbal Intervention

Nonverbal intervention employs teacher movement and gestures to communicate to students. The goal of nonverbal interventions is low-profile correction of misbehavior, promotion of positive behavior by student self-correction, and minimal disruption to the learning of others. Low-profile correction does not interrupt the learning activity or focus the classroom's attention on a student's misbehavior. Conversely, high-profile controls are explicit, and the learning activity is temporarily set aside to deal with a specific incidence of misbehavior.

Shrigley suggested that minor misbehavior likely to stop quickly of its own accord should be ignored. Only behavior that is particularly disruptive or likely to continue should require teacher intervention. If the teacher notes a series of minor behaviors that the student quickly self-corrects, the teacher may inform the student during a noninstructional time that his or her behavior was observed and request that such behavior be avoided in the future.

The next weakest intervention makes the student aware that the teacher disapproves of the student's current behavior. Signals such as gesturing, pointing, or nodding can prompt a student and allow the student time to self-correct. Some signals can be high profile but effective. Some teachers use a rhythmic hand clap or a music box as a general signal for alerting the group about their misbehavior or for encouraging conformity to a classroom routine.

Proximity is a slightly more powerful response. Moving toward the misbehaving student generally prompts the student toward appropriate behavior. Frequent monitoring by the physical presence of the teacher helps students realize that they will be held accountable for their own behavior.

Touch control involves touching children in ways that are supportive. Touching reinforces the notion that the teacher is aware. Everyone likes the literal pat-on-the-back that acknowledges his or her contribution. In this way, touch control can be proactive in preventing misbehavior and encouraging quality work. However, a teacher's hand on the shoulder of a misbehaving child is a strong signal to stop and desist. Touch control can be controversial. With concerns about sexual and physical abuse of children, touching children must be done with care and thoughtfulness. Should the teacher choose to use touch control, touching should be limited to the shoulders and the back of hands. Children often spontaneously give hugs as a show of appreciation, and the teacher need not avoid receiving these rewards. The teacher is cautioned to limit the hug to a second or so, smile at the child, and express appreciation. Teachers should be aware that local norms, the age of students, gender differences, and cultural backgrounds all affect the appropriateness and the use of touch in the classroom.

Verbal Interventions

Verbal interventions tend to be high-profile controls because of the public nature of the classroom. When the teacher uses verbal interventions, usually all students can hear. High-profile interventions tend to disrupt the flow of the classroom, although cautious use can invoke a ripple effect and increase attentiveness and task orientation for the whole class. Verbal interventions can be minimally disruptive when the teacher combines the intervention with a low-profile control such as the use of proximity or touch.

Telling students directly that the current behavior is unacceptable by devices such as an "I-message" or direct appeal can gain compliance quickly. Telling a student "When you throw food on the floor, it cannot be eaten, and this upsets me!" or "Food on the floor makes the custodian's job harder; please stop" is forceful, yet not degrading to teacher or student. The use of these strategies is reserved for spontaneous and impulsive behavior of otherwise disciplined students.

Accelerating in severity and slightly more direct is the use of the "is not for" statement. Telling a student "Food is not for throwing. Food is for eating" may seem awkward at first but clearly communicates to students what behavior is not acceptable and what the acceptable substitute is. This is a versatile intervention that focuses more on the situation than on the person. All of the interventions up to this point require minimal follow-up, such as a subsequent statement of appreciation for compliance.

If students do not choose to control their behavior after a minimal intervention or if the behavior is recurring, more direct and restrictive measures may be required. However, at this point, teachers can make students aware that the negative sanctions to come are a direct result of deliberate repetitive activity of the student. Invoking logical consequences ("Throw food on the floor, and you sweep the cafeteria floor before you go to the playground") is a major intervention that consumes teacher time while providing the student with an opportunity for a power struggle. When consequences are logical, they are rationally related to the student's misbehavior. In the case of food on the floor, sweeping up the peas is directly related to student misbehavior. The solution ("Be more careful with your food, or you must clean up the mess") resides more within the logic of the situation than the teacher's authority. An almost universal natural consequence of student misbehavior is loss of teacher trust. Thus, in the elementary classroom setting, student movement and self-direction can be restricted.

When a student refuses to exercise appropriate control, stronger measures are necessarily required. Contrived consequences (sanctions not related to the student's misbehavior) may be required. Following the food-throwing incident, the teacher may say to the student, "Throw food, and you go to detention" or "You are making a choice: Eat the food and stay; throw the food and lose your privilege to eat here." Contrived consequences are coercive actions reserved for the chronic and defiant offender and must be used with care. No one wins in a confrontation. Teachers risk open defiance and loss of credibility. Students risk loss of face and have lingering feelings of resentment. Confrontations take time that can best be used for learning. They also have a dampening effect on the learning environment and the focus of the classroom.

Developing a Personal Plan

Each teacher's classroom should reflect his or her goal, values, and skills as well as the personality of the students and the climate of the school. Teachers must take charge of developing a happy, healthful, and productive classroom climate. Management plans such as those developed by Shrigley (1985) are helpful in initiating or revitalizing a classroom management plan that assists in developing a positive climate. However, for teachers to meet the needs of their students, their management plan must focus more precisely on their teaching skills in concert with their students' needs within the specific learning environment. The following set of suggestions can assist teachers in developing a plan:

- Talk to students about the purpose of school.
- Involve students in developing classroom goals and methods of achieving them.
- Focus on the remedy of problems rather than on assigning blame.
- Learn to forgive. Genuinely try to heal each misunderstanding every day.
- Think carefully about the results of each day's instruction in relation to long-term goals.
- Take time to recognize and celebrate successes. Be a "good-finder" and create an environment of support and excitement.
- Keep a log of ideas. By recording ideas on paper, thinking is focused, and ideas are clarified.
- Continually reevaluate and rejuvenate the teaching plan.

In closing, it is important to recognize that managing the classroom is a significant task that requires continual effort and assessment. By using the ideas of others, by developing personal skill, and by maintaining optimism and energy, every teacher can be successful.

◆ ◆ ◆

Summary

1. Management and discipline continue to be critical issues for successful teachers and remain key elements to successful instruction.

2. Six primary areas of successful classroom management are use of time, group management strategies, lessons that engage students, classroom communication, beginning the school year, and handling misbehavior.

3. Theorists on classroom management who conclude student behavior can be directly influenced by specific teacher acts are called *instrumentalists*.

4. Theorists on classroom management who conclude that teacher acts are appropriate because they allow students to develop responsibility, self-control, and morality are called *developmentalists*.

5. Kounin identified key teacher behaviors that have a predictable influence on student behavior. These included "withitness," overlapping, proximity control, and signal alerting.

6. Kounin argued that carefully created desists can have a positive influence on the entire class. He called this the *ripple effect*.

7. Jones concluded that a teacher's body language can be used to influence children in

positive ways. Being businesslike, remaining calm, and actively moving about the room are key elements of successful management.

8. Incentive plans can be used to promote cohesive effort among the class and employ peer influence to maintain task orientation.

9. Canter argued that clearly stated consequences to misbehavior, when used consistently, bring about greater conformity to classroom rules.

10. Ginott defined the central element of successful management as congruent communication in that the person in authority explores feelings instead of judging and defending judgments.

11. Communication is enhanced when effort is directed toward cohesion, acknowledgment of feelings, emphasis on solutions, and understanding of others' points of view.

12. Dreikurs demonstrated that student misbehavior is a result of mistaken goals: attention, revenge, power, and feelings of inadequacy.

13. Central to successful management are strategies that promote personal respect among students, acceptance of responsibility, and self-control of behavior.

14. Glasser maintained that only students can control their behavior; therefore, teacher efforts should be directed toward assisting students to make good choices.

15. Students attempt to make choices to satisfy needs. Only a classroom management plan that focuses on satisfaction will work.

16. Teachers who consider recurring events, develop strategies for dealing with all of them, and redirect students positively are more successful in promoting student responsibility.

◆ ◆ ◆

Activities and Questions for Further Understanding

1. List the five basic needs described by Glasser. Make a list of teacher activities that can work toward fulfilling those needs on a daily basis.

2. Develop strategies to resolve Mrs. Donald's problem presented in "A Slice of Life." Develop one set of strategies using the instrumentalist ideas and a second using the developmentalist ideas. Compare the two strategies.

3. Create several examples of an appropriate desist as defined by Kounin for the following common student misbehaviors.
   a. Passing a note during class discussion
   b. Whispering to another student
   c. Pushing other students while lining up
   d. Loud talking in the hall

4. Create a chart showing the basic assumptions of the six theorists presented in the chapter.

5. Create a list of natural consequences for each misbehavior listed in question 3.

6. Create your own classroom management philosophy. Include the purpose of classroom management, the causes of student misbehavior, and appropriate redirection.

7. Develop a "ladder of alternatives" that outlines your personal beliefs of successful interventions. List them in ascending order with the solution involving the least teacher efforts and power first. What is the effect of high levels of teacher credibility on these strategies?

◆ ◆ ◆

References

Black, S. (1994). Throw away the hickory stick. *Executive Educator. 16*(4), 44–47.

Canter, Lee. (1979). *Assertive discipline: Competency based guidelines and resource materials.* Los Angeles: Canter & Associates.

Canter, Lee. (1992). *Assertive discipline: Elementary workbook, Grades K–5.* Santa Monica, CA: Lee Canter & Associates.

Canter, Lee, & Canter, Marlene. (1989a). *Assertive discipline: Resource materials workbook elementary, K–6.* Santa Monica, CA: Canter & Associates.

Canter, Lee, & Canter, Marlene. (1989b). *Assertive discipline: Middle school workbook, Grades 6–8.* Santa Monica, CA: Canter & Associates.

Curwin, Richard L., & Mendler, Allen N. (1988). Packaged discipline programs: Let the buyer beware. *Educational Leadership, 46*(2), 68–71.

Dreikurs, Rudolf; Bronia, Grunwald; & Floy, Childers. (1982). *Maintaining sanity in the classroom: Classroom management techniques* (2nd ed.). New York: Harper & Row.

Dreikurs, Rudolf, & Cassel, Pearl. (1974). *Discipline without tears.* New York: Hawthorn Books.

Dreikurs, Rudolf, & Grey, Loren. (1968). *Logical consequences: A handbook of discipline.* New York: Meredith Press.

Dreikurs, Rudolf, & Soltz, Vickie. (1964). *Children: The challenge.* New York: Hawthorn Books.

Educational Research Service. (1996). *What we know about: Classroom management to encourage motivation and responsibility.* Arlington, VA: Author.

Evertson, C. M., & Harris, A. H. (1992). What we know about managing classrooms. *Educational Leadership, (49)*7, 74–78.

Freiberg, H. J. (1996). From tourists to citizens in the classroom. *Educational Leadership, 54*(1), 32–36.

Ginott, Haim G. (1965*). Between parent and child: New solutions to old problems.* New York: Macmillan.

Ginott, Haim G. (1972). *Teacher and child: A book for parents and teachers.* New York: Macmillan.

Glasser, William. (1965). *Reality therapy: A new approach to psychiatry.* New York: Harper & Row.

Glasser, William. (1968). *Schools without failure.* New York: Harper & Row.

Glasser, William. (1986). *Control theory in the classroom.* New York: Perennial Library.

Glasser, William. (1990). *The quality school: Managing students without coercion.* New York: Perennial Library.

Glasser, William, & Wubbolding, Robert E. (1994). *Managing the disruptive classroom: Strategies for educators* [videorecording]. Bloomington, IN: Phi Delta Kappa.

Jones, Fredric H. (1987). *Positive classroom discipline.* New York: McGraw-Hill.

Keillor, Garrison. (1987). *Leaving home.* New York: Viking.

Kohn, Alfie. (1993). *Punished by rewards: The trouble with gold stars, incentive plans, A's, praise, and other bribes.* Boston: Houghton Mifflin.

Kounin, Jacob. (1977). *Discipline and group management in classrooms.* Huntington, NY: R. E. Krieger Pub. Co.

Landers, Ann. (1968). *Ann Landers says truth is stranger.* Englewood Cliffs, NJ: Prentice Hall.

Morris, R. C. (1996). Contrasting disciplinary models in education. *Thresholds in Education, 22*(4), 7–13.

Shrigley, Robert L. (1985, March). Curbing student disruption in the classroom—Teachers need intervention skills. *NASSP Bulletin, 69*(479), 26–32.

Name Index

Subject Index